THE CONNOISSEUR'S GUIDE TO THE

MOVIES

Other Books by James Monaco

The New Wave: Godard, Truffaut, Chabrol, Rohmer, Rivette

How to Read a Film

Celebrity

Media Culture

Alain Resnais

American Film Now: The Power, the People, the Money, the Movies

Who's Who in American Film Now

The French Revolutionary Calendar

THE CONNOISSEUR'S GUIDE TO THE MOVIES

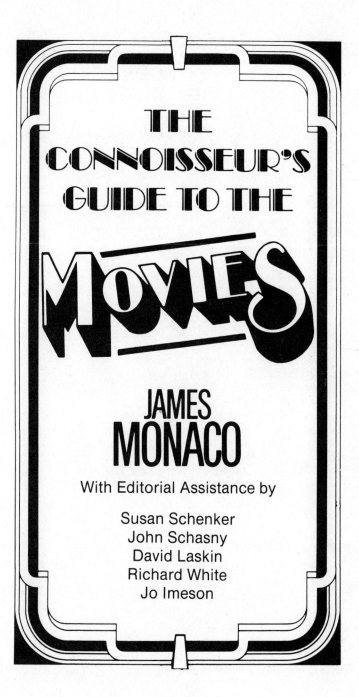

JAMES MONACO

With Editorial Assistance by

Susan Schenker
John Schasny
David Laskin
Richard White
Jo Imeson

Facts On File Publications
New York, New York • Oxford, England

**For Andrew, Charles, Margaret,
Megan, Susan, Kristin, . . .**

some good memories for the future.

THE CONNOISSEUR'S GUIDE TO THE MOVIES

Library of Congress Cataloging in Publication Data

Monaco, James.
    The connoisseur's guide to the movies.

    1. Moving-pictures--Reviews.   I. Title.
PN1995.M567 1985   791.43'75   85-10153
ISBN 0-87196-964-5
ISBN 0-87196-963-7 (pbk.)

Printed in the United States of America

10 9 8 7 6 5 4 3 2 1

CONTENTS

INTRODUCTION

For a long time during the sixties and seventies, whenever François Truffaut would come to town, a reporter from *The New Yorker* would be sent to interview him for "The Talk of the Town" column. The short, precise notes that then appeared in the magazine conveyed the flavor of pleasant, affectionate, and intelligent conversation which marked Truffaut's excellent movies. The chatter dealt with Truffaut's impressions of New York and Paris, his works in progress, and his plans for the future, but it always seemed to center on news of his children, Eva and Laura. The anonymous reporter seemed instinctively to know the dilemma of Truffaut's life—a conundrum that Truffaut himself finally put into words in *Day for Night*: "Are films more important than life?"

François Truffaut was pulled between the two throughout a life that, like his films, turned out to be too short and modest. His sudden death in the fall of 1984 from a brain tumor was the sort of poignant, abrupt, dramatic twist that might very well have ended one of his own movies.

The New Yorker reporter always asked him how many films he'd seen in the two or three years since their last meeting and what the total was to date. On last report he'd seen some 8,000 films. By the end of his life the total couldn't have exceeded 12,000, which means that even a dedicated cineaste like François Truffaut was able to see less than one-fifth of the total number of extant movies from the US, Europe, and the Third World that we now have records of.

The Connoisseur's Guide is intended to make your life a little easier than Truffaut's. We are all overwhelmed with a wealth of culture—not only in film but in music, literature, and other arts as well, and we are thus faced with the difficult task of separating out some of the good stuff from the vast mountains of chaff. Life is too short and art is too long.

Like any effort of this sort, *The Connoisseur's Guide* must of necessity be personal and idiosyncratic. There's no doubt in my mind that at least one of your favorite movies is sure to be missing from the list that follows. (If you'll write to me describing it, we'll certainly consider it for inclusion in the next edition.) In no sense is this a complete list of good or interesting or otherwise remarkable movies. That's a Sisyphean and silly task; however, the 1,463 films included here should yield some pleasant discoveries. It's my hope that you'll find a couple—or a couple of hundred—enjoyable surprises, and perhaps be warned away from a few of the tired products that somehow always make lists of best films.

Considering the nature of the enterprise, you may be interested in my own background. I was born in the radio era and cut my teeth on sounds without pictures. Although, proverbially, we were one of the first in our neighborhood to get a TV, a kid's experience of television in the early fifties was quite different from what it is today. All that mattered really was George Burns and Gracie

Allen, Sid Caesar, Milton Berle, and a diet of 1930s cartoons.

The first film I remember seeing in a theater was the very adult *Five Fingers*. (My grandmother took me.) In the mid-fifties, like a number of other bored suburban kids, I spent a lot of hot summer afternoons in cool neighborhood theaters gorging myself on westerns, 3-D adventures, sci fi, and swashbucklers. It was a good time for junk movies. By the time I was fourteen I had a job as an usher in the Squire Theater in Great Neck, New York. Watching movies five or ten times on a weekend I began to notice how they were made.

I never considered myself a "film buff" and a number of years went by in college when I had more interesting things to do. Like a lot of other graduate students in the mid-sixties, however, I escaped from some dull classrooms at Columbia University to discover the explosion of film talent in the art houses downtown, where they often served espresso and pastries rather than popcorn and coca-cola. By 1970 I was teaching film at New York's New School for Social Research and learning more about it myself—both from my students and from William K. Everson's unique Friday night series of unknown movies. Everson remains the most important American conservator of film culture, and a number of the lesser-known older films you'll find listed here owe their continued existence to Bill Everson's unsung, but important work.

As a working journalist a few years later I started watching movies in the unnatural but welcome environs of screening rooms. Like other critics, I got a distorted sense of the filmgoing process: the seats were comfortable, the audiences generally well-mannered, and the films actually projected in focus, most of the time.

By the late seventies, I was impatient with movies. I was angry with the rigidity of the medium. I found myself intentionally going late to screenings, leaving early, and taking breaks. The film experience changed most radically for me—and for us all—in the early eighties with the popularization of the videocassette recorder. The VCR gives us all a welcome degree of control over the medium. That control forever alters our perception of film and shifts the balance of psychological power over to us, the viewers.

In the winter of 1985 *American Film* magazine queried a bunch of film critics. They asked them for their choice of the most influential filmmaker, film, or event of the last ten years. The answer, I think, is "None of the above"; it's Sony. Their invention of the VCR will prove to be as important as the invention of the film projector and of television. While it's true that an important element of filmgoing has always been the communal experience of the theater, today's movie houses on the whole aren't much larger than our living rooms. What we lose in visual quality at home we more than make up for with control. Moreover, the image is only part of the experience. In the film equation, people and ideas loom large and the fact is they sometimes work better on a TV screen. (The VCR, too, should help us overcome our prejudices against film—and video—products that don't classify as "features.")

Certain principles guide the choices in this book:

●   **Movies are where you find them.** Much of the best filmmaking of the twentieth century never appeared in theaters. It's in television commercials, travelogues, industrials, and a host of other small forms. We haven't listed them all here but we've tried to indicate the range.

●   **The medium is not the message.** Ideas and character, people and intelligence, are the life of any good movie. Appreciating esthetics for their own sake alone seems to me to be an adolescent trait.

●   **Doing is better than watching.** Paradoxically, one of the aims of *The Connoisseur's Guide* is to free you from slavery to the screen to which we are all subject to one degree or another. If the book works, it is to be hoped you will have more time to. . . get out in the sun, play with your kids, talk to people, or even make your own movies. They may not have 30 to 40 million Hollywood dollars behind them but they're your own work with your own people and often to be preferred to the professional product that overwhelms us.

●   **Comedy is smarter and better.** This is the one immutable rule. We agree with George Bernard Shaw that it's certainly much too easy to portray the death force at work in the world. The heroic enterprise—the achievement to applaud and treasure—is the support and affirmation of the life force. The intelligence and spirit of comedy is much to be preferred to the cruder emotions of lesser forms.

Finding your way around

We have alphabetized the entries according to the following rules: Spaces between words count, so *Bad News Bears* comes before *Badlands*, for example. Initials are considered to be words, so *J. W. Coop* comes at the start of the J's, not the end. With the exception of hyphens, punctuation is ignored; hyphens are considered spaces. Dr., Mr., Mrs., M., and Mme. and all numbers and symbols are alphabetized as if they were spelled out. Finally, all articles—including L', Le, La, Les, Il, I, Une, Un, Uno, Der, Die, Das, and El, as well as The, A, and An—are ignored, with two exceptions: *De Duve* and *El Dorado*.

All films are referred to by their common American release titles except in cases where another title seems to be preferred by the majority of critics and filmgoers. Most alternate titles, including UK release titles and original titles in German, French, Italian, Polish, Czech, Swedish, Danish, Russian, Japanese, Greek,

Bengali, and Spanish, as well as unofficial but common "nicknames" have been included in the alternate title list at the back of the book. Capitalized titles in the text are cross-references. The year given for each film is generally the year of its first commercial release. The country of origin listed is the country with which the film is most likely to be associated, not necessarily the home base of the production company. Full credits and data on all films are available from the BASEline Information Service, 80 East 11th Street, New York, NY, 10003.

Acknowledgements

I'm grateful to my wife Susan Schenker Monaco for her always interesting advice and much-needed support. I'm thankful, too, for my children, Margaret, Charles, and Andrew, to whom, with their cousins, this book is dedicated. They've contributed some interesting opinions on some of the kids' films mentioned here. Andrew and Charles designed most of the special symbols for the book, using an Apple IIc.

John Schasny's professional expertise was a vital element in the completion of this project and I'm grateful to him, and to Jo Imeson for her editorial help. David Laskin read the manuscript and provided conscientious and valuable suggestions, as did Richard White, who also took charge of typesetting. Michael Pollack of New Video, Inc., New York, graciously provided the data on cassette availability.

John Thornton, editor-in-chief at Facts on File, was directly involved in the development of *The Connoisseur's Guide* and has gone beyond the call of duty to lend support and advice.

A note on the type.

The Connoisseur's Guide is set in 10-point Plantin. Named after the famous Antwerp printer, Christophe Plantin, this face was designed by F.H. Pierpoint for the Monotype Corporation, and modelled on a popular sixteenth-century face. Type was set on a Monotype Lasercomp at Oxford University Computing Service under the direction of Catherine Griffin, to whom much thanks.

James Monaco
New York City
February 1985

LEGEND

✳ A true masterpiece: these are the 40 great films in history.

✛ A "minor" masterpiece: worth repeated viewings.

🚩 A landmark in film history, for technical or other reasons.

◐ A classic film, or otherwise remarkable. "Good of its kind."

↘ A personal favorite.

⬆ Overlooked and underrated: "sleepers."

⬇ Overrated. See it only if you must.

☺ Recommended for kids—of any age.

♪ Outstanding music or soundtrack.

‼ A comedy, good for your health!

▼ As of February, 1985 available on videocassette or disc.

A NOS AMOURS. France. 1984. Director Maurice Pialat in a lighter and more relaxed mood than in past films like *LA GUEULE OUVERTE*, studies teenagers and their sexual adventures from the girl's point of view.

A NOUS LA LIBERTE. France. 1931. The precursor of Chaplin's *MODERN TIMES*, Rene% Clair's film matches it in its satire of industrial civilization and exceeds it in its experimentation with novel uses of the soundtrack. It's only lacking the presence of Charlot at the center. This is a more politicized treatment of Chaplin's theme of industrial dehumanization.

ABSENCE OF MALICE. US. 1980. This is another solid job by one of the more underrated directors of the seventies, Sydney Pollack: a melodrama that attempts to investigate media abuse of power. Sally Field is the reporter. Paul Newman is the slightly shady character under investigation. The movie doesn't really tell us very much about the issues involved in the power media wields, but at least it introduces them. ▼

ABSENT-MINDED PROFESSOR, THE. US. 1961. A Disney movie with Fred MacMurray and Keenan Wynn that set the style for a long series of PG live-action films from the Disney studio. Robert Stevenson directed. MacMurray invents "flubber" (flying rubber) here and it's a better idea than the flying Volkswagen Beetle that made so much money for Disney later on.

ACCATTONE. Italy. 1961. Pier Paolo Pasolini's first feature is a classic Neorealist study of the Roman underworld of poverty and petty thievery. It is based on his novel and it supposedly mirrors his own experiences. It's ironic that his life was to come full circle: he died years later in the same milieu.

ACCIDENT. UK. 1967. Joseph Losey's staging of this Harold Pinter script gives us a chance to observe the interplay between Pinter's quintessentially theatrical dialogue and the visual medium of the movies. The two men worked several times together after this but never as effectively as in *Accident*. It's just a little domestic melodrama, but it has the kind of chic that was popular in the late sixties. Dirk Bogarde stars with Stanley Baker, Delphine Seyrig, Michael York, and Vivien Merchant. Representative of its kind. ▼

ACE IN THE HOLE. US. 1951. Billy Wilder at his bitterest here is no match for Wilder at his funniest, but *Ace In the Hole*, with Kirk Douglas and Jan Sterling, offers an interesting comparison with the Wilder comedies. Douglas is a cynical reporter who milks a local tragedy.

ACROSS 110TH STREET. US. 1972. Star Anthony Quinn was behind this production, a tough cop drama, also starring Yaphet Kotto and Anthony Franciosa. It's Blacks versus cops versus Mafia in a film which makes great and extensive use of Harlem locations and neatly translates the urban underworld experience. ∨

ACROSS THE PACIFIC. US. 1942. It's those wonderful *MALTESE FALCON* folk together again in a World War II romp. Sydney Greenstreet, Humphrey Bogart, and Mary Astor star under the direction of John Huston.

ACT OF THE HEART. Canada. 1970. This is a simple little story of a young girl (Geneviève Bujold) who falls in love with a priest (Donald Sutherland). It can't be, so in the end she immolates herself. I suppose most people will find it rather silly and certainly egregiously romantic. I suppose most people will be right; however, *Act Of the Heart* stays in the mind. Partly it's Geneviève Bujold, a very interesting actress; partly it's the strong sense of funky, Canadian realism that permeates the film; and partly it's the neat dramatic trick of ending a very mundane story with a very dramatic event. To my knowledge, this was done better only once—in *L'ALLIANCE*.

ACTS OF THE APOSTLES. Italy. 1970. Another in Rossellini's brilliant series of historical television films. This one provides a platform for a commentary on religion.

ADAM'S RIB. US. 1949. No two actors in Hollywood ever worked better together than Spencer Tracy and Katharine Hepburn and this may be their best film as a couple. She's a defense attorney, he's the prosecutor, and the witty case fashioned by writers Ruth Gordon and Garson Kanin gives them every opportunity to do verbal battle, from the bedroom to the courtroom. Film students think movies are a visual medium. That's true until you're confronted with a film like *Adam's Rib*, which strongly suggests that—at least since 1929—dialogue has been the essential key to any

Katharine Hepburn and Spencer Tracy as lawyers Amanda and Adam Bonner in a courtroom scene from *Adam's Rib*.

superior movie.

⊘ ADVENTURES OF ROBIN HOOD, THE. US. 1938. The elan and exhilarating charm that Errol Flynn brought to his movies is just the sort of feeling that recent movies like *RAIDERS OF THE LOST ARK* have tried to revive. Spielberg and other contemporary directors can reproduce the mise-en-scene but not the spirit. Neither Harrison Ford nor Michael Douglas has the esprit of Flynn. The only actor who has come close is Peter O'Toole in *MY FAVORITE YEAR* doing a parody of Flynn. Anyway, *The Adventures Of Robin Hood* is quintessential Errol Flynn with more tongue-in-cheek than its modern imitators.

ADVENTURES OF ROBINSON CRUSOE. Mexico. 1952. The best of Luis Buñuel's Mexican period, this is really a Hollywood film, starring Dan O'Herlihy and Jaime Fernandez. It's an absorbing adventure in color that fully captures the mythic Crusoe experience.

⊤⊘ ADVENTURES OF SHERLOCK HOLMES, THE. US. 1939. TV has almost entirely taken over the genre of the mystery. You very seldom see it on the large screen anymore. *The Adventures of Sherlock Holmes* is a classic of its kind. There's not much to say about it. You probably already know Basil Rathbone. Alfred Werker directed. This is just good solid thirties story-telling.

ADVENTURES OF TOM SAWYER, THE. US. 1938. Norman Taurog directed this superior thirties children's film of the classic Mark Twain story. It's got spirit and life enough for any ten Shirley Temple vehicles.

ADVISE AND CONSENT. US. 1962. Part of the wave of Washington melodramas that seemed inspired by the Kennedy years (see also *SEVEN DAYS IN MAY*), *Advise and Consent* attempts an inside story of senate wheeling and dealing. Otto Preminger directs Henry Fonda, Charles Laughton, Peter Lawford, Franchot Tone, Lew Ayres, and Burgess Meredith. In the seventies, Watergate and its ilk gave us far better dramatic material for the same genre.

AFRICAN QUEEN, THE. US. 1952. If you look at all of Humphrey Bogart's 70-odd movies chronologically, you see the development, rise, and eventual decline into parody of the Bogart character. This one came very near the end and it provided a reprise and respite. In fact, it's Bogart at his best. Watching the interaction between Bogart and Katharine Hepburn, you learn a very simple secret of the movies: put two interesting actors together and let them talk and work. This is one of the half dozen films that assures director John Huston an important place in American film history.

AFTER A LIFETIME. UK. 1969. Kenneth Loach directed this British television film in the late sixties and it's highly unlikely that you'll ever be able to see it. As far as I know, only one copy of the film exists. But Loach is an important force in film art and *After a Lifetime* is a superb example of his work. It's a very simple story about a death in a working class family and one laborer's reminiscences of union struggles all the way back to the great strike of 1926. Loach usually uses people who are not professional actors but who have some acting experience. The result is an uncanny duplication of reality. Many of his other films have been criticized for their heavy regional accents. Yes, the accents are thick enough to cut with a knife, but it's worth taking the trouble to try to understand the dialogue.

AFTER THE FOX. US/Italy/UK. 1966. Another unusual combination of international talent from the mid-sixties. Vittorio De Sica directed the Neil Simon script about an over-the-hill movie star. Peter Sellers and Victor Mature star in a comedy that totters on three legs planted in three very different cultures. ▾

⇩ **AGE D'OR, L'**. France. 1930. This is Luis Buñuel's second film (after *Le Chien Andalou*) and a clear statement of his surrealistic principles. It's a film-school classic but the cold violence and contempt that it exhibits suggest that it's been much overrated for its esthetics. Buñuel's later films were suffused with a sense of humor and humanism that is entirely missing here. He grew a lot.

⊘ **AGUIRRE: THE WRATH OF GOD**. West Germany. 1972. The ultimate Werner Herzog movie follows Klaus Kinski (Nastassja's dad) as the crazy Spanish conquistador of the sixteenth century who goes off on his own up Amazonian tributaries. Herzog did this himself in order to film the story—so who's crazier? For a possible answer see Les Blank's *THE BURDEN OF DREAMS*.

⇧ **ALEX & THE GYPSY**. US. 1976. John Korty, the director, has probably had more success in television (*THE AUTOBIOGRAPHY OF MISS JANE PITTMAN*) than in theatrical films. *Alex & the Gypsy* is not a memorable movie, but it has two good performances: Geneviève Bujold, as a gypsy, and Jack Lemmon as her bail bondsman. Look at it as a sequel to *THE APARTMENT* and you'll find it of some interest.

⊘ **ALEX IN WONDERLAND**. US. 1970. This is Paul Mazursky's version of *8 1/2*. After *BOB & CAROL & TED & ALICE* he seems to have decided to make a movie about a director who doesn't know what to make a movie about. Donald Sutherland plays Mazursky; Fellini plays himself. But even the visit to Fellini and the experiment with drugs don't help. *Alex In Wonderland* has one great scene as the director shoots a fantasy war on Hollywood Boulevard. It's one of Mazursky's lesser films, but if you're interested in movies you are probably interested in movies about movies.

✛▜ **ALEXANDER NEVSKY**. USSR. 1938. Sergei Eisenstein was under strict control here but still managed to produce an exciting visual and aural experience. The music is by Sergei Prokofiev. The theme is the Russian resistance to a medieval German invasion. It's full of cinematic and patriotic power and sweep and did the necessary job of propaganda in the days just before World War II. At the time of the German/Soviet friendship pact in 1939, it was abruptly pulled from theaters. ▾

◐§ **ALFIE**. UK.. 1966. Lewis Gilbert directed this classic with Michael Caine. It's got a good theme song that people still remember. It was Caine's step up to stardom. (He's a Cockney ladies' man.) Representative of the mid-sixties, *Alfie* is a kind of upbeat color version of the black-and-white working-class melodramas that preceded it. Cockney chic.

ALICE ADAMS. US. 1935. Katharine Hepburn and Fred MacMurray star under the direction of George Stevens in a version of the famous Booth Tarkington romance. MacMurray's persona of the decent, honest guy next door was forged here. ▽

⇩ **ALICE DOESN'T LIVE HERE ANYMORE**. US. 1975. This is a pleasant but very old-fashioned story about a woman (Ellen Burstyn) who tries to make a life for herself after her husband dies. Kris Kristofferson is the new love interest. The film is nicely staged by Martin Scorsese, but it would be unremarkable if it hadn't presented itself as a feminist statement. Like *AN UNMARRIED WOMAN* it's a male fantasy of a "feminist statement." ▽

◐↘ **ALICE IN THE CITIES**. West Germany. 1974. During the seventies, Wim Wenders was more interesting than Rainer Fassbinder (and while we're at it, Volker Schlöndorff was more interesting than Werner Herzog). *Alice In the Cities* is perhaps his best film. Wenders makes very sad and perhaps pointless movies, but he represents very well a certain strain of German culture after the war: the generation that was born in the late forties must deal with the pervasive American cultural presence in Germany. Perhaps Wenders's downbeat realism is the correct response. *Alice* is more interesting than some of his other films simply because it stars a young girl. She brings life to the movie. It is, if you can believe it, a forlorn road movie for kids.

☺ **ALICE IN WONDERLAND**. US. 1951. Walt Disney's contributions to the art of animation are undeniable, but the legend often seems to pale in the face of real evidence. Mickey Mouse is still stuck in the thirties, a pretty dull character all around today—and even back then greatly overshadowed by Max Fleischer's ingenious inventions. I've never been able to understand more than one word in any Donald Duck sentence, and as a character he makes Mickey look bright and lively. (Scrooge McDuck was a far more interesting invention but never got star billing.) On the whole, more lively and—forgive the expression—"animated" cartoons emanated from Chuck Jones and the Warner Bros. Looney Tunes factory. Disney did undeniably succeed where he was most ambitious: in feature animation. *Alice In Wonderland* comes at the tail-end of the fifteen-year period in which he extended this form to new limits. It's not the best of them, but still worth watching.   ▼

ALICE'S RESTAURANT. US. 1969. If there's one movie that distills the cultural experience of the late sixties, this may be it. Not so much because director Arthur Penn understands what our generation went through in those days, more because he carefully captures the spirit of Arlo Guthrie's "talking blues" record of the same name. It's a shaggy dog story and not very dramatic, but enormously nostalgic if you're in your late thirties or early forties. This is *not* a source of the TV sitcom.
▼

ALIEN. US. 1979. Film is a medium of enormous psychological power. *Alien* is the most famous of a number of recent films to exploit that power obscenely. It's not a bad idea to make a horror space movie, but the end product in *Alien* is distinctly sadistic, catering to the latent masochism in audiences who go to films simply to be moved—it doesn't matter in which direction, or why, or how. This kind of facile audience manipulation is a real and present problem for contemporary film.   ▼

ALL ABOUT EVE. US. 1950. Joseph L. Mankiewicz knew better than most of the Hollywood directors of his time how to put together a solid piece of craftsmanship. *All About Eve* has interesting characters, solid dialogue, proper pacing: all in all, a course in classic filmmaking. Bette Davis, Anne Baxter, and George Sanders star in this classic story of stardom. It's especially interesting because the characters are uniformly uninviting.   ▼

ALL QUIET ON THE WESTERN FRONT. US. 1929. Erich Maria Remarque's novel (and Lewis Milestone's ambitious film of it) is an important landmark in antiwar literature of the first World War, especially powerful for Americans because the story is told from the "enemy" German point of view.

ALL THAT JAZZ. US. 1979. This is supposedly Bob Fosse's autobiography on film. The whole seems to add up to more than the sum of the parts. The dancing, especially by Ann Reinking, is interesting. Fosse's choreography is interesting. The music is okay. Roy Scheider's performance is feverish. None of these elements by themselves catches fire, but put them together and you've got an unusual attempt at a musical. How many times do you see graphic open heart surgery in a musical anyway? ▽

ALL THE KING'S MEN. US. 1949. Robert Rossen directed Broderick Crawford in this superb adaptation of the Robert Penn Warren novel about a populist senator very much like Huey Long.

ALL THE PRESIDENT'S MEN. US. 1976. Dustin Hoffman, Robert Redford and director Alan J. Pakula: this is probably one of the US films of the 1970s that should go first in the time capsule. It's a relentless, real, and thrilling docudrama about reporters Woodward and Bernstein—an unusually successful attempt to take undramatic material and give it life on the screen. Comparing it with ABC's Watergate miniseries *Washington: Behind Closed Doors* is interesting. *All the President's Men* shows you what film can do well: distilling an experience into a few hours. *Washington* shows you what TV can do well: elaborating an experience over many nights. It is unclear yet whether the film will keep its power as Watergate and Richard Nixon recede into the mists of history. ▽

ALL THE RIGHT MOVES. US. 1983. Shot on location in Johnstown, Pennsylvania, this ingratiating movie about teenage football players, their coach, and their future in the dying coal towns of the northeast is full of local color and flavor. A good movie for older kids. Tom Cruise and Craig T. Nelson star under the direction of Michael Chapman. ▽

ALL THIS AND HEAVEN TOO. US. 1940. Superior light Gothic by Anatole Litvak. Bette Davis and Charles Boyer ensconced in French settings of the last century romance it in the face of certain trouble.

ALLIANCE, L'. France. 1972. It's unlikely you'll ever see this film by Christian de Chalonge. It hasn't surfaced again since it was originally released. A simple and rather interesting domestic story about two people simply living their lives, *L'Alliance* leaves you totally unprepared for the shock of the ending. All of a sudden, in the middle of the drama,

with no warning—and no connection to the story—
the bomb drops. *L'Alliance* is important because it
shows in filmic experience the absurdity of nuclear
war. It is "the day before." If you can find a copy,
run it together with *THE DAY AFTER*.

ALLURES. US. 1963. Along with the Whitney
Brothers (see *PERMUTATIONS*), Jordan Belson
extended the form of the abstract film of the 1960s.
This is one of his most representative efforts: a
hypnotic and rhythmic short exercise in patterns that
is quite enjoyable.

◥◯ ALPHAVILLE. France. 1965. This is Jean-Luc
Godard's science-fiction film noir starring Anna
Karina and Eddie Constantine, the American actor
and tough guy who had starred in a number of
French imitations of Bogart films in the fifties and
the sixties. It's Godard's attempt to explode genres
by combining them and it is at least mildly
humorous. Godard's city of the future was Paris in
1965. This is another Thing That We Know about
Her. Compare this film to *BLADE RUNNER*;
Alphaville comes out way ahead. ▽

╲♪ ALWAYS FOR PLEASURE. US. 1978. Les
Blank's celebration of the food and music of the
Louisiana bayou is enormous fun and a great record
of some American "folk" music you might not
otherwise be exposed to. When Blank shows this film
himself he usually cooks up a mess of red beans and
rice—and you should, too. If you write to him at
10341 San Pablo Avenue, El Cerrito, CA, 94530,
he'll send you the recipe. ▽

◕♪ AMADEUS. US. 1984. Miloš Forman's staging of
the popular Peter Shaffer play is an interesting filmic
realization of an unusual historical drama pitting
Wolfgang Amadeus Mozart against his real-life
nemesis. Starring Tom Hulce, F. Murray Abraham,
and Elizabeth Berridge.

⬩╪⬩ AMARCORD. Italy. 1973. This is restrained,
elegiac Fellini, but it's Fellini nevertheless.
Amarcord is Fellini's reminiscence of boyhood and it
should have been done by a man twenty years older
than he was in 1973. Nevertheless, the Fellini
elements are still here and so is Nino Rota. ▽

◥⬇ AMERICAN DREAM, AN. US. 1966. This is an
egregious worst movie mis-directed by Robert Gist.
The film has interest mainly because it was based on
a Norman Mailer novel that was quite famous at the
time but seems to have been forgotten since. All the

choices are wrong, all the blocking is wrong, the dialogue is awful. It's a film school course in itself.

⬠ **AMERICAN FRIEND, THE**. West Germany. 1977. Because it's in color and it's based on a novel, this may be Wim Wenders's most approachable movie. Because it's about Americans and Germans, it's probably his most representative film. It has, as we used to say, great mise-en-scene. In other words, the way the characters work in the setting is interesting. You'll remember it for excellent shots of La Défense and the French suburban railway system in Paris. ▾

⬠❀☺✿ **AMERICAN GAME, THE**. US. 1978. Directors Jay Freund and David Wolf produced a great little documentary about two basketball players—one from Brooklyn and one from Indiana, one white and one Black—who use the sport to gain a leg up on life as well as enjoying it immensely. The contrast is superb. If this film has survived, it will eventually become a classic. It shows you how documentary can be every bit as exciting and moving as fiction.

AMERICAN GIGOLO. US. 1979. Writer/director Paul Schrader had an interesting career for a while in the 1970s. After producing a series of very successful scripts for other directors (*TAXI DRIVER* was the most notorious of these) he got the chance to direct himself. Formerly a film scholar (author of a critical tome—*Ozu Bresson Dreyer*), Schrader's directorial efforts were highly Europeanized. If *American Gigolo* had come to us from France or Sweden, we might have accepted it. As it is, set in L.A., it's a curiously out of place story. Richard Gere, dressed by Giorgio Armani, did set brief fashions as the Gigolo. ▾

⟡❀ **AMERICAN GRAFFITI**. US. 1973. As a director, George Lucas made three movies. First came *THX-1138*, a workmanlike but lifeless science-fiction effort based on a student film of his. Last came *STAR WARS*. *American Graffiti* appeared in the middle and it's undoubtedly the best of the three. He was in the right time and the right place to celebrate the early sixties for the generation that had just left that decade behind. For anyone who remembers being a teenager in the late fifties or early sixties, *American Graffiti* is a touchstone that will last for a long time. ▾

⬠§ **AMERICAN IN PARIS, AN**. US. 1951. Gene Kelly directed and starred in this film, and as far as I'm concerned any movie with Gene Kelly is worth going out of your way to see. The American musical is one of our great artistic inventions and Kelly is at the center of it. The actor/director did standard Hollywood shtik just as well as his more ambitious artistic exercises like *An American In Paris* and *Invitation to the Dance*. Pretentious? Perhaps. But the French element in an American musical more than makes up for it. ▽

AMERICANIZATION OF EMILY, THE. US. 1964. This typically cynical Paddy Chayefsky script was remarkable in the mid-sixties, but it would pall now were it not for the presence of James Garner and Julie Andrews as the romantic leads. Arthur Hiller staged Chayefsky's story of mistrust and double-crossing during World War II.

AMOUR FOU, L'. France. 1972. Jacques Rivette was the most difficult of the New Wave directors (and the least interesting) but he made films about the intensity of French intellectualism that at least rank as landmarks of anthropology and ethnography. Here are people who spend almost all their time thinking about thinking. They don't get much accomplished. They're not likeable, but the film is an intense experience.

ANCHORS AWEIGH. US. 1945. Frank Sinatra and Gene Kelly sing and dance as sailors during World War II. It seems as if they're practicing for *ON THE TOWN*. If you see this first, it looks good. George Sidney directed.

AND GOD CREATED WOMAN. France. 1956. Brigitte Bardot burst upon the world in this color CinemaScope celebration of her eroticism by her then-husband Roger Vadim. Shot on location in St. Tropez, the film was considered quite erotic and daring at the time, and deserves attention even today as part of the vanguard in the battle of the late fifties and early sixties for a new popular culture.

‼ **AND NOW FOR SOMETHING COMPLETELY DIFFERENT**. UK. 1971. This is a film anthology of half a dozen or so well-known Monty Python skits. Enough said. The upper class twit of the year playoffs are here, the dead parrot sketch, and if you aren't familiar with them by now, you probably wouldn't be too interested in this film. Useful until you can tape a complete run of at least the first season of Monty Python off the air. ▽

AND THE SHIP SAILS ON. Italy. 1983. Fellini places his gallery of characters on an oceanliner early in this century. More abstract and fantastic than any of his films during the last twenty years, it provides a refreshing variation on familiar Fellini themes of love, character, and community. ☒

ANDERSON TAPES, THE. US. 1971. This is another one of those solid, precise, and enjoyably well-made Sidney Lumet New York movies. It's a caper film, one of the last of that dying breed. Sean Connery is the master heister, Dyan Cannon is the heistee. ☒

ANDREI RUBLEV. USSR. 1966. This is one of those films that you don't necessarily want to watch so much as you need to know about. Director Andrei Tarkovsky has repeatedly been the target of Soviet persecution. This is an intentionally arty film about medieval Russian icons that looks important to critics mainly because of the paucity of ambitious style in Soviet cinema during the last fifty years.

ANDROCLES AND THE LION. US. 1952. How often do you get to see George Bernard Shaw on film? For this reason alone *Androcles And the Lion* would be worth including. Jean Simmons, Alan Young, Victor Mature, and Maurice Evans work well together. A good adult story for kids about ancient Rome.

ANGELS WITH DIRTY FACES. US. 1938. There are so many good, solid, well-made and entertaining genre movies from the thirties and forties that they are bound to be vastly under-represented here. For more than fifteen years now, a man named William K. Everson has been rediscovering the small and not-so-small gems of Hollywood's so-called Golden Years in a series of courses at New York universities, including the New School for Social Research. During that time he has shown well over 500 movies, most of which were hardly known to any but the most ardent buffs before. As the system of film distribution shifts over the next few years to video cassettes and discs, the lifelong work of Everson and others like him is going to open a cornucopia for the rest of us. *Angels With Dirty Faces* isn't an unknown film at all, but it's a good representation of the studios' factory output of B-movies. Directed by Michael Curtiz, this is a super Warner Bros. movie with what is perhaps the definitive James Cagney gangster performance and Pat O'Brien as the priest. Ann Sheridan, Humphrey Bogart and many other favorites appear in supporting roles. ☒

ANIMAL CRACKERS. US. 1930. We'll list

nearly all of the Marx Brothers films here for what I hope are obvious reasons. A hundred years from now when American culture of the twentieth century is pretty well codified by the academics, it's going to be clear that the core of our cultural contribution to the world—and it is an enormous contribution—has been the American comic tradition that started with vaudeville, made a brief appearance in the so-called legitimate theater in the 1920s, moved west to Hollywood as soon as the movies found their voice, and was later to nourish the new medium of television. The Marx Brothers carried us from one end of this journey to the other. It's more than a bit sad to think of Groucho, the last survivor, standing behind his schlock podium on TV waiting for that forlorn duck to come down out of the flies, but *Animal Crackers* brings us back to a happier time, just as the brothers were finding their voice on film. "Hooray for Captain Spaulding!" ☑

ANNIE HALL. US. 1977. This is Woody Allen's most successful film to date. It made Diane Keaton a star, nicely expressed an inveterate New Yorker's view of Los Angeles, and by implication the rest of the country, set clothing fashions that lasted until Keaton's performance in *REDS*, and just generally showed off the Woody Allen persona at its best. Ever since *Annie Hall* he's surrounded himself with much less interesting women and therefore written, produced, directed, and starred in, much less interesting films. ☑

ANNO UNO. Italy. 1975. This was one of Roberto Rossellini's last theatrical features and it exhibits the usual Rossellini attractions. Like no one else except Godard, Rossellini was an intelligent, even wise, essayist who attempted to bend the intransigent medium of film to his own ends. *Anno Uno* is about the founding of the Christian Democratic party in Italy after the war. Though its historical concerns may not be of interest to some viewers today, the way that Rossellini makes dramatic characters develop a drama of ideas is well worth watching.

ANTONIO DAS MORTES. Brazil. 1970. From a contemporary vantage point this doesn't look like much of a film, but it was important historically as one of the first of a new wave of what looked like art movies coming out of the Third World. Glauber Rocha directed. Now we can tell that he'd been seeing too many French films and may have lost touch with his Brazilian roots.

ANTS IN YOUR PLANTS OF 1939. US. 1939.

Director John Lloyd Sullivan was known during his extremely brief career in the late thirties as "the cailiff of comedy," and you see why from this classic comedy. Sullivan's only known other film was *Hey, Hey in the Hayloft*. Neither survives. *Ants* stands here to remind us of all those other films and filmmakers who exist only as subjects of other people's movies.

⊘ **APARAJITO**. India. 1956. The second in Satyajit Ray's trilogy of films about Apu, the low-caste Indian boy who lifts himself by his own bootstraps. Here Apu goes to college. See *PATHER PANCHALI* and *THE WORLD OF APU*. ▽

✛↘ **APARTMENT, THE**. US. 1960. When I was in college, *The Apartment* was a great romantic touchstone. Partly this was the happy responsibility of Shirley MacLaine, not quite a pinup (that was the ideal of forties and fifties), but the new intellectual protofeminist's idea of an attractive and, yes, sexy heroine. More important, probably, was the Jack Lemmon persona. He's the schlump insurance company employee; she's everybody's girlfriend. Lemmon seems to have a unique place in the history of American film characters, bridging the gap between the heroes of the thirties and forties and the antiheroes of the seventies and eighties. (In the fifties we had parodies of heroes, like Randolph Scott and Victor Mature.) With a lot of location footage on the streets of New York before this became popular, and a great cast of supporting characters, and director Billy Wilder's usual wonderfully sour wit, *The Apartment* showed us way back in 1960 that American movies were going to recover from the doldrums of the fifties. It may seem archaic now, but *The Apartment* made a feminist statement in its day. Perhaps that just shows you how bad things had gotten by 1960. ▽

🚩⇓ **APOCALYPSE NOW**. US. 1979. Although this is not a good movie, and in fact politically it presents a lot of problems, it is still to the credit of Francis Coppola that he tries to capture the Vietnam experience on film. Unhappily, the great metaphor from Joseph Conrad's *Heart of Darkness* that he chose simply defuses the issues. Along with *The Deer Hunter*, *Apocalypse Now* made it impossible to make a movie about the issues, and therefore the real experience, of Vietnam. It's not a good movie, but it's full of extraordinary cinema. Coppola's notorious budgetary extravagance pays off in details: the swarms of helicopter gun ships, the villages, and Kurtz's elaborate hideaway in the jungle. Come to think of it, *Apocalypse Now* is the obvious antecedent of *RAIDERS OF THE LOST ARK* and that new-old genre of the eighties. That's exactly its problem. It trivializes Vietnam by turning it into just another movie. One day, a few years after the film premiered, I interviewed Francis's father, Carmine Coppola, who was responsible for the music for *Apocalypse Now*. Carmine told me he had rights to the music for the movie and graciously insisted that I come up to the Coppola family suite at the Sherry Netherland. He played for me a tape of himself singing what he called "the love theme from *Apocalypse Now*." It's the music you hear while the helicopters are thwupping. He said it had been a big success in Italy. (The song, that is.) ▼

APPRENTICESHIP OF DUDDY KRAVITZ, THE. Canada. 1974. This is one Canadian film that doesn't look like a Canadian film, which I suppose is praising with faint damns. Ted Kotcheff directed Richard Dreyfuss in the adaptation of the classic Canadian novel by Mordecai Richler. It's still interesting because it's about Canadian Jews, there's a good flavor of Montreal in the forties and fifties, and it remains Dreyfuss's most manic and most effective role. He never matched it again. ▼

AROUND THE WORLD IN 80 DAYS. US. 1956. Michael Anderson directed this Mike Todd extravaganza. Movies in the fifties were simple. There were classic horror films, a few classic science fiction films, a goodly number of forgettable melodramas (and an even greater number of excellent westerns, most of which have been forgotten). Then, at least once a year, there was the attempt to make Cinerama (or in this case Todd-AO) blockbusters that would get people out of the house away from their TVs. *Around the World in 80 Days* doesn't have much to recommend it in the way of drama, but it's a good collection of fifties stars moving in stately procession across the gorgeous scenery. ▼

ARSENIC AND OLD LACE. US. 1944. Frank Capra directed this film during the war when his mind was obviously on more important things. It's a well-known staple of television reruns but I don't like it. It's supposed to be a black comedy, but none of the actors (Cary Grant, Raymond Massey, James Gleason, Edward Everett Horton, Peter Lorre, Boris Karloff) nor Capra have a light enough touch. It may have been a pretty good stage play in its time but it seems as if the kind, thoughtful Frank Capra was overwhelmed by the blackness of the comedy. ▼

‖ **ARTHUR**. US. 1981. Steve Gordon's only directorial effort before his untimely death is a kind of laid-back, romantic screwball about a rich drunk (Dudley Moore) and a nice girl (Liza Minnelli) with John Gielgud in a memorable supporting role as Moore's valet. ▽

ASHES AND DIAMONDS. Poland. 1958. Early Andrzej Wajda study of the Polish resistance movement during World War II which introduced star Zbigniew Cybulski to western audiences. In this and several other films in the early sixties before his early death, Cybulski looked to a number of critics like the Polish answer to Marcello Mastroianni. It seemed he might have a chance at stardom in international film.

ASPHALT JUNGLE, THE. US. 1950. John Huston's slick and solid gangster movie with Sterling Hayden, Sam Jaffe, and a bit of Marilyn Monroe.

ASSAULT ON PRECINCT 13. US. 1976. Before he became famous as a director of horror movies, John Carpenter wrote and directed a kind of hommage to the Howard Hawks western *RIO BRAVO*. It takes place in a police station under siege. It's a decent thriller that was quite a cult hit at the time. ▽

AT LONG LAST LOVE. US. 1975. One of the worst movies ever made! Peter Bogdanovich attempted to put people like Burt Reynolds, Cybill Shepherd, and John Hillerman in a 1930s ersatz Cole Porter musical. They do it so incredibly badly that it's wonderful to watch. The cinematography is equally awful. Very few bad movies are really worth more than twenty minutes. We've included here the few that are.

ATALANTE, L'. France. 1934. Michel Simon is the hero at the center of this human and lyrical romance set in the wintery barge canals north of Paris. The film's power is enhanced by great location shooting and director Jean Vigo's very particular sensibility. This was his last film.

ATLANTIC CITY. US. 1980. If you pay attention to that strange byway of cinema history, European films about the US, you'll very much appreciate Louis Malle's vision of the decaying New Jersey resort town as it's about to turn into Las Vegas East. Burt Lancaster is an old gangster. Susan Sarandon is

Chico and Harpo square off balletically in *Animal Crackers* as Groucho looks on.

a young dreamer. Playwright John Guare wrote the script.

⇩ **ATTACK OF THE KILLER TOMATOES**. US. 1978. No one ever went broke underestimating the intelligence of the American public and this cult favorite "bad movie" proves it once again. The title is terrific. The movie is a bore, and it stands here for all the *Rocky Horror Picture Show* midnight favorites whose only redeeming grace is that they give you a chance to flaunt it in front of your professor of cinema history—since he's probably sitting in the row in front of you.

ATTICA. US. 1974. A superior, straightforward, and moving documentary by Cinda Firestone about the revolt at the Attica State Prison in upstate New York in 1971 and Governor Nelson Rockefeller's tragic and uncourageous reaction to it. Compare it with. . .

⊘ **ATTICA**. US. 1980. Marvin J. Chomsky directed this superb docudrama about the events at Attica. At the center is the slaughter of almost forty inmates and hostages, but the real strength of the film is its expression of the human and political elements. George Grizzard plays New York Times journalist Tom Wicker.

AUNTIE MAME. US. 1958. This is a stolid and

stagey film of the Broadway play about the free-spirited, middle-aged flapper Mame, directed by Morton DaCosta, but it does give us Rosalind Russell's tour-de-force performance and nice bits by Forrest Tucker, Fred Clark, and Peggy Cass. ◪

AUTHOR, AUTHOR. US. 1982. Playwright Israel Horovitz wrote the script for this Al Pacino movie. Pacino is a playwright/father with a large collection of kids by various mothers and fathers, and a wife, Tuesday Weld, and a girlfriend, Dyan Cannon, who both leave him. The real secret of this movie is that Horovitz has captured a very contemporary male fantasy. Pacino gets the whole lot of kids to himself when the women leave. This kind of fantasy may have come up in some male consciousness-raising group in the late seventies, but it's one that you never see mentioned in the media. With all the deserved talk during the last twenty years about women jealous of their husband's roles in the outside world, no one mentions the obverse. As a playwright Pacino gets to hang out with the kids whenever he wants, and he lives in a big house in Greenwich Village! What a wonderful idea. ◪

AUTOBIOGRAPHY OF MISS JANE PITTMAN, THE. US. 1974. One of the great made-for-TV movies, this set a style for the genre that made it superior to much of American feature filmmaking over the next ten years. It tells the story of a 110-year-old woman who remembers the Black experience in the US from Civil War to Civil Rights. Although this is fiction, it extends the boundaries of the docudrama to treat historical subjects more broadly. *Roots*, one of the most significant film experiences since World War II, started here. John Korty directed; Tracy Keenan Wynn wrote the script.

AVVENTURA, L'. Italy. 1960. This was one of a group of films made in 1959 and 1960 (others include *LA DOLCE VITA*, *THE 400 BLOWS* and *BREATHLESS*) that heralded the new age in cinema. It may look archaic now, but at the time it was a stunning development. Everyone who saw it left the theater thinking, "now cinema is one of the high arts." This artiness proved to be a diversion in the history of the movies, but it was a very exciting and interesting one while it lasted. You have to remember when watching things like this that once upon a time people who talked about the arts in colleges and universities never considered movies (or popular music for that matter) within their purview. It was only when intellectuals like Bergman and

Antonioni loaded down films with symbolism, metaphor, litotes, and other such scholarly concerns, that they began to understand the power of the medium. In *L'Avventura* "nobody comes and nobody goes. It's awful." It's certainly not the kind of "adventure" we were used to before or since, but in 1960, boy, was this important! ◼

⊘‼ AWFUL TRUTH, THE. US. 1937. A model screwball comedy, Leo McCarey's movie gives us Cary Grant and Irene Dunne as a newly-divorced couple screwing up each other's new wedding plans.

☺ BABES IN TOYLAND. US. 1934. This is the Victor Herbert operetta as interpreted by Stan Laurel and Oliver Hardy. It's a classic film for kids, redolent of the thirties.

↑ BACH TO BACH. US. 1965. This is an animated short by Paul Leaf illustrating a classic comedy routine by Mike Nichols and Elaine May. The sketch follows the conversation of a man and woman in bed. It turns out they have met in a bar and they have a lot in common. They "allay each other's anxieties": "I think we're going to have a relationship," Elaine May declares at the end. The routine dates from the late fifties and it's enormously instructive. Nichols's and May's sharp characterizations of hip West Side New Yorkers a quarter of a century ago dates not at all, and that's extraordinary. Actually, the film doesn't matter at all, it's the routine that matters—but this is a book about film.

BACK AND FORTH. Canada. 1969. Another of Michael Snow's structuralist experiments. This time he puts the camera in a classroom and pans quickly back and forth, back and forth, in rhythmic succession for quite enough time. It's really a study for *LA REGION CENTRALE*.

BAD AND THE BEAUTIFUL, THE. US. 1952. Vincente Minnelli's inside story of Hollywood, with Kirk Douglas, Lana Turner, and William Powell.

☺ BAD COMPANY. US. 1972. Robert Benton directed this absorbing western about young people. Nothing special, but like all westerns a wonderful way to spend a Saturday afternoon. ◼

⊘ BAD DAY AT BLACK ROCK. US. 1954. This was a tough little western about the fragility of the social contract, with Spencer Tracy, Robert Ryan, Dean Jagger, and Anne Francis. It was made memorable by gorgeous color and CinemaScope photography. John Sturges directed.

BAD NEWS BEARS, THE. US. 1976. This is a really solid Michael Ritchie film that does great justice to the Little League children who are its stars. Any movie that treats kids like human beings deserves to be treasured. Ritchie's great coup was to cast Walter Matthau as the coach. If anyone defines middle age for us these last ten years, it's Matthau, and the contrast between him and the kids is exciting.

BADLANDS. US. 1973. Terrence Malick has made two stunning painterly movies about the US landscape. Call *Badlands* and *DAYS OF HEAVEN* "post-westerns" and you'll have some idea of what he's up to. No American filmmaker working today (is he working today?) has a better sense of the mythic quality of the American landscape. *Badlands* contrasts the beauty of the countryside with the blithe human waste of mass murderer Charles Starkweather and his girlfriend Carol Ann Fugate.

BALLAD OF GREGORIO CORTEZ, THE. US. 1982. Director Robert M. Young has been doing interesting if little-noticed work for many years now. This is a turn-of-the-century story of a young Mexican who was pursued for weeks by a 600-man posse. The authentic recreation of historical milieus is a hallmark of recent filmmaking, but Young's ballad set new levels for historical authenticity.

BALLET MECANIQUE. France. 1924. Fernand Léger directed this landmark abstract film (with the assistance of Dudley Murphy). As Léger himself put it: "the repetition of forms and various rhythms—slow or fast—presents possibilities that are extremely rich." This is a basic source of the power of movies. Compare *TIME PIECE*.

BANANAS. US. 1971. Like *TAKE THE MONEY AND RUN*, *Bananas* is uncultured Woody Allen and therefore funnier and with more kick to it than the later pasteurized spread. Howard Cosell has his best movie role covering Woody's Central American revolution. Of course this was long before recent tragic events in Nicaragua and El Salvador, and parts may seem a little hard to take today.

BAND WAGON, THE. US. 1953. You probably can't find a better American musical than this. Vincente Minnelli directed. Betty Comden and

Adolph Green wrote it. Howard Dietz and Arthur Schwartz provided the music, and Fred Astaire starred with Cyd Charisse in this story of a movie star returning to the Broadway stage. Of course it's in gorgeous early-fifties Technicolor. Charisse was, I think, Astaire's best dancing partner, as well as his most attractive. This is the sort of film you want to buy rather than rent. ▼

BANDE A PART. France. 1964. This is one of Jean-Luc Godard's lesser-known films but an important one because it's a more direct and simpler exploration of some of the themes—musicals, gangsters, and Americana—he was dealing with in the early sixties. Claude Brasseur, Sami Frey, and Anna Karina are enamoured of American gangster movies and plan a robbery. Along the way they do the Louvre in a new world record: 9 seconds. ▼

BANG THE DRUM SLOWLY. US. 1973. Everybody's favorite baseball novel, by Mark Harris, was turned into a fine film by director John Hancock. Robert DeNiro and Michael Moriarty star as the ballplayers. (Moriarty's parody of Tom Seaver was written years before that intelligent ballplayer's advent.) Phil Foster and Vincent Gardenia provide useful support. ▼

BANK DICK, THE. US. 1940. This is quintessential W. C. Fields. Here he's a bank detective. Fields's movies were much looser than the Marx Brothers' and depended far less on plot, if you can believe that. They were stages for him to do his vaudeville routines. Many of his shorts work just as well as the longer features. We've listed a few of the features here, but frankly, anything by Fields that you can get your hands on is worth watching. ▼

BAREFOOT IN THE PARK. US. 1967. One of Neil Simon's early Broadway hits was nicely staged by director Gene Saks. It's a classic New York stage comedy that has developed an extra dimension after almost twenty years as it stars a very young Robert Redford and Jane Fonda, both of whom were soon to become Hollywood's most outspoken and thoughtful filmmaker/politicians. What was once just a better-than-average Broadway comedy about a pair of newlyweds making do in a Greenwich Village garret now has historic dimensions: we are witnessing the birth of the yuppies! ▼

BARRY LYNDON. UK. 1975. Between 1965 and 1975 Stanley Kubrick made three very important and very different films: *2001: A SPACE ODYSSEY*, *A CLOCKWORK ORANGE*, and

Barry Lyndon. The first two have received their due. *Barry Lyndon* remains the least known of the three. It is very simply the closest anyone has come to making an eighteenth-century movie. The music, the lighting, the structure of the frame, even the acting of Ryan O'Neal and the rest of the cast bring another time to life. Like all Kubrick films, it's cerebral, even cold, but well worth watching out for. ▼

BATTLE OF ALGIERS, THE. Algeria/Italy. 1966. Often mistaken for a documentary, Gillo Pontecorvo's *The Battle of Algiers* was a seminal film in the mid-sixties. It's about the Algerian battle for independence from France in the fifties. The film struck a responsive chord among the political generation of the sixties. Purely as a movie, it's most interesting for its adept combination of documentary and fictional techniques.

BATTLE OF CHILE, THE. Chile. 1977. By Patrizio Guzman, this is a superb historical documentary about the gut-wrenching experience of the coup against Allende in Chile in 1973. As a dramatic historical occurrence, Allende's overthrow was not only exceptionally well covered by filmmakers, but also bore all the elements of a political and human drama of the highest caliber. Not since the Spanish Civil War were filmmakers or writers and other artists so involved in a political situation. Never has history come alive on film with more feeling.

BATTLE OF MIDWAY, THE. US. 1942. This is John Ford's very personal view in 16mm Technicolor of the battle for that crucial Pacific island during World War II. It's unusual because Ford was not aided and abetted by a large crew. It's almost as if these were home movies.

BEAT THE DEVIL. US. 1954. The longest running cult favorite in history, *Beat the Devil* has a rather funny script by Truman Capote. John Huston directed the fascinating combination of Humphrey Bogart, Peter Lorre, Gina Lollobrigida, and Robert Morley in a parody of forties adventure movies.

BEAUTY AND THE BEAST. France. 1946. I don't know whether it's a good idea for poets to fool around with filmmaking, but Jean Cocteau came close to success here with this artful fable. ▼

BECKY SHARP. US. 1935. The first full Technicolor feature is an adaptation of Thackeray's *Vanity Fair*, starring Miriam Hopkins, Cedric

Hardwicke, and Billie Burke, under the direction of Rouben Mamoulian.

BED AND BOARD. France. 1970. This is the fourth chapter in the saga of Antoine Doinel (Jean-Pierre Léaud) which began with *THE 400 BLOWS*, continued with *Love at 20* and reached a breathtaking climax with *STOLEN KISSES*. We are on the down side of the drama now. Doinel is married to Christine (Claude Jade) and he can't handle the new responsibilities. He's the perennial kid after all. The climax of the film is the birth of their child. Antoine died with his creator. It's a pity, therefore, that we'll never see him come to terms with his existence or watch his children grow. (The final Doinel film was *LOVE ON THE RUN*.)

BED-SITTING ROOM, THE. UK. 1969. During the sixties, Richard Lester made an extraordinary series of movies beginning with *THE MOUSE THAT ROARED* and ending with *The Bed-Sitting Room*. This is a fascinating morality tale which can best be described as Monty Python and *The Goon Show* meet *THE DAY AFTER*, as written by Samuel Beckett and Lewis Carroll. The bomb has dropped on Britain. All that is left are deserts and some of the London tube trains. The BBC (only one man is left) comes to your house to stick its head in your empty television set and give you the news. More important, people are mutating— often into bed-sitting rooms. This is a remarkable approach to the problem of dealing with nuclear war in the arts: perhaps the surreal is the only way to deal with such an absurd occurrence. Nobody could make a feature film like this now, and in fact, it was five years before Richard Lester was able to make another feature.

BEDAZZLED. UK. 1967. One of the remarkable qualities of Stanley Donen was his ability to shift gears. Throughout the sixties and seventies and now in the eighties he's produced contemporary comedies that are very much of their time. This one, a modern Faust, starred Peter Cook, Dudley Moore, Raquel Welch, and Eleanor Bron. Somebody should put Cook and Moore back together again (and while we're at it, let's throw in Jonathan Miller and Alan Bennett, the other members of the original *Beyond the Fringe* comedy team). ▽

BEDTIME FOR BONZO. US. 1951. You think this is here only because of the recent notoriety of its star, Ronald Reagan. Well, you're right. But it's also a nice little comedy typical of its time about a professor who adopts a chimp to prove (successfully) his theory that environment is more important than heredity. In his current role, Ronald Reagan must regard *Bonzo* as ideologically suspect. Frederick de Cordova directed. ▾

BEFORE THE REVOLUTION. Italy. 1964. Bernardo Bertolucci directed this film from his own script when he was in his early twenties. It's an unusually rich document, mixing politics and family drama in a way that is as fresh today as it was twenty years ago. I don't know whether it has a useful political point to make, but for Americans it's an instructive illustration of the deep roots of European intellectual politics.

BELLE DE JOUR. France. 1967. The first of Luis Buñuel's extraordinary series of moral fables that stretched on through the seventies. Catherine Deneuve, Michel Piccoli, and Francisco Rabal star in the story of a young wife who works in a smart brothel. Buñuel's satiric wit is under control here in a way it never was before. This new balance makes this film and the ones that follow memorable. ▾

BELLES OF ST. TRINIAN'S, THE. UK. 1955. In the fifties and very early sixties, what we used to call art theaters showed an occasional intellectual experience from Ingmar Bergman or Michelangelo Antonioni. They survived in between on a steady diet of British comedies. This one, a classic, is by Frank Launder and Sidney Gilliat. It stars Alastair Sim and a host of fiendish little girls (St. Trinian's is a girls' school). The same sort of intense cathartic humor that we've come to expect from the likes of Monty Python is evident in these fifties comedies, but as befits the time, here it's encased in a set of much more rigid social mores. ▾

BELLS ARE RINGING. US. 1960. Nobody has written better musical comedies than the team of Jule Styne, Betty Comden, and Adolph Green. We sometimes take them for granted. This one, directed by Vincente Minnelli, stars Judy Holliday in her last role as an answering service operator pitted against Dean Martin as the leading man.

BELLS OF ST. MARY'S, THE. US. 1945. Leo McCarey's followup to *GOING MY WAY* pairs Bing Crosby as Father O'Malley with Ingrid Bergman. The ads at the time announced, "Hubba, hubba! Ingrid Bergman as a nun?!" Enough said. ▾

BEN-HUR. US. 1926. This side of *IN-*

TOLERANCE, *Ben-Hur* was the spectacular blockbuster of silent films, exceeding anything Cecil B. De Mille produced. Directed by Fred Niblo it compares quite well with the more recent nostalgic favorite. . . .

◉ **BEN HUR**. US. 1959. The big picture of the late fifties directed by William Wyler stands halfway between *THE ROBE* at the beginning of the period of CinemaScope spectaculars and *CLEOPATRA* at the end. It's a solid historical romance/adventure about Roman times starring Charlton Heston (of course), and a host of minor stars. It's great entertainment—you'll never forget the chariot race—but compare it to *SPARTACUS*, made about the same time, to understand the difference between good filmmaking and great filmmaking.

✦╍▆◥ **BERLIN—SYMPHONY OF A GREAT CITY**. Germany. 1927. A very significant achievement in the history of the development of abstract cinema, this one is the result of a confluence of three major but contrasting talents. Cinematographer Karl Freund collected a bushelful of documentary sequences shot without much artificial light. Director Walter Ruttmann edited the footage into a mesmerizing rhythmic montage which shows the influences of his Russian contemporaries. Producer Carl Mayer insisted on social commentary. The unusual combination was influential in all three areas for years to come.

⇪ **BERNICE BOBS HER HAIR**. US. 1976. Joan Micklin Silver directed this short adaptation of an F. Scott Fitzgerald story. Shelley Duvall stars as Bernice, a young lady in the 1920s who decides to bob (cut short) her hair. Not much else happens, but it's perfectly done and it reminds you of the value of the short story form, a form that lends itself all too seldom to treatment on film. The closest we ever get, and some of them are great, is the television commercial where, in 30 to 60 seconds, we see vignettes that tell us all we need to know about the characters and their situations.

⇪ **BEST FRIENDS**. US. 1982. Burt Reynolds and Goldie Hawn are screenwriters who have been living together for a number of years and finally convince themselves, against their will, to get married. This sends them back to their roots in the east for the predictable encounters with their families. The film goes off in too many directions but it does deal with an interesting contemporary problem: how many people do you know who have been living contentedly together for years whose relationship is destroyed by the threat of marriage (and growing up)?   ◪

BEST MAN, THE. US. 1964. Franklin Schaffner directed this film of the Gore Vidal play about contemporary American party politics. Henry Fonda and Cliff Robertson star. It evinces a good bit of the wit of Vidal.

✛ **BEST YEARS OF OUR LIVES, THE**. US. 1946. Sometimes reality rears its dishevelled head even in Hollywood. William Wyler's lengthy exposition of the situation of returning veterans after World War II not only works as melodrama, it also touched a highly responsive chord right after the war. There's a liberal tinge to it now. It has scenes, for example, the only purpose of which is to show us how non-actor Harold Russell uses the hooks that have replaced his hands. But it made a strong point after the watershed emotional experience of the war.

◒ **BETRAYAL**. UK. 1983. A nicely done film record of one of Harold Pinter's more interesting plays, directed by David Jones and starring Jeremy Irons, Ben Kingsley, and Patricia Hodge. Perhaps influenced by the ingenious and entertaining experiments in stage space and time by Alan Ayckbourne (*The Norman Conquests* trilogy) during the last few years, Pinter here structures his drama as a series of seven scenes that run backwards in time. It's about a woman, her husband, and her husband's best friend with whom she has had a long-standing affair. It's an intriguing change and the little domestic drama has the usual Pinter touches.   ◪

◒☝ **BETWEEN THE LINES**. US. 1977. This is a just-above-ground movie with lots of good actors, including John Heard, Lindsay Crouse, Jeff Goldblum, Jill Eikenberry, and Gwen Welles. Under Joan Micklin Silver's direction these people come very close to giving us a true story about the generation in its twenties in the early seventies. Lawrence Kasdan later achieved some considerable commercial success by putting pretty much the same group of characters in *THE BIG CHILL*, 1983. By this time they were entering middle age and could look back ruefully and dramatically on the time when they were kids in *Between the Lines*.   ◪

◒ **BICHES, LES**. France. 1968. Another of Claude Chabrol's remarkably absorbing melodramas that is also an essay in film craftsmanship. Starring Jean-Louis Trintignant, Jacqueline Sassard, and of course, Stéphane Audran, this one is a simple story of an older woman (Audran) who picks up a young girl, and the man who comes between them.

BICYCLE THIEF, THE. Italy. 1948. I don't think film was ever more exciting and exhilarating than it was in Italy just after World War II. Neorealism, as it was called, managed to distill the art to its two essential elements: the uncanny reproduction of reality, and the breathtaking portrayal of human drama. *The Bicycle Thief* by Vittorio De Sica is a very simple film about a poor father and his son with no great meaning. However, the background of Italy just after the war and the foreground of people struggling to survive make an unbeatable combination. A classic, if that word means anything.

BIG BROADCAST, THE. US. 1932. Perhaps on the theory that if it was ignored it might just go away, the American film business rather seldom exploited the possibilities of movies about radio—the other big cultural revolution of the twenties and thirties. The series of "big broadcasts" (1936, 1937, and 1938 followed) included a number of successful treatments of the radio theme. The first was best. George Burns and Gracie Allen appear, which is reason enough to watch. Bing Crosby is star and Kate Smith, Cab Calloway, and the Mills Brothers make appearances. Calloway sings a song about a cocaine addict that shows you a little of what was possible in the pre-Code days. After enjoying one of these surprisingly sophisticated "exploitation" movies you'll wonder as I do why American film history doesn't show greater evidence of the grand American tradition of Vaudeville and variety.

BIG BUS, THE. US. 1976. This is a takeoff on *Airport* and *The Poseidon Adventure* and those other descendents of *GRAND HOTEL* that populated the early seventies. It's a very funny movie and it should have received the acclaim that *Airplane!* did later. Our characters are gathered together on a giant bus traversing the US and run into all manner of cliff-hanging adventures including an actual cliff-hanging. Directed by James Frawley.

BIG CHILL, THE. US. 1983. If you're in your thirties now, this is probably a personal favorite. If you're in your forties you're wondering why those people who were kids in the early seventies think so much of themselves when you remember the excitement of the sixties. Lawrence Kasdan's *The*

Big Chill is a very well mounted nostalgic look back at lost youth. It shows us the kinds of lives many of us lead but very seldom see in the movies. I suppose that was the reason for its success late in 1983. But basically it's a simple melodrama. It doesn't attempt to criticize the way these people have led their lives, nor does it want to. It's a *THE WAY WE WERE* for young folks. ▼

BIG DEAL ON MADONNA STREET. Italy. 1958. A big international success at the time, this is a parody of all caper films at the same time that it's a very good example of the genre itself. Mario Monicelli directed Vittorio Gassman, Marcello Mastroianni, and Toto. See it together with *RIFIFI*. ▼

BIG HEAT, THE. US. 1953. If *THE BIG SLEEP* is the best of the forties/fifties films noirs because of its wonderful humor, *The Big Heat* is perhaps the most representative because of its passion and pessimism. Fritz Lang directed Glenn Ford, Gloria Grahame and Lee Marvin in this story of a righteous city cop. ▼

BIG PARADE, THE. US. 1925. America's emblematic World War I battle movie was directed by King Vidor, with grace, precision, and spirit which still impress. John Gilbert is the hero, Renee Adoree the heroine.

BIG RED ONE, THE. US. 1980. Lee Marvin in one of the last great Second World War dramas. And by Samuel Fuller, master of tough-guy movies. Nothing fancy here, just a good old-fashioned war story, but it's refreshing to see contemporary actors work it out. ▼

BIG SLEEP, THE. US. 1946. If there's a perfect film noir, this is it; it may not be the blackest, but it's certainly the most richly textured and most humorous. Raymond Chandler, Howard Hawks, Leigh Brackett, William Faulkner, Jules Furthman, Humphrey Bogart, and Lauren Bacall: this group is peerless. Nobody knew what the title meant, nor could the writers and director figure out why the plot twists the way it does, but it didn't matter. It's hard, fast, tough, laconic, sullen, and hip. It's full of the strong women Hawks had a knack for in the forties. It's got dialogue you can spread with a spatula. *The Big Sleep* is the best proof—if anyone still needs it—that Chandler is a major writer (and Hawks a great director). ▼

BILLY LIAR. UK. 1963. Tom Courtenay is a young cockney full of daydreams. Julie Christie debuts as "the girl." John Schlesinger directed this seminal British working-class film of the early-sixties, based on Keith Waterhouse's play about a young man who escapes into fantasy. ☑

BINGO LONG TRAVELING ALL-STARS AND MOTOR KINGS, THE. US. 1976. John Badham later solidified his reputation with *BLUE THUNDER* and *WARGAMES*. This early film by Badham is a very solid and exceptionally enjoyable paean to the era of the Negro baseball leagues. Combining Blacks and baseball is probably still a prescription for commercial failure in Hollywood. The film was not successful, but it's well worth searching out if you have any interest in either. ☑

BIRDS, THE. US. 1963. It seems everybody paid attention to Alfred Hitchcock during the last twenty years of his career for the wrong reasons, namely *The Birds* and *PSYCHO*. I don't think he would have ranked either very high on his list and I don't either. *The Birds* is mildly interesting for technical reasons: working with the now primeval special effects techniques at his command in 1963, he manages to convince us that flocks of birds are attacking Bodega Bay in northern California. The film is interesting from an historical point of view because Tippi Hedren was the last and least of Hitchcock's wan blonde heroines. The life and humor that mark his best films aren't here, however. ☑

BIRTH OF A NATION, THE. US. 1915. This is a great film, but not a good one. The history books have it down as the moment when American filmmaking came of age. The scope, the drama, the technique; yes, they're all there, but they're all ultimately at the service of the profoundly racist story line. Griffith did better later and he did better before. Others did nearly as well. ☑

BITTER HARVEST. US. 1981. Ron Howard plays a young dairy farmer whose cattle are dying—and he can't tell why—in this made-for-television movie directed by Roger Young. The State Agricultural Extension Department won't help. His neighbors don't know. He is left alone to discover with real-life heroism that a minor mixup at the feed company has resulted in the shipment of untold numbers of sacks of poisoned feed. And now the poison is everywhere. His neighbor, Art Carney, is sick from it. It's in his cows' milk, it's in his wife, it's in his wife's milk, it's in the infant she is breast-feeding. *Bitter Harvest* is a gripping moral story that stands as a model for films of this kind. There is a proper balance between heroism and victimization.

BITTER RICE. Italy. 1949. Silvana Mangano in a landmark of Neorealism about labor in the rice fields of northern Italy. Giuseppe De Santis directed.

BLACK HOLIDAY. Italy. 1973. Marco Leto directed this understated but powerful story of resistance to Mussolini's fascism in the late-thirties. An idealistic college professor gets sent to a detention camp: a simple story but a gripping one.

BLACK NARCISSUS. UK. 1946. Over the years, thousands of British filmmakers from Alfred Hitchcock on down have migrated from the chilly isles to the warm sun of the Hollywood raj. The remarkable team of Michael Powell and Emeric Pressburger often seemed as if they were guarding the reputation of native British cinema double-handedly. They knew how to do what Hollywood does at least as well as any of their American contemporaries, but they insisted on operating from home. *Black Narcissus* is a classic Hollywood movie, gorgeously photographed in Technicolor and full of the melodrama you might expect. (It's about nuns in a remote Himalayan village.) Deborah Kerr and Jean Simmons star.

BLACK ORPHEUS. Brazil/France. 1958. The Brazilian samba is one of the great musical forms of the twentieth century, rivalling American jazz. The French know this much better than we do. *Black Orpheus* was the first of a number of French productions to celebrate the samba and its tradition. A simple story set during Carneval, *Black Orpheus* is pleasant to watch and lots of fun to listen to.

BLACK STALLION, THE. US. 1979. If the Disney studio's live-action movies cranked out month after month were A-grade instead of B+-grade, they'd look like *The Black Stallion*. It's a classic children's story told unpretentiously and with considerable cinematic panache by Carroll Ballard. Mickey Rooney, the old man here, connects us with an earlier generation of children's movies. You don't even have to like horses.

BLACKBOARD JUNGLE. US. 1955. Richard Brooks directed this film which made a considerable impact in the mid-fifties. At the time the subject

Frank Sinatra, Gene Kelly and friends on the town for the first time in MGM's *Anchors Aweigh*.

would have been described as "juvenile delin-quency," but what we were really discovering then and have realized since is that it's about class differences: middle-class teachers versus working-class students. Every once in a while Hollywood filmmakers in the fifties ventured into the outside world; *Blackboard Jungle* was a landmark here as well, with a few shots of subway trains and New York streets. To understand what the fifties were about, you have to look not only at the paranoid horror movies but at *Blackboard Jungle* as well.

BLACKMAIL. UK. 1929. Hitchcock's first talkie started out as a silent film. It's exhilarating to watch him discover the possibilities of the new medium right before your eyes. There are sections obviously shot as silent to which one telling sound has been added, then we segue into full-blown dialogue scenes. A woman kills a man and then gets caught between the detective investigating the murder and the blackmailer. Anny Ondra stars.

BLADE RUNNER. US. 1982. This is only slightly less a dislikeable movie like director Ridley Scott's earlier *ALIEN*, but you have to give it credit for the clash of genres. It's film-noir science fiction, with a vengeance. Harrison Ford is a futuristic bounty hunter. He comes across okay, but you have to wonder why people would enjoy spending a couple of hours in this very dark, depressing, dirty, and downbeat future. A movie has got to be more than sets and an idea. ☑

BLAISE PASCAL. Italy. 1972. Another in Roberto Rossellini's landmark series of absorbing and intellectually involving historical essays. This one studies the seventeenth-century French philosopher who found himself caught in the dilemma of religion at the dawn of the age of science.

BLAZING SADDLES. US. 1974. Mel Brooks found a groove here that he travelled in happily for ten years: parodying genres. *Blazing Saddles* is a western with a Black hero and there are a number of good jokes, and some not so good as well. Interestingly, Richard Pryor was scheduled to star at one point but never hired because of a reported cocaine problem. If you know this when you watch the movie it's a disappointment. You keep thinking what Pryor could have done. He is exactly what's missing from *Blazing Saddles*. ☑

BLITHE SPIRIT. UK. 1945. David Lean directed this film version of the classic Noel Coward comedy about a man (Rex Harrison) who is haunted by the ghost of his dead wife. Margaret Rutherford steals the show as the medium, Madame Arcati.

BLOW-UP. UK. 1966. This may have been Michelangelo Antonioni's most popular film. It certainly was a landmark of the new intellectual cinema in the mid-sixties. Pauline Kael hated it and lost her job at *The New Republic*. The new breed of cineastes loved it. It was mysterious and metaphysical and thrillingly cinematic. Antonioni is one of the few directors who can really make it on style alone. At a time when people were beginning to be fascinated by the power of the camera, he gives us a philosophical essay on just that theme, based on the Julio Cortazar novel about appearance and reality. The essay doesn't say much, but his camera says a lot. ☑

BLUE ANGEL, THE. Germany. 1930. Josef Von Sternberg's best film is a good balance between style and subject. Marlene Dietrich is the cabaret singer. Emil Jannings is the repressed professor who falls longingly in love with her. This is a model of Weimar decadence which is still influential. ☑

BLUE COLLAR. US. 1978. This is Paul Schrader's attempt at a working-class drama set in Detroit, starring Richard Pryor, Yaphet Kotto, and

Harvey Keitel. The film hasn't aged well, even in the few short years since it was released, but it's worthwhile to catch for Pryor's extraordinary acting as the renegade factory worker. ▼

BLUE THUNDER. US. 1982. John Badham established himself in 1982 as a director to watch with *Blue Thunder* and *WARGAMES*. *Blue Thunder* has a mild political point (Big Brother is watching), a great machine (the Blue Thunder Helicopter), and a very nicely paced action story as renegade cop Roy Scheider takes out after the bad guys. The film is a great combination of genres: a little film noir, a bit of political melodrama, and lots of aerial battles—only this time they're in the skies above Los Angeles. It's us versus us! Don't miss it. ▼

BLUME IN LOVE. US. 1973. This is probably Paul Mazursky's best movie. It's certainly George Segal's best movie. It's about a middle-aged guy who loses his wife and gets her back again, and it's a romantic classic, especially interesting since you probably think you can't do romances anytime after 1968. Not true. It's got the usual Mazursky gently satiric touch and it's a warm story that leaves you feeling abashedly silly at the end, like a fond tickle. ▼

BOB & CAROL & TED & ALICE. US. 1969. This was Paul Mazursky's first directorial effort and is still his most popular film. It struck a chord at the end of the sixties. For the first time in an American movie someone was dealing with the sexual revolution of the sixties in a fairly intelligent way. It was one of those landmark films that seemed to be speaking at least some of the truth in a new way. Elliott Gould was a hip sixties type at the time as was Robert Culp. Natalie Wood shows herself to be a much better actress than most people gave her credit for. Dyan Cannon debuted. "What the world needs now is love, sweet love." ▼

BOB LE FLAMBEUR. France. 1955. A landmark in French appreciation of American film forms, this slightly noir, mildly gangster study by director Jean-Pierre Melville influenced a generation of French filmmakers by showing them how to do American genres in French settings. ▼

BOCCACCIO '70. Italy. 1962. During the sixties the Italians loved to make anthology films. The main reason was that three or four directors could be put to work simultaneously. The investors' money was tied up for a much shorter period of time. *Boccaccio '70* was the grandest of these, with episodes by Fellini, De Sica, and Visconti. It's best remembered for the Fellini episodes starring Anita Ekberg in a summary of her role in *LA DOLCE VITA*. She's a billboard figure that haunts the Fellini everyman, inviting him with her voluminous breasts to "drink more milk." Better yet is Romy Schneider in the Visconti episode, as a little rich girl, pointless but beautiful to watch. She writes English poems, too: "I love you cypress tree because your melancholy resembles unto me."

BODY AND SOUL. US. 1947. Director Robert Rossen's best film may also be actor John Garfield's summa. He stars as a boxer battling his way to the top by fair means and foul. ▽

BODY HEAT. US. 1981. Writer Lawrence Kasdan made an auspicious directorial debut with this hommage to 1940s film noir starring William Hurt, Kathleen Turner, and Richard Crenna in a typically steamy murder plot. Kasdan shows an interesting flair and point of view and bears watching in the late eighties. ▽

BOMBAY TALKIE. India. 1970. The team of James Ivory and Ismail Merchant has gone on for more than twenty years making their unique brand of Anglo-Indian cinema. *Bombay Talkie* is about an enormously popular genre of movie—the Indian musical—that you'll probably never be exposed to otherwise. Like so many Merchant/Ivory films, it shows us a culture that we seldom have an opportunity to experience.

BOMBSHELL. US. 1933. Jean Harlow in the title role in an unusually early movie about Hollywood social and professional lifestyles. Victor Fleming directed this sharp satire of the town that still fascinates the world.

BONNES FEMMES, LES. France. 1960. Claude Chabrol's study of the everyday lives of three shop girls was an important film early on in the French New Wave. Its treatment of Paris cityscapes still impresses.

BONNIE AND CLYDE. US. 1967. Arthur Penn is not an easy director and he's pretentious, but he struck a vein here with this seminal script by Robert Benton and David Newman about mythic gangsters of the thirties. You may not see what all the fuss was about now, but at the time *Bonnie and*

Clyde was hailed as a new mark of maturity in American filmmaking. What survives is great acting by Warren Beatty, Gene Hackman, Estelle Parsons. The poetic final shootout was unusual at the time. Now it's a cliche. (Compare *THIEVES LIKE US*.) ◩

BOOMERANG. US. 1947. Elia Kazan's docudrama about a priest's murder is tough and rhythmic and a worthy precursor of *ON THE WATERFRONT*. Dana Andrews, Lee J. Cobb, and Jane Wyatt star.

BOOT, DAS. West Germany. 1982. This elaborately produced genre movie gives us a Nazi submarine crew in the North Atlantic in World War II. It's good of its kind, and especially interesting for American audiences who have seen so many films shot from "the enemy's" (the "Allies'") point of view. ◩

BORING AFTERNOON, A. Czechoslovakia. 1968. During a brief period in the mid-1960s, Czechoslovakian filmmakers experienced a rush of freedom under the Dubček regime just before the Russian invasion. Miloš Forman is now the most famous of these directors (nearly all of them moved to the US eventually), but at the time Ivan Passer appeared to be equally interesting. *A Boring Afternoon* is a short film about just that. Passer makes people sitting around doing nothing extraordinarily humorous. It's well worth watching out for. Unlike Forman, he was never able to find his stride again in the English language.

BORN YESTERDAY. US. 1950. George Cukor directed Judy Holliday in this film version of the Garson Kanin play that made her famous as America's nicest dumb blonde since Jean Harlow. Broderick Crawford is almost as memorable as her boyfriend, the self-made man who hires William Holden to educate her into respectability. ◩

BOUCHER, LE. France. 1969. Claude Chabrol's series of bourgeois dramas from *LES BICHES* through *JUST BEFORE NIGHTFALL* constitutes quite an accomplishment. Studies of middle-class mores most often phrased as murder melodramas, they are all humorous, elegant, and telling. In *Le Boucher* Stéphane Audran is a provincial school teacher who is being courted by Jean Yanne, the butcher of the title. When she puts him off, he turns to a series of murders. It's all quite pleasant and the sunny locales add to the drollness of the story. Each of these films is set in a different provincial location and the story goes that Chabrol and his wife, Audran, made the series at least in part to have the opportunity to sample local cuisines. Let's revive the series at some cinematheque equipped with a good kitchen and combine showings with full course dinners. See also *LA FEMME INFIDELE* and *THIS MAN MUST DIE.*

BOUDU SAVED FROM DROWNING. France. 1932. Jean Renoir provided actor Michel Simon with a classic role—Boudu, the tramp who falls into the Seine and is saved by his opposite number, the very middle-class Lestingois (Charles Granvil). Like *THE CRIME OF MONSIEUR LANGE*, *Boudu* is a Renoir masterpiece that deserves as much attention as his more famous films. ▽

BOUND FOR GLORY. US. 1976. This is Hal Ashby's reverent and sumptuous biopic of Woody Guthrie. It is as it should be, a celebration of the American countryside and Guthrie's music. It's not a great film but it should remain with us for a long while because of its subject.

BOY FRIEND, THE. UK. 1971. Ken Russell's staging of the play about musicals in the 1920s starring Tommy Tune and Twiggy. Russell later went on to much more outrageous stylistic extravagances, but this remains his best film: a real celebration of the musical from a camp point of view. And let it be said Russell discovered Tommy Tune many years before Broadway did.

BRAINSTORM. US. 1983. Special effects master Douglas Trumbull came up with a novel and ingratiating plot to showcase his flamboyant visual displays. Scientists Louise Fletcher and Christopher Walken devise a way to record memory (on a wonderfully glitzy golden tape). Walken gets into trouble with the authorities, and with the help of his wife, Natalie Wood, outwits them. Wood died during the filming. ▽

BRANIFF/1975. US. 1969. It was common in the sixties and seventies for filmmakers abroad to earn spare cash shooting commercials. (A number of American feature filmmakers, for their part, trained in commercials.) Richard Lester directed this three-minute extravaganza for Braniff Airlines in the late sixties. It was made especially for showing during end-of-season football games. It envisions a future in faraway 1975 when everyone flies on supersonic jets, and passengers aim funny little flashlights in their eyes when they have headaches, while robot valets cruise the aisles collecting soiled clothing. A bunch of guys with half an eye on the commercial at the two-minute warning wouldn't have seen the humor, but in fact, this little film is very intentionally witty. You'll probably never see it but it stands here for all those thousands of tiny jewels of the filmmaker's art known as commercials. Anthologies of prize-winning commercials are already staples of network television. Let's hope the day is not so far off when the shelves of videostores are stocked with commercial collections put together with taste and purpose.

BREAKER MORANT. Australia. 1979. A good court-martial drama in the old-fashioned style about exploited soldiers, this film uses the novel location of South Africa during the Boer War. Bruce Beresford directed. Compare it to *PATHS OF GLORY*. ▼

BREAKFAST AT TIFFANY'S. US. 1961. This was the romantic touchstone of the early sixties, thanks to Henry Mancini's Moon River theme song, Audrey Hepburn at the height of her career, and Blake Edwards's lively celebration of the Manhattan milieu. Truman Capote's source novel is a thin story but for some reason we were all enthralled by George Peppard's attempt to bring Hepburn's call girl into the real world. On the other side of town *THE APARTMENT* was happening. See them together. ▼

BREAKING AWAY. US. 1979. This is a simple story about a kid and a bicycle and a very pretty town in Indiana. The lesson here is that's all you need to make a very good movie. With this film Peter Yates brought cycling to our attention in 1979. Five years later US cyclists walked off with a bunch of medals at the Los Angeles Olympics. It was a sport that few in this country had ever paid much attention to. The power of movies. ▼

BREAKING THE SOUND BARRIER. UK. 1952. David Lean directed Ralph Richardson, Ann Todd, and Nigel Patrick in this very British movie about a landmark in aviation. It's fun, but don't trust the history: it's not certain the filmmakers knew much about aerodynamics. Compare *THE RIGHT STUFF*.

BREATHLESS. France. 1960. The New Wave didn't start here, but it came of age on the Champs Elysées with Jean Seberg in her *New York Herald Tribune* T-shirt selling papers. *Breathless* neatly and remarkably summarized romantic imagery for the generation of the fifties in France caught up with the aura of Bogart, Hollywood, and America. (Belmondo plays Bogart's patented existential gangster.) It also stands as an emblem for the romantic concerns of a generation of Americans in the early sixties: Paris, Bogart, film noir, and the very exciting (at that time) art of the cinema. The jump cuts in Jean-Luc Godard's *Breathless* aren't important, although they're always mentioned. The romance of culture and the culture of romance, are. We still hark back to Bogart through Belmondo for our models.   ▼

BREATHLESS. US. 1983. Former underground director Jim McBride directed this strange American remake of the French film that celebrated American movies from a script he wrote with Kit Carson. In the set of Chinese boxes that passes for culture in the eighties, the *Breathless* remake is worth a look for people who are interested in the strange phenomenon of how we repeat ourselves again. And again.   ▼

⚠️🏠 **BRIDE OF FRANKENSTEIN**. US. 1935. Another admirable classic "programmer" from James Whale, this was a sequel to the original *FRANKENSTEIN*—and many think superior. Boris Karloff stars with Ernest Thesinger and Elsa Lanchester in the title role.   ▼

📌 **BRIDGE ON THE RIVER KWAI, THE**. UK. 1957. With this film, and *LAWRENCE OF ARABIA* in the early sixties, David Lean established himself as the king of the epic filmmakers, inheriting the mantle of C. B. De Mille. The film is remembered for Alec Guinness's performance and the famous theme song, but it also deserves mention as an interesting approach to an unusual war story.   ▼

⚠️ **BRIEF ENCOUNTER**. UK. 1945. Everybody's favorite end-of-the-war love story stars Celia Johnson and Trevor Howard as two people who fall for each other in a train station and enjoy a brief romance. Noel Coward wrote it, David Lean directed it, and it has served for forty years as a model for this sort of romance: a prime fantasy of married people.

💲 **BRIGADOON**. US. 1954. Gene Kelly, Van Johnson, and Cyd Charisse star under the direction of Vincente Minnelli in this film of the durable Alan Jay Lerner and Frederick Loewe musical about a magical Scottish village.

The "Triplets" number from *The Band Wagon:* Fred Astaire, Nanette Fabray, and Jack Buchanan.

BRINGING UP BABY. US. 1938. It's mentioned on everyone's list of top screwball comedies and probably deserves to be. Cary Grant is the stuffy scientist; Katharine Hepburn the nutty rich girl who invades his life with her pet leopard "Baby". Compare *WHAT'S UP, DOC?*

BRITANNIA HOSPITAL. UK. 1983. Once in a great while, Lindsay Anderson, the English stage impressario, turns his hand to cinema. When he does, it is worth stopping to watch. In the sixties it was *IF. . .*, in the seventies *O LUCKY MAN!* *Britannia Hospital* follows the Malcolm MacDowell character once again. This time he's set down in the middle of a bureaucratic British hospital. Anderson's brand of social satire is unusual, and probably deserves our attention. ▽

BROADWAY DANNY ROSE. US. 1984. This is a very interesting movie by Woody Allen: an hommage to standup comics that lets a bunch of them, including Corbett Monica, Milton Berle, and Sandy Baron appear on screen telling old stories about that crazy (fictional) agent Danny Rose. Allen himself plays Danny Rose but he's thoroughly miscast. He's just not brash or self-confident enough to carry off the ever-optimistic theatrical hanger-on that Rose is supposed to be. Danny has all the qualities Woody lacks, so maybe it was excellent therapy for the director/star. Mia Farrow is his girlfriend. The film made a smalltime club singer named Nick Apollo Forte into a temporary but very engaging movie star. ◩

BUDDY HOLLY STORY, THE. US. 1978. Steve Rash directed this biopic of the great rock and roll singer of the fifties. Gary Busey stars. It's an unpretentious, well-told, absorbing story and the music is worth the price.

BUGSY MALONE. UK. 1976. Alan Parker is a consistently interesting director. This was his first feature. It's a musical about pint-sized gangsters starring children playing adult's roles. The score by Paul Williams is full of catchy tunes and the conceit is interesting, very nearly until the end. With *Bugsy* and *FAME*, Englishman Parker can lay claim to being the leading innovator in film musicals during the last ten years.

BULLITT. US. 1968. This is a landmark cop movie by the consistent and intelligent Peter Yates. It's most memorable for the wild car chase through the streets of San Francisco. When people get around to making tape and disc anthologies of bits and pieces of movies, they'll save the *Bullitt* car chase. Compare *THE FRENCH CONNECTION*. ◩

BURDEN OF DREAMS. US. 1982. Les Blank's fascinating study of Werner Herzog during the obsessive shooting of his South American epic, *Fitzcarraldo*, tells us a lot about post-modernist filmmaking in which the artist is a more important work than the art. If Werner Herzog is more interesting than his movies, that must make Les Blank's movie more interesting than Herzog's. ◩

BUS, THE. US. 1963. Directed by Haskell Wexler, this is an important documentary record of the Civil Rights movement at its dramatic height.

BUTCH CASSIDY AND THE SUNDANCE KID. US. 1969. The western is a haunting form. It's useful dramatically because it's so simple: good and evil, men and nature, earth and sky. But there's more to it than that. Westerns have a lot to do with the myth that is still America, and so long as that myth survives, so will the western. *Butch Cassidy and the Sundance Kid* is a landmark in the history of the form. George Roy Hill and screenwriter William Goldman put the modern hero of the sixties, Paul Newman, and of the seventies, Robert Redford, together and killed them off at the end to provide us with a morality tale that caught the temper of the times in 1969. ⬇

⬆ **BYE, BYE BRAVERMAN**. US. 1968. Sidney Lumet is a great director, but he is probably a regional talent. His films are about the essence of New York City. *Bye, Bye Braverman* is even more local than that. It's about the kinds of intellectuals who live on the upper west side of Manhattan. There's a paradox that's always operating in literature and the arts: humor is a matter of precision, but the more precise you get the more limits you place on the audience you can reach. Perhaps you have to know these people to enjoy this film. A corollary to that paradox is that viewers and readers who want to appreciate the best in comedy should develop an understanding of cultures other than their own.

⬂ §⬆ **CA VA, CA VIENT**. France. 1970. This is a little-known, unpretentious, but thoroughly ingratiating French film from 1970. Written and directed by Pierre Barouh, *Ça Va, Ça Vient* follows the fortunes of a loosely-knit bunch of young French workers during the month of June. It doesn't mean to go very far, but it's full of good music and redolent of, well, "savoir vivre." Life goes on and *Ça Va, Ça Vient* has the pulse. Barouh appeared as the guitar-playing husband in *A MAN AND A WOMAN* and was in fact the source for much of the music in that famous film. Recently returned from Brazil, he was instrumental in introducing the Samba to the French. *Ça Va, Ça Vient* carries that mood of "Saravah."

⚑ § **CABARET**. US. 1972. A technically proficient musical with lots of good songs by Kander and Ebb. *Cabaret* is probably most notable for being a film version of a Broadway musical based on a film based on a play based on some short stories (by Christopher Isherwood, about Berlin in the thirties). For us to have recycled the British novelist's work so often in the past thirty years must mean something. In fact, *Cabaret* revived the Weimar decadence of the 1920s as an acceptable cultural style that has been with us for more than fifteen years now. With Liza Minnelli, Joel Grey, and Michael York. ⬇

⚑ § **CABIN IN THE SKY**. US. 1943. Today, the racial attitudes may make you cringe, but at the time this was applauded as a Hollywood effort to bridge the gap between Blacks and whites. Eddie Anderson, Lena Horne, Ethel Waters, Louis Armstrong, and Duke Ellington star in a slight plot that gives lots of time to the music. Vincente Minnelli directed, starting on a long and productive career.

CABINET OF DR. CALIGARI, THE. Germany. 1919. A key film in silent history directed by Robert Wiene, this set the style for what was to become known in the next ten years as German Expressionism. Caligari is a hypnotist one of whose victims commits murder. The sets are painted flats. Perspective is distorted. The lighting is harsh chiaroscuro and the effect is still eerie and moving today.

CABIRIA. Italy. 1914. A saga of the Punic Wars, this first real feature film lasted close to four hours in its original version. It served as a source not only of subject matter for spectacular films (see *BEN-HUR* and *INTOLERANCE*) but also as a model of lavish film production. Traveling shots were first used to good effect here.

CALIFORNIA SPLIT. US. 1974. Robert Altman's funkiest movie stars George Segal and Elliott Gould as a pair of inveterate gamblers, with Ann Prentiss and Gwen Welles as two sublimely happy-go-lucky goodtime girls. Perhaps it's a bit too loosely structured, but the film is so good-natured it wins you over.

CANDIDATE, THE. US. 1972. Michael Ritchie and Robert Redford made this film, hoping to have an effect on the 1972 presidential elections. They didn't, of course, but it's still a fascinating document about the relationships between politics and movies. Redford isn't yet Ronald Reagan, but he is clearly, along with Jane Fonda, a leading Hollywood politician. Pols in San Francisco, who helped stage rallies for the fictional character Redford plays in the film, assured him they'd have no trouble getting him elected. It's full of insight, and offers unusually precise vignettes of political figures and workers of the time. It's a fascinating essay on contemporary political media machinations. *Footnote*: In the fall of 1984, polls indicated that there was someone who could have beaten Ronald Reagan: Robert Redford.

CARABINIERS, LES. France. 1962. This is Godard's attempt at straightforward Brechtian story-telling with a political moral. Two young men go off to war leaving their women behind. It's most memorable for a stunningly Godardian scene: they return carrying suitcases full of postcards. They think the images are deeds to the properties. "Look what we've brought you: the Taj Mahal, the Eiffel Tower, St. Peter's Basilica, the Venus de Milo. . . ."

CARMEN. Germany. 1918. This is Ernst Lubitsch's first feature and one of the great international hits of the early silent period. It made Pola Negri an international star and set a fashion for lavish sets and costumes.

CARNAL KNOWLEDGE. US. 1971. Mike Nichols directed this Jules Feiffer script following two college roommates from the forties into the seventies as they continually fail with women. It's notable for Ann-Margret's performance; Jack Nicholson and Art Garfunkel just sort of stand there. Nevertheless, this very well represents the anxieties of people in their forties in the early seventies, bypassed by the sexual revolution of the sixties.

CARWASH. US. 1976. This looks like a simple teenage exploitation movie, but director Michael Schulz, together with a fine cast of actors from Richard Pryor on down, brings real life and verve to the subject. These are just a bunch of guys who work at a car wash but they're very real, and by the end of the film we feel as if we've known them for a long time.

CASABLANCA. US. 1942. This is obviously the ultimate Humphrey Bogart movie, greatly enhanced by the presence of Ingrid Bergman. Throughout her life, to the very end, Bergman was able to project unusual intelligence and humanity, as well as sexuality. In this she has few peers among actresses in American films. Bogart came close to this fantasy again with Lauren Bacall. This is where the fire was first lit.

CASE OF THE MUKKINESE BATTLE HORN, THE. UK. 1958. The British surreal humor that marked Monty Python in the seventies actually had its start on a radio show, *The Goon Show*, in the early fifties. Peter Sellers starred along with Spike Milligan and other favorites. The Goons never had much chance to make films, but *The Case of the Mukkinese Battle Horn*, a short, remains a rare opportunity to watch Sellers the comedian strut his radio stuff. This was before he became a serious actor.

CASINO ROYALE. UK. 1967. This is a landmark sixties film by John Huston and a number of other directors, starring most of the people who were in movies in the 1960s. It's the only James Bond film that didn't fit the James Bond mold. It's a wild melange of styles and approaches; just the sort of thing that was thought to be "kicky" in the 1960s. There's also a catchy score by Burt Bacharach.

CASQUE D'OR. France. 1952. The Paris underworld at the turn of the century as masterfully staged by Jacques Becker. Simone Signoret stars with Serge Reggiani and Claude Dauphin.

CATCH-22. US. 1970. The Joseph Heller novel had been such a bible for the generation of the sixties that there was no way Mike Nichols or anyone else could bring it to the screen without disappointing. First, since he can't include the whole thing, he's bound to leave out your favorite parts. Second, you've spent five or ten years envisioning the characters and it's unlikely that you saw Nichols's actors in the roles. Nevertheless, it's a good try and a very well-mounted and expensive production. The sight of a squadron of B-24s rumbling to take-off is something we shall not see again in our lifetime.

CELINE ET JULIE VONT EN BATEAU. France. 1973. Jacques Rivette has always been a difficult director. His experiments with film time and his obsession with existential ennui certainly don't make for popular cinema. Here he is at his lightest with a fantasy of two women (Juliet Berto and Dominique Labourier), friends in Paris enjoying their confusion of make-believe and reality. Bulle Ogier and Marie-France Pisier assist.

CESAR. France. 1936. See *MARIUS*.

CESAR AND ROSALIE. France. 1972. Michel Piccoli, Sami Frey, and Romy Schneider star in this reasoned and evocative romance about a menage a trois directed by Claude Sautet. It's a solid middle-class comedy.

CHANG. US. 1927. Filmmakers Ernest B. Schoedsack and Merian C. Cooper continued their documentary career for Paramount with this story of an Indo-Chinese family on their own in the jungle and the elephant who was as important to their lives as a horse is to a cowboy's. In order to understand the full impact of films like these in the twenties you have to realize how novel and refreshing such travelogues and ethnographical portraits were. This was a world which lacked the thousands of hours of well-made documentary footage that we take for granted on television now. The climax of the film, an elephant stampede, was projected in a process called

Magnascope. An enlarging lens was placed in front of the projector which increased the image to fill a screen four times normal size. It's a simple technique, but it was and still is very effective.

⚑ CHANGING MAN, THE. US. 1935. This Warner Bros. biopic came as close as anyone thought possible to capturing the ephemeral character of its subject, Leonard Zelig, the faddish chameleon personality of the 1920s. Shot in an early duotone process, the film hasn't lasted any longer than its subject's fleeting fame. By the early 1960s, when the sole remaining print was unearthed in the closet of an Upper West Side movie buff, it had faded to a barely perceptible pallet of gray on gray. In 1983, when Woody Allen recreated Zelig for his cool and clever existential meditation of the same name, master film technician Garrett Brown was able to restore several clips of *The Changing Man* using modern computerized image enhancement techniques. It's the only evidence that we have that Leonard Zelig, no matter who he looked like, always looked like Woody Allen. Allen's own film seems to me to be flawed by the heavy influence of John Morton Blum's academic study of the man, *Interpreting Zelig*. Allen misses the moderne savoir faire that was a key to Zelig's personality—what there was of it. This variegated character was perfectly captured by *The Changing Man*. It stands here for all lost films, and those which we know only from clips and quotes.

⊘ CHANT DU STYRENE, LE. France. 1958. Alain Resnais celebrated the manufacture of plastic in this wittily shot and sharply edited essay. It stands here for all industrial films.

‖↘ CHARADE. US. 1963. Stanley Donen was unique in being a fifties director who scored some of his most successful hits in the sixties. *Charade* is a classic romance of the sixties, perhaps the ultimate Audrey Hepburn film, and probably Cary Grant's last best effort. What more could you ask for? Paris, of course. You got it. And a small role by Walter Matthau. ▼

CHARIOTS OF FIRE. UK. 1981. I don't know why this film about amateur Olympic sports in the twenties caught on the way it did. I guess it's because it deals with values of another time and was so well mounted by director Hugh Hudson. Sports movies notoriously do poorly. I've never understood why. They're inherently dramatic and anyone who enjoys the sport should have half a leg up on the movie. The main problem with watching *Chariots of Fire* now is the theme song. It's been burned into our brains. ▽

⛫ **CHARLEY VARRICK**. US. 1973. This is a Don Siegel movie starring Walter Matthau. A very well-made caper film full of action and rich with character. A great B-movie of the seventies.

⬛ **CHARLIE BUBBLES**. UK. 1968. Not a great movie but an absorbing one about a writer who becomes suddenly successful, finds it very boring, and has an affair with his secretary. Albert Finney and Liza Minnelli starred in a fantasy of escape that remains unique. Finney directed. This was a romantic touchstone for some in the late sixties.

◬ **CHARLIE CHAN AT THE OPERA**. US. 1936. Yes, Charlie Chan is a caricature of the Oriental personality and questions of racism do arise, but in his heyday in the 1930s the character of Chan presented an Oriental hero on the screen in what is perhaps the longest running series in movies. (The first *Chan* film was made in 1926 and the most recent in 1981.) There's something else going on here besides the caricature. Chan is probably unique in being a family detective and his collaboration with his sons is one of the attractions of the character. As with Nick and Nora Charles in *THE THIN MAN* movies, we're often more interested in the relationship than in the mystery. A number of actors have played Chan. Warner Oland, who starred in this one, was generally regarded as the best. This film is as good as any in the series. H. Bruce Humberstone directed.

‖◬ **CHARLIE CHAPLIN FESTIVAL**. US. 1938. Chaplin put together several compilations of his earlier shorts (*Charlie Chaplin Cavalcade* and *Charlie Chaplin Carnival* also appeared in this year). This one includes *THE IMMIGRANT* and *EASY STREET*. All are, of course, prime candidates for inclusion in even the smallest home video library.

ℊ⟍☺ **CHARLOTTE'S WEB**. US. 1972. This is a very good animated film. It is of course a version of the E. B. White classic, a strange and wonderful story, of a pig named Wilbur and a spider named Charlotte who gives vocabulary lessons. Debbie Reynolds plays the voice of Charlotte and I believe every word. If you have kids and a tape of *Charlotte's Web*, you will have to listen to it hundreds of times during the next few years. It's greatly to the film's credit that you will seldom regret it when your kids pop the cassette into the machine. The music is superior for a film of this sort. "Some terrific, radiant, humble pig!" ▽

⊕ CHASSE AU LION A L'ARC, LA. France. 1965. Film is a tool as well as an entertainment medium (although critics pay very little attention to it as such). Jean Rouch is a French anthropologist and ethnologist who, more than anyone else, has made great use of the technique of film to capture cultures on celluloid. He has spent most of his career with certain African tribes. This film is a simple document of a group of hunters on the Niger/Mali border chasing a lion with bows and arrows. It's representative of numerous films that he's made with the same people over many years. An interesting paradox has developed during this time: Rouch's aim is to preserve culture on film, but a person who spent some time as an assistant to the filmmaker once told me that by the mid-seventies many of the younger tribe members, when they wanted to know, for example, how a certain dance or ritual was performed, watched old Rouch movies of their parents and grandparents! Apparently by preserving the culture, he has taken the life out of it. For hundreds of years these people had preserved their rituals, but also modified, extended, and changed them to fit the times. They can no longer do that: the Rouch films have become the authority and their culture is now frozen in time. Dead.

⊐ CHELSEA GIRLS, THE. US. 1966. In the sixties, when it was chic to make movies, a number of non-filmmakers tried their hand at it. Norman Mailer was poorest at this. Andy Warhol in his quirky way, perhaps the most successful. His arty films like *Empire* (eight hours of the Empire State Building in a static shot) are more interesting conceptually than the later films which attempted some sort of drama, but if you have to watch an Andy Warhol movie, you might as well catch a few minutes of *The Chelsea Girls*. It's just a bunch of the Warhol characters sitting around the Chelsea Hotel in Manhattan, talking. *The Chelsea Girls* is significant for one major innovation; when it was first shown, two projectors were run at the same time. They weren't in sync; it didn't matter. There were two movies going on in front of you. What an excellent way to deal with long, boring films!

◑ CHEYENNE AUTUMN. US. 1964. No one had a greater love of the west than John Ford, and it is maybe best represented in this, one of his last westerns. In Hollywood it was unusual, even striking at the time, to do a western from the point of view of the Indians. Ford is given credit for a lot of talents. But seldom do critics point to his emerging sensitivity to more advanced cultural viewpoints than the old-fashioned Hollywood Cowboys-and-Indians cliches.

⇓ **CHILDREN OF PARADISE**. France. 1945. This is one of the classics that gives movies a bad name. Theatrical and rhythmless, it stars Jean-Louis Barrault and Arletty in a drawn-out love affair. Like most films of the mid to late forties, it goes on for a very long time. It seems people needed any excuse then to spend time in a theater.

◓ **CHIMES AT MIDNIGHT**. Spain/Switzerland. 1966. This is certainly Orson Welles's most interesting late effort: a version of Falstaff from the Shakespeare history plays with the great man himself as the rotund classic character. Jeanne Moreau, Margaret Rutherford, and John Gielgud helped. It's probably the role Welles was born to play—and how often is a successful commercial theatrical film based on Shakespeare?

✛ **CHINA SYNDROME, THE**. US. 1979. This is an exceptionally well made political melodrama about the potential danger of nuclear plants that seems to have had a direct impact on public consciousness—a rarity. Of course it was helped greatly by good timing: a few weeks after the film was released reality imitated art at Three Mile Island in Harrisburg, Pennsylvania. Because the drama is so real it is close to unbearable. Director James Bridges had done a similarly pessimistic fantasy about computers almost ten years earlier with *Colossus: The Forbin Project*. ▼

⚑ ⇓ **CHINATOWN**. US. 1974. Though I'm not too fond of this, it's probably the best example of the remake/redo frame of mind that has obsessed Hollywood since the early seventies. Screenwriter Robert Towne fashioned an excellent imitation of Raymond Chandler, and Roman Polanski put every inch of it on the screen with the help of Jack Nicholson as the detective Jake Gittes on the trail of corruption and dark family secrets in L.A. in the thirties. But it's ersatz, and Hawks and Chandler finally did it better. Why do it again so often? That's a question we've been asking Hollywood filmmakers for fifteen years now. So far there is no answer except a lack of contemporary imagination.   ▼

⚑ **CHINOISE, LA**. France. 1967. Jean-Luc Godard was just getting politicized at this time and he was very proud that *La Chinoise* was shown at Columbia University shortly before a student revolt there. With hindsight it's a much more prescient film than we may at first have noticed: the French student revolt started at the Nanterre campus of the Sorbonne, just as Godard had suggested. For all his reputed political commitment, Godard nevertheless paints a balanced and reasoned portrait of young revolutionaries. A document of its time.

CHLOE IN THE AFTERNOON. France. 1972. This is the sixth and final of Eric Rohmer's moral tales. These *contes moraux* aren't "moral" in the English sense of the word; they are rather concerned with sensibilities and the life of the mind. This is the last episode in the series: our male hero has finally made the commitment to a woman (he's been avoiding it throughout the series) and is only mildly distracted by Chloë (Zouzou). Rohmer surprised everyone with the success of these moral tales internationally; he's the true Henry James of the cinema. See also *MY NIGHT AT MAUD'S*, *CLAIRE'S KNEE*.

CHRIST STOPPED AT EBOLI. Italy. 1979. With all the attention that we paid to the fantasies of Federico Fellini and Michelangelo Antonioni in the sixties and seventies, it now turns out that the great strength of Italian film during the last half century remains Neorealism. Francesco Rosi directed this version of the famous novel with extraordinary attention to the details of everyday life and it really comes alive.

CHRISTMAS CAROL, A. UK. 1984. Purists preferring the 1938 MGM version with Reginald Owen or the 1951 Alastair Sim rendering of the Scrooge fable will cringe, but, in all, this recent Clive Donner television film with George C. Scott and David Warner seems to capture the spirit of Dickens with more precision. "God bless us everyone."

CHRISTMAS IN JULY. US. 1940. It's one of the tenets of this book that any film written by Preston Sturges ranks very high indeed. His view of America was unique and his sense of humor is one of our great national assets. It is so fresh and vivacious, so liberating and infectious, that it makes an awful lot of what came after in the fifties and sixties and seventies look cramped and neurotic. In addition, Sturges was one of very few humorists to succeed on film only as writer/director, without having to act in his films as well. *Christmas in July* is based on a simple concept: William Powell thinks he's won a lot of money and goes off to spend it. Money is usually at the heart of Sturges's concerns. Sturges took screwball comedy and achieved its apotheosis.

CHRISTMAS STORY, A. US. 1983. Humorist Jean Shepherd started on radio in the fifties where he gained some notoriety with a local New York show. His work is sometimes cloying, but at its best is in the grand tradition of American humor that started with George Ade. Shepherd's problem is that he has never found a proper medium since leaving radio. *A Christmas Story* comes as close as anything he's done to capturing the special Shepherd midwestern sense of humor. He narrates the autobiographical story of a kid in the thirties who lives only for the BB gun he wants for Christmas. Somewhere, Will Rogers is smiling.

CHRONICLE OF A SUMMER. France. 1961. This is the film that founded the impersonal, unnarrated style of documentary known as cinéma vérité. Anthropologists Jean Rouch and Edgar Morin set their cameras down in Paris in the summer of 1960 and recorded life as it passed by in the persons of a handful of unpretentious Frenchmen. They kept—or tried to keep—themselves out of the picture and thus was born cinéma vérité.

CITIZEN KANE. US. 1941. If you're a young novelist you have dreams of writing the Great American Novel. If you're a young filmmaker, sadly, the corresponding dream is not available: it's already been done. *Citizen Kane* is, without a doubt, the Great American Film and will remain so for the forseeable future. It takes all the elements of popular movies—character, dialogue, story—and does them as well as anyone has before or since. The acting by Welles, Joseph Cotten, Everett Sloane, Agnes Moorehead, Dorothy Comingore, Ray Collins, George Coulouris, William Alland, and Paul Stewart is as good as you'll find in an American movie. At the same time, *Citizen Kane* stretched the boundaries of film art in a fascinating and exhilarating way. At a young age, Welles had apparently forgotten more about the strange craft of narrative than most masters of the cinema ever learned. Not until Godard did anyone tell stories in such an interesting way. It's essential to note, however, that these "esthetics" never get in the way of the human drama of ideas. They're always at the service of it. If *Citizen Kane* did no more than this— combine popular moviemaking with advanced cinematic techniques—it would stand certainly as one of the best American movies of all time. But it does much more. William Randolph Hearst, the subject of the film, is perhaps the quintessential American character of the twentieth century, outranking even Richard Nixon. Welles and company not only captured this character live on film, they also seemed to understand it. We learn something. If one film is to be preserved for a thousand years to explain America in the twentieth century, there's no question it's *Citizen Kane*. One final note: Welles is known as the great American genius of the cinema, and there's no doubt that his work in film and radio and theater ranks him at the top, but it's ironic and interesting to note that he never did quite as well again. The reason? Despite his real individual genius, I think he very much needed the company of actors, writers, and technicians who came together with such transcendent power in *Citizen Kane*. The work of writer Herman J. Mankiewicz, cinematographer Gregg Toland, and composer Bernard Herrmann was integral to the success of the film. ▼

CITIZEN'S BAND. US. 1977. Like people, movies seem to divide themselves into two categories: ambitious on the one hand, and good-natured and unpretentious on the other. *Citizen's Band* is a fine example of the latter style of filmmaking. Director Jonathan Demme is not well known, but he's made a number of good-natured, finely observed stories like this one about a group of people addicted to their citizen's band radios. A good document of its time.

CITY LIGHTS. US. 1931. This is the ultimate Charlie Chaplin film, the movie in which Charlie's tramp was raised to the level of paragon. Charlot is in love with a blind flower girl here. It's a silent film with sparing use of music written by Chaplin. We have a problem that still haunts us nearly one hundred years after the end of the Victorian era. In the twentieth century we find it impossible intellectually to accept sentiment. This is a serious failing and if we are ever to overcome it the films of Charles Chaplin should be of great aid. ▼

CLAIRE'S KNEE. France. 1970. Eric Rohmer had some considerable success with international audiences in the late sixties and early seventies with his series of "moral tales." He doesn't mean the word "moral" the way you may think. In French a "moraliste" is someone who's greatly concerned about psychological motivation: Rohmer's very attractive series of films is fascinating in that respect. This is pure intellectual comedy: we are interested in how people think about what they think about what they do. In *Claire's Knee*, the hero (Jean-Claude Brialy) is surrounded by five women, including Claire, whose knees impress him inordinately, and Laura, equally young, who has a crush on him. A simple film with a lot to think about. See also *MY NIGHT AT MAUD'S* and *CHLOE IN THE AFTERNOON*.

⇧ **CLEO FROM 5 TO 7**. France. 1962. Agnès Varda made this little-known film just at the beginning of the New Wave. It exhibits all the qualities: the contemporary characters, the realistic setting in the streets in Paris, the concern with thought and action. It's also interesting because the real time of the film takes just two hours, as the title indicates.

🚩 **CLEOPATRA**. US. 1934. This is the gargantuan Cecil B. De Mille/Paramount spectacular. Don't miss Claudette Colbert's bath. You may also want to take a look at the 1916 Theda Bara *Cleopatra*.

🚩 ⇧ **CLEOPATRA**. US. 1963. *Cleopatra* is more famous for the events surrounding its production than any film since *GONE WITH THE WIND*. It brought Richard Burton and Elizabeth Taylor together in what was, at that time, an enormously expensive production. When the film was released, critics and audiences laughed a lot. Joe Mankiewicz did a rather good job of working around Burton and Taylor, and *Cleopatra*, on second viewing years later, proves to be a worthy epic. ▽

☺ **CLOAK AND DAGGER**. US. 1984. An honest and interesting film for kids about kids. Henry Thomas stars as a boy who loves videogames who gets to be a real-life hero playing out his fantasies and stepping into the shoes of his fictional hero. Richard Franklin directed. Dabney Coleman and Michael Murphy play the adults. ▽

⋅⋅🚩 **CLOCKWORK ORANGE, A**. US/UK. 1971. This is probably a nasty film but Stanley Kubrick brilliantly presaged the cultural phenomena of the late seventies and eighties a good number of years before teenagers discovered the punk style. At the time, however, the film looked outdated. *A Clockwork Orange*, based on Anthony Burgess's pessimistic novel of the early sixties, talks about "milk bars" but we already had "juice bars" back in the late sixties. The punk phenomenon of the past few years may thus best be viewed as a cultural remake of a 20-year-old novel and a 10-year-old film. ▽

Ryan O'Neal and Marisa Berenson form a tableau worthy of Jacques-Louis David in Stanley Kubrick's elegant *Barry Lyndon.*

⇩ **CLOSE ENCOUNTERS OF THE THIRD KIND.** US. 1977. Director Steven Spielberg is brilliant at capturing quick sketches of contemporary American characters. They're always pleasurable to watch. The trouble is they don't ever seem to add up to much. Spielberg's movies are always a little fuzzy. *Close Encounters* has a great spirit at its heart, but it goes off in many directions. It's ostensibly about visitors from another planet, but for most of its length it pretends to be a kind of thriller—or maybe a domestic drama—or perhaps a horror movie. . . . Nevertheless, it's nice that such humane, friendly, and good-natured films as *Close Encounters* and *E.T.* have become blockbusters. ☒

‼ **CLOWNS, THE.** Italy. 1971. Federico Fellini turned here to mock documentary to celebrate the circus clowns and the joy of humor and parody which is at the heart of his movies. It's almost like a self-critique: a pleasant hommage to a worthy theatrical tradition. ☒

COAL MINER'S DAUGHTER. US. 1980. The story of the rise to fame of country singer Loretta Lynn is a good solid musical biography written by Tom Rickman and directed by Michael Apted. Sissy Spacek stars with Tommy Lee Jones, Beverly D'Angelo, and Levon Helm, former drummer of The Band, who's made a second career for himself as an admirable character actor in the eighties.　▽

COME BACK AFRICA. US/South Africa. 1959. American Lionel Rogosin shot this landmark study of South African apartheid mostly on the sly. It's a combination of documentary and fictionalized scenes that was striking at the time and sadly remains as relevant today as it was more than twenty-five years ago.

COMES A HORSEMAN. US. 1978. Alan J. Pakula, master of paranoia, directed this unusual film-noir western with James Caan as a cowhand, Jane Fonda as a ranch owner, and Jason Robards as the evil oil tycoon. An unusual staging of the American west.

CONFIDENTIALLY YOURS. France. 1983. Very late Truffaut in the Hitchcock mold. Much lighter and more enjoyable than most of Truffaut's films in the seventies, this is a classy black-and-white movie about a man falsely accused of murder. Jean-Louis Trintignant and Fanny Ardant star.

CONFORMIST, THE. Italy. 1970. Bernardo Bertolucci's best film makes an interesting comment on the relationship between repressed sexual desires and fascist politics. It's a moody study of the twisted Italian character of the thirties starring Jean-Louis Trintignant, Stefania Sandrelli, and Dominique Sanda. Elegantly photographed and memorable. ▽

CONTRACT ON CHERRY STREET. US. 1977. A solid policier with a good sense of New York City. It gives Frank Sinatra his first movie-made-for-television role as a New York cop who takes on the gangsters after his partner is killed. Based on Philip Rosenberg's novel.

CONVERSATION, THE. US. 1974. This Francis Coppola experiment does for tape recorders what *BLOWUP* did for cameras. Gene Hackman is a private eye caught in the paradoxes of his profession, trying to piece together a conversation on tape. It pre-echoes Watergate. It's not a pleasant film, but it was made with some style.　▽

COOGAN'S BLUFF. US. 1968. Another evocative action cop film from Don Siegel. This time Clint Eastwood is a western lawman who shows up the big city cops in New York. Siegel has an unparalleled ability to breathe life and interest into simple stories like this one.　▽

COOL WORLD, THE. US. 1964. Shirley Clarke directed and Frederick Wiseman produced this landmark in American documentary which depicted the struggles, often unsuccessful, of teenagers in Harlem slums. In the mid-sixties it was important for showing real Black kids on film in a way we had never seen them before. It's sobering that the drugs, violence, and racism are just as much a part of the scene twenty years later.

CORNER IN WHEAT, A. US. 1909. A significant D. W. Griffith short based on Frank Norris's "A Deal In Wheat" this dramatic political tract parallels the tough life of the farmers with the easy life of the "wheat king." It's magnificently photographed by Billy Bitzer and a striking example of Griffith's development of parallel editing. It also makes a useful point.

COSIMO DE MEDICI. Italy. 1973. This is one of the grand string of historical "docudramas" that Rossellini made at the end of his life for Italian television: a study of the powerful renaissance family. No one before or since has known better how to get ephemeral ideas into the physical medium of film. Bringing history to life has been at the heart of cinema since the very beginning and Rossellini has done it better than anyone.

COTTON CLUB, THE. US. 1984. The story behind the making of *The Cotton Club* as chronicled by Robert Daly in *New York Magazine* is so full of high drama, eccentric character, and Hollywood madness that the film itself has to pale in comparison. The battle between producer Robert Evans and director Francis Coppola, the extreme budget overrun, and the shady financial dealings cry out for a screen treatment. The film itself is listed here more for what it might have been than what it is. Evans's original idea was to present a story about white gangsters in the 1930s against the exciting historical setting of the Cotton Club and its Black musicians and dancers. When the film focuses on its Black background it's an enthralling recreation of one of the wellsprings of American music. It is as good to look at as it is to listen to. However, this "background" material is interrupted far too often by the gangster story. Coppola apparently shot far more footage of the Cotton Club milieu than actually appears on screen. Shortly after the film's release at the end of 1984, disappointed collaborators laid plans to reconstruct the extra footage. Precedents exist, and *The Cotton Club* may yet show up as a miniseries with Black entertainers in the foreground and white gangsters in the background. That's how it should have been from the beginning.

COTTON COMES TO HARLEM. US. 1970. For a very brief period in the early seventies, it looked as if Black American cinema was going to develop with as much vigor and interest as Black American theater. This did not come to pass, as Hollywood moguls learned that they could get just as much money out of the Black audience with more general films. *Cotton Comes to Harlem* was directed by Ossie Davis from the well-known series of novels by Chester Himes. Godfrey Cambridge was the private eye. Lots of local atmosphere and a workmanlike job of direction.

COURT JESTER, THE. US. 1956. This Danny Kaye vehicle is a lovely musical comedy—and one of the very best children's films ever made. First, it has Kaye at the peak of his form. Next, it has some delightful patter songs by Sylvia Fine. ("The Chalice with the palace has the brew that is true.") It has color and action and heart. And, as if that weren't enough, it makes a strong feminist statement. That's right! In 1956! Glynis Johns is the hero. Jester Kaye needs and defers to her. Considering the time, it's almost incredible.

COUSIN, COUSINE. France. 1975. In the seventies, popular French films were marked by a new concern for middle-class lives. Gone were the rebels of the sixties, to be replaced by working people very much like all those people who still go to the cinema. Director Jean-Charles Tacchella scored with *Cousin, Cousine*, a comedy about family matters which set attendance records for French movies in the US at the time. It's witty and mildly charming and—most important—stars the nonpareil Marie-France Pisier.

COUSINS, LES. France. 1959. This is Claude Chabrol's second feature, often regarded as the first film of the French New Wave. It's about the relationships of Parisian university students and thus echoes the actual background of several New Wave directors in the fifties. Compare it with *PARIS BELONGS TO US*.

CRAIG'S WIFE. US. 1936. Under the direction of Dorothy Arzner, Rosalind Russell had her first success here as the coldly ambitious wife who dominates her husband in a classic melodrama. It's much more a Joan Crawford role than a Rosalind

Russell character but luckily she moved on to far more positive and engaging roles later in her career.

⇩ **CRIES AND WHISPERS**. Sweden. 1972. Harriet Andersson, Liv Ullmann, and Erland Josephson in Ingmar Bergman's impressively photographed poem about death. By 1972 Bergman was no longer a mystical foreign art filmmaker for us; in *Cries and Whispers* his depressive morbidity became clear. ∨

✳\ **CRIME OF MONSIEUR LANGE, THE**. France. 1935. Other films by Jean Renoir are more famous; I think this is his best. It's a heady realist fantasy of a community. Workers at a publishing house form a cooperative after the shady owner absconds, and have fun making a success of publishing popular novels by Monsieur Lange. When Batala, the owner, returns to claim his "property," Lange kills him. The action takes place in and around a classic Paris apartment house and celebrates the architectural idea of community inherent in those buildings with central courtyards, concierges, public laundries, and a mixture of shops, businesses, and living quarters. Jacques Prévert wrote the script, and historically the film is considered a tract for theories of the Popular Front during the thirties, but Renoir gives it such vivacity and humanity that the ideology springs to life—a rare thing.

‼ **CRITIC, THE**. US. 1963. Ernest Pintoff directed this short animated illustration of a routine by Mel Brooks. Brooks on the soundtrack is an elderly Jewish gentleman stuck in an art house forced to watch some abstract cartoon before the feature begins. Brooks is a brilliant standup comic and it's always hard to capture this sort of particular genius on film. This is one of the few relics that we have.

⇪ **CROSS CREEK**. US. 1983. Director Martin Ritt has a particular fascination with the mores of the American south. In *Cross Creek* he gives us Mary Steenburgen as the author Marjorie Kinnan Rawlings abandoning the high life of Long Island to hack out a new life for herself all alone in the swamps of Florida. It's such an unusual premise, and Steenburgen is so good at the role, that the film holds your interest for longer than you might expect. ∨

🚩 **CROSSFIRE**. US. 1947. This tough cop story by Edward Dmytryk about a crazy ex-G.I. was given more credit than it deserved at the time because it injected commentary on anti-Semitism into the plot.

Ironically, the novel by Richard Brooks on which it was based used homosexuality, not Jewishness, as a plot element. ▼

CROWD, THE. US. 1928. King Vidor's landmark drama treats a realistic theme—the inhumanities of urban civilization—with expressionistic techniques, giving us snapshots of the day-to-day lives of everyman and everywoman.

CUBA. US. 1979. Richard Lester is such an interesting and varied director that even his lesser works are worth spending some time with. There's always something to think about and look at. *Cuba* is a vague film which should have had a much more specific political sense, but it's the closest he has yet come to equaling his success with *PETULIA*. It's a strange melodrama set in Cuba during the final days of the Battista regime in late 1959, just as Castro comes to power. As usual with Lester, much of the interest is around the edges. He's still better at detail than anybody else working today.

CUTTER'S WAY. US. 1981. Director Ivan Passer has never matched in the US the success he had in his native Czechoslovakia, but *Cutter's Way*, with Jeff Bridges, John Heard, and Lisa Eichhorn, has become a cult favorite. It's about the psychological aftermath of Vietnam and the possibilities of taking political action, and it has much admirable detail. ▼

DAMN YANKEES. US. 1958. It's a classic fifties stage musical brought to the screen by George Abbott, the dean of the American musical stage, and Stanley Donen. It's Tab Hunter's best movie, and probably Gwen Verdon's, too. "Whatever Lola wants, Lola gets!" The anti-Yankee baseball politics, valid in the fifties, are all the more valid today in the era of Steinbrenner. ▼

DANTON. France. 1982. Over the years Polish director Andrzej Wajda has established himself slowly and surely as one of the masters of European cinema. *Danton* is a wise and insightful historical melodrama starring Gérard Depardieu as the hero/villain of the French revolution. Of course the film has contemporary political resonance as well. ▼

DARK CRYSTAL, THE. US. 1983. Jim Henson's muppets have been so much with us these last fifteen years that we often ignore the significance of his work. Henson and his colleagues are as important in the history of puppeteering as, say, Walt Disney is in the history of animation. They've raised the craft to an entirely new level and established muppets and other characters that are remarkably alive. *The Dark Crystal*, sans muppets, is Henson's attempt to take the craft of puppeteering in new directions yet again, as he experiments with a mixture of puppets and special effects. ▽

DARK VICTORY. US. 1939. The ultimate Hollywood soap opera and the definitive Bette Davis role combine to make a film which is enjoyable from two entirely opposite points of view. You'll enjoy either crying or laughing at Davis as the spoiled rich girl with the mysterious fatal disease. George Brent, Humphrey Bogart, and Ronald Reagan surround her. ▽

DARLING. UK. 1965. John Schlesinger directed this landmark of British cinema in the 1960s from a Frederic Rafael script. Dirk Bogarde and Julie Christie star in a chic, nicely-tuned domestic drama about a poor girl's numerous affairs and eventual marriage to a rich Italian. At the time it was released, critics saw in it evidence that British cinema was catching up to French and Italian. ▽

DARLING LILI. US. 1970. Overlooked at the time, this is a Blake Edwards/Julie Andrews collaboration set against the background of World War I that has a nicely restrained sense of humor and some good music. She's a German spy in London posing as a singer.

DATE WITH JUDY, A. US. 1948. We have several series about boy teenagers from the golden years of Hollywood, but very few films about girl teenagers (aside from Deanna Durbin). Here's one starring a wonderfully young Elizabeth Taylor together with Jane Powell, Carmen Miranda, and Wallace Beery. Richard Thorpe directed. The theme song is memorable.

DAVID AND LISA. US. 1963. Before the European New Wave broke on American shores in the late sixties, the more ambitious independent American "films" (as opposed to traditional Hollywood "movies") almost always dealt with social problems centering on the disadvantaged and disabled in society. The emblem for this is Harold Russell, the double amputee with the hooks in *THE BEST YEARS OF OUR LIVES*. The aim, intentional or not, was to give audiences someone to feel sorry for. *David and Lisa* was one of the last and, in fact, one of the best in this independent filmmaking tradition. Keir Dullea and Janet Margolin starred as disturbed teenagers. Frank and Eleanor Perry directed and wrote the film.

DAVID COPPERFIELD. US. 1935. A solid and fairly faithful Hollywood rendition of the Charles Dickens novel about a boy growing to self-made manhood, directed by George Cukor. Starring Freddie Bartholomew, W. C. Fields, and Lionel Barrymore. It still holds up.

DAY AFTER, THE. US. 1983. Everyone here had good intentions: to make an effective anti-nuclear political statement by showing the aftermath of nuclear war in one American city. The film was among the most watched and controversial television events of the last fifteen years, but a major question remains: does such a shocking and depressing portrayal of nuclear war have any lasting political effect or is it simply just another more sophisticated form of psychological exploitation? *DR. STRANGELOVE*, and even Peter Watkins's *THE WAR GAME*, did it much better and much earlier.

DAY AT THE RACES, A. US. 1937. Most connoisseurs regard this as the third best Marx Brothers film. Groucho is Dr. Hackenbush here, quackily treating Margaret Dumont.

DAY FOR NIGHT. France. 1973. This is François Truffaut's movie about moviemaking. There's no great drama here. Rather, like the films Truffaut loved best to watch and make, it's a quiet study of people. But there's no denying Truffaut's pleasure in showing us how movies are made. Many in-jokes and cross-references.

DAY OF THE JACKAL, THE. UK/France. 1973. This is a classic thriller from a classic Frederick Forsyth novel. It's about an attempt to assassinate Charles de Gaulle and it's about as good a job as you can do in this genre. "Thriller" is perhaps the wrong word, because what's fascinating about films like these is watching how things happen: They're a combination of thriller and caper. The question is: what's he going to do next? Watching people work out the logic of a situation is one of the major attractions of any film.

DAYBREAK EXPRESS. US. 1963. This is a superb, rocking piece of music by Duke Ellington to which D. A. Pennebaker had added footage of New York subway trains hurtling around the city. It's only three or four minutes long, but it's a pleasure. It also reminds you that the form of the music video was invented a long, long time ago.

DAYS AND NIGHTS IN THE FOREST. India. 1969. Satyajit Ray is to western eyes India's great filmmaker. His films open a new world to us. He deals with contemporary Indian characters with aplomb and insight, and Indian characters are of considerably more interest to westerners than characters of other oriental cultures because of the still pervasive effect of the historical British presence in India. *Days and Nights in the Forest,* a gentle story of four young men on holiday in the country, may be Ray's quintessential study of contemporary intellectual Indians.

DAYS OF HEAVEN. US. 1978. *Days of Heaven* is a film about wheat and locusts, crickets and blue sky. There's an interesting historical drama at its core— the settling of the west—but what you really want and get from this film is a celebration of the American countryside. Almost alone among American filmmakers, director Terrence Malick has the power to make scenery, images, and sounds as exciting as dialogue, character, and action. He's no slouch in those departments, either. The dialogue here, for Linda Manz, in particular, is one of the great glories of the movie. See it in 70mm if you possibly can.

DAYS OF THRILLS AND LAUGHTER. US. 1961. A compilation by Robert Youngson of clips and shorts from the silent days including Chaplin, the Keystone Kops, Laurel and Hardy, and others.

DAYS OF WINE AND ROSES. US. 1962. This is the third great romantic touchstone for the class of 1963 (along with *THE APARTMENT* and *BREAKFAST AT TIFFANY'S*). Another great theme by Henry Mancini, and Jack Lemmon and Lee Remick in a downbeat story of alcoholism. At the time it seemed a new, more adult sort of drama. Blake Edwards directed. It may not hold up today.

DE DUVE. US. 1969. Three people named Sidney Davis, George Coe, and Anthony Lover made this sublime 15-minute parody of all of Ingmar Bergman's movies. Like any great parody, it's really indescribable: be there if you can. If you've ever seen a Bergman movie you'll spend the next three years quoting bits of mock-Swedish dialogue from *De Duve*. The whole film is in Swedish-English and you learn a lot about the mistakes we make in judging foreign films simply because we can't understand the language. Frankly, it's doubtful you'll ever be able to take Bergman seriously again after seeing *De Duve*. Like all great satire it "severs the head from the body and leaves it standing," as John Dryden once said. Madeline Kahn appears.

DEADLIEST SEASON, THE. US. 1977. A good solid sports film dealing with pro hockey. Michael Moriarty is confronted with the dilemma of the contemporary sports star: he doesn't know whether he's there to play the game or to entertain the fans. Meryl Streep, Kevin Conway, Jill Eikenberry, and Patrick O'Neal round out the superior cast of this rather serious melodrama. Compare it to the more lively and irreverent *SLAP SHOT* and you'll see the difference between television movies and theatrical movies in the seventies. Script by the earnest and responsible Ernest Kinoy.

🚩 ⌂ DEADLY AFFAIR, THE. UK. 1967. This is a superior John le Carré novel filmed by Sidney Lumet with an interesting international cast: James Mason, Simone Signoret, Maximilian Schell, Harriet Andersson, Harry Andrews, and Lynn Redgrave. The downbeat spy story captures the mood that made *Tinker, Tailor, Soldier, Spy* so popular fifteen years later. It's also of interest technically because Lumet experimented with "flashing" techniques, exposing the film stock before shooting to give it unusually subdued color. These techniques later became common.

DEALING. US. 1972. Paul Williams directed this interesting essay on the way young people lived then on the edge of the drug culture. The full title is *Dealing, or the Berkeley to Boston 40-Brick Lost Bag Blues*. Compare it with *THE BIG CHILL*, which shows us more or less the same folks ten years later on.

⇩🚩 DEATH IN VENICE. Italy. 1971. Luchino Visconti's most operatic movie, based on the classic novel by Thomas Mann, with a score by Gustav Mahler, is static and often tiresome. The film, which portrays the obsession of an old man for a young boy, was important at the time because it expressed a gay sensibility early on in the current period of gay political activism. The pictures of Venice are the best you'll ever see, and that alone makes it worth looking out for. ◼

DEATH OF A SALESMAN. US. 1951. With

Fredric March and Kevin McCarthy, this is a very good record of the classic American stage play. Arthur Miller never did as well again.

DEFIANT ONES, THE. US. 1958. Tony Curtis and Sidney Poitier are handcuffed together as white and Black escaped convicts in the south in this classic liberal adventure from Stanley Kramer. The political lesson drives the movie but the action is good, too, as they flee from their oppressors. In a strange way, this is a model for numerous Black/white partnerships over the years, from Cosby and Culp in *I Spy* to Michael Warren and Charles Haid in *Hill Street Blues*.

DENTIST, THE. US. 1932. Another fine W. C. Fields vehicle. Collect 'em and trade 'em with your friends.

DESTINATION TOKYO. US. 1943. This is a superior World War II submarine drama that exhibits two other points of interest. First, Cary Grant is the sub commander. He's supposedly from Kansas, and it's interesting to watch him play so much against type. He brings it off. Secondly, the film stops about two-thirds of the way through for a fifteen- to twenty-minute propaganda essay as Grant writes a letter home to the wife and kids. We learn in this mini-documentary how the Germans and the Japanese, our enemies, are ethnically and racially simply no-goodniks, and how the Russians and the Chinese, our allies, are good, solid, strong folk who will always do right. Of course, ten years later these racially motivated evaluations would be reversed. By the mid-seventies, many, if not all, prints of the film were lacking this fascinating sequence. Make sure you get the full-length version.

DESTRY RIDES AGAIN. US. 1939. A classic western sendup starring James Stewart and—of all people—Marlene Dietrich. Stewart is the lawman who takes control of his town without shooting it up. Dietrich is the chantoosie who sings "See What the Boys in the Back Room Will Have." George Marshall directed.

DEVIL AND DANIEL WEBSTER, THE. US. 1941. William Dieterle's staging of Stephen Vincent Benet's story gives room to Edward Arnold and Walter Huston to act up a storm. Good—not great— Hollywood filmmaking with an excellent score by Bernard Herrmann.

DIABOLIQUE. France. 1955. Directed by

Henri-Georges Clouzot, this is a thriller about a conspiracy to murder with a few good twists that's almost worthy of Hitchcock. At the time it was released in the US in the mid-fifties, it was also a shock of a different sort: we discovered that "intellectual" European directors were capable of good old-fashioned American genre moviemaking. ▽

DIAL M FOR MURDER. US. 1954. In film school they teach you that if you make a movie of the stage play you have to "open it up." Alfred Hitchcock knew better. His record of the popular thriller stays put on the set. It's one of Ray Milland's finest performances and stars Grace Kelly and John Williams, too. The show belongs to Milland, who relishes the dialogues. You've never met a more pleasant and ingratiating would-be murderer. That's the secret of the film. ▽

DIARY OF A COUNTRY PRIEST. France. 1950. Director Robert Bresson's work is no doubt a specially acquired taste. His minimalist cinema can be mesmerizing if you give it a chance. *Diary of a Country Priest*, one of his first efforts, follows the unhappy career of the eponymous hero slowly and strikingly. ▽

DIARY OF A MAD HOUSEWIFE. US. 1970. Eleanor Perry wrote and Frank Perry directed this early protofeminist drama about a middle-class New York couple. Carrie Snodgress is so meek and unassuming as the wife that Richard Benjamin, the chauvinist husband, is more memorable, which makes for pointed irony. Frank Langella plays the lover. ▽

DINER. US. 1982. In its own quiet way, this unpretentious but wonderfully detailed exploration of adolescence in the 1950s by Barry Levinson is every bit as good as *AMERICAN GRAFFITI*. It lacks the music that was the secret of *AMERICAN GRAFFITI*'s popularity, but it's got much more detail. If you were there, you'll appreciate it. Levinson's kids are growing up on the east coast— Baltimore; *GRAFFITI*, of course, is west coast. It's interesting to compare: cars are less important here, for instance, and diners more. ▽

DINNER AT EIGHT. US. 1933. George Cukor mounted this star-studded film version of the classic thirties play about parvenus at a dinner party. It's a pleasure to watch Jean Harlow and Wallace Beery at work.

Lauren Bacall and Humphrey Bogart on the lookout in *The Big Sleep,* ever-vigilant against the dangers of the film-noir night.

DIRECTED BY JOHN FORD. US. 1971. This is a documentary interview and essay by Peter Bogdanovich, with one of America's great directors. Bogdanovich, the former journalist, interposes himself too often, and Ford, in the interviews, seems annoyed at this, but Bogdanovich has unearthed so many great clips from Ford movies, and they are reproduced with such special care, that the film is invaluable as an anthology of Ford's work.

DIRTY DOZEN, THE. US. 1967. In this landmark downbeat, but humorous caper film, twelve criminals get a chance to do what they do best, but this time in the service of the US Army in World War II. It's the quintessential Robert Aldrich film with Ernest Borgnine, Jim Brown, John Cassavetes, Lee Marvin, Charles Bronson, Robert Ryan, Donald Sutherland, Telly Savalas, Ralph Meeker, George Kennedy, and Trini Lopez. (Trini Lopez?!)

DIRTY HARRY. US. 1971. This is the film that made Clint Eastwood a star (again) in the US. Sure, the tough macho detective Eastwood plays was the main reason for the success of this film and its several sequels, but I don't think it would have come off with such force and effect without Don Siegel's direction. I can't think of a better film course than simply to study Siegel's movies: he takes everyday material and finds just the right choices to make it most effective on the screen. ◪

✛ **DISCREET CHARM OF THE BOURGEOISIE**. France. 1972. Working most often with screenwriter Jean-Claude Carrière, Luis Buñuel fashioned not one but several great films in the mid-seventies at the end of his career. By this time he had got control of the surrealist impulse and was able to combine it with a wonderful tongue-in-cheek narrative that makes these films as appealing as they are masterful. *The Discreet Charm of the Bourgeoisie* sets the tone for this series. An egregiously bourgeois dinner party gives Buñuel a chance to ring surrealistic changes on some old themes. Fernando Rey, Delphine Seyrig, Stéphane Audran, Jean-Pierre Cassell, Bulle Ogier, and Michel Piccoli star. This is the kind of film that makes you wish we didn't use the word "masterpiece" quite so indiscriminately.

DISPATCH FROM REUTERS. US. 1940. William Dieterle, always reliable, was responsible for this classic example of the Warner Bros. biopic genre, with Edward G. Robinson in the title role. Not quite as good as *DR. EHRLICH'S MAGIC BULLET*, made the same year by the same people.

⬤ **DISRAELI**. US. 1929. If you've never seen a George Arliss vehicle, this is the one to see: a theatrical biopic about the colorful Victorian Prime Minister. Arliss did a special kind of B-grade drama in the late twenties and early thirties that is the sort of stuff your high school dramatic coach would have taken you to see. It's interesting evidence of the effect of the stage on early talkies.

DISTANT THUNDER. India. 1973. Satyajit Ray turns here to a story set in a small Bengali village in 1942. The title refers to the shock waves emanating from the war in the Pacific. The Brahmin hero and his wife gradually have to realize their connection with the rest of the world.

⬤\‼ **DIVORCE ITALIAN STYLE**. Italy. 1961. Comedies from anywhere else but the US or England always come as a surprise. This one, set in a lugubrious Sicily, did. In fact, director Pietro Germi gave Marcello Mastroianni a meatier role than he ever had with Fellini. "Divorce Italian Style," of course, is murder.

⬤ **DR. EHRLICH'S MAGIC BULLET**. US. 1940. Perhaps the best of the Warner Bros. biopics.

Directed by William Dieterle, and starring Edward G. Robinson, it's interesting history about the invention of a cure for venereal disease. Isn't it surprising that in 1940 Hollywood took on such a story?

⬤ **DOCTOR IN THE HOUSE**. UK. 1954. If you're interested in British comedy series, the "Doctor" films, starring Dirk Bogarde, and directed by Ralph Thomas, probably rank near the top of the list. This was the first. The idea of setting a bunch of young doctors down in a hospital with a stern overseer (James Robertson Justice) certainly trumped the Dr. Kildare concept (old doctor versus young doctor). It formed the model in numerous movies and television series up to and including *St. Elsewhere*.

⬤ **DR. JEKYLL AND MR. HYDE**. US. 1931. There are several good films of this classic novel about the ultimate split personality. We have chosen the Rouben Mamoulian version, starring Fredric March and Miriam Hopkins. It's a good example of early thirties Hollywood style.

DOCTOR KILDARE'S WEDDING DAY. US. 1941. The Doctor Kildare series was one of the most successful of all time and the one film series in which we can most easily see television serial styles developing. Several actors played Kildare at one time or another; Lew Ayres made the role his own in the early forties. With Lionel Barrymore as the crusty Dr. Gillespie and Laraine Day as the love interest, the ensemble was at its height in this film. Laraine Day left the series afterwards.

⬇🚩 **DR. MABUSE**. Germany. 1922. This is a classic: Fritz Lang's most influential work, and the epitome of the German expressionist style. It is also the precursor of the film noir style that Lang did so well later. *Mabuse* is the master criminal nonpareil, but this is a decadent, cold film that has more style than sensibility.

⬤ **DOCTOR NO**. UK. 1963. Watching a James Bond film, whether it's Sean Connery or Roger Moore, is like watching *The Tonight Show* with Johnny Carson. They're very comfortable and they've been around forever. We forgive Bond his archaic sexual attitude because we know it dates back to the fifties. And we also know that Connery and Moore are a lot smarter than that. *Doctor No*, the second Bond film, seems to me to be one of the best. There was still some freshness to the form then, and the tricks and plot devices mesh nicely with a colorful story. ▽

✳🚩 ╲ **DR. STRANGELOVE; OR, HOW I LEARNED TO STOP WORRYING AND LOVE THE BOMB**. UK. 1964. Not only is this one of the best films ever made, it's also one of the most important. Its intelligence is supreme and its art transcendent. Stanley Kramer's *ON THE BEACH*, 1959, was the only major attempt before *Strangelove* to deal with the subject of nuclear war. Kubrick and screenwriter Terry Southern understood that a satiric tone was necessary for subject matter beyond comprehension. To take nuclear war seriously is to reduce it, to make it comprehensible, and therefore thinkable. The only way to think about the unthinkable is to use the leverage of satire and comedy. The genius of *Dr. Strangelove* echoed down the years. For example, when Henry Kissinger moved into the public consciousness in the 1970s, people remembered that Peter Sellers had done him better as Dr. Strangelove. The film is certainly Sellers's best work: he plays triple roles, each one illuminating the others. George C. Scott, Sterling Hayden, Slim Pickens, Keenan Wynn, Peter Bull, and James Earl Jones also contribute. Listen to Sellers as the President (a version of Adlai Stevenson) on the phone with Soviet Premiere Peter Bull. Watch Sterling Hayden disintegrate as he worries about the purity of our bodily fluids. Enjoy Slim Pickens's ride 'em cowboy as he bombs the bejesus out of Mother Russia right between the legs. The real shock of *Dr. Strangelove* is not in the film itself but in cinematic history. There were five or six major anti-nuclear war films made in the early sixties, but it was then fifteen years before the subject was taken up again in the public consciousness. None of the recent films comes close to capturing the absurdity of the situation the way *Dr. Strangelove* did, although most make supporting contributions to the anti-war effort. *Dr. Strangelove* is the only film that realizes this special style of early sixties black comedy to its full extent. Ultimately the film is thrilling because it is powerfully affirmative: we will survive because collectively we have the intelligence to make films like this. ◢

DOCTOR ZHIVAGO. UK. 1965. This is a huge romantic melodrama whose theme song lingered all too long throughout the sixties. The novel, by Boris Pasternak, had been famous; the film was more famous. By this time David Lean had so mastered the style of grand romance that it was beginning to turn in on itself in parody. If the setting were anywhere else but Russia, people would have laughed. ◢

⬤ **DODGE CITY**. US. 1939. Perhaps the definitive Warner Bros. western, this classic was directed by Michael Curtiz and stars Errol Flynn, Olivia de Havilland, and most of the Warner Bros. contract character actors. It's a B-movie with A-talent. ◪

DODSWORTH. US. 1936. The film version of the famous Sinclair Lewis novel directed by William Wyler and starring Walter Huston, Ruth Chatterton, Mary Astor, and David Niven. Huston is Dodsworth, the midwestern American businessman, who discovers a new set of values when he visits Europe. It's a talky film and sometimes the rhythms are lost, but it's important because it shows that the intellectual urge operating in Hollywood in the thirties every once in a while bubbled up to the surface.

¶⁃⬤ **DOG DAY AFTERNOON**. US. 1975. What a terrific movie this is: it's Al Pacino's best role, and under athletic syncopated direction by Sidney Lumet. Pacino, John Cazale, and friends try to hold up a Brooklyn bank one hot afternoon. They get stuck, take hostages, and manipulate the media. The film was based on a true story. One of the real-life people sued the filmmakers for a larger cut of the profits and thus was born New York State's "Dog Day Law," which limits the amount of money a convicted felon can earn from his or her life story. ◪

⬤⟍ **DOGS OF WAR, THE**. UK. 1980. John Irvin directed this film of a Frederick Forsyth novel about a group of mercenaries who are hired to perform a coup in a small African country. Forsyth reputedly did hire a bunch of mercenaries to do the same, purely as research for the novel. Christopher Walken stars as the head mercenary. Once again, the pleasure here is in watching very well-delineated characters work at a job. Half the fascination is in the modern weaponry, the other half in the surprising political content. In a way, Christopher Walken's character parallels Humphrey Bogart's in *CASABLANCA*: cynical through to the end, when he throroughly redeems himself with a grand gesture. ◪

⁃⁃§ **DOLCE VITA, LA**. Italy. 1960. After what we've seen of decadence during the last twenty-five years, *La Dolce Vita* now seems tamely absurd, but people wasting time in night clubs, dancing in the fountains of Rome, and just generally hanging out, seemed a bit of a shock at the turn of the decade between the fifties and the sixties. If *La Dolce Vita* still works, it's because of Marcello Mastroianni. More than any American actor, he inherited Bogart's mantle. ◪

$. US. 1972. An unusual departure for Richard Brooks, the master of the downbeat film noir, *$* is a comedy that has the good sense to star Warren Beatty together with Goldie Hawn. It's an excellent caper film with what may be the longest and certainly one of the best chase scenes in movies.

DOLLMAKER, THE. US. 1984. Directed by Daniel Petrie, this is a Jane Fonda project. (She stars with Levon Helm and Geraldine Page.) If you ever had any doubts that so-called made-for-television films could equal the power and scope of theatrical films, *The Dollmaker* should lay these to rest. It's a classic and evocative mythic tale of a young woman from the Kentucky hills (Fonda) who follows her husband (Levon Helm) to the ramshackle auto worker's housing developments of Detroit during the war, and eventually returns home to the country. It's based on a true story. Of course, the husband goes to Detroit to earn money. The irony is that the wife earns more relying on her country skills as a woodcarver. This is the "Foxfire" moral: stick to your roots. Fonda's performance is exciting and heroic.

DON'T CRY WITH YOUR MOUTH FULL. France. 1974. I nearly stopped watching movies once my kids were born. Much of what we want from movies—character, drama, language, love, and emotion—we get in quite a different way from our children. You would think we would make a lot more movies about children, but of course the way children portray these emotions and feelings is evanescent and almost impossible to capture on film. A young director named Pascal Thomas succeeded very well at just this difficult feat with *Don't Cry With Your Mouth Full*. It's in the excellent French tradition that goes back through Truffaut's *400 BLOWS* to Jean Vigo.

DON'T LOOK BACK. US. 1967. D. A. Pennebaker was probably the leading American documentarian of the fifties and sixties. *Don't Look Back*, an essay on Bob Dylan, is one of his best. If the name Bob Dylan means something to you, you'll love it.

DON'T LOOK NOW. UK. 1973. Nicolas Roeg has done a couple of mildly interesting experiments in the vaguely supernatural (for example, *The Man Who Fell to Earth*). *Don't Look Now*, set in Venice, with

Julie Christie and Donald Sutherland as the haunted parents of a dead child, is his most interesting. The film has a great love scene and a very accurate sense of place. ▽

DOUBLE INDEMNITY. US. 1944. Raymond Chandler script, James M. Cain novel, Billy Wilder direction, Fred MacMurray, Edward G. Robinson, and Barbara Stanwyck, all combine for a classic film noir. Fred's an insurance man lured by Barbara into committing murder, and investigated by boss Edward G.

DOWN TO THE SEA IN SHIPS. US. 1922. The story, about a New England whaling family, is not especially interesting, but the location photography in New England and on board real whalers is remarkable, especially for the time, and often breathtaking. Clara Bow debuted here.

DOWNHILL RACER. US. 1969. This magnificent film about sports provides Robert Redford's first big role, as well as Michael Ritchie's debut as a director of features. Redford is a skier, not a very nice guy. Gene Hackman is the coach. Camilla Sparv is "the girl." The film has an extraordinary realistic feel to it and that's not just because of the excellent downhill skiing photography. It set a fashion for sports films that has lasted till this day. ▽

DRACULA. US. 1931. For reasons that aren't quite clear, the Dracula myth has proved one of the most durable in movies. There are numerous versions in many languages. This, the original, starred Bela Lugosi under the direction of Tod Browning and it should be required viewing before you see any of the remakes, takeoffs, hommages, and sendups. ▽

DRAGNET. US. 1969. This is in fact the pilot for the second television series of *Dragnet*, conceived and directed by Jack Webb. The TV series is so important that this film, a relic of it, deserves to be seen. Jack Webb invented a type of TV drama that's had a pervasive effect on the medium and has really never been surpassed for stylishness. *Dragnet* should play on a double bill with something by Harold Pinter.

DRAUGHTSMAN'S CONTRACT, THE. UK. 1982. This is an exceptional film: the first in probably fifteen years that's really avant garde. That is, it pushes back the limits of cinema and seems to do things in an entirely new way. Nominally about an artist hired to immortalize a piece of property, it's set in the eighteenth century and does very well as a period piece, but that's not the point. The images are full of visual puns and the dialogue is even more complex: a melange of Joycean word play that leaves an audience breathless. Director Peter Greenaway had done some short films before this; he was known in England as a "structuralist" filmmaker. But nothing prepares us for the high humor of *The Draughtsman's Contract*. If you've been sitting in movie theaters for years waiting for the excitement you felt in the early sixties, *The Draughtsman's Contract* may provide it.

DRIVER, THE. US. 1978. Ryan O'Neal and Bruce Dern in a curious film noir by Walter Hill, who always takes an unusual point of view. O'Neal is the renegade driver; Dern, his nemesis, the cop.

‼ **DUCK SOUP**. US. 1933. In this one Groucho is Rufus T. Firefly, ruler of Freedonia. It wasn't very popular when it was released, perhaps because politics is not the best topic for the Marx Brothers, but it's gained a reputation over the years and now probably ranks second only to *A NIGHT AT THE OPERA*. "Remember, you're fighting for this woman's honor, which is probably more than she ever did." ▼

⬇▜ **E. T.: THE EXTRATERRESTRIAL**. US. 1982. Okay, this Steven Spielberg blockbuster is a well-made story that children will enjoy (which is nice because they can't escape it). Young Henry Thomas scores as the all-American kid who shares his Reese's Pieces with the visitor from space. But the emotional deck is stacked: what if a character from another planet doesn't look like such a cute Walter Keene drawing?

⊹ **EARTH**. USSR. 1930. This celebration of collective peasant life starts out ideology-ridden but director Alexander Dovzhenko really knows these people and their world and makes it a moving experience: a paean to the relationship between farmers and their land.

⊹▜ **EAST OF EDEN**. US. 1954. James Dean in his best role in Elia Kazan's version of the John Steinbeck novel about two brothers' rivalry. It's a colorful, searing domestic drama that became a touchstone for the 1950s. ▼

§ **EASTER PARADE**. US. 1948. Fred Astaire and Judy Garland, Peter Lawford, and Ann Miller in an Irving Berlin musical. That's all you need to know, but if you want another hook, notice the commentary the plot makes on Astaire's own career: like the character he plays here, he never stayed long with one dancing partner.

EASY LIVING. US. 1937. Mitchell Leisen directed, but it's really screenwriter Preston Sturges's film. The least known, but perhaps the best of the late screwball comedies, with Jean Arthur, Ray Milland, Edward Arnold, Franklin Pangborne, and William Demarest. The next time a fur coat drops on your head when you're riding on top of the Fifth Avenue bus you'll know what to do.

EASY RIDER. US. 1969. This is the great semi-underground emblem of the generation of the hippies. Peter Fonda and Dennis Hopper take out across America. Now when you look at it, you see that these two paragons of late sixties hipdom are whiney and self-pitying. It's certainly instructive that Fonda and Hopper never got very far after this, but Jack Nicholson, as the semi-straight tagalong on this odyssey, developed the brightly cynical, humorous persona that has been admired for a generation. We were much squarer than we knew then. ◢

EASY STREET. US. 1917. Charlie Chaplin, as a recent convert to the cause, becomes a policeman and deals magnificently with the terrors of the slum neighborhood. Run it on a double bill with an episode of *Hill Street Blues*. See *CHARLIE CHAPLIN FESTIVAL*.

ECSTASY. Czechoslovakia. 1932. This is a simple story—a young woman takes a lover in the country—that became a significant international success because its star Hedy Lamarr appeared nude for ten minutes. It's not at all pornographic but it is a very erotic movie.

EDUCATING RITA. UK. 1983. This is a very old-fashioned film that's been done many times before, but director Lewis Gilbert and stars Michael Caine and Julie Walters do it very well again. Willy Russell wrote the play on which it's based, and it reveals its stage origins mostly in the thickness of the dialogue. Caine is a boozy college professor who falls for Rita, the hairdresser looking to educate herself. She rises as he falls. He explains his obsession to Walters this way: "Life is such a rich and frantic form that I need the drink to help me step delicately through it." That's the kind of line an actor waits a lifetime for. ◢

8 1/2. Italy. 1963. This is Federico Fellini's magnum opus, well-deserved of its rank in the pantheon. It's about a director who can't get it together for his next film, and of course we don't watch it for its subject matter. I suppose in the sixties, people may have cared somewhat more than they do now about the plight of the poor benighted film director with nothing to say, but now we recognize that *8 1/2* is important not for what it says but how it says it. Fellini remains the great circus master of movies, cramming all the joys and heartaches that this flesh is heir to onto the screen in an operatic profusion, accompanied by the necessary melodies of Nino Rota. What makes Fellini a supremely important filmmaker is that he captures the life force. It bubbles off the screen and we partake of it. Chaplin did that—and precious few others. The Germans have a word: "weltschmertz." Like all such intellectual terms, it's supposedly untranslatable, but it has something to do with world pain, a kind of pervasive sadness. There's a little of that in Fellini but there's much, much more of what we might call "weltfreude," the *joy* that suffuses life. It has to do with food and drink and sex and children and art, not necessarily in that order. I guess it's Italian. ◪

◬ **EL DORADO**. US. 1966. Howard Hawks's western comedy with a script by Leigh Brackett allows the new Hollywood to meet the old: John Wayne and Robert Mitchum star; James Caan and Edward Asner have small roles. ◪

◬ **ELEANOR AND FRANKLIN**. US. 1976. Edward Herrmann and Jane Alexander starred in this Daniel Petrie TV movie about the President and his wife. There were numerous docudramas on TV in the seventies that probably meet or exceed the standards for inclusion here. In fact, the form itself was probably the most interesting thing happening in movies in the seventies, either on the large screen or the small. *Eleanor and Franklin* is a good example of the success of the genre, and will have to hold a place for those we've missed.

◬ **ELECTRIC HORSEMAN, THE**. US. 1979. One of the sadder things that's happened to American movies in the last twenty years is the decline and fall of the western. There aren't any real ones left anymore, so any semi-western that comes along, like *The Electric Horseman*, is bound to be appreciated. Robert Redford has probably done more for the genre than anyone else during the last fifteen years: here he plays the neon cowboy symbol quite nicely, with Jane Fonda's media-hype reporter as foil. Sydney Pollack directed; Willie Nelson contributes. Like a couple of other earlier post-westerns, *The Electric Horseman* suggests that the dream is dead, preserved only in Las Vegas neon and television commercials.

§ **ELVIRA MADIGAN**. Sweden. 1967. This was a very popular film at the time and—whatever else it did—made Mozart acceptable for the world's teenagers. It's rather a silly love story of two adolescents, but prettily photographed and, although we don't like to admit it, even grownups occasionally like to watch this sort of jejeune adolescent romantic fantasy. Those were legitimate feelings when we were fifteen, and there's nothing wrong with reliving them for an hour or two. A decade later a whole genre was spawned on this model—*The Blue Lagoon* for example—bringing the level down to proto-kiddy-porn pre-teen. ☑

EMIGRANTS, THE. Sweden. 1970. Director Jan Troell's three films of the early 1970s, *The Emigrants*, *THE NEW LAND*, and *ZANDY'S BRIDE*, form a trilogy about the experience of the founding of America. They are superior to any other films on that subject I can think of. Starring Liv Ullmann and Max von Sydow as peasant farmers in Sweden who can barely make a go of it, *The Emigrants* sets the stage for the saga of the journey to America. This is a realistic, not romantic, retelling of the myth of immigration and the balance which Troell provides between the old world and the new is an important new wrinkle on the tale. *The New Land*, also called *THE IMMIGRANTS*, follows the same characters as they arrive in the new world to find a place in the midwest. The third film, *ZANDY'S BRIDE*, is rather a coda to the story than a continuation. It follows the trek from the midwest to the west coast.

END OF THE GAME. West Germany. 1976. Whenever Europeans try to do an American genre it's usually worth taking a look. Things we take for granted, they interpret in a new light. This is a Friedrich Dürrenmatt novel, a policier that's complex and involuted. Martin Ritt plays a dying policeman, Robert Shaw plays the object of his hunt, Jon Voight is Ritt's assistant, and Donald Sutherland is the dead man. Maximilian Schell directed.

ENFORCER, THE. US. 1950. A Humphrey Bogart sleeper that pits him as D. A. against crime boss Everett Sloane. Zero Mostel also appears. ▽

ENTER THE DRAGON. US. 1973. This is Bruce Lee's last complete film, and probably his best. It's pure martial arts action unsullied by much attention to plot or character. Lee was so good at this sort of thing that even if you are uninterested in action pictures and the physical violence repulses you, you may find it worthwhile: the choreography of the martial arts has been an important influence on other dance styles during the last fifteen years. ▽

ENTERTAINER, THE. UK. 1960. Laurence Olivier's tour-de-force as Archie Rice, the over-the-hill vaudevillian who antagonizes everyone around him in John Osborne's play directed for film by Tony Richardson. Albert Finney and Alan Bates support.

ENTRE NOUS. France. 1983. Director Diane Kurys remembers a tangled bit of family history composed of equal parts of sex and ego. It's about the friendship of two women. It goes on perhaps too long but remains in the mind as a psychological study that is equally as knotty and complex as everyday life. It stars Miou-Miou and Isabelle Huppert. ▽

ERNIE KOVACS: BETWEEN THE LAUGHTER. US. 1984. Ernie Kovacs was one of the first true television artists. This made-for-television film deals not with his career as a comedian, but rather with his search for his daughters after a bitter custody struggle with his ex-wife. Jeff Goldblum plays Kovacs; veteran B-movie director Lamont Johnson mounted the production.

ESCAPE FROM ALCATRAZ. US. 1979. Don Siegel directed this simple and gripping story, with roots in reality, about an escape from the supposedly escape-proof Alcatraz. Siegel is awfully good at this sort of thing and if you like to watch people doing a job, you won't find it done better elsewhere. Clint Eastwood and Patrick McGoohan star.

EVERY MAN FOR HIMSELF AND GOD AGAINST ALL. West Germany. 1974. This is the Kaspar Hauser legend as retold by Werner Herzog. Confined since birth, Kaspar offers a unique view of the world when he joins it in nineteenth-century Nuremberg. It's probably Herzog's best film, restrained but incisive. Compare *THE WILD CHILD*. ▽

"Bevete piu late," says the billboard: "Drink more milk." Anita Ekberg's voluptuous figure tempts Dr. Antonio in Fellini's episode of *Boccaccio '70.*

EXORCIST, THE. US. 1973. The sado-masochistic trend in horror films, which culminated with *ALIEN* and films of that ilk in the late seventies and early eighties, began here with this remarkably obscene exercise in special effects. Linda Blair is the infected child victim, Max von Sydow the title character. The film is anti-child, anti-human, and anti-audience, but hang on, *GHOSTBUSTERS* are coming!

EXTERMINATING ANGEL, THE. Mexico. 1962. Classic Luis Buñuel surrealism about a group of dinner party guests who can't go home and gradually begin to die from starvation. Buñuel improved markedly on the concept with *DISCREET CHARM OF THE BOURGEOISIE* by adding humor and humanity.

FACE IN THE CROWD, A. US. 1957. In the late sixties Andy Warhol declared: "In the future everybody will be famous for fifteen minutes." Writer Budd Schulberg and director Elia Kazan understood this truth much earlier. This is a film about the power of TV to confer celebrity and the unusual results that power entails. Andy Griffith is the bum who becomes a TV star. Run it on a double bill with *NETWORK*.

FACES. US. 1968. Like *SHADOWS* before it,

Faces was hailed at the time as a great accomplishment of American independent cinema. John Cassavetes, his friends, and family, took several years to shoot the film on very grainy 16mm black-and-white stock. As usual, it's about marriages and the war between men and women. Cassavetes did much better later in the seventies with a little more money (see *HUSBANDS*, for example), but *Faces* remains as a cultural document of the late sixties.

FAHRENHEIT 451. UK/France. 1966. François Truffaut took a great chance shooting this film of the Ray Bradbury novel in English. Delicately portraying a world in which books are illegal and it's the job of firemen to find and burn them, the film wasn't successful at the time, but the images are haunting. They remain in the memory. This is the most restrained and elegiac of science-fiction films, full of poignant moments: a paean to the physical importance of books. Julie Christie, Oscar Werner star.

FAIL-SAFE. US. 1964. Shot at about the same time as *DR. STRANGELOVE*, Sidney Lumet's melodrama *Fail-Safe* was released a few months later and all but ignored in the competition with Kubrick's more successful treatment of a similar subject. *Fail-Safe* handles nuclear war in dramatic—not satiric—fashion, and in its own way, makes its point strongly. Henry Fonda and Walter Matthau star.

FAME. US. 1980. This is a wonderfully simple idea that succeeds very well indeed: take a bunch of kids from New York's High School of the Performing Arts and let them do their stuff. A lot of music, a few desultory plotlines, and you've got the contemporary version of the Mickey Rooney/Judy Garland "Hey kids, let's put on a show!" movie. *Fame* shows us how much life there is in genres like the musical that we thought were moribund. While everybody else in Hollywood was trying to duplicate the forms of the past, director Alan Parker took a refreshing new slant here.

FANNY. France. 1932. See *MARIUS*.

FANNY AND ALEXANDER. Sweden. 1983. Ingmar Bergman says this is his last film, and even if it turns out not to be it nevertheless provides a fitting period to his career. Thematically it takes him back to his beginnings and presents a carefully remembered childhood in Sweden at the turn of the century. Erland Josephson and Harriet Andersson, who have worked with him so often before, are here to remind us of Bergman's history, but *Fanny and Alexander* transcends the pain and neuroses of most of Bergman's great movies. It's a magnificent conclusion. ◻

FANTASIA. US. 1940. Probably the Disney Studio's most ambitious experiment in animation, *Fantasia* uses images to illustrate music, and has become a cult and children's classic. It is, perhaps, the progenitor of today's pop video form.

FANTOMAS. France. 1913. Louis Feuillade took an important step in 1913 when he shot several episodes of a very popular detective novel series of the time. We are more than halfway to the feature film here. *Fantomas* is the arch-criminal pursued by Juve, the detective, and Fandor, the reporter. The cinematography is unusually contemporary in style. Feuillade later did a number of other *Fantomas* stories, and thus the serial was born.

FAR FROM VIETNAM. France. 1967. In the midst of the Vietnam embroglio, French filmmakers Alain Resnais, Jean-Luc Godard, Claude Lelouch and others, attempted a composite essay film on the subject. Remember that the French had been through the Vietnam experience fifteen years before the Americans. *Far From Vietnam* remains a very unusual political document that's worth studying even today for the attitudes it represents. As the title indicates, we are left mainly with a sense of existential irresponsibility. The film is full of cinematic ironies: the "romantic" Claude Lelouch comes closest to producing a segment of political value; the "political" Jean-Luc Godard is most clearly paralyzed by his art; and Alain Resnais's segment makes a sharp commentary on the kind of intellectual bad faith exhibited by people with very reasonable excuses for doing nothing. It's a self-critique of the film.

FAREWELL TO MANZANAR. US. 1976. Here is a classic seventies docudrama, directed by John Korty, about a Japanese-American family's internment in the World War II Manzanar camp. It's a subject that was all but invisible before the film, but has since become a part of the American public's consciousness due in no small part to the efforts of Korty and crew. The more we gain perspective on the last fifteen years in American filmmaking, the more we see how important so-called television movies were. Films like *Farewell* *to Manzanar* gain in importance every year as the glossier theatrical product fades.

FATHER BROWN. UK. 1954. Alec Guinness is the perfect G. K. Chesterton character, the likeable clerical detective on the trail of art thieves. Joan Greenwood, Peter Finch, Bernard Lee, and Sidney James assist under the direction of Robert Hamer.

FATHER OF THE BRIDE. US. 1950. Spencer Tracy is dad and Elizabeth Taylor his daughter in this homey but perceptive portrait of family life at the moment of celebration. Director Vincente Minnelli captures the post-war suburban milieu perfectly. Compare it with *LOVERS AND OTHER STRANGERS*.

FELLINI SATYRICON. Italy. 1969. One of the more interesting developments in international film in the seventies was the attention to a new level of detail in historical films. The aim was to go "on location" in time. *Fellini Satyricon* was one of the first of the historical films in which a new level of historical authenticity appears. It was especially surprising coming from a director like Fellini, who had been so closely associated with contemporary themes. The film, which was celebrated at the time only for its risque subject matter, presents a startlingly Roman view of classical Roman times. It's as interesting to classicists and historians as it may be to voyeurs. There are contemporary echoes as well, of course: in 1969 Fellini was forecasting our entry into a new period of decadence. In an important way, this film, along with Kubrick's *A CLOCKWORK ORANGE*, set a cultural tone that has lasted fifteen years. *Fellini Satyricon* is more ambitious than we knew at the time.

FEMME DOUCE, UNE. France. 1969. Based on a story by Dostoyevski but set in modern Paris, this is another mesmerizing exercise in understatement by Robert Bresson. He did his best work after the age of sixty.

FEMME FATALE, UNE. France/West Germany. 1975. Although Jacques Doniol-Valcroze was one of the founders of *Cahiers du Cinéma*, he was never an integral part of the New Wave and has always been an outsider. *Une Femme Fatale* is a very striking but simple movie that stays in the mind. It's a classic bourgeois triangle—Jacques Weber and Heinz Bennent are the men—with Anicée Alvina at the apex. It's a situation that Chabrol might have been proud of, except that food is far less important here than sex. Alvina radiates a quiet sexuality that is fully the match of the "noisier" film personas of such predecessors as Brigitte Bardot and Clara Bow. A sleeper.

FEMME INFIDELE, LA. France. 1968. Claude Chabrol has made a great many movies during the last twenty-five years, a number of them rather pedestrian. But at his best, as in *La Femme Infidèle*, he's an extraordinary and much underrated filmmaker. This is a very mundane blood triangle: a husband, a wife, and her lover. What Chabrol does better than anyone else is to take the cliches of the melodramas that we know so well and turn them in upon themselves. His droll sense of humor is not to everyone's taste but it makes an important and ironic comment on what we consider the drama of daily life in the twentieth century. There's one scene in *La Femme Infidèle* that stands out in the mind: Michel Bouquet has clomped his wife's lover (Maurice Ronet) on the head. He's dead. There's so much blood to wash up and the body is so bulky and difficult to handle that it seems to take forever to clean up after the murder. This may be the reality of murder, not the forced drama we attend to every night on TV. In fact, the murder doesn't make much of a difference in the plot of the film. It's just another event.

FFOLKES. UK. 1980. Andrew McLaglen directed this entertaining action film. Roger Moore is the title hero, an eccentric expert in terrorism, hired by the British government to save their North Sea oil rigs. James Mason and Anthony Perkins also star.

FILM. US. 1968. Stage director Alan Schneider mounted this film essay by playwright Samuel Beckett. It was one of the last appearances of Buster Keaton. During the sixties, Beckett wrote a series of short plays and scripts which attempted quite successfully to describe in action the essence of various media forms. *Film* is a small jewel which, upon study, reveals the heart of cinematic expression. (*Play* does the same thing for the theatrical experience, and *Eh, Joe* does the same for TV.) Film, for Beckett, is a matter of the interplay between camera and character, and isn't that what so many people spend years in film school trying to discover? (*Note*: There's also a kinescope available of the original production of the teleplay *Eh, Joe*, an even more pointed distillation of style.)

FINDERS KEEPERS. US. 1984. Richard Lester rediscovers the farcical style he used so well twenty years ago in a nice little con-artist movie starring Michael O'Keefe, Beverly D'Angelo, and Louis Gossett Jr.

§ **FINIAN'S RAINBOW**. US. 1968. The Lane and Harburg musical debuted on the Broadway stage twenty years before Francis Coppola made this film version starring Fred Astaire. In the late forties, *Finian's Rainbow* seemed to be an important statement against racial injustice. At the same time, songs like "How Are Things in Gloccamorra?" entered the American consciousness. Coppola's film adaptation is a decent one. It's important to have a record of this play on film and it's one of Fred Astaire's last musical performances. ▽

✛ **FIREMEN'S BALL, THE**. Czechoslovakia. 1967. Miloš Forman's last Czechoslovakian film is perhaps the ultimate film of the Czech renaissance before the political crackdown forced most directors into exile. It's a more thorough realization of the same kinds of themes that directors like Forman and Ivan Passer developed in several films in the mid-sixties: invigorating essays in everyday life. Not much happens here except the firemen have their ball. It might as well have been a bar mitzvah or a wedding. The people and their day-to-day loves and minor tribulations are thoroughly ingratiating. ▽

FIST IN HIS POCKET. Italy. 1965. Marco Bellochio directed this unusual tragi-farce about a family of crazy epileptics. It relies a little too heavily on the outrageous subject matter, but it has an underlying sense of humor which makes it worth watching.

▼ **FISTFUL OF DOLLARS, A**. Italy. 1964. This is the one that made Clint Eastwood a star and "spaghetti western" a household phrase. Sergio Leone directed "the man with no name," and Ennio Morricone did the music for this Italian version of an American western. How many American-born stars of the first magnitude, like Eastwood, got their start overseas? ▽

▼ **FIVE EASY PIECES**. US. 1970. Once upon a time in the late sixties, a director named Bob Rafelson was an important member of the American directorial new wave, along with his associates in the BBS production group. *Five Easy Pieces* was their keystone movie. Hardly anybody ever talks about it now, but it's still worth taking a look at. It remains the classic late sixties Hollywood attempt at the new moviemaking (this was before *STAR WARS*, boys and girls) and it's got at least one great scene. Jack Nicholson in a diner wants toast. The waitress says it's not on the menu. Nicholson complains. The waitress stands fast and then, in the kind of frustrated, intelligent, and gleeful manner which was Nicholson's trademark, he talks her into it. He orders a cheese sandwich, "hold the cheese, hold the lettuce, hold the mayo." All that's left is toast. Gotcha! It's certainly pretentious, but we must preserve these relics of the late sixties and early seventies.

FIVE FINGERS. US. 1952. James Mason stars as the spy working for the Germans during World War II. Michael Rennie and Danielle Darrieux assist in the Joseph L. Mankiewicz film. *THE THIRD MAN* is better known, and probably a better film, but *Five Fingers* is the sleeper of its kind from the same period.

FIVE GRAVES TO CAIRO. US. 1943. Billy Wilder directed this superior Warners wartime drama from a script he and Charles Brackett wrote. Franchot Tone, Akim Tamiroff, and Erich von Stroheim have a good time with above-average dialogue and a plot set in a Sahara oasis. A genre film with a real sense of humor, *Five Graves to Cairo* shows you the possibilities.

FIVE PENNIES, THE. US. 1959. Coming near the end of Danny Kaye's series of PG comedies, this isn't among his best, but still worth looking at. It's the biopic of trumpeter Red Nichols. The music is decent and you get a chance to watch Shelley Manne, Bobby Troup, Louis Armstrong, and Bob Crosby— to say nothing of Tuesday Weld.

FLASH OF GREEN, A. US. 1984. Director Victor Nuñez is a virtuoso of authentic local color. His first film, *Gal Young 'Un*, nicely caught the flavor of Marjorie Kinnan Rawlings's unique vision of rural Florida. This one, based on a novel by John D. MacDonald, deals with the .period of the early sixties. It's a story of the first days of the environmental movement interpreted by Hollywood stars Ed Harris, Blair Brown, and Richard Jordan (he also produced), that you'll enjoy for its honesty and restraint. Harris is a local journalist who is torn between the powers that be and the environmentalists fighting them.

FLYING DOWN TO RIO. US. 1933. It doesn't take much to make a memorable movie. *Flying Down to Rio* has that famous scene of chorines dancing on airplane wings; it's got Astaire, and it's got Rogers, as well as Delores del Rio. Otherwise, it's rather thin. ▽

⬥＼ **FOG OVER FRISCO**. US. 1934. "Programmers" were B-movies designed to fill the bottom half of double bills and had at most an hour-and-a-quarter to do their job. Since the plots were usually just as complicated as those of their companion features (which lasted half an hour or more longer), directors of programmers had to work fast. Their speed and efficiency remains among their main charms. *Fog Over Frisco* is the fastest one I know. William Dieterle puts Bette Davis, Lyle Talbot, and other Warner Bros. contract players through their paces in a story of the San Francisco underworld with breathless and exhilarating abandon.

§ **FOLLOW THE FLEET**. US. 1936. Mark Sandrich directed Astaire and Rogers as well as Randolph Scott and Harriet Hilliard (later Mrs. Ozzie Nelson) in this classic musical. Irving Berlin provided songs like "Let's Face the Music and Dance" and "Let Yourself Go." ▽

＼§ **FOOTLIGHT PARADE**. US. 1933. In any Busby Berkeley catalogue, *42ND STREET* always comes first—but *Footlight Parade* proves to be a very close second. Ruby Keeler, Dick Powell, James Cagney, and Joan Blondell carry the thin story quite well for a while. It winds up with three terrific Berkeley dance numbers: "Honeymoon Hotel," "By a Waterfall," and "Shanghai Lil." The plot is the simplest excuse for the staging of the numbers and no attempt is made to disperse them throughout the film. Cagney plays a director who, like Berkeley, is trying to match an earlier success. No pretensions here.

＼‖ **FOR HEAVEN'S SAKE**. US. 1926. A masterful Harold Lloyd comedy about a spoiled young millionaire in love with a mission girl, with one of the greatest chase sequences ever filmed. When the citizens of Los Angeles built their freeways, they lost an important natural resource for film. The broad local streets of the teens and twenties provided magnificent settings for careening car chases like this one.

⊹§ **FOR ME AND MY GAL**. US. 1942. Busby Berkeley provides a simple stage for Judy Garland, Gene Kelly, and others to sing and do vaudeville turns. The story concerns the classic vaudevillians' dream: to play the Palace. Once again, no pretensions, just good music and dance.

FOR WHOM THE BELL TOLLS. US. 1943.
Ingrid Bergman brings this version of the
Hemingway novel alive; Gary Cooper as an
American fighting in the Spanish Civil War couldn't
carry it by himself. It's a grand love story, forties
style, but no one has done fully successful films of
the great Hemingway novels *The Sun Also Rises*, *A
Farewell to Arms*, and *For Whom the Bell Tolls*.
Perhaps that just tells us that too much depends
upon his literary style.

FORBIDDEN GAMES. France. 1952. René
Clement's most famous film shows us children
creating an imaginary world entirely separate from
the adult world. It allows the children an existence of
their own without relationship to adults, and that is
an essential fantasy for kids.

FORBIDDEN PLANET. US. 1956. In science
fiction, the fifties was the great age of paranoia. From
THE THING to *INVASION OF THE BODY
SNATCHERS* American SF traded heavily in
neurotic fear. Only *Forbidden Planet* tries to explain,
to educate. Turns out, the monster is our very own
creation; in fact, the reflection of our id. The fault,
therefore, is not in our stars but in ourselves. Robbie
the Robot became the model for countless less
inventive filmmakers during the next twenty years
(including George Lucas in *STAR WARS*). And
then there's Anne Francis....

FOREIGN CORRESPONDENT. US. 1940. This
wartime spy melodrama is Hitchcock at his second
best, which puts it head and shoulders above most
movies of this type. It's interesting to see Hitchcock
work with B-actors like Joel McCrea and Laraine
Day. The windmill! The windmill!

FORT APACHE. US. 1948. This is the first of
John Ford's cavalry trilogy with John Wayne (of
course), and Henry Fonda in an unusual role as the
stiff, tough officer so distant from his men. See *SHE
WORE A YELLOW RIBBON*.

FORTUNE, THE. US. 1975. Jack Nicholson and
Warren Beatty, together with Stockard Channing, in
a very much underrated comedy by Mike Nichols. I
think the film failed at the box office because of
Nichols's "discovery," Stockard Channing.
Although she later went on to have a respectable
career in television and theater, she can't match
Nicholson and Beatty here. Nichols needed an
actress with real star quality to play off against his

two larger-than-life male stars. Nevertheless, the film was a pleasure to watch for its good script, mise-en-scene, and above all, the performances of Nicholson and Beatty, very near their best here.

FORTUNE COOKIE, THE. US. 1966. The productive partnership between Walter Matthau and Jack Lemmon began here. They are at their seediest as a smalltime lawyer and his brother-in-law out to make a buck off the insurance companies. Billy Wilder had the perverse humor to shoot the film on location in Cleveland, quite an event in the mid-sixties. ▽

48 HRS. US. 1982. The always-ambitious Walter Hill found this debut vehicle for television comedian Eddie Murphy, who co-stars with Nick Nolte and Annette O'Toole. It's all on the surface, but Nolte and Murphy cook together as the crazy cop and the con he springs to help him close a case. Murphy has the ability like no other Black comedian before him to parody white dialects and lifestyles, and that opens up enormous new opportunities for him. Watch him here put the make on a bar full of working-class whites. ▽

FORTY-NINTH PARALLEL, THE. UK. 1941. Another superior Michael Powell and Emeric Pressburger film—a war drama about Nazi U-boats off the Canadian coast—starring Leslie Howard, Laurence Olivier, Raymond Massey, Anton Walbrook, and a young Glynis Johns.

42ND STREET. US. 1932. This, of course, is the classic Busby Berkeley musical and probably needs no introduction. "You're going out there a youngster, but you've got to come back a star!" If Ruby Keeler in hot pants isn't enough, how can you resist a show where the boy sings to the girl: "I'm young and healthy and so are you!" Certainly one of the US's great contributions to popular culture, not to put too fine a point on it, is the musical comedy, and *42nd Street* will serve as well as any other as an emblem of that form. ▽

FOUR FRIENDS. US. 1981. Playwright and screenwriter Steve Tesich constructed an ambitious panorama of the sixties based on the experiences of a Yugoslavian immigrant. Arthur Penn filmed the script with a good deal of understanding. It goes off in many directions, and at times its sentiment goes over the edge into sentimentality, but it probably comes as close as any movie to capturing the experience of the sixties, something a lot of people have tried to do, almost always without applause from the critics. ☒

400 BLOWS, THE. France. 1959. No one else has made films about children with the sensitivity of François Truffaut, and Truffaut never made a better one than this, his first. Based loosely on his own experiences, it begins the five-film saga of Antoine Doinel, one of the great characters in contemporary movies—and the only one actually to have grown up on the screen. The boy loved Balzac, hated school, and found nowhere to run in the fifties. One of the first films of the French New Wave to get out in the streets of Paris with handheld cameras, *The 400 Blows* has a sense of freedom which is the antidote to its own claustrophobic story. The images stick in the mind for many years: the line of schoolboys snaking through the streets of Paris, seen from a rooftop, as first one, then another, then another, peels off to go his own way; Doinel in the last freeze frame caught at the edge of the water with nowhere to go, looking plaintively at us. The music by Jean Constantin is an integral part of the bittersweet effect.

FOUR MUSKETEERS, THE. UK. 1974. See *THE THREE MUSKETEERS*. ☒

FOUR NIGHTS OF A DREAMER. France. 1971. As with *UNE FEMME DOUCE* made two years earlier, Robert Bresson here sets a simple Dostoyevski story in the streets of contemporary Paris. It's a romantic poem to youth and elegantly filmed in luminescent color.

FOUR SEASONS, THE. US. 1981. This is Alan Alda's paean to middle age, a tremendously popular film about couples vacationing together which showed that you could still make movies for grownups. Although it usually stays just this side of cloying, Alda's people are so nice, so ingratiating, that it might put you off. ☒

FOXES. US. 1980. Adrian Lyne directed this rather messy film starring Jodie Foster, which attempts to capture the experience of growing up in the Los Angeles suburbs of the San Fernando "Valley." It's too melodramatic and not humorous enough, but any film that tries to deal with teenagers on their own terms deserves some attention. ☒

FRANKENSTEIN. US. 1931. If you've been exposed to other versions of the Frankenstein legend during the last fifty years, you may be surprised at the freshness of the original, directed by James

Whale. The real question here is why the myth has been so powerful since the early years of the last century when Mary Shelley created it. Remember that Frankenstein is the scientist and not the monster. Perhaps the myth is an emblem of our own fears of our newly magnified creative powers: in a sense, every film director is a Frankenstein, creating life he can't control. ▼

FRENCH CONNECTION, THE. US. 1971. Other films were antecedents, but *The French Connection* set the style for action films for a generation now. Loosely based on a famous sixties New York City drug bust, it's gutsy, seedy, lively, direct, relevant, tough, and exciting. The chase scenes here have never been surpassed. Gene Hackman and Roy Scheider star.

FRENCH POSTCARDS. US. 1979. This is a small film, directed by Willard Huyck with a script by his wife, Gloria Katz. It's about a bunch of nice young American kids spending their junior year in Paris under the supervision of Marie-France Pisier. It's too special a subject to be very popular, but the theme is an important link between US and French culture that's been very significant in the development of movies during the last twenty years. The cast includes such (at the time) unknowns as Mandy Patinkin and Debra Winger.

FRENCH, THEY ARE A FUNNY RACE, THE. France. 1956. Preston Sturges's last film is about the marriage of a Britisher and a Frenchwoman and their continual cultural clashes. Clearly not as successful as his earlier films, but it's interesting to watch such a quintessentially American talent at work in a French milieu.

FRENZY. UK. 1972. Hitchcock's last films were disconcerting because he used so many of the techniques that worked well in the forties and fifties at a time when we expected greater realism and a different, if not better, style. *Frenzy* works best of the last films because it's intentionally stagey. Playwright Anthony Shaffer wrote the script. ▼

FRESHMAN, THE. US. 1925. People know all about Charlie Chaplin and Buster Keaton. They're far less aware of the third member of the comic triumvirate of the 1920s, Harold Lloyd. *The Freshman* may be his most fully realized film. He matches his two more famous colleagues step for step in physical humor. His stunts are still legendary. In addition, I think he surpasses Keaton and comes close to matching Chaplin with the human sensibility of his character. In fact, because he's middle class, and clearly twentieth-century, the Harold Lloyd character is probably more germane than Keaton's and Chaplin's nineteenth-century clowns.

FRIENDLY FIRE. US. 1979. Based on the nonfiction book of the same name, this made-for-television film by David Greene, starring Carol Burnett, Ned Beatty, Sam Waterston, and Timothy Hutton, is another example of the value of the docudrama form. Hardly anyone in the feature film world has been able to capture the Vietnam experience in a meaningful and intelligent way. *Friendly Fire* at least attempts this, carefully tracing the history of an American family who try to find out how their son has died in Vietnam.

FRIENDLY PERSUASION. US. 1956. This elegiac drama of a Quaker family during the Civil War may be the ultimate Gary Cooper film. He doesn't act any better here than he did elsewhere, but somehow it's the character he was born to play (in addition to Sergeant York). Composer Dimitri Tiomkin was the musical voice of the fifties in American film, and this may be his best score. William Wyler directed.

FROG PRINCE, THE. US. 1982. Produced originally for the Showtime pay-TV network, Shelley Duvall's Fairie Tale Theatre series of fairy tales for adults has become quite popular with kids on videocassettes. *The Frog Prince*, starring Robin Williams as the anthropomorphical toad, is the best of these. Written and directed with fine wit by Eric Idle (formerly of Monty Python) *The Frog Prince* also stars Teri Garr. *Pinocchio*, with Carl Reiner as Giapetto, and kid's komedian Pee Wee Herman as the little wooden boy, is a close runnerup. All the tapes star major Hollywood figures and each succeeds to one degree or another. These are nice thoughtful retellings of classic stories that are appealing equally to children and adults.

FROM HERE TO ETERNITY. US. 1953. It was a classic novel by James Jones, and it's a classic romantic film about Army life in Hawaii just before the war, when things were simpler. Fred Zinnemann directed Burt Lancaster, Deborah Kerr, Donna Reed, Montgomery Clift, Frank Sinatra, and Jack Warden.

FROM   NOON   TILL   THREE. US. 1976.

Playwright Frank D. Gilroy tried his hand at film directing in the mid-seventies with this simple, very novelistic, and pleasant story about a crook, Charles Bronson, and the woman with whom he has an affair (Jill Ireland) in a western setting.

⚑ FROM RUSSIA WITH LOVE. UK. 1963. This is the James Bond film you may remember best. It's the Connery Bond at the very beginning with Robert Shaw and the evil Lotte Lenya. What Bond always missed after this were wizened and worn fully-dimensional characters like the one Lenya plays here.   ▽

⊙ FRONT PAGE, THE. US. 1931. Playwright/screenwriter Ben Hecht's contribution to American film in the thirties and forties is as underrated as anybody's. *The Front Page* (directed by Lewis Milestone), a classic story of newspapering in the 1920s, with Adolphe Menjou and Pat O'Brien, is about the only work of his most people are familiar with. It's been remade several times, most notably as *HIS GIRL FRIDAY*.   ▽

§ FUNNY FACE. US. 1957. Fred Astaire, as a fashion photographer, turns the dowdy Audrey Hepburn into the epitome of chic in a superb Stanley Donen staging of Gershwin tunes.

§ FUNNY GIRL. US. 1968. The role Barbra Streisand was born to play: Fanny Brice. (And she did it on Broadway, too.) The Merrill/Styne musical isn't really as winning as it might be but certainly this remains one of the memorable film musicals of the sixties.   ▽

❋＼⇧§ FUNNY THING HAPPENED ON THE WAY TO THE FORUM, A. UK. 1966. This ranks with the best musicals ever made, and it's probably the most underrated musical film of the last thirty years. Richard Lester mounted Stephen Sondheim's version of a classic farce by Plautus with a gallery of comedians that runs from Buster Keaton, through Phil Silvers, Zero Mostel, and Jack Gilford, to Michael Hordern. It's an interesting combination of US and British talents, with the young Michael Crawford playing the juvenile lead. It's a classic farce in both meanings of that term, and Lester's free style mise-en-scene fits perfectly, although that seems to be the reason most critics reject the film. The songs by Sondheim—"Everybody Ought to Have a Maid," "I'm Lovely," "Comedy Tonight"— are among his best. If you'll forgive the conceit of basing a contemporary musical on a play

Jean Harlow and Marie Dressler in *Dinner at Eight*. Jean: "Did you know that the guy said that machinery is going to take the place of every profession?" Marie: "Oh, my dear, that's something you need never worry about!"

written thousands of years ago, it is his work with the least pretense. Give Lester credit for heightening and refining what was already a superb Broadway play. Compare the recordings of the stage and film scores and you'll see that the musical numbers Lester does faster, work better faster, and the ones he does slower, work better slower. "Was 1 a good year?" You bet!

GAI SAVOIR, LE. France. 1967. Jean-Pierre Léaud and Juliet Berto as two mouthpieces discuss the joy of knowledge in what may be Jean-Luc Godard's most demanding film essay. This is pure discourse; the two people just talk. Since the film was made for television, it fits: the interview is the basic TV form. This is as close as anyone has come to "pure" film, or at least to talk about and representations of pure film, as Godard would put it. It's also certainly Godard's most poetic and philosophical movie. It's the beginning of sixties political dialectic in French film and that was a very special historical point just before the events of May 1968. Certainly only for people who care about the philosophy of movies—or "fauxtographie" as Godard puns—*Le Gai Savoir* is a riveting convolution of images and sounds.

GANDHI. UK. 1983. This is one of those films you have to include in a book like this simply because it's so ambitious, grand in scope, and popular. How could you gainsay director Richard Attenborough's longtime ambition to put the life of Mahatma Gandhi on film? How could you criticize the brilliant acting of Ben Kingsley in the title role (except to suggest that perhaps the role might have been more properly played by an Indian)? How could you belittle the sweep and grandeur of this very important life story? You can't. ▽

GANG'S ALL HERE, THE. US. 1943. A vivid Technicolor Busby Berkeley original with Alice Faye, Carmen Miranda (the lady in the tutti-frutti hat), Charlotte Greenwood (the longest high-kicking legs that side of Cyd Charisse), Edward Everett Horton, and Benny Goodman. In the early seventies, a new color print of the film was struck and it introduced a new generation to the glories of early Technicolor. If you're unaware of the charms of Alice Faye, this is your chance to catch up, too.

GANJA   AND   HESS.   USA.   1973. Playwright/actor/director Bill Gunn took a contract for a simple Black exploitation film in the early seventies and turned it into one of the most remarkable film documents of the Black outlook that we have ever had. Put succinctly, *Ganja and Hess* is an upper-middle-class Black vampire story. When you're upper-middle-class and a vampire, where do you go for blood? You go down to the local blood bank and heist a few pints. Gunn is trying to deal with so many issues here; intellectualism, the Black revolution, anthropology—even "roots"—that the film rewards repeated viewings. It's unsettling and evocative in a way that no ordinary horror movie ever could be because it's such an ambitious attempt to investigate how we got to where we are. There are very few prints of the film extant, but the Museum of Modern Art does have one, and it is to be hoped that it will find its way to video cassette. Black or white, if you have the chance, don't miss it. It's a remarkable demonstration of the Black artistic sensibility on film.

GARDEN OF THE FINZI-CONTINIS, THE. Italy. 1971. Vittorio De Sica directed Dominique Sanda and Helmut Berger in this story of an aristocratic Jewish Italian family confronting the realities of World War II. The film is elegantly mounted, but after you've left the theater, you begin to wonder if the experiences of the Finzi-Continis might not be unrepresentative in the extreme. ▽

GARLIC IS AS GOOD AS TEN MOTHERS. US. 1981. Les Blank concentrates on food here as he surveys the contemporary culinary fascination with the magical herb garlic. Lots of good recipes here and an insight into the inner workings of the seminal Berkeley restaurant, Alice Waters's "Chez Panisse," together with a visit to the famous Gilroy, California Garlic Festival. I'd like to see something like this as a television series: this week basil, next week tomatoes. At the very least, Blank should be encouraged in this new genre. ▽

⇓ **GASLIGHT**. US. 1944. I don't much like this classic because it's so heavily dependent on gothic cliches, but George Cukor directed Ingrid Bergman in what is for many one of her most memorable roles. ▽

§ **GAY DIVORCEE, THE**. US. 1934. Astaire and Rogers under the direction of Mark Sandrich, with Edward Everett Horton and Betty Grable. Numbers include "Night and Day" and "The Continental." ▽

⊹‖ **GENERAL, THE**. US. 1926. Like Charles Chaplin and Harold Lloyd, Buster Keaton is under-represented in the present volume because so much of his work was done in short films. *The General* is full of the physical grace and deadpan panache that made Keaton's character so significant. Perhaps there's too much plot in *The General* (supposedly based on a true story about a stolen union train during the Civil War), but it's a good long stretch of Keaton doing the physical work that he does best. ▽

⇑ **GENEVIEVE**. UK. 1953. This is an unusual film for connoisseurs of 1950s British comedy. First, it's in color; second, it's a domestic comedy about a group of people and their sports cars in a cross-country race; and third, it doesn't star Alec Guinness, but rather Kenneth More, who was later to achieve considerable success in television. The famous comediennes Kay Kendall and Joyce Grenfell assist.

GENTLEMAN'S AGREEMENT. US. 1947. Gregory Peck pretends to be Jewish and discovers how prevalent anti-Jewish feeling really is. This was important in its time as a document against and about anti-semitism. The attitude may seem out of date now, but the subject is still quite real.

⇑ **GETTING STRAIGHT**. US. 1970. This was one of a group of films (including *The Strawberry Statement* and *R.P.M.*) about the generation of the sixties that appeared shortly after the close of that decade. Like those other films, and nearly every film since about the generation of the sixties, it received poor reviews. In most cases, I think those reviews were treating the subject, rather than the film. As a member of the sixties generation still in good standing, I always found something interesting— even in *The Strawberry Statement*—to look at. *Getting Straight* stars Elliott Gould as a disaffected, over-the-hill graduate student. For me, the orals exam scene in which Gould attemps vainly to deal with the silliness of a Professor obsessed with proving his own point of view, was one of those special moments in the movies where you seem to become part of the action on the screen. Every word rang true. Director Richard Rush later achieved some fame and cult status for *The Stunt Man*. ▽

GHOST AND MRS. MUIR, THE. US. 1947. Rex Harrison, George Sanders, Gene Tierney, and even Natalie Wood, directed by Joseph L. Mankiewicz, with a score by Bernard Herrmann: the ingredients of a classic romantic fantasy. It's a nice, positive ghost story. Play it on the same bill with *THE UNINVITED*. Both are about houses and seashores and improving our relations with the past.

GHOSTBUSTERS. US. 1984. As producer of such films as *NATIONAL LAMPOON'S ANIMAL HOUSE* and more recently as a director, Canadian Ivan Reitman has had nearly as profound an influence on American culture in the early eighties as the more famous Steven Spielberg and George Lucas. He just hasn't had the credit so far. On the whole, Reitman's enterprises are probably more interesting than Spielberg's and Lucas's. *Ghostbusters* is his most notable success to date, both at the box office where it scored as the number one film in the summer of 1984, and with critics. What looks like a simple teenage vehicle for Bill Murray and Dan Aykroyd, turns out to be much more. *Ghostbusters*—scripted by Harold Ramis and Dan Aykroyd—is the final exorcism of *THE EXORCIST*. The only thing to do when confronted with the flying pea soup and moving furniture and all those devilish, scary, sadistic tricks that moviemakers have been playing on us for more than 10 years, is laugh. *Ghostbusters* is a triumph of the life force and it will be with us long after those nasty little horror films of the seventies have disappeared. "We came, we saw, we kicked its ass!"

GIANT. US. 1956. An unusually long film for the 1950s, this was the western romantic classic of the decade: based on Edna Ferber's generational Texas saga, it was James Dean's last film and one of Elizabeth Taylor's and Rock Hudson's best. Today, Ferber's novel would be grist for the miniseries mills.

GIDGET. US. 1959. The successful series about *Gidget* never starred the same actress twice. This Gidget is Sandra Dee, and she's torn between James Darren and Cliff Robertson. It's a classic of late fifties/early sixties teenagerdom, about life on the beach. Paul Wendkos directed.

GIGI. US. 1958. Vincente Minnelli's authoritative staging of the Lerner and Loewe musical of the fifties with Leslie Caron radiant at its center of the turn-of-the-century story. With Maurice Chevalier, Louis Jourdan, Hermione Gingold, and Eva Gabor. It's a sentimental classic of the fifties based on Colette's story of a courtesan in training. "Thank heaven for little girls!"

GILDA. US. 1946. This is Rita Hayworth's famous movie. It's a silly plot—a combination of melodrama and film noir—but the triangle of Glenn Ford, Hayworth, and George Macready, lit fires at the time.

GIMME SHELTER. US. 1972. Well-reputed 1960s/70s documentarians David and Albert Maysles shot this record of the Rolling Stones infamous Altamont concert. It's important not only because Altamont marked the end of the sixties dream, but also because if you can divorce the murder that took place there from the musical events surrounding it, you can enjoy the Rolling Stones at the height of their talent.

GIRL FRIENDS. US. 1978. Claudia Weill's feature debut as director stars Melanie Mayron as a young woman establishing an independent life for herself after her roommate leaves. The contrast between the married and independent lifestyles is key here. A feminist classic of the seventies.

GIRL WITH GREEN EYES, THE. UK. 1963. A nicely done romantic drama about country girl Rita Tushingham falling in love with famous writer, Peter Finch. Lynn Redgrave is the girlfriend. Desmond Davis directed on location in Dublin. There was a freshness to this film at the time that's still notable.

GIRLS, LES. US. 1957. George Cukor directed.

Gene Kelly, Kay Kendall, Mitzi Gaynor, and Taina Elg starred. Cole Porter provided the music. A solid parlay. The story's interesting, too. The three women recount flashbacks about Kelly—sort of a Parisian *RASHOMON*.

△ **GLASS KEY, THE**. US. 1942. Alan Ladd, Veronica Lake, Brian Donlevy, and William Bendix in a nicely-turned, hardboiled second try at the Dashiell Hammett political murder mystery. (George Raft and Edward Arnold starred in the earlier 1935 version, also of interest.) Stuart Heisler directed.

🎬💲 **GLENN MILLER STORY, THE**. US. 1954. This is a solid biopic about the swing bandleader. James Stewart stars, and all the swing hits ("String of Pearls," "PEnnsylvania 6-5000") are well reproduced. A newly-struck print has just been reissued by Universal with a restored stereophonic soundtrack. It was apparently the first film recorded in stereo, although at the time it was not released in stereo since few theaters had equipment. The result is that we have a better experience of this film in the 1980s than we did thirty years earlier. (You'll still have to deal with June Allyson, however.)

✳ 🎬💲 **GODFATHER, THE**. US. 1972. Most critics agree that this is one of the central American films of the last twenty-five years, perhaps approaching *CITIZEN KANE* in its significance. Great movies aren't planned as such; they happen through an unusual confluence of talents and qualities. *The Godfather* is no exception. Francis Coppola had set out simply to redeem a faltering career when he started to shoot the popular Mario Puzo mafia novel. His talent brought him luck. First he collected an extraordinary number of the great actors who made American filmmaking interesting during the seventies and eighties: Marlon Brando, James Caan, Al Pacino, John Cazale, Diane Keaton, Robert Duvall. Then he spiced the mixture with some accomplished character actors: John Marley, Al Lettieri, Sterling Hayden, and Coppola's sister, Talia Shire. He had the eminent good sense—or good luck—to get Nino Rota to write Rota's last great score. He got a finely crafted script from author Puzo, then he worked obsessively pushing these people to the limits of their abilities, and sometimes beyond. The screen crackles with the intelligence of acting. Coppola and his crew paid extraordinary attention to detail. Coppola did, after all, have some memory of the Italian-American world of New York of the 1940s. The novel by Puzo (which also redeemed a faltering career) provided not one but several mythic elements that Coppola was canny enough to reinforce in the film. The Godfather is a generational saga; it's also an action film; but above all it caught the imagination of audiences because it suggests that the career of a gangster is not so very different from the career of a businessman or a politician. This had an important resonance for the generation of the early seventies. The film is dark— Coppola had the courage intentionally to underlight each scene; the mood is dark; and the climax in which son Michael operatically indulges in blood vengeance would simply be horrific were it not for the ironic melodies of the Rota score which underline the human and humane sensibility of the storyteller and keep us at a distance. ◩

✳\ **GODFATHER, PART II, THE**. US. 1974. Sequels were beginning to become all the rage in the early seventies, so it's not surprising that a film as popular as *THE GODFATHER* gave birth to what might have been just a followup exploitation. What is remarkable, perhaps unique, is that *The Godfather, Part II* not only expands upon and amplifies its predecessor, but also comes close to superseding it. It's a courageous conceit to tell two stories in the same film: here we have both the early years of Don Corleone in Sicily and the succeeding years of his son, Don Michael, before he assumes his father's title; and it does work. Something like this could only have happened in the mid-seventies when Hollywood was still in awe of directors and their "art." A good part of the film is in Italian with English subtitles and this also bespeaks the remarkable "sprezzatura" the movie evinces. The themes of the two films are the same: *Godfather II* simply amplifies and expands upon the equation of politics, business, and crime. But there was enough in that myth and in our fascination with vengeance and the mundanity of evil to keep the series going. Several years later, both films were recut in chronological order for a television miniseries. The story told in sequence was of less interest. We need to know the heart of the matter first. The few additional scenes that were interpolated for the TV version might just as well have been left on the cutting room floor. ◩

GOIN' DOWN THE ROAD. Canada. 1970. Director Donald Shebib gained some acclaim south of the border for this classic Canadian tale of the road. US road movies usually follow the hero as he leaves the city to find at least some temporary peace of mind in the countryside. Canadian road movies, motivated by social concerns, usually find a couple of country boys going off to the big city (Montreal or Toronto). These boys are from Nova Scotia, and they nearly make it.

GOIN' SOUTH. US. 1978. Jack Nicholson directed this fine little western starring himself and Mary Steenburgen in her first film role. As a dissolute and very funny crook, Nicholson saves himself from the gallows by marrying Mary.

GOING IN STYLE. US. 1979. An unusual little caper film about a bunch of retirees who decide to rob a bank to help stretch Social Security. George Burns is the ringleader, as we might expect; Art Carney and Lee Strasberg are the sidekicks.

GOING MY WAY. US. 1944. This is the great Oscar-winning sentimental classic of the forties which makes the unusual proposition that priests are just like you and me. Bing Crosby is the Padre who's a regular guy; Barry Fitzgerald is the crusty but loveable older priest. Bing gets the gang of kids to straighten up and fly right, and also wins over Fitzgerald. "Would you like to swing on a star?"

GOLD DIGGERS OF '33. US. 1933. Along with *FOOTLIGHT PARADE*, this is a close runner-up to *42ND STREET* for Busby Berkeley dance routines. Mervyn LeRoy directed Joan Blondell, Ruby Keeler, and Dick Powell. *The Gold Diggers* sequels became progressively less interesting.

GOLD OF NAPLES, THE. Italy. 1954. Four short stories directed by Vittorio De Sica and starring Sophia Loren, De Sica, Toto, and Silvana Mangano. The Italians have kept the short form in film alive since 1954 with numerous other anthology features. This is one of the best.

GOLD RUSH, THE. US. 1925. Although this is feature length, it's a good emblem of Chaplin's many great short films of the teens and twenties. This is the one where he eats his shoe.

GOLDEN AGE OF COMEDY, THE. US. 1957. This is an excellent compilation film that gathers many of the best comedy bits by Harry Langdon, Laurel and Hardy, Will Rogers, and numerous others. Everybody learns literature from anthologies, why can't we learn film the same way?

GOLDEN COACH, THE. Italy/France. 1952. Anna Magnani in Jean Renoir's highly stylized film about acting and color. A group of actors on tour in the raucous eighteenth century discover numerous love interests for their leading lady.

GOLDFINGER. UK. 1964. This was the third of the Bond films, and the one with the most entertaining gadgets. Gert Frobe was the title villain and "Oddjob" his henchman. ☒

GONE WITH THE WIND. US. 1939. So much Hollywood hoopla surrounds *Gone With the Wind* that it's difficult to analyze objectively. It was as much an event as a film, capping the Hollywood Golden Years. It's full of great moments in moviemaking from the burning of Atlanta on the back lot, to "Frankly, my dear, I don't give a damn." If I don't seem more excited, it's perhaps because when confronted with Scarlett O'Hara's problems, I never gave a damn myself. Perhaps you do. There's no denying the scope of this Civil War drama. Victor Fleming mounted the film for producer David O. Selznick, and Max Steiner provided what is perhaps his best score. ☒

GOOD EARTH, THE. US. 1937. Pearl Buck's classic novel about Chinese peasants is decently brought to the screen with Paul Muni and Luise Rainer starring. Of course you need a willing suspension of disbelief.... Compare *EARTH*. ☒

GOODBYE, MR. CHIPS. UK. 1939. Robert Donat and Greer Garson give some life to this classic story of a dedicated schoolmaster. The genre dates back to the Victorian classic novel *Tom Brown's School Days* and has been done many times since on film and in television. There's no doubt that teachers have a special relationship with students. Compare *EDUCATING RITA*. ☒

GOSTA BERLING'S SAGA. Sweden. 1924. Mauritz Stiller's four-hour version of the classic novel by Selma Lagerlöf tells a story that's halfway between Strindberg and Bergman of a defrocked pastor who falls in love with his student. He winds up marrying Greta Garbo. The film introduced Garbo to international audiences.

GRADUATE, THE. US. 1967. When you look at *The Graduate* now, it seems like a rather tame story. It's hard to tell what all the fuss was about. Young Benjamin (Dustin Hoffman) has a fling with an older woman (the redoubtable Anne Bancroft), steals a bride (Katharine Ross) away from the altar, and rides off happily ever after into the future in the back seat of a bus. Perhaps it was slightly shocking that the older woman was the mother of the bride; perhaps it was simply the disparity in age of the participants; whatever it was, director Mike Nichols's work was hailed as a landmark. On reflection, there's nothing much hip about Benjamin. In fact, he could just as easily come out of a forties or fifties novel. But *The Graduate* was hailed as the lead film of the sixties generation. Certainly the elegant mise-en-scene was remarkable at the time, but the measure of success may very well have had a lot to do with the poetical score by Simon and Garfunkel. For the first time, a filmmaker used the music of the new generation to great advantage to set the mood of a film. I still don't really know what it means, but that famous line from "Mrs. Robinson" still brings a lump to the throat: "Where are you now, Joe DiMaggio? A nation turns its lonely eyes to you!" (Whoo, whoo, whoo.) ▣

GRAND HOTEL. US. 1932. Not just a great early sound movie with the likes of Greta Garbo, John Barrymore, Wallace Beery, Lionel Barrymore, Joan Crawford, and Lewis Stone, *Grand Hotel* also founded an important genre—a genre which films do much better than novels. Much of what we enjoy about movies (not to mention television) comes from spending a few hours with some interesting characters who talk with each other in interesting ways. The *Grand Hotel* genre strips film narrative of any extraneous details; it simply puts a bunch of people together in one place so that we can watch them interact. One advantage of *Grand Hotel* over its successors (*THE HIGH AND THE MIGHTY*, *The Poseidon Adventure*) is that there isn't a suspenseful disaster impending. It's been done many times since, but never better.

GRAND ILLUSION. France. 1937. Jean Renoir's classic anti-war drama gives us a group of French prisoners of war during World War I under their interesting German commandant, Erich von Stroheim. Class conflicts loom larger than national differences, and the relationships between these "enemies" are so intensely intertwined that the idea of the present conflict becomes absurd.   ▣

GRAPES OF WRATH, THE. US. 1940. This is the ultimate John Steinbeck story, passionately mounted by John Ford. Henry Fonda, John Carradine, and Jane Darwell are the Okies moving doggedly through the Depression to California and what may—or may not—be a better life. Essential Americana.

GREASED LIGHTNING. US. 1977. Richard Pryor in an early dramatic role as Wendell Scott, the first successful Black race car driver. Directed by Michael Schultz. Nothing unusual here, except for a fine cast, including Cleavon Little and Pam Grier. Play it on a double bill with *HEART LIKE A WHEEL*.

GREAT DICTATOR, THE. US. 1940. This is Charlie Chaplin's first complete talkie and it's fascinating to see the way the structures of his silent movies are translated into a unique blend of slapstick, wordplay, parody, and pointed political commentary. Chaplin plays Adenoid Hinkel the dictator, Jack Oakie his rival Benzino Napolini. It's one of the salient ironies of the twentieth century that Charlot (the Chaplin everyman) and Adolf Hitler, the transcendent arch-villain, were similar enough in physical appearance that they might have been brothers.

GREAT GILBERT AND SULLIVAN, THE. UK. 1953. Sidney Gilliat directed Martyn Green, Maurice Evans, Robert Morley, and others in a celebration of the lives and music of the well-known composers. It's a curious fact that the wit and satire of Gilbert and Sullivan's Victorian operettas are nearly as pointed and certainly as entertaining today as they were one hundred years ago. More attention should be paid.

GREAT EXPECTATIONS. UK. 1946. If you're looking for a film adaptation of a great Victorian novel, you can't do much better than this treatment of the Dickens classic. John Mills, Alec Guinness, and Jean Simmons are excellently orchestrated by David Lean.

GREAT McGINTY, THE. US. 1940. This is Preston Sturges's first time in the directorial chair. Brian Donlevy is the tough guy of the streets who's groomed by the political machine and eventually elected Governor. Then he has the audacity to turn straight. Actually, Sturges did better later, with such films as *THE PALM BEACH STORY* and *THE LADY EVE*.

GREAT MUPPET CAPER, THE. US. 1981. This one got lost in the shuffle. Jim Henson himself directed the muppets along with Charles Grodin, John Cleese, Robert Morley, and other English types. There's a plot this time—the famous "Baseball" diamond has been stolen—and the music is even better than *THE MUPPET MOVIE*. That first film with the muppet crew had to be a success; this time it was more difficult. Nonetheless, the caper plot Henson and company worked out manages to hold our interest for quite a while. ▽

GREAT TRAIN ROBBERY, THE. US. 1903. It's exciting now to watch a film from the earliest days of cinema history like *The Great Train Robbery* and realize that more than eighty years ago pioneers like director Edwin S. Porter blithely foreshadowed so much of what was to come. In the US, France, England, and Germany, the inventors of cinema quickly discovered its major artistic assets: its ability to capture reality, its converse power to bring fantasies to life, its unique humanness, and the intelligence and drama that springs from montage: putting two shots side by side. *The Great Train Robbery* is one of those films now seen only in university classes, which will become common experiences for more of us as the videocassette industry matures. ▽

GREAT ZIEGFELD, THE. US. 1936. A long and entertaining biography of the eminent showman provides numerous opportunities for fully developed thirties-style musical numbers. Myrna Loy, William Powell, Fanny Brice, Luise Rainer, Ray Bolger, and many others contribute to the grand hommage.

GREED. US. 1923. In the early days, Hollywood fed upon itself and believed in itself with such delirious passion that the characters behind the camera often exceeded in interest and melodramatic style the characters in front of the camera. In the twenties there were two great directors who each attempted the role of independent rebellious artist. Josef von Sternberg did it in a way that was more acceptable to the studio establishment: he made relatively popular films, notable now mainly for their stylishness and sexuality. Erich von Stroheim attempted more interesting work, but was less successful in Hollywood terms. *Greed* was his donnybrook. He filmed Frank Norris's novel *McTeague* faithfully, with a cast that included ZaSu Pitts, Jean Hersholt, and Gibson Gowland. The result was a legendary ten-hour film that would have been the very model of a modern miniseries. Irving Thalberg at MGM cut it in half, then had it cut in half again, and the two-and-a-half-hour long film that remains is a vestige of great ambitions and a milestone in silent cinema.

GREEN FOR DANGER. UK. 1946. The team of

Robby the Robot with humans Leslie Neilsen, Walter Pidgeon, and Anne Francis in *Forbidden Planet*.

Sidney Gilliat and Frank Launder produced numerous representative British film dramas during the forties. This policier, directed by Sidney Gilliat, and starring Alastair Sim, is one of the best. Solid casting, solid acting, finely-paced dialogue—all the elements that a film connoisseur can savor—contribute to this mystery set in a World War II hospital.

GREETINGS. US. 1968. This is a very early effort by Brian De Palma, starring Robert DeNiro. It's very much the semi-underground film and gives you a portrayal of what used to be known as the counter-culture, the likes of which you will never find in a Hollywood film. The "Greetings" are from Uncle Sam, and they are not welcome. De Palma later got stuck making rigidly generic movies. If he'd gone back to this sort of naturalism, it certainly would have been refreshing.

GREGORY'S GIRL. Scotland. 1981. With two films in recent years, Scottish director Bill Forsyth has shown that there is still life in the classic British comedy thirty years after its heyday. *Gregory's Girl* gives us a romance between two teenagers, and it's got all the elements: the wry tone, the low-keyed but strong affection for its characters, the finely-tuned sense of place and time. See also *LOCAL HERO*.

⊘ **GREY FOX, THE**. Canada. 1982. Here's a transition western set in the early twentieth century, in a Canadian locale. Richard Farnsworth plays real-life highwayman Bill Minor, who switched to robbing trains after a long spell in prison. Great scenery. ▽

GREY GARDENS. US. 1975. The Maysles brothers shot this notable portrait of a couple of Jacqueline Bouvier Kennedy Onassis's dotty relatives. The two women, mother and daughter, are interesting in themselves, but let's face it, the film got made because they were related to Jackie.

⊘＼⇪ **GROUP, THE**. US. 1966. By now *The Group* should be a well-known classic. It's based on Mary McCarthy's biting portrait of a group of eight Vassar College graduates. Sidney Lumet brings it alive on screen with the considerable help of a cast which includes Joan Hackett, Shirley Knight, Joanna Pettet, Jessica Walter, Kathleen Widdoes, Candice Bergen, Elizabeth Hartman, and Mary Robin-Redd. This is the film in which Joan Hackett blushes on cue, which alone should be worth the price of admission. A couple of these actresses went on to minor careers. A couple were never heard from again. Larry Hagman, Richard Mulligan, and Hal Holbrook provide the male support. It's an important feminist document. ▽

⊹▼＼ **GUERRE EST FINIE, LA**. France/Sweden. 1965. An extraordinary film; one of the great ones. Novelist Jorge Semprun wrote the script for Alain Resnais's study of political commitment and thirties radicals in their middle age. We didn't know it at the time, but *La Guerre Est Finie* was an important cautionary tale for sixties political activists. Yves Montand is the professional revolutionary coming to terms with a life spent in the struggle against fascism in Spain. Ingrid Thulin and Geneviève Bujold are the women.

⊘⇪ **GUEULE OUVERTE, LA**. France. 1974. Maurice Pialat's fictional study of how a family copes with death focuses on a woman slowly dying of cancer. It sounds more lugubrious than it is because Pialat manages to convey a strong sense of the life force: paradoxically, this death becomes life-affirming. See *ME*.

⊘ **GUMSHOE**. UK. 1971. Here's a British view of the film-conscious generation of the sixties and seventies. Albert Finney plays a small-time British comic who's as impressed in his way with the persona of Humphrey Bogart as Woody Allen was. Stephen Frears directed.

GUNGA DIN. US. 1939. Cary Grant, Victor McLaglen, Douglas Fairbanks Jr., and Sam Jaffe in a high adventure that has something to do with India. George Stevens directed. ▼

HAGBARD & SIGNE. Iceland. 1968. This is a fascinating film which deserves your attention. First of all, it's bound to be the best Icelandic film you've ever seen. More important, it's a novel attempt to capture the spirit of an Icelandic saga on film. Outside of Monty Python, nobody pays much attention to the medieval world. But the saga is an important artistic form, and here it works in the film medium. Director Gabriel Axel gets credit for an ambitious and unique undertaking.

HAIL THE CONQUERING HERO. US. 1944. One of the great things about Preston Sturges was how well he did with actors in lead roles who would've been lucky to get second billing anywhere else. Here, Eddie Bracken is the 4-F stay-at-home who gets mistaken for a war hero. Who else but Sturges would have thought to do this kind of counter-heroic comedy very near the end of World War II? The film is full of the sardonic, apoplectic touches that we love in Sturges.

HAIR. US. 1979. This was the hippy fantasy musical, first off-Broadway, then on Broadway, in the late sixties. It finally made its way to film ten years later. Miloš Forman does a good job of making a very stagey play an effective film. *Hair* also boasts choreography by Twyla Tharp. The trouble is the theme songs of a generation have a strange period ring a decade later. ▼

HALLELUJAH, THE HILLS. US. 1963. Once upon a time in the early sixties there was a movement known as the New American Cinema. Jonas Mekas was its prophet in a weekly column in the *Village Voice*. He and his brother, Adolfas, who directed *Hallelujah, the Hills*, were among its practitioners. Most of this underground cinema consisted of arty shorts. (Perhaps Kenneth Anger's *Scorpio Rising* was the best known of these.) The Mekas brothers produced more traditional feature-length films. This one is an interesting confluence of Hollywood structures and home-movie techniques: a document of its time, in part.

HANDS ACROSS THE TABLE. US. 1935. Carole Lombard, Fred MacMurray, and Ralph Bellamy in an underrated thirties comedy by Mitchell Leisen. She's a manicurist looking for a husband coiffed by Fred and Ralph.

HANOVER STREET. UK. 1979. This may not be a very good movie, but it is a very strange one. Director Peter Hyams comes as close as anyone has to making a 1940s movie thirty-five years later. *Hanover Street* is a World War II romance starring Harrison Ford and Lesley Anne Down, as well as Christopher Plummer and Alec McCowen. There is very little here except the color that would have been out of place on a movie screen at the end of the war. It's an interesting genre experiment.

HANS CHRISTIAN ANDERSEN. US. 1952. Danny Kaye as the storyteller for children. The score by Frank Loesser includes "Inch Worm" and "Ugly Duckling." The scenery is nice, but elsewhere Kaye was able to entertain adults as well as children.

HARD DAY'S NIGHT, A. UK. 1964. This magnificent, exciting, noteworthy musical by Richard Lester was an important step in the Beatles' career. After this they were actors, writers, and personalities, as well as musicians—never again to be compared with the Dave Clark Five. Lester's free-form style established a format for film musicals for two generations culminating in the rock video form of the mid-eighties. Understandably, it was never so fresh, vivacious, and liberating as it was here at the beginning. ◩

HARDER THEY COME, THE. Jamaica. 1972. Perry Henzell directed this unusual and entertaining cult favorite. Jimmy Cliff stars as the country boy who comes to Kingston to make his name in music. The film introduced reggae to a wide spectrum of American audiences. It works as a musical, and, more important, it works as a drama. There were a number of films like this made in Jamaica in the seventies, but *The Harder They Come* was the only one to survive the Caribbean crossing. "You can get it if you really want." ◩

HARLAN COUNTY, U.S.A. US. 1976. Film-maker Barbara Kopple spent more than a year living with a group of miners in the hills of Kentucky, and this extraordinary document of their strike against the mines is the result. If you've ever wondered whether "documentary" could provide the same sort of drama and character that fiction films do, *Harlan County* should put those fears to rest. One of a number of remarkable historical nonfiction films made in the US in the mid-seventies, *Harlan County* provides a necessary contemporary counterpoint to movies like *THE WOBBLIES* and *THE LIFE AND TIMES OF ROSIE THE RIVETER*. The struggle continues. ∇

‼ **HAROLD LLOYD'S WORLD OF COMEDY**. US. 1962. Lloyd himself compiled this collection of some of his best bits and it's highly recommended, assuming you can't afford a set of the original films. ∇

⏶⏏ **HARPER**. US. 1966. Paul Newman is the down-and-out private eye in this film of a Ross MacDonald novel. The film has a good laconic script and a fine cast that includes Lauren Bacall, Julie Harris, Shelley Winters and Janet Leigh. Newman isn't Humphrey Bogart, but then neither was Jean-Paul Belmondo. This genre continues to show surprising signs of life forty years after its heyday. From our vantage point, *Harper* is midway between Bogart and Clint Eastwood. ∇

⏶ **HARRY & TONTO**. US. 1973. These days when George Burns is seen almost as often on the screen as Brooke Shields, it's difficult to remember a time when old people were as rare as infants in American movies. Paul Mazursky's *Harry & Tonto* broke that barrier in 1973 with its portrayal of oldster Art Carney setting out on a trek across America to the west coast to see each of his grown children in turn. With Ellen Burstyn and Larry Hagman, and Geraldine Fitzgerald as the love interest. ∇

⏷ **HARVEY**. US. 1950. James Stewart is Elwood P. Dowd, the drunk with a six-foot invisible rabbit friend. Probably only Stewart could bring this off: the subject is too cutesy and stagey to make a good film otherwise.

⏏ **HEAD OVER HEELS**. US. 1979. There was a significant subculture in the 1970s—people in their twenties, leftovers of the generation of the sixties—whose stories seldom made it to the screen. *Head Over Heels*, based on the popular seventies novel by Ann Beattie, *Chilly Scenes of Winter*, is one of the few times that they did. Director Joan Micklin Silver had a special feel for this sort of material. You may object to the self-concerned, rather forlorn passivity of the characters, but they represent a generation. John Heard is trying to win the heart of Mary Beth Hurt. Peter Riegert, Gloria Grahame, and Kenneth McMillan assist. *THE BIG CHILL* had much more success with similar characters, and for a very old-fashioned Hollywood reason: Lawrence Kasdan's group, unlike Joan Silver's, is upper-middle-class, and that gives a brighter tone to the proceedings overall. Silver's people are probably more representative, if downbeat.

HEART LIKE A WHEEL. US. 1983. Bonnie Bedelia as Shirley Muldowney, the real-life woman drag racing hero, directed by Jonathan Kaplan. This is a solid biopic made memorable by its subject. It's one thing for a woman to succeed in the corporate boardroom, or in one of the professions; it's quite something else for a woman to make it as a leading drag racer. If the idea intrigues you, the movie will. ☑

HEARTBREAK KID, THE. US. 1972. The Jewish boy and the WASP girl, directed by Elaine May from a script by Neil Simon from a story by Bruce Jay Friedman. These are the three people you'd pick as experts on the subject. Charles Grodin and Cybill Shepherd star. May's daughter, Jeannie Berlin, is caught in the middle. ☑

HEARTLAND. US. 1979. This was an independent sleeper that kept coming back again and again in the early eighties and finally gave rise to a mini-genre: the "country" movie. Richard Pearce directed Rip Torn and Conchata Ferrell in the independent Montanan production based on a true story. Ferrell is the tough pioneer woman who comes to keep house for the incredibly taciturn Torn. This is something of a feminist document as well. Run it on a double bill with *ZANDY'S BRIDE*. ☑

HEARTS AND MINDS. US. 1974. During the last twenty years fiction films have made quite a poor showing in treating the subject of the Vietnam war. Nonfiction filmmakers, on the other hand, have done a brilliant job in capturing the issues, the experience, the pain, and the doubts and fears of the war. No one has done it better or more concisely than Peter Davis in this remarkable essay. For Americans, this film, even more than Marcel Ophuls's *THE SORROW AND THE PITY*, demonstrates the surprising power the medium of film has in treating complicated ideas. Davis doesn't shirk on the details, nor does he hide behind them. The film is a poweful indictment of the American experience in Vietnam. ◩

◭ **HEARTS OF THE WEST**. US. 1975. This is, so far as I know, the only comedy about making grade-Z westerns in Hollywood in the 1930s. Jeff Bridges is the star. Blythe Danner is the girl. Howard Zieff directed Alan Arkin as the director. If you like grade-Z westerns, you'll love *Hearts of the West*.

HEAVEN CAN WAIT. US. 1943. Ernst Lubitsch directs Don Ameche, Gene Tierney, and Charles Coburn in a color fantasy, not to be confused with Warren Beatty's remake of *HERE COMES MR. JORDAN*. Ameche is the sinner who has to come to terms with his mortality. ◩

⚑ **HEAVEN'S GATE**. US. 1980. Michael Cimino reputedly spent more than $40 million on this overblown western. When the film was released it fell thoroughly flat. A little while later, producer/distributor United Artists effectively went out of business, merging with MGM. This is the only film in history to have brought down a major studio.

◭ **HEIRESS, THE**. US. 1949. Here's a fascinating, ambitious Hollywood experiment that succeeds. William Wyler directed Olivia de Havilland, Ralph Richardson, and Montgomery Clift in this film based on Henry James's novel *Washington Square*. The Jamesian sensibility is the very antithesis of Hollywood style: internal, introspective, and psychological. Wyler shows, with considerable panache, how it can be expressed on the screen.

HELL'S ANGELS. US. 1930. This is Howard Hughes's gift to himself: an expensive hymn to airplanes in the Great War, combining Hughes's first love with his second. It makes you wish he'd made a movie starring the "Spruce Goose," his great aeronautical engineering accomplishment.

⚑⛫ **HELL'S HINGES**. US. 1916. Hell's Hinges is a town—"a good place to ride wide of" according to the titles. It's also a classic William S. Hart western. He generally played a western badman who saw the light, usually under the influence of a pure-minded young girl. *Hell's Hinges* is a good example of the melodrama that Hart did so effectively and to such popular acclaim, but it also shows the psychological complexity of character that audiences at the time didn't notice but that means so much to us now.

‼ **HELLZAPOPPIN**. US. 1941. Ole Olsen and Chick Johnson were far ahead of their time as absurdist comedians in their Broadway performances. Here they try to fit into a Hollywood movie but the anarchy of their humor sloughs over the edges. This is an important precursor of contemporary comic concerns.

HELP! UK. 1965. Could Richard Lester and the Beatles do it again? Yes indeed! *Help!* is a worthy followup to *A HARD DAY'S NIGHT*. The style of the film is comparable and the music is of similar vintage, but this time they had color to work with and a wonderfully corny plot, aided and abetted by comedians like Leo McKern, Victor Spinetti, and Roy Kinnear. Our only disappointment is that this is the last of the real Beatles films. After this they got arty.

HENRY V. UK. 1945. Laurence Olivier turned this rather static conclusion to Shakespeare's historical tetralogy into a magnificent colorful hymn to patriotism—a gift to the people of Britain at the end of the war. This will remain for a long time the ultimate staging of the play.

HERE COMES MR. JORDAN. US. 1941. You probably know this better from its remake, Warren Beatty's *HEAVEN CAN WAIT*. Not to underrate Beatty's work, but the original still wins out on points: it's the kind of ripe fantasy that doesn't work well in contemporary settings. Robert Montgomery is the fighter who dies before his time here and returns to life in a new body. If you want to do fantasy, certainly this conceit is as good as you can get. Alexander Hall directed.

HI, NELLIE! US. 1934. There are so many great little B-movies, or "programmers," from the 1930s and early forties, that they must perforce be vastly under-represented here. At an hour-and-a-quarter running time, *Hi, Nellie!* , directed by Mervyn LeRoy, is a superb example of the fast-paced programmer art. Paul Muni is an independent-minded muckraker who gets stuck writing the Lonely Hearts column for his newspaper. It's a device that would be repeated a thousand times again in film and television. Watch how breathlessly and stylishly LeRoy and company handle the task.

HIDE IN PLAIN SIGHT. US. 1980. For the last fifteen years while most critics in America have been celebrating the same eight or ten boy wonder directors, something strange has been happening. Actors, who used to be the kings of Hollywood until dethroned in the late sixties by perversions of the auteur theory, have been putting themselves in the director's chair, as if in revenge. What's remarkable is that their track record is excellent. Warren Beatty, Jack Nicholson, Richard Benjamin, and here James Caan, are proving that the craft of directing is not so terribly hard to learn. This is an absorbing little film about a divorced man, Caan, searching for his missing children. Jill Eikenberry, Kenneth McMillan, and Danny Aiello work well together with Caan.

HIGH AND THE MIGHTY, THE. US. 1954. William Wellman directed this classic *GRAND HOTEL* of the air. It's the precursor of all the disaster films to come, and still the best. The latter examples are always a little self-conscious about their silliness. *The High and the Mighty*, set on a doomed airplane flight with John Wayne at the controls, is unself-conscious. Another great theme song by Dimitri Tiomkin gives the film its special fifties aura.

HIGH NOON. US. 1952. "Do not forsake me, oh my darling." Here is the apotheosis of the western. Gary Cooper is the lonely sheriff counting down to the showdown with the gunfighter. All extraneous details have been swept away. It's just the hero and the girl (Grace Kelly) and the idea of order on the plains. Fred Zinnemann directed. Dimitri Tiomkin wrote the memorable score.

HIGH PRESSURE. US. 1931. A good con-man story by Mervyn LeRoy, starring William Powell. One of the unsung programmers of the thirties.

HIGH SOCIETY. US. 1956. This is a musical remake of *THE PHILADELPHIA STORY* with very little of the energy of the original. Watch it for the Cole Porter songs and for Bing Crosby, Grace Kelly, Frank Sinatra, and Louis Armstrong, all settling quietly and comfortably into middle age.

HIRED HAND, THE. US. 1971. Peter Fonda directed this weird western starring himself, Warren Oates, and Verna Bloom. It's often pretentious but magnificently photographed and worth a look.

HIRED WIFE. US. 1940. This is a magnificent, if little known, screwball comedy directed by William A. Seiter, and starring Rosalind Russell at the peak of her early form, and Brian Aherne. Even more than *HIS GIRL FRIDAY*, *Hired Wife* shows us how women were succeeding in business forty-five years ago. Aherne is the boss; Rosalind Russell is the gal Friday who runs the whole show. For business reasons, and business reasons only, it appears, they marry. You know what happens. He falls in love with her at the end. What you may not suspect is that she doesn't retire to the country house. She's still running the show. That little plot twist is refreshing.

HIROSHIMA, MON AMOUR. France/Japan. 1959. Along with *L'AVVENTURA*, and *LAST YEAR AT MARIENBAD*, this was one of the great art house classics of the late fifties/early sixties. Alain Resnais's artistically leveraged study of war and its effects shows us a brief affair between a French woman and a Japanese man, each of whom remembers his or her war. She was pilloried as a collaborator; he remembers Hiroshima. This may seem arch or involuted, but how else to deal with such an intense subject?

HIS GIRL FRIDAY. US. 1940. Howard Hawks directed this markedly superior remake of *THE FRONT PAGE* with Cary Grant and Rosalind Russell and a host of excellent minor actors. Grant is the boss, Russell is the star reporter, and the script by Ben Hecht, Charles MacArthur, and Charles Lederer shows not only that you can go back to old material again, but sometimes you can do it much better than you did the first time. 1940 was a great year for Rosalind Russell (see *HIRED WIFE* above).

HOLIDAY INN. US. 1942. At Christmas, after the umpteenth showing of *IT'S A WONDERFUL LIFE*, you have your choice between two films in which Bing Crosby sings "White Christmas:" *Holiday Inn* and *WHITE CHRISTMAS*. Choose the former. Even though it's cluttered up with other holidays, this Mark Sandrich staging of Irving Berlin songs is an excellent way to celebrate. With Crosby singing and Astaire dancing, you'll mark the change of years in style.

HOOPER. US. 1978. The partnership of Burt Reynolds and director Hal Needham has produced some of the more entertaining genre films of the late seventies and early eighties. *Hooper* gives us a perspective on all the *SMOKEY AND THE BANDIT* movies, since it comes home to Hollywood to study the world of stuntmen, so important to the success of that genre. Reynolds is

Hooper, an aging stuntman, and Sally Field is his girlfriend. Jan-Michael Vincent is the young turk. It's got lots of good in-jokes, the most notable of which is Robert Klein playing a pompous Peter Bogdanovich director. No one knows better than Needham, the ex-stuntman, and Reynolds, the actor/producer/director, that the cult of the auteur is a crock. ▨

⬆ **HOPSCOTCH**. UK. 1980. This one came and went rather quickly, but it's been developing an underground reputation ever since. Ronald Neame directed, Walter Matthau and Glenda Jackson star. Matthau is an out-of-place CIA agent who decides to publish his memoirs to get back at the system. ▨

‼ **HORSE FEATHERS**. US. 1932. The Marx Brothers again. This time Groucho's head of Huxley College and they play football. Make this number four on the Marx list. ▨

◉§ **HORSE'S MOUTH, THE**. UK. 1958. This is the classic novel by Joyce Cary as staged by Ronald Neame with a script by, and starring, Alec Guinness as the renegade painter. It's about the demands and responsibilities of art, and it's still charming.

⬆ **HOT ROCK, THE**. US. 1972. William Goldman wrote the screenplay from the novel by Donald Westlake. Peter Yates directed and Robert Redford, George Segal, Paul Sand, and Zero Mostel star in this well-paced, efficient, and ingratiating caper film from the Donald Westlake novel about bungling jewel thieves. The caper movie was probably the leading genre of the 1960s and it's a shame it's fallen out of favor.

HOT SATURDAY. US. 1932. A programmer about smalltown life, with Cary Grant and Randolph Scott, directed by William A. Seiter. It's interesting to watch Grant feel his way at the beginning of his career.

⬗◉ **HOUND OF THE BASKERVILLES**. US. 1939. This is the beginning of the Basil Rathbone/Nigel Bruce Sherlock Holmes series, and, therefore, a landmark. The atmosphere of the books was captured here better than in any of the other numerous Sherlock Holmes films and television series.

⬗ **HOUSE CALLS**. US. 1978. Walter Matthau and Glenda Jackson (together with Art Carney and Richard Benjamin) in a signal middle-aged romantic comedy that started a fad for grownup films that has lasted since. Matthau is a doctor, Jackson the independent women he tries to win. Howard Zieff directed. ◹

HOUSE OF ROTHSCHILD, THE. US. 1934. Here's another chance to look at stage star George Arliss. Together with Boris Karloff, Loretta Young, and Robert Young (Florence Arliss gets in here, too), he stars in an elaborate biopic of the Rothschild family in the nineteenth century.

HOUSE OF WAX. US. 1953. Garish fifties color and the lugubrious Vincent Price and Frank Lovejoy from TV combine to make this a linchpin movie of the 1950s. Directed by Andre de Toth, it was apparently the most popular of the 3-D movies during that two-year fad. Price is the mad entrepreneur who uses real bodies for his wax museum.

HOUSE ON 92ND STREET, THE. US. 1945. Hollywood became so enamoured of the studio system in the 1930s that it was rare indeed that we had a glimpse of the outside world. Occasionally Warner Bros. would shoot on location because it cost less, and they're to be applauded for that. But it wasn't until after World War II and the advent of television and the wide cinema screen that locations became important again as they had been in the very early days. *The House on 92nd Street* is a World War II spy drama directed by Henry Hathaway and starring Lloyd Nolan, Gene Lockhart, and Leo G. Carroll, that is notable for its considerable location photography in New York City. It started the move out of the studio backlot and into the real world. American Neorealism? Perhaps.

HOW GREEN WAS MY VALLEY. US. 1941. This is the Welsh coal miner classic directed by John Ford, and starring a couple of Brits and a host of Americans with rather poor British accents. Walter Pidgeon and Maureen O'Hara lead the cast. This sort of film adaptation became BBC fodder in the 1970s, and you may agree it's been done better as a British television series, but perhaps it's unfair to compare such different times and places. At the time it was notable as a human drama and seemed ambitious for Hollywood.

HOW I WON THE WAR. UK. 1967. Richard Lester was getting ambitious here, and not without success—critically at least. Michael Crawford, John Lennon, Roy Kinnear, and Jack MacGowran combined forces for an abstract and fairly surrealist

Jean-Pierre Léaud as Antoine Doinel in Truffaut's *The 400 Blows*.

anti-war film. Lester and screenwriter Charles Wood had the good sense to use World War II as the setting. If you can criticize the good war successfully, you've criticized every war. ▽

HOW TO MURDER YOUR WIFE. US. 1965. Richard Quine directed and George Axelrod wrote the screenplay for this vivid, invigorating, and slightly black comedy. Jack Lemmon is a rich cartoonist, Virna Lisi the Italian woman he marries by accident, Terry-Thomas is the butler, and Eddie Mayehoff the garrulous lawyer. Jack Albertson is the doctor who provides the "alphadexabenzath-erapotathalamine." Just push the button, Eddie, that's all you have to do. Push the button. The film has an excellent score by Neil Hefti.

HUBBA-HUBBA. US. 19??. It's an axiom in Hollywood that movies are made by chance. For every produced and released film there are a dozen interesting projects that don't make it to the screen for one reason or another. Since 1967 when their BONNIE & CLYDE premiered, and throughout the seventies, the screenwriting team of Robert Benton and David Newman ranked high with Hollywood producers. But that didn't necessarily make it easy for them to get their scripts produced. There are at least four of their scripts still sitting on producers' shelves gathering dust that David Newman thinks would still make very good movies.

"Money's Tight" is a caper comedy about five
people who rob banks. "Floreana" is about an
eccentric German dentist in the Gallapagos Islands,
and based on the true story of a crime which took
place there. By himself, Newman once wrote a film
called "Tom & Jerry." A take-off on the famous
cartoon cat-and-mouse act, it would have been a
live-action movie, reproducing all of the classic
tricks and cliches of cartoons—certainly an
intriguing idea, at least. The best of the "un-made"
Newman and Benton scripts must be *Hubba-Hubba*,
about the Hollywood film community during the last
months of 1941. Norman Lear was to have produced
and Bud Yorkin was scheduled as director. It was the
last script Benton and Newman turned out under a
three-picture contract with Warners. A shady fellow
named Lou Schindell inherits a down-and-almost-
out Hollywood studio when his seventy-year-old
father croaks during his birthday party after a roll in
the hay with a starlet. Lou battles his mother Sylvia
for control of the studio and bets the whole shebang
on a high-class production starring Nora Duke, the
hottest young actress in town, and Dennis
Blanchard, Momma Schindell's fading lover.
Grandma Schindell holds the balance of power: Lou
sends her back home to Rivington Street on New
York's lower East Side-except it's really the back lot
at the studio. *Hubba-Hubba* is fast, furious, funny
and delightful. If it had been made, it would have
ranked along with *SINGIN' IN THE RAIN* as a
classic movie about Hollywood. It stands here for all
those legendary non-films that exist only on paper--
and in our imaginations.

⊘ **HUD**. US. 1963. Not the first, but perhaps the best
of the nouveau westerns of the sixties, with Paul
Newman and Patricia Neal, as well as Melvyn
Douglas. Martin Ritt directed.

✛ **HUNCHBACK OF NOTRE DAME, THE**. US.
1923. Lon Chaney, the master of makeup
characterization, was never more striking than as
Quasimodo, the deformed bell-ringer cursed by
love, in this American silent. It matches its European
contemporaries for atmosphere and photography.
Wallace Worsley directed this first adaptation of the
Victor Hugo novel. Compare. . .

⊘ **HUNCHBACK OF NOTRE DAME, THE**. US.
1939. William Dieterle directed Charles Laughton in
the Lon Chaney role. Maureen O'Hara, Cedric
Hardwicke, and Thomas Mitchell also star.   ▽

HURRICANE, THE. US. 1937. John Ford's

fantasy of south-sea island life, starring (of course) Dorothy Lamour, with Mary Astor and Raymond Massey. The storm is built of superb special effects.

HUSBANDS. US. 1970. If you have a taste for John Cassavetes's very personal films, *Husbands* is quite attractive. Nearly all of Cassavetes's work has to do with families and the war between the men and women. Here he comes closest to his own situation, casting himself and friends Ben Gazzara and Peter Falk as three suburban husbands caught on the treadmill and escaping for a brief moment to London. There is one long indulgent scene where the three of them improvise in a bar that summarizes all that's best in Cassavetes's work.

HUSTLER, THE. US. 1961. Robert Rossen made very few films in his short career. He was the first of the modern "art" Hollywood directors and, therefore, a precursor of the auteur generation of the seventies. *The Hustler*, with Paul Newman and Jackie Gleason as rival pool sharks, was a cult classic at the time. The gritty pool hall atmosphere was as much a star as the actors. It still holds up.

HUSTLING. US. 1975. Joseph Sargent directed this made-for-television movie that gives Lee Remick and Jill Clayburgh a chance to act up a storm as investigative reporter and prostitute, respectively.

I AM A CAMERA. UK. 1955. We are already halfway through the long transmogrification of Christopher Isherwood's *Berlin Stories* here. The film was based on John Van Druten's play, which was based on the book. Henry Cornelius directed Julie Harris, Laurence Harvey, Shelley Winters, and Patrick McGoohan. You know the story because you're familiar with it from the musical *CABARET*, either the play or the film or the soundtracks. At the time it was considered mildly daring.

I AM A FUGITIVE FROM A CHAIN GANG. US. 1932. This is the great realistic classic of the Warner Bros. studio from the early thirties. Paul Muni stars as the unjustly accused man nearly destroyed by brutal prison practices. Mervyn LeRoy directed. The tough, gutsy style became a hallmark of the Warner studio. ◪

I AM CURIOUS (YELLOW). Sweden. 1967. Vilgot Sjoman directed this movie, ostensibly about a sociologist studying sex, but notable mainly for its considerable nudity. It's not a good film, but it was a landmark at the time. It was met with a storm of moral outrage which will seem odd after our experience of the seventies. ◪

◬ **I. F. STONE'S WEEKLY**. US. 1973. Jerry Bruck Jr.'s affectionate and informative portrait of veteran iconoclastic political journalist I. F. Stone was well received at the time and has become a classic of recent nonfiction filmmaking. It stands here for all the thousands of hours of film portraiture which preserve real heroes and villains and ordinary folk for our children and their children's children.

⬆ **I KNOW WHERE I'M GOING**. UK. 1945. More a portrait than a drama, this typically unusual point of view from Michael Powell and Emeric Pressberger stars Wendy Hiller as a girl who thinks for herself but nevertheless falls in love. Great Scottish locales.

⬛‼ **I LOVE YOU, ALICE B. TOKLAS**. US. 1968. Paul Mazursky and Larry Tucker wrote the script for this comedy about a middle-class lawyer (Peter Sellers) who discovers pot and the counter-culture. It's a significant comedy, introducing the sixties themes to the Hollywood establishment. Hy Averback directed. ◪

I MARRIED A WITCH. US. 1942. René Clair's fantasy gave tousle-haired Veronica Lake her most memorable role. Compare it with *THE GHOST AND MRS. MUIR*.

⬋⬆ **I OUGHT TO BE IN PICTURES**. US. 1982. Neil Simon, on whose play this is based, gets bad press he doesn't deserve. He's been responsible for so many plays and film scripts during the past twenty years that some of them are bound to be bombs. But *I Ought to be in Pictures*, directed by Herbert Ross, who often works with Simon, is as good a Simon film as you can find. Walter Matthau is an over-the-hill screenwriter, and the film captures the middle-class Hollywood milieu very well indeed. The subject of the film, and its star, is Matthau's daughter from New York whom he hasn't seen in many years. She's played by Dinah Manoff, a superb young actress (and the daughter of Lee Grant). This is the kind of role that makes a kid a star, and Manoff is more than up to it. This also happens to be the film in which Ann-Margret, as Matthau's mistress, finally proved that, years after her image began to change in *CARNAL KNOWLEDGE*, she is not just a big-boobed broad. She gives a very intelligent, restrained performance that anchors the whole film.

I WANNA HOLD YOUR HAND. US. 1978. Robert Zemeckis directed, and Bob Gale wrote this original comedy about Beatlemaniacs circa 1963. It's well done, considering the budgetary limitations, but it's included here mainly for the idea, not for the execution. The shoestring budget meant that closely cropped Hollywood streets had to stand in for the real New York. That hurts.

I WANT TO LIVE. US. 1958. Susan Hayward is Barbara Graham, a convicted woman who goes to the gas chamber, in what remains a powerful indictment of capital punishment. Robert Wise directed. A solid, naturalistic late-fifties film noir, the film remains in memory for the superb score by Gerry Mulligan and his group. As a fifteen-year-old usher, I sat through this movie ten times one weekend. It changed my musical tastes forever—and for the better.

IF. . . UK. 1968. This is the first in Lindsay Anderson's trilogy starring Malcolm McDowell. (Followups: *O LUCKY MAN!* and *BRITANNIA HOSPITAL*.) Here he's at a British Public School plotting revolution. It's notable for its rather daring surrealist style and for its music.

ILLUMINATION. Poland. 1973. Director Krzysztof Zanussi made a series of films in the seventies about the moral and intellectual dilemmas of people who work in the sciences. Not only is this interesting in a Polish setting, it's not likely to be rivalled elsewhere in the world for its treatment of intellectual subject matter. *Illumination* is an important film about the way choices are made.

I'M ALL RIGHT, JACK. UK. 1959. A superior Boulting brothers comedy with Ian Carmichael, Peter Sellers, Terry-Thomas, Richard Attenborough, and Margaret Rutherford. It's ostensibly about labor relations (hence the title). The only people in the film crookeder than the workers are the bosses.

I'M NO ANGEL. US. 1933. If you want to take two Mae West films with you to that desert island, make *SHE DONE HIM WRONG* your first choice and *I'm No Angel* your second. This is the one where Mae and Cary Grant work in the circus sideshow.

IMMIGRANT, THE. US. 1917. Like *EASY STREET*, this classic Chaplin short has autobiographical overtones and more than a hint of social commentary. See *CHARLIE CHAPLIN FESTIVAL*.

IN COLD BLOOD. US. 1967. With films like this, director Richard Brooks carried the forties tradition of film noir well into the sixties and seventies. *In Cold Blood* was an icy, quietly dramatic version of the famous (at the time) "nonfiction novel" by Truman Capote about the random murder of the Clutter family in a Kansas farmhouse. The controversy that surrounded the writing of the book carried over to the film.

IN THE HEAT OF THE NIGHT. US. 1967. Without a doubt, Sidney Poitier's best role and he lights into it with an actor's relish: he's a big city detective caught up in a case in a small southern town. Because it showed a Black hero in what is essentially a white film, and because the racial undertones could hardly be avoided given the setting, *In the Heat of the Night* was a landmark in raising racial consciousness in the late sixties. Norman Jewison directed.

IN WHICH WE SERVE. UK. 1942. It's difficult to avoid throwing around superlatives in a book of this sort, but *In Which We Serve*, the British wartime drama about a naval crew, written, produced, and directed by Noel Coward (with assistance from David Lean), is unique. It's extraordinary because it's an excellently crafted film, just as exciting and involving today as it was nearly half a century ago. It's extraordinary because it so perfectly captures the ideals of the British character, which were so important to that country's success during World War II. And it's extraordinary moreover because it's such an unexpected work from Noel Coward, who is best known as a brilliant songwriter and light playwright. One of the admittedly lesser lessons of *In Which We Serve* is that film is perhaps too important a medium to be left solely to the professionals.

INADMISSIBLE EVIDENCE. UK. 1968. When you think how important the theater of the early years of this century was in founding and forming the traditions of sound film, it's surprising to realize that so little of what's considered excellent in contemporary theater has managed to find its way successfully onto celluloid. In nearly every case, what we wind up with is nothing more than a filmed record and a pale shadow of the theatrical experience. Sad to say *Inadmissible Evidence*, directed by Anthony Page, is no exception. When the play by John Osborne premiered on Broadway in the mid-sixties, starring Nicol Williamson, it was a near perfect theatrical experience, heavily dependent on Williamson's charged brilliance. Though Page may not have captured the full measure of the reality on film, at least we have a warm shadow of Williamson's performance for future generations. It's an essential document of the compromises and disappointments of middle age.

INCREDIBLE SHRINKING MAN, THE. US. 1957. One of the B-grade classics of science fiction in the mid-fifties, this is a film that depends almost entirely for its success on one special effect: the use of larger-than-life model sets. Isn't it surprising that with the current sophistication of blue screen techniques, which allow combining images at will, nothing more ambitious has been done in this way?

INDIAN MASSACRE, THE. US. 1913. Thomas Ince may be the least-known of the filmmakers who founded Hollywood. His westerns, many with William S. Hart, began what may be the most enduring and is certainly the most original native American genre. This one has a freshness and wisdom about it that was unsurpassed for many years. For decades after, native Americans were seldom more than barbarian villains in most westerns. Here, they're the central characters. Compare *CHEYENNE AUTUMN*.

INFORMER, THE. US. 1935. John Ford's strong dark brew of loyalty, betrayal, and other deep emotions during the Irish battle for independence in the early years of this century, starring Victor McLaglen.   🔽

INHERIT THE WIND. US. 1960. The always serious and moral Stanley Kramer brought this stage play about the notorious Scopes "monkey" trial of the twenties to the screen. Spencer Tracy and Fredric March star as Clarence Darrow and William Jennings Bryan. It seems incredible that a quarter of a century after the film and play and sixty years after the trial, the theory of evolution is still under attack from Bible fundamentalists.

INSIDE DAISY CLOVER. US. 1966. Natalie Wood, Christopher Plummer and Robert Redford in an insider's story about Hollywood in the thirties. Full of great shots of the locale and a wonderful tongue-in-cheek sense of humor. I don't think it's yet become a cult film, but it should. Robert Mulligan directed.

⇓ **INTERIORS**. US. 1978. One of the saddest events in recent film history was this attempt on the part of Woody Allen to achieve what he hoped would be a new level of intellectual acceptance with this egregiously serious, thoroughly non-comic New York pastiche of Ingmar Bergman. *Interiors* is a study in tense anxiety about the relationships of several women. It's a well-made film and Allen certainly understands the soul of Bergman, but *Interiors* reminds us how infinitely poorer is the tradition of twentieth-century "serious" drama (we can no longer call it tragedy) when compared with the richness of comedy. That lesson is even sharper here, since Allen is such a masterful comedian. ⊠

INTERMEZZO. US. 1939. A romantic classic about an affair between violinist Leslie Howard, and a young star, Ingrid Bergman, directed with a quick light touch by Gregory Ratoff. Any film with Ingrid Bergman. . . . ⊠

❋▜ **INTOLERANCE**. US. 1916. David Wark Griffith's monumental answer to the furor surrounding *THE BIRTH OF A NATION*, *Intolerance*, as its title indicates, is an act of atonement—and a model for all grand films that come after it. Not only because it deals with one of the great themes of human understanding, but also for its structure, which interweaves four separate stories. Above all else Griffith was, like Chaplin, a man of the Victorian era. The sentiment and the religiosity of that age are captured perfectly here on film. Be aware that you're watching a document from another time. ⊠

▜◔ **INVASION OF THE BODY SNATCHERS**. US. 1956. Beware the pods! There were many paranoid science-fiction fantasies in the 1950s, most of them more or less morally contemnable. Don Siegel's great and scary movie has a much more sophisticated and political point to make. In the fifties it did seem to a lot of us that everybody else in town was being replaced by zombie pods. And, sad to say, it looks like those pods are still with us in the eighties. Siegel and crew strikingly illustrate here the rule of "polynoia": the irrational belief that one is *not* being persecuted. An important political lesson. The remake in the seventies was satisfactory. ⊠

⬆ **INVESTIGATION OF A CITIZEN ABOVE SUSPICION**. Italy. 1970. This is an outstanding member of the group of politically motivated movies made in the sixties and the seventies by actor Gian

Maria Volontè. A politically well-situated police chief commits murder—with apparent impunity. Elio Petri directed this eerie study of the relationship between class and guilt.

INVISIBLE MAN, THE. US. 1933. Another thirties science-fiction classic directed by James Whale, this is based on the H. G. Wells novel. Claude Rains is the unwrapped unmummy who terrorizes a village.

IPCRESS FILE, THE. UK. 1965. Sidney J. Furie directed this first and best of the Len Deighton thrillers. A young Michael Caine plays the almost-brainwashed agent, Harry Palmer. Careful attention to detail and fine use of London sites adds to the pleasure. Palmer is a gourmet. Watch him make coffee in his elegant "caffetière," a very chic device at the time. (Little more than a year later Paul Newman's *HARPER* also made coffee—this time by retrieving last night's Chemex filter from the garbage and sloshing some warm water through it into a cup.) "A word in your shell-like ear."

IRMA LA DOUCE. US. 1963. The musical is such an American form that, whenever anybody else does it, it's curious. This is a French musical, the only one in memory that has played on the US stage. Billy Wilder directed the film version starring Shirley MacLaine and Jack Lemmon. Putting such thoroughly American stars in French roles further confuses the tone, but the songs are good. In fact, the film turns out to be very much an American parody of French musical culture.

IT. US. 1927. Elinor Glyn's book upon which this film is based was a popular and seminal novel of the twenties. It defined for all time the Flapper: the girl who had "it," or sex appeal. Clara Bow stars. She became, of course, the "it girl." If you've never seen a Clara Bow film, you're in for a treat. She explodes off the screen with sex appeal and personality that were hardly ever matched again. Her only competition during the twenties was Louise Brooks.

IT HAPPENED HERE. UK. 1966. Scholars Kevin Brownlow and Andrew Mollo were responsible for this vision of what Britain would have been like had the Nazi invasion actually taken place in 1940. Shot as an ersatz documentary, the film is unique and makes an incisive point about politics and nationality: the British would have got along quite nicely under Nazi rule, just as the French did. "I'm all right, Jack." Compare *THE SORROW*

AND THE PITY.

✳‖ **IT HAPPENED ONE NIGHT**. US. 1934. If you had to pick one classic Hollywood film of the thirties, this may be it. Frank Capra directed Clark Gable and Claudette Colbert in what is quite likely the most sublime romantic comedy. He's a reporter, she's an heiress, and they hitchhike back from Florida. They also fall in love, of course. 〔∨〕

‖ **IT'S A GIFT**. US. 1934. W. C. Fields on his way west under the capable direction of Norman Z. McLeod has one perfect routine: Fields, trying to sleep on a back porch, has to listen to the neighbors make noise: "Don't forget the ipecac!" "I'm looking for Carl LaFong! Capital L, small a, capital F, small o, small n, small g!" Fields's barely controlled rage against the absurdity around him is a special treasure of American movies. "Yes, but tomorrow I'll be sober and you'll still be crazy."

✳＼ **IT'S A WONDERFUL LIFE**. US. 1946. This wasn't an especially great success at the time, but it seems to get better every year. In the early seventies the annual Christmas showings of this movie began and people became addicted to it. The film represents an extraordinary confluence of events and themes. In the first place, it's sublimely sentimental. Only Frank Capra can bring this sort of thing off on film. There are several times in the movie when Jimmy Stewart's high-pitched, cracking voice breaks your heart. More important, it's an interesting political statement. That's probably the reason it carries the force that it does forty years later. In case you don't already know the story, Stewart is Harry Bailey, the kid who's left behind during World War II in Bedford Falls—small town America. His brother goes off to be a war hero. The film centers on Harry's mid-life crisis. He thinks his life has been a failure. He's spent a good number of years running the local Savings & Loan Association and battling Lionel Barrymore, the capitalist banker across the street. He's married Donna Reed and had a bunch of fine children—everybody's dream after the war, and still. With the help of an angel, Henry Travers, Harry has a fantasy vision of what life in Bedford Falls would have been like without him. Without him it has turned into a crass, neon jungle, for the banker has won. Now, what this is saying in the late forties, right after the war when nobody was thinking about things like this, is that a sense of community is far more important than individual well-being. Harry Bailey at the head of the Savings & Loan Association has battled to build the kind of community all Americans can be proud of. When the whole town comes by at the end of the film with their piggy-banks and cookie-jar savings it's hard not to shed a tear. In Capra's world we're all in this together, and we can make it, so long as we can successfully challenge the greed of the rich. "Everytime the bell rings, an angel gets his wings." ▼

§ **IT'S ALWAYS FAIR WEATHER**. US. 1955. Gene Kelly and Stanley Donen directed this unusually pointed post-World War II musical about a group of war buddies ten years later whose lives have diverged. Kelly, Dan Dailey, and Michael Kidd star. Betty Comden and Adolph Green wrote the script. The garish fifties color is an important element, even today. Why aren't Comden and Green studied in college drama classes (and Hecht and MacArthur, as well)?

IT'S NOT JUST YOU, MURRAY. US. 1962. Martin Scorsese made this film as a student at NYU in the early sixties. It won a prize and it stands here as a representative of all the good movies by film school students who later won fame and fortune in Hollywood and maybe overreached themselves. It's a solid, simple, funny character study of a guy named Murray, and it reveals none of the pretensions that later characterized too many of Scorsese's (and others) commercial movies.

§ **IT'S TRAD, DAD!** UK. 1962. Although this is basically a run-of-the-mill rock-and-roll film, it's fascinating considering what came later in its director Richard Lester's career. He's practicing for the Beatles here, with the able assistance of Chubby Checker, Dell Shannon, Gary "US" Bonds, Gene Vincent, and Aker Bilk, among others. With hindsight, we can see *It's Trad, Dad!* as the precursor of *IT'S A HARD DAY'S NIGHT* and, therefore, of twenty years of musical films.

▼ **IVAN THE TERRIBLE, PART I**. USSR. 1943. Solid, plodding, but magnificent historical recreation of Czar Ivan's career by Sergei Eisenstein past the peak of his career. A necessary text for both filmmaker and film viewer. ▼

⌂ **J. W. COOP**. US. 1972. Cliff Robertson wrote, directed, and starred in this winning yarn about an ex-con who wants to be a rodeo star but has trouble competing with well-financed rodeo businessmen. Run it on a double bill with *JUNIOR BONNER*.

§ **JAILHOUSE ROCK**. US. 1957. Probably Elvis Presley's best movie, because it's the role he was born to play: he graduates from prison to become a rock star. Richard Thorpe directed. ▾

JANE EYRE. US. 1943. Another classic Brontë novel becomes a film. This has the slow pace of the middle forties, redeemed somewhat by Orson Welles's performance. Robert Stevenson directed. Compare *WUTHERING HEIGHTS*.

JAWS. US. 1975. Steven Spielberg, the kid who used to hang around Universal City Studio's gates waiting for a chance to get in, showed with this movie that the young people had thoroughly absorbed the lessons of their elders. Forget about the mechanical shark terrifying a seashore resort town. Focus instead on the scene in which people on the beach first view the threat. Spielberg uses here a combination track in and zoom out as simple punctuation. The effect is to increase the sense of depth. This is the device that Hitchcock spent half a lifetime trying to create. When he finally accomplished it in *VERTIGO*, it cost him 20,000 1957 dollars to do so, and it was the culmination of the movie's dramatic point. Spielberg uses the technique as a throwaway. That's what had happened to movies in a mere seventeen years. ▾

§ **JAZZ ON A SUMMER'S DAY**. US. 1959. With all the successful rockumentaries over the last fifteen years, it's worthwhile remembering that jazz used to be the subject of films, too. This is a record of the 1958 Newport Jazz Festival with the likes of Louis Armstrong, Thelonious Monk, Gerry Mulligan, Anita O'Day, and Dinah Washington. Bert Stern directed. An excellent musical film.

JAZZ SINGER, THE. US. 1927. Okay, this is here mainly because it's the first all-sound film, but nevertheless, Al Jolson as the Jewish kid who wants to get into show business is an emblem for several generations of entertainers. Since Jolson (and the jazz singer) were most famous for singing "Mammy" in blackface, the film can also be seen as a symbol of the aspirations of Blacks in entertainment. Put the Jewish experience and the Black experience together and you've got 90% of American entertainment in the twentieth century. ▾

JE T'AIME, JE T'AIME. France. 1970. This is a brilliantly cinematic movie by Alain Resnais. The excuse is science fiction: Claude Rich volunteers for an experiment in time travel and gets stuck. The real aim here is to experiment with editing techniques. It's an experiment successfully carried out with great genius. Because our hero is stuck in time, scenes are repeated again and again. Bits and pieces of this life are revealed to us in no particular order, thus giving director Alain Resnais a chance to do what every editor has probably dreamed of doing: create a portrait in pure cinema without regard to drama, without regard to time, without regard to location. The scenes are juxtaposed in a brilliant cacophony of a man's life. For anyone who cares about the essence of cinema, *Je T'aime, Je T'aime* is not to be missed.

⬧ **JEANNE DIELMAN, 23 QUAI DU COMMERCE, 1080 BRUXELLES**. Belgium. 1976. Here we have one of the last of the truly avant-garde films (before film artistes began repeating themselves). Director Chantal Akerman gives us a painstaking portrait of her eponymous heroine, played by Delphine Seyrig. She gets up and goes over to the sink and washes the dishes and prepares the dinner and walks in and walks out and goes in and goes out and "nobody comes, nobody goes, it's awful," as Samuel Beckett once wrote. As a feminist statement about housework, it can't be matched. As a structuralist statement about film time and space, it's an extraordinary document. It goes on a long time and it becomes mesmerizing. The rhythms of everyday life have been captured for once and for all.

JEREMIAH JOHNSON. US. 1972. Robert Redford took tight control of his film enterprises from very early in his career. This was one of his earliest productions. Directed by Sydney Pollack, it's a contemporary western about a mountain man in the icy wilds of Utah. Not much happens but look for one of Will Geer's last performances. ▽

JEZEBEL. US. 1938. William Wyler directed Bette Davis and Henry Fonda in this classic exercise in southern camp. This is what they used to call "a woman's film." For Davis fans mainly. ▽

JOE HILL. Sweden. 1971. It's always interesting when Europeans attempt American themes. Swedish director Bo Widerberg shot this historical movie about the famous labor leader of the title. It's often affecting. Joe Hill was an interesting character, but the uniqueness of the film lies in its slightly Swedish view of America.

⚐ **JOHNNY GUITAR**. US. 1953. This was an

enormous favorite of the New Wave critics of France in the fifties, and other Europeans, because it's such a cockeyed western. First, the main characters are women (Joan Crawford runs a gambling establishment), then there's the very idea of casting Crawford in a western, and finally, because of the psychological overlay, it's one of the first "adult" westerns. Nicholas Ray directed and gained a cult following ever after. ▽

JOLSON STORY, THE. US. 1946. A landmark in the history of entertainment biopics, of interest mainly because of its subject, played by Larry Parks. See *THE JAZZ SINGER*.

JONAH, WHO WILL BE 25 IN THE YEAR 2000. Switzerland. 1975. In the long, dark period of the seventies while the best that mainstream European cinema could come up with was *Das Neue Kino* in Germany, Swiss filmmaker Alain Tanner distinguished himself for two films which were both charming and politically salient, *THE MIDDLE OF THE WORLD* and *Jonah, Who Will Be 25 in the Year 2000*. *Jonah* probably tells the story of the sixties generation better than any American film on the subject. It gives us eight characters left over from the sixties trying to deal with the seventies as best they can. They find hope, as a thousand generations before them, in the child. Swiss actor Jean-Luc Bideau stands out along with French actress Miou-Miou.

JOUR DE FETE. France. 1948. French comedy is very much like Dr. Johnson's dog. We're surprised, not that they do it well, but that they do it at all. Comedy is the great strength of the English/American culture and doesn't seem to fit continental cartesian coordinates. Jacques Tati stands out as the quintessential French comedian, very much a man of ideas. But also very physical, and moreover, firmly rooted in an earthy sense of humanity. This one, his debut, gives us a whole series of jokes based on everyday smalltown events. Not to be missed.

JOURNEY INTO FEAR. US. 1942. An early Orson Welles effort based on an Eric Ambler spy novel. Welles was only partly responsible for the final result, but it's still an unusual, mysterious movie. With the Mercury Players, including Joseph Cotten, Agnes Moorehead, and Everett Sloane.

JOURNEY TO THE CENTER OF THE EARTH. US. 1959. The fifties was the great age of Jules Verne in movies, and *Journey to the Center of*

Muppets remarkably riding bicycles through a London park in the underrated *Great Muppet Caper.*

the Earth, directed by Henry Levin, may be the best of these adaptations because it understands the cartoon nature of Verne's narrative. With James Mason and Pat Boone as the intrepid adventurers, it's a great movie for kids.

JUDGMENT AT NUREMBURG. US. 1961. Another solid, socially conscious movie from Stanley Kramer. Burt Lancaster, Marlene Dietrich, Maximilian Schell, Montgomery Clift, Spencer Tracy, Richard Widmark, Judy Garland, and others delineate the German war criminal trials. Montgomery Clift did his nervous wreck act here to a fare-thee-well. ▽

▽ **JUGGERNAUT**. UK. 1974. This is the film that brought Richard Lester back to features after a five-year absence. It's a thriller/caper movie about demolition experts working on an oceanliner. The caperers are Richard Harris, David Hemmings, and Anthony Hopkins. Old Lester hands like Shirley Knight and Roy Kinnear show up as well to provide comic relief and dramatic background. It's fascinating to see what an interesting director like Lester does with this standard genre fare.

✳§ **JULES AND JIM**. France. 1961. Jeanne Moreau, Oscar Werner, and Henri Serre in the finest love triangle of three generations (and don't forget Marie Dubois!) directed by François Truffaut. Everyone

knows this is a masterpiece, but it's sometimes hard
to tell exactly why. Partly it's Jeanne Moreau at the
shining center of the film, on screen nearly all the
time. (The film really isn't about Jules and Jim, it's
about Catherine, a most intransigently self-
possessed woman.) Partly it's a sense of nostalgia for
the years before and after World War I. Partly it's—
no doubt—Truffaut's elegant mise-en-scene. But
perhaps the heart of *Jules and Jim* is more ephemeral:
it delineates the spirit that we would like to think
represents the twentieth century. These three
characters look for new ways of living, and they try
to do it with intelligence and affection. The film is so
good that Truffaut never again matched this scope
and resonance. ◩

JULIA. US. 1977. Whether or not Lillian Hellman
ever really had a friend like "Julia" (a dashing anti-
Fascist political activist at the start of World War
II), this film is worth watching. Jane Fonda is
Hellman, Vanessa Redgrave the eponymous heroine,
and Jason Robards is Dashiell Hammett. What's
interesting here is exactly what gave pause to critics
of Hellman's memoirs: the rakish combination of
reality and fantasy. Julia's no doubt a great hero (not
a heroine), but the film spends most of its time with
the relatively unheroic people who surround her.
◩

◉ **JULIET OF THE SPIRITS**. Italy. 1965. Federico
Fellini's paean to his wife and star, Giulietta Masina.
In violent color, the film was almost too much to look
at at the time. The story, about a wife who fears her
husband is cheating on her, is meant to be an
evocation of feminine psychology. The problem is,
of course, that Fellini, not Masina, wrote the script.
But the result is an interesting clash of masculine and
feminine sensibilities, nevertheless. ◩

✛ **JULIUS CAESAR**. US. 1953. Joseph L.
Mankiewicz directed and John Houseman produced
this outstanding film of the Shakespeare play—
second only to *RICHARD III* as a cinematic
adaptation. Marlon Brando, James Mason, Louis
Calhern, and John Gielgud star. A remarkable
achievement for Hollywood film.

⇡ **JUNIOR BONNER**. US. 1972. This is a sleeper.
Steve McQueen is an over-the-hill rodeo star.
Robert Preston and Ida Lupino are his parents in
this funny and likeable comedy by Sam Peckinpah
about the compromises of middle age and our
collective attempt to keep the western myth alive.
Run it on a double bill with *THE ELECTRIC
HORSEMAN*.

JUST BEFORE NIGHTFALL. France. 1971. A kind of variation on the themes of *LA FEMME INFIDELE*, this is another of Claude Chabrol's remarkable series of bourgeois murder stories from the late sixties and early seventies. Great photography by Jean Rabier adds to the effect. Starring Michel Bouquet as the murderer, Stéphane Audran as the wife, and François Perier.

JUST TELL ME WHAT YOU WANT. US. 1980. This is as close as anybody has come to making a screwball comedy recently. Sidney Lumet directed Ali McGraw (if you can believe it) and Alan King from a sharp, catchy script by Jay Presson Allen. He's a high-powered businessman, she's his off-again, on-again girlfriend. Myrna Loy and Keenan Wynn provide continuity with the past. What is captured here is a vivid New York sensibility that may seem overly garish, but it's a reality nevertheless. Once again, Lumet proves he is New York's great native filmmaker.

KAGEMUSHA. Japan. 1980. A sixteenth-century historical movie from Akira Kurosawa near the end of his career that finally captures his sense of historical color and drama. These historical Japanese films, whether they're samurai epics or not, come surprisingly close to the spirit of the American western. The close parallelism between the two genres seems a curious and salient fact about Japanese film. ▽

KANCHENJUNGA. India. 1966. One of Satyajit Ray's most completely realized human portraits, the first time he worked in color, and a film with an interesting structure: Ray juxtaposes the India of the valleys with the India of the hill stations in the mountains to interesting symbolic effect.

KARATE KID, THE. US. 1984. Here's a real old-fashioned movie about teenagers, bullies, and the development of self-consciousness. Ralph Macchio is the kid, Pat Morita is the coach, and John G. (*ROCKY*) Avildsen is the director. The story is about learning how to deal with bullies and learning that you have a strength of your own in the world. It is such a common plot in kids' films and literature that it ought to be a genre with a name. As useful to kids as it is entertaining to them (and us); it's a political lesson as well as a moral one. ▽

KES. UK. 1970. Here's an extraordinary film about a young boy who doesn't get along too well in school and finds a sense of purpose and joy training a kestrel hawk. *Kes* has the accuracy and precision that director Ken Loach is famous for, which means that the dialect may pose a problem for a lot of American viewers.

KEY LARGO. US. 1948. This is a theatrical sub-genre (gangster holds characters captive) that's static and potentially boring, but the cast, including Humphrey Bogart, Edward G. Robinson, Lauren Bacall, Lionel Barrymore, and Claire Trevor, is so interesting to watch in John Huston's adaptation of the stage play, that they more than compensate. ∨

KHARTOUM. UK. 1966. This is a solid and intriguing historical biopic about General "Chinese" Gordon, hero of the African Colonial wars, with Charlton Heston, Laurence Olivier, and Ralph Richardson. Gordon was an extraordinary Victorian character, and the more you know about Victorian history and the sensibility surrounding the film, the more you'll enjoy it.

KID, THE. US. 1921. *The Kid*, as you probably know, is a four-year-old Jackie Coogan. The foster parent is director and star Charlie Chaplin in one of his first features.

KID BROTHER, THE. US. 1926. A Harold Lloyd classic in which Lloyd's physical derring-do is made part of the plot. All his brothers are stronger than he is but the kid brother gets a chance to prove himself at the climax.

KILLERS, THE. US. 1946. Robert Siodmak directed Burt Lancaster and Ava Gardner in this version of the famous Hemingway story about a murdered ex-fighter. This is solid, well-made film-noir stuff.

KILLERS, THE. US. 1964. Don Siegel directed another version of the Hemingway story with Lee Marvin and John Cassavetes. Ronald Reagan appears in his last role (on film) as a tough old gangster. That's the only reason it's a cult classic.

KILLING, THE. US. 1956. An early film by Stanley Kubrick and a strange and enjoyable genre movie about a complicated robbery. Sterling Hayden stars with a bunch of fifties character actors and there's a great surprise ending.

KIND HEARTS AND CORONETS. UK. 1949.

Alec Guinness plays all eight murder victims in this film directed by Robert Hamer. Fans of British comedy of the fifties rank this very high on the list, but it seems weighed down by the concept. Guinness and the others did better later. ⊻

KIND OF LOVING, A. UK. 1962. John Schlesinger directed this classic of kitchen-sink realism in the early sixties. Alan Bates and June Ritchie are the working-class kids who are forced into marriage by her pregnancy. It's an old story, but a classic one.

KING KONG. US. 1933. New prints of this all-time favorite are now available with restored footage and far better reproduction of the elegant black-and-white photography. The big ape is such an important part of our folklore, and Kong on the Empire State Building is such a memorable image that maybe we should just ignore the deeper meanings (and likely racist sub-text) and enjoy. It's not generally known, but filmmakers Merian C. Cooper and Ernest B. Schoedsack were intent on making great location films—exciting travelogues—not the special-effects cartoons that we take them for. See *CHANG*, perhaps a better movie. ⊻

KING OF MARVIN GARDENS, THE. US. 1972. Not especially well-received at the time, this was director Bob Rafelson's followup to *FIVE EASY PIECES*—with Jack Nicholson again. It's pretentious, there is no doubt, but it has some wonderful scenes, especially Nicholson as a disc jockey in a monologue at the beginning: "I promised to tell you why I don't eat fish." Since it uses the Atlantic City milieu to the same effect as Louis Malle's later film named after that reborn resort, it might make an interesting double bill, at least in New Jersey. Come to think of it, the plot now seems strangely prophetic: Nicholson's brother, Bruce Dern, is involved in crazy business deals.

KING SOLOMON'S MINES. US. 1950. Certainly the best reason to go to the movies in the fifties was to see striking color movies like this one shot in strange, faraway places. The fifties was the great age of the adventure/travelogue, and *King Solomon's Mines*, with Stewart Granger and Deborah Kerr, is representative of its kind: a jungle quest for a missing person that uses its settings to great effect.

KINGS OF THE ROAD. West Germany. 1976. Here's the ultimate Wim Wenders movie: a lanky, laconic, contemporary German road movie that follows a couple of Wenders' non-heroes from town to town as they try to deal with the American presence, their love of movies, and their alienation from contemporary German culture.

⚠ **KING'S ROW**. US. 1941. Here's another sub-genre that ought to have a name. Call it the *Our Town* school: a multi-character study of a community. Robert Cummings, Ronald Reagan, and many others get mixed up in small-town America in the early years of this century.

▜ **KINO-PRAVDA**. USSR. 1922. This is a series of experiments in editing by Dziga Vertov using thousands of newsreel shots taken by numerous other filmmakers. Vertov had a grand sense of the possibilities of film editing and mise-en-scene that has not been exceeded since.

KIPPS. UK. 1941. Carol Reed directed this version of the H. G. Wells story about a man who inherits money and tries to use it to change his social class. Michael Redgrave stars.

⚠ **KLUTE**. US. 1971. One of the really memorable films of the seventies: Jane Fonda is a prostitute, Donald Sutherland is the detective who falls for her while investigating a case in which she's involved. Charles Cioffi and Roy Scheider also contribute. Alan J. Pakula directed this portrait of a strong woman very much on her own. It's an interesting structural combination of detective story and human portrait. The script was by Andy and Dave Lewis.
▽

⟍‼ **KNACK. . . AND HOW TO GET IT, THE**. UK. 1965. A great mid-sixties play by Ann Jellicoe is made even better in Richard Lester's film version with Rita Tushingham, Michael Crawford, Ray Brooks, and Donal Donnelly. On stage and screen in the sixties, Crawford was a brilliantly physical light comedian, and it's a shame he isn't better represented on film after this. Rita Tushingham, of course, was everybody's comic vision of the young English girl. In the sixties, this was the perfect vehicle for them. Crawford, the knackless one, learns from his roomies, Brooks and Donnelly, how to catch a girl. This is a better celebration of youth in the sixties than even Lester brought us in the Beatles films, which flank it on either side chronologically.

KNIFE IN THE WATER. Poland. 1962. There's an argument to be made that this is a more interesting movie than any its director, Roman Polanski, made in the west after he left his native Poland. It's a simple triangle story, brilliantly told, and Polanski's half-tongue-in-cheek lugubrious and sinister filmic style was refreshing at the time. ▽

KNOCK ON WOOD. US. 1954. Danny Kaye is a ventriloquist in love with Mai Zetterling and the plot leaves him considerable room for some of his best hijinks. Norman Panama and Melvin Frank directed.

KNUTE ROCKNE, ALL AMERICAN. US. 1940. Certainly the best biopic of a star football coach, this one includes one of the most famous lines in all film history. Ronald Reagan is the doomed football player. Pat O'Brien is the legendary Notre Dame coach. After you see it you'll also want to win one for the Gipper. ▽

KON-TIKI. US. 1951. Adventurer Thor Heyerdahl made a career out of tracing ancient sailing routes. This masterful and influential documentary of the early fifties shows us Heyerdahl's raft trip from Peru to Tahiti. A lot of kids in the fifties fell in love with this real-life adventure, and you will, too.

KRAMER VS. KRAMER. US. 1979. This is certainly the most famous and best mounted example of what seems to be a newly developing genre: the paternity fantasy. The film was celebrated as a study of a couple (Dustin Hoffman and Meryl Streep) breaking up. In fact, I think audiences flocked to it not to see a divorce but rather to see a father getting a kick out of raising his kid: that's the paternity fantasy. (See also *AUTHOR, AUTHOR.*) ▽

KUEHLE WAMPE. Germany. 1932. The great playwright Bertolt Brecht wrote the script for this film directed by Slatan Dudow. Brecht's remarkable and influential dramatic technique—distancing audiences from the action in order to bring the ideas into focus—is not nearly so evident on the screen as it is on the stage. Yet the film remains important for the opportunity it provided him to experiment with another medium.

LADY EVE, THE. US. 1941. Preston Sturges's best-remembered film, not only because it's a perfectly paced screwball, but also because it's one of the few times he worked with A-stars. This time Henry Fonda and Barbara Stanwyck join the stock Sturges company. But the plot is fairly mundane—for Sturges, at any rate: Stanwyck is the con artist who cons then falls for the child-like Fonda on a cruise: girl gets boy, girl loses boy, girl gets boy back.

⇩ **LADY FROM SHANGHAI, THE**. US. 1948. Despite the powerful dramatic presences of himself and Rita Hayworth on the screen, this is the film in which Orson Welles ignored the drama, mesmerized instead by the power of the camera. Nevertheless, the hall of mirrors climax has to be included in any anthology of great shots from the cinema. Compare it with the mirror scene in Joseph Losey's *Eva* (with Jeanne Moreau).

⇧ **LADY SINGS THE BLUES**. US. 1972. Richard Pryor in one of his first roles, and Diana Ross in her debut as Billie Holliday in this musical biopic. Maybe this isn't such a great biography but any attention paid to Billie Holliday is worth notice. ◺

⊹·↘ **LADY VANISHES, THE**. UK. 1938. Probably the ultimate British Hitchcock, with a script by Launder and Gilliat. Dame May Whitty gets lost on a train ride. This is the one where Naunton Wayne and Basil Radford score as a pair of wonderfully dopey twits.

‼ **LADYKILLERS, THE**. UK. 1955. Another in the long string of successful and enduring Ealing comedies, this one pits Alec Guinness, Peter Sellers, Herbert Lom, Cecil Parker, and Frankie Howerd as crooks against an awfully nice little old lady (Katie Johnson) who turns out to be hell on wheels.

⇧ **LANDLORD, THE**. US. 1970. Bill Gunn (director of *GANJA AND HESS*) wrote the script for this sharp, comic, and perceptive view of Black ghetto life. Hal Ashby directs Pearl Bailey, Diana Sands, Louis Gossett, Lee Grant, and Beau Bridges. Bridges is the rich kid who buys a Black apartment house planning to gentrify it. The tenants have other ideas. A real sleeper.

⇧ **LAST HURRAH, THE**. US. 1958. All you need to know is that John Ford directed Spencer Tracy, Basil Rathbone, Pat O'Brien, Frank McHugh, and a veteran cast in a version of the popular novel loosely based on the real-life Boston politics of the Mayor Curley era. It's Golden-Age filmmaking twenty-five years later.

⬆ **LAST LAUGH, THE**. Germany. 1924. A landmark of silent cinema, this efficiently and ingeniously tells the simple story of an old hotel porter as he sinks into the slough of despond. Produced by Carl Mayer and photographed by pioneer Karl Freund, the film is a classic of silent cinematography and made the international reputation of its director, F. W. Murnau.

LAST METRO, THE. France. 1980. Late Truffaut, but still absorbing, this is a forties-like movie about Paris theater during the German occupation, starring Catherine Deneuve and Gérard Depardieu as actors attempting to ply their trade in the face of Nazi power and French complicity. Compare Peter Yates's *The Dresser*.

⬆ LAST OF SHEILA, THE. US. 1973. One of the more curious films of the last fifty years, this is ostensibly a shipboard murder mystery, and Dyan Cannon, James Mason, Joan Hackett, and the rest of the cast mount it quite well. What's really interesting, however, is that the script by Stephen Sondheim and Anthony Perkins is written as a British-style crossword puzzle. If you're familiar with the puns, anagrams, and wordplay of that form, *The Last of Shiela* is a breathtaking exercise in language: every inch a clue. The title tells all, if you hang on to the end. If James Joyce had made movies they might have looked something like this. Unique.

§ LAST OF THE BLUE DEVILS, THE. US. 1979. Long before there were pop videos there were dedicated filmmakers who had the good sense to understand that the pleasures of music aren't limited to the ear. Jazz especially benefits from our experience of the performance. Filmmaker Bruce Ricker set his camera down during a party of legendary Kansas City jazzmen, including Count Basie and Big Joe Turner, and let it roll. The result is a masterful summation of an important jazz tradition, and we're grateful for the record. *The Last of the Blue Devils* is a restrained film that lets its subjects speak eloquently for themselves. It stands here for hundreds of filmed records of musical performances. ◪

⬥ LAST PICTURE SHOW, THE. US. 1971. A curiosity because it was shot in black and white at a time when color had become nearly universal, this is also Peter Bogdanovich's best movie, based on Larry McMurtry's novel about a small town in Texas when the movie theater closes in the 1950s. Cast includes Timothy Bottoms, Sam Bottoms, Jeff Bridges, Cloris Leachman, and Ellen Burstyn. Grizzled Ben Johnson is the anchor.

LAST TANGO IN PARIS. France. 1972. This was an intellectual favorite of the early seventies that in retrospect marked the end of the bright period of the sixties New Wave in filmmaking. (How interesting that Jean-Pierre Léaud is here at the end as he was at the beginning.) American and European intellectuals alike hailed *Last Tango* as innovative and daring. In fact, the film is thoroughly exploitative and sexist and perhaps, therefore, truly obscene. Marlon Brando stars as an American suffering from a curiously French malaise who takes up with a young Maria Schneider and commits a buttery buggery which shocked audiences (although it was modestly shot). The film exploits Schneider, both as actress and character. It exploits Brando's star celebrity: we would have been much less interested in the sex scenes if someone less famous were faking them. And it exploits audiences because it fools them into thinking they're watching something of substance when in fact they're not even getting honest porn. It is, we'll admit, nicely photographed, but it marks the end of a beautiful era in filmmaking in quite an ugly way. ▣

LAST WALTZ, THE. US. 1978. Martin Scorsese directed this rather pretentious "rockumentary" about The Band's last performance. Staged studio numbers are included. We would have preferred a funkier approach to the music of this group. Bob Dylan, Eric Clapton, Muddy Waters, and Emmylou Harris appear. ▣

LAST WAVE, THE. Australia. 1977. Australian director Peter Weir made an international reputation for himself with this film and *PICNIC AT HANGING ROCK*, two unusual exercises in the occult that benefit greatly from a simple Hitchcockian trick: it's easy to be eerie at night; it's much more effective in broad daylight. The "broad daylight" here is the milieu of middle-class Australians. Richard Chamberlain is a lawyer who gets involved in an aboriginal case. . . and then, it starts to rain . . . . The Apocalypse comes, not with a bang, not with a whimper, but as a surfer's nightmare. ▣

LAST YEAR AT MARIENBAD. France. 1961. This may seem almost laughable now but at the time, along with *HIROSHIMA, MON AMOUR* and *L'AVVENTURA*, it was a great art house hit. At the time, those of us who were discovering the "art" of film figured if you couldn't understand it, it had to be great, or at least fired with ambition. Nobody can figure out whether they met last year at Marienbad or this year at Marienbad or maybe even next year at Marienbad, and who cares? Director Alain Resnais was feeling his way in these early films, so they do bear study, and the cinematography is quite startling. ◹

LATE AUTUMN. Japan. 1960. Late Yasujiro Ozu, but as mesmerizing as his earlier films. This one is about a father and his unmarried daughter.

◬ **LATE SHOW, THE**. US. 1977. During the seventies so many younger American directors turned back to the thirties and forties, not only for their inspiration but for their subject matter and sometimes even for their scripts, that it's refreshing to come across a film that pays hommage to the Golden Age with a high degree of intelligence and originality. Robert Benton, who came to directing the long way after writing a bunch of seminal scripts with David Newman, is responsible for this startling mix of seventies style and humor with the forties private-eye genre. He doesn't mimic the genre, he recreates it and breathes fresh life into it. It's the ultimate Lily Tomlin film, and the pairing of Tomlin with Art Carney was inspired. ◹

◬§ **LAURA**. US. 1944. The theme song may be the ultimate forties ballad, and the film still seems to live up to it: just the right balance of romance and mystery, with a very witty script. Gene Tierney is the nearly-murdered title character; Dana Andrews is the detective; and Clifton Webb is Waldo Lydecker, the bitchy columnist. ◹

📡‼ **LAVENDER HILL MOB, THE**. UK. 1951. Alec Guinness has figured out how to rob a bullion van and is aided and abetted by Stanley Holloway, Sidney James, and Alfie Bass. Guinness's string of comedies in the fifties is a singular achievement. It's almost a shame he took so many serious roles thereafter. ◹

◬ **LAWRENCE OF ARABIA**. UK. 1962. Director David Lean, at the height of his career, developed an almost pathological obsession with epic romance. Once or twice it worked, most notably in this film. Peter O'Toole's Lawrence, a Britisher quite at home in the politics of the Arab world, manages to convey the same kind of burning obsession. O'Toole holds the film together with the help of Alec Guinness and Anthony Quinn. There are a lot of cut versions of this floating around; to get the full effect, you need all three-and-a-half-hours plus. ◹

⊙❨§ **LEADBELLY**. US. 1976. Late in life, photographer Gordon Parks directed several fascinating movies during the brief opening in the seventies in Hollywood for Black films. Roger Moseley stars as the influential folk singer and guitarist who led a life that makes the blues seem optimistic. The music is solid, the cinematography is incisive—sometimes breathtaking. Any aspiring cinematographer should spend a lot of time with Gordon Parks's movies.

⚐ **LEARNING TREE, THE**. US. 1969. Gordon Parks's first feature, like *LEADBELLY*, is a lesson in restrained, effective cinematography. The film is based on his own autobiographical novel about growing up in Kansas. He's not as dramatic a figure as Leadbelly, so the result is more elegiac.

LEATHER BOYS, THE. UK. 1964. Rita Tushingham, Colin Campbell, and Dudley Sutton in another and rather late example of the kitchensink school. It's again about a failed marriage, with some homosexual undertones that were unusual at the time. Sidney J. Furie directed.

⊙ **LENNY**. US. 1974. Dustin Hoffman gives his best performance by far in Bob Fosse's intelligent but harrowing biography of Lenny Bruce, from the stage play by Julian Barry. The career and humor of Bruce are crucial to understanding the true meaning of the radical and lasting cultural revolution we underwent in the 1960s. ▼

LEOPARD, THE. Italy. 1963. Luchino Visconti's long, gorgeous celebration of a ruling class in decline, based on the famous novel by Giuseppe de Lampedusa. It's about Sicilian nobility at the end of the nineteenth century at the end of their sway. Burt Lancaster is surprisingly effective as "the leopard," the aristocratic hero. Visconti's sense of operatic decadence was put to best use here.

‖ **LET'S TALK ABOUT WOMEN**. Italy. 1964. Ettore Scola directed this series of comic episodes, all starring Vittorio Gassman as different men chasing or running away from a host of interesting women.

LETTER, THE. US. 1940. For Bette Davis fans, it's a Somerset Maugham novel set on a rubber plantation. The lady shoots her lover. Is it self defense? Considering the setting, it doesn't matter. ▼

⚠︎↘ **LETTER TO JANE**. France. 1972. If you want to know what Jean-Luc Godard was trying to do during his "Dziga-Vertov" political period, this is the film that explains it. What he was trying to do was quite interesting, and even important, although you might not know it from looking at the other films he made during that time. For Godard, politics are never separate from language, and he is fascinated by the relationship between the two. *Letter to Jane* was mildly controversial when it was released, although most people paid it little attention. But it remains a gem of a film essay about film form and film style. Forget Jane Fonda (to whom it was addressed) and the politics of the Vietnamese war in the early seventies and listen to Godard and collaborator Jean-Pierre Gorin on the soundtrack describe images and sounds and the way they relate to one another. If you want a course in film theory, you could do no better than to watch *Letter to Jane* a dozen times. In addition, the film (and Godard) both display a vital sense of humor.

⬆︎ **LIAISONS DANGEREUSES, LES**. France. 1959. Director Roger Vadim was the point man for the New Wave. He didn't in any way share the concerns and interests of directors like Truffaut and Godard, but in two films—this one and *AND GOD CREATED WOMAN*—he was able to épater les bourgeois and soften them up for a new kind of film in the sixties. *Les Liaisons Dangereuses* stars Gérard Philipe and Jeanne Moreau in a sexy version of the eighteenth-century novel by Choderlos de Laclos. A husband and wife tempt each other with stories of their infidelities. Quite a good movie, it deserves to be re-seen.

⚠︎↘ **LIFE AND TIMES OF ROSIE THE RIVETER, THE**. US. 1980. Filmmaker Connie Field put together this combination of historical footage and present-day interviews with a number of women who worked in defense plants during World War II. It's an entertaining and involving example of the seventies documentary style that produced so many important nonfiction films.

↘ **LIFE IS A BED OF ROSES**. France. 1983. One of the many fascinating things about Alain Resnais is that he seems to get better as he gets older. Here is another essay in time and memory and editing that parallels two stories: one from the past, one from the present, both full of thought. Jean Gruault wrote it; Vittorio Gassman, Geraldine Chaplin, and Fanny Ardant star.

LIFE OF EMILE ZOLA, THE. US. 1937. Paul Muni, Gale Sondergaard, Joseph Schildkraut, Morris Carnovsky, and other stage actors under the direction of William Dieterle in an unusually detailed biopic of the nineteenth-century French writer so closely associated with the Dreyfus Case.

LIFE WITH FATHER. US. 1947. This is a film version of the smash hit Howard Lindsay/Russel Crouse Broadway play, with Irene Dunne and William Powell. There is something especially attractive about this theatrical sub-genre: family sagas like *Life with Father*, *I Remember Mama*, and *The Four-Poster*, are a kind of exercise in tribal memory, the point of which is to remind us that we're here only for a very short while, bound between the generations before and those to come, and that our duty is to the continuity. A cliche? Perhaps. But when Yasujiro Ozu does it in Japanese, we think it's art.

LIFEBOAT. US. 1944. Despite the presence of Tallulah Bankhead, William Bendix, Hume Cronyn, and Walter Slezak, this isn't first-class Alfred Hitchcock. But it is a fascinating experiment. All the action takes place aboard a lifeboat, about as un-cinematic a setting as you could devise. Hitchcock mostly brings it off. He even gets to put in his customary appearance. Can you guess how?

LILI. US. 1952. "The song of love is a sad song," nowhere better captured than in this American version of French sentiment directed by Charles Walters and starring Leslie Caron, Jean-Pierre Aumont, and Mel Ferrer. She's a waif who joins a small circus and falls for Aumont. I don't know about you, but I had two film crushes when I was a kid and one was Leslie Caron. Fine score.

LIMELIGHT. US. 1952. Late Chaplin, but Chaplin nevertheless. He's a music-hall clown, and this offers him the opportunity to reprise his own early career. Claire Bloom is the ballerina he saves. This is where you get to see Chaplin and Buster Keaton work together.

LITTLE BIG MAN. US. 1970. After the adult westerns of the fifties and early sixties there was nowhere for the genre to go to except full-blown symbolic epics. *Little Big Man* is the classic post-adult western, based on a Thomas Berger novel. Dustin Hoffman scored as the incredibly old

Leslie Caron with Mel Ferrer's puppet in the still-charming *Lili*.

man who remembered his involved and epic past. Chief Dan George scored as a real native American Indian. Arthur Penn directed. Lots of scope, but you can't help longing for Randolph Scott. ▢

LITTLE CAESAR. US. 1930. This is the classic gangster movie of the very early years of talkies, rivalled only by *SCARFACE*. Edward G. Robinson is the crime boss. Mervyn LeRoy directed. ▢

LITTLE FOXES, THE. US. 1941. The combination of director William Wyler, playwright Lillian Hellman, and actress Bette Davis provides an unusual matching of intelligent melodramatic talents. This is among Davis's best: she lets out all the stops as the ultimate southern bitch.

LITTLE THEATRE OF JEAN RENOIR, THE. France. 1970. Jean Renoir's envoi to the cinema is a collection of little stories perfectly told and nostalgically reminiscent of a great career.

LITTLE WOMEN. US. 1933. George Cukor directed Katharine Hepburn, Joan Bennett, and others in this film adaptation of the famous Louisa May Alcott novel which is a children's (and grownup's) classic.

LOCAL HERO. UK. 1982. Director Bill Forsyth seems single-handedly to have revived the great tradition of eccentric British comedy of the fifties. *Local Hero* is a quiet little movie about an oil company executive who's about to environmentally rape an incredibly beautiful Scottish fishing village, but falls in love with it. It's full of interesting characters doing interesting things in ingratiating ways. In genre terms, it's even more interesting because it stars Americans Peter Riegert and Burt Lancaster. In that respect it's a moral tale about ugly Americans who turn out not to be so ugly.   ⩔

LODGER, THE. UK. 1926. Hitchcock's first thriller stars Ivor Novello as the unjustly accused hero. It was a theme he would repeat again many times. It's fascinating from a contemporary perspective to watch Hitchcock at work in his silents. Only half-a-dozen directors spanned half a century of cinematic history as Hitchcock did, and he alone made films over such a long period of time with such consistency.   ⩔

LOLA. France. 1961. Anouk Aimée became one of the favored actresses of the New Wave fringe after starring in this fantasy by Jacques Demy. This *Lola* is a cabaret dancer in Nantes whose idealized life and loves create a romantic mood that is particularly French. Raoul Coutard was the cinematographer.

LOLA MONTES. France. 1955. The great Max Ophüls romantic classic is more a filmmaker's film than an audience movie. It's not that the story of the historical *Lola*, a circus performer and romantic idol, is uninteresting (Martine Carol stars): it's that Ophüls's camerawork is so much more stunning than the story.

LOLITA. UK. 1962. Vladimir Nabokov's novels were so intensely concerned with language that you'd think they would be particularly difficult to translate to the screen. *Lolita*, the great grey comedy of the 1950s, carefully sets up and knocks down the shibboleths of the silent generation. James Mason is the European professor, Humbert Humbert, in love with the little American nymphette (Sue Lyon). Shelley Winters is the wife, and Peter Sellers, in a great American accent, is Quilty. The scene in which he explains himself to Mason is a small masterpiece of the acting art.

LONEDALE OPERATOR, THE. US. 1911. If all you know of D. W. Griffith is the features, the early shorts come as a great surprise. They have a freedom and freshness and directness which is very modern and appealing—something you don't necessarily get from the ambitious, longer films. There were scores of them. *The Lonedale Operator* stands out.

LONELINESS OF THE LONG DISTANCE RUNNER, THE. UK. 1962. It was considered chic among cinephiles in the 1960s to denigrate British stage and film director Tony Richardson, but on balance he was responsible for as many important British films in those years as anyone else. *Loneliness of the Long Distance Runner* stars Tom Courtenay as the rebellious kid who turns into a track star. This is classic kitchen-sink realism from the landmark story by Alan Sillitoe. Compare Sillitoe's *SATURDAY NIGHT AND SUNDAY MORNING*.

LONELY ARE THE BRAVE. US. 1962. Dalton Trumbo wrote this elegy to the western. Kirk Douglas is an out-of-place cowboy in the modern west—almost like a time traveller. There's one memorable scene as he and his good old horse attempt to cross a busy highway with the eighteen-wheelers barrelling by. It will stay with you forever. ☑

LONG GOOD FRIDAY, THE. UK. 1980. When the French make gangster movies they become essays in existential esthetics. When the British make gangster movies (even more rarely) they're exciting exercises in character. Actor Bob Hoskins scored here as the crazy, wonderful underworld boss engaged in a gutsy, bloody battle for supremacy on the London scene. Helen Mirren is the girlfriend, and Eddie Constantine appears to make the connection with the traditions of continental imitations of American gangster movies. John Mackenzie directed. ☑

LONG GOODBYE, THE. US. 1973. One of Robert Altman's most interesting movies, this is a modern version of the Raymond Chandler novel with Elliott Gould as a down-and-out Phillip Marlowe. Leigh Brackett, of *BIG SLEEP* fame, worked on the script. Sterling Hayden, Nina Van Pallandt, and even Jim Bouton pull out all the stops. The score is a wonderful joke, too.

LONG RIDERS, THE. US. 1980. A good late western by the always idiosyncratic Walter Hill. The gimmick here is that all the outlaw brothers are played by actor brothers: the Carradines, the Keaches, the Quaids, and the Guests. ☑

LONG SHOT. UK. 1980. Although films about

filmmaking occur regularly on the American scene, it's all too rare to see the subject discussed abroad. Maurice Hatton is a longtime British filmmaker who's responsible for one of the most unusual and significant political movies of the sixties and seventies: *PRAISE MARX AND PASS THE AMMUNITION*. He hadn't been able to put together the financing for a commercial feature in years, so he scrounged several thousand pounds and a lot of out-of-date film stock, called up his friends, and took off for the Edinburgh Film Festival, where he mainly improvised this charming story of a filmmaker trying to put together a project. It has roots in reality, but it's much funnier than the real hard work of making movies.

LONGEST DAY, THE. US. 1962. One genre that clearly had a beginning, a middle, and an end, was the World War II movie. Near the end, as here, the custom was to assemble a huge international cast and celebrate the glory of the good war by re-enacting some famous (or not-so-famous) event. This one is D-Day, of course. John Wayne, Robert Ryan, Henry Fonda, Robert Mitchum, and Sean Connery are our heroes. ▟

LOOK BACK IN ANGER. UK. 1959. John Osborne's play set the tone for the generation of the fifties: the angry young men. A young Richard Burton stars in the film version as Jimmy Porter, the rebellious antihero, with Claire Bloom and Mary Ure. Tony Richardson directed.

LORD LOVE A DUCK. US. 1966. This may be a minor film, but it's an important one, nevertheless. George Axelrod wrote and directed what amounts to an underground comedy made in Hollywood. Tuesday Weld, Roddy McDowall, and Ruth Gordon star in a satiric essay on southern California lifestyles. It would be years before the rest of us caught on to this.

LORD OF THE FLIES. UK. 1963. William Golding's novel about a group of schoolboys stranded on an island who slowly but inexorably return to their tribal roots, was a classic of college fiction in the 1960s. Peter Brook did a workmanlike job of bringing it to the screen. Here's the case of a work of fiction and film that achieved considerable fame simply because it broke the pattern of story-telling. On reflection, I think I'd much rather watch, or show my kids, or read, *THE SWISS FAMILY ROBINSON* or *ROBINSON CRUSOE*. Left to our own devices we needn't disintegrate: it's much more interesting to cope and survive.

LORDS OF FLATBUSH, THE. US. 1974. This film about Brooklyn teenagers in the mid-fifties was directed by a couple of locals and starred a couple of unknowns named Sylvester Stallone and Henry Winkler. It's remarkable that both of them went on to such considerable acclaim playing those fifties roles on television and in film. I'll bet filmmakers Stephen F. Verona and Martin Davidson have wished many times during the past ten years that they were receiving royalties on the characters. The only thing missing here is John Travolta.

LOST HONOR OF KATHARINA BLUM, THE. West Germany. 1975. This is Volker Schlöndorff's film version of the famous Heinrich Böll novel. Katharina Blum is a housemaid who gets caught up with a political radical on the lam. A journalist paints her as a fearful gangster character herself, much against her will and the truth. It's a powerful indictment of the Springer press in Germany and a fascinating examination of the way media and politics intertwine these days. Böll was writing from personal experience. Several years earlier Springer newspapers had had a field day McCarthyizing the Baader-Meinhof gang. Böll protested in print, and for his troubles he was branded a Commie sympathizer in the Springer press.

LOST HORIZON. US. 1937. Frank Capra's fantasy about the lost paradise of Shangri-La remains a romantic classic for its scenery and for the performance of Ronald Colman.

LOST WEEKEND, THE. US. 1945. When Billy Wilder got serious . . . whew! Ray Milland is the ultimate alcoholic, weaving from bar to bar along 3rd Avenue. Because the film is so unrelenting, it was hailed at the time as a great advance in seriousness. I'm not sure about that, but Milland's performance is not to be beat.

LOVE AFFAIR. US. 1939. Leo McCarey directs Irene Dunne and Charles Boyer in an above-average shipboard romance story.

LOVE AFFAIR, OR THE CASE OF THE MISSING SWITCHBOARD OPERATOR. Yugoslavia. 1968. In the late sixties, Yugoslavian filmmaker Dusan Makavejev gained some notoriety with this film because it seemed to treat modern

western themes in an eastern European setting. It
also was considered sexually daring.

LOVE FINDS ANDY HARDY. US. 1938. The
combination of Mickey Rooney, Judy Garland, and
Lewis Stone in the *Andy Hardy* series is a landmark
in American filmmaking. Mickey was everybody's
all-American teenager in the late thirties and forties,
and that was the time when teenagerdom had been
raised to the level of myth. Judy was his equal as a
bobbysoxer. And Stone provided a masterful
fatherly anchor. Our fantasies of boys and girls and
growing up still date from that time. Archie Andrews
still pursues Veronica in the comic books even if
Andy Hardy and Henry Aldrich have receded into
the mists of history.

LOVE ON THE RUN. France. 1979. This is the
final episode of François Truffaut's Antoine Doinel
series, once again starring Jean-Pierre Léaud, the
only actor to play a single role on film from
childhood to adulthood. His first love, Marie-France
Pisier, shows up here. Claude Jade is the wife he's
divorcing. The film includes clips of the four Doinel
movies which preceded it (*THE 400 BLOWS*, *Love
at 20*, *STOLEN KISSES*, *BED AND BOARD*)
which gives it an eerie sense of history. ▢

LOVE STORY. US. 1971. Everyone likes to
condescend to this movie about a tempestuous
romance and it is silly, no doubt, but writer Erich
Segal was able to parlay his script into an extremely
successful novel before the film was made (and that's
good for screenwriters). I've always enjoyed Ali
McGraw's dotty, naive, and wonderfully unpolished
film persona. Ray Milland also makes an appearance.
It's all quite funny.

LOVE WITH THE PROPER STRANGER. US.
1963. Robert Mulligan is one of the more underrated
directors of the sixties. Here he puts working girl
Natalie Wood and jazzman Steve McQueen through
their paces in what was considered at the time to be a
very adult romance since it suggested the possibility
of pre-marital sex and abortion. Great location
shooting in New York City made it an interesting
companion to *THE APARTMENT* and
BREAKFAST AT TIFFANY'S as romantic
classics of the early sixties.

LOVED ONE, THE. US. 1965. If you've ever
wondered precisely what "black comedy" was all
about, this Tony Richardson adaptation of the
Evelyn Waugh novel defines it for you. Specifically,

Robert Morse, Jonathan Winters, Rod Steiger, Milton Berle, John Gielgud, Roddy McDowall, Robert Morley, and numerous others give us the Britisher's view of the strange never-never land of southern California. Run it on a double bill with *LORD LOVE A DUCK*.

LOVERS, THE. France. 1958. This film by Louis Malle is often credited with beginning the French New Wave. It was considered at the time a very adult sexual drama and the glimpse that we catch of Jeanne Moreau's left breast was startling in 1958. Through the sixties and much of the seventies, Malle was eclipsed by Godard and Truffaut but he's kept working with intelligence and personality. The tortoise may still win the race: see *ATLANTIC CITY*.

LOVERS AND OTHER STRANGERS. US. 1970. Playwright/actor husband and wife team Renee Taylor and Joseph Bologna produced a couple of classic middle-class comedies dealing incisively and memorably with family life. This one with Gig Young, Anne Jackson, Harry Guardino, Richard Castellano, and others, celebrates a wedding. You've probably been there yourself which is why you're going to laugh a lot. It's one of Gig Young's last roles. He's the wonderfully forlorn father of the bride. Castellano is the father of the groom: "So what's the story?"

LOVES OF A BLONDE. Czechoslovakia. 1966. It's just a little romance, but for westerners it marked the debut of the shortlived Czech cinematic renaissance. Miloš Forman directed with freshness and originality. ▣

LOVESICK. US. 1983. A former Woody Allen collaborator, Marshall Brickman, made a gem of a movie his second time out with *Lovesick*. Dudley Moore had made a quick succession of unmemorable comedies after *10*. *Lovesick* shows him to best advantage as a sick psychiatrist in love (and understandably so) with Elizabeth McGovern. This is a classic New York romantic comedy, well situated in its time. ▣

LOVING. US. 1970. Irvin Kershner directed this striking mid-life-crisis drama. George Segal is the commercial artist with the wife in the suburbs (Eva Marie Saint) and the mistress in the city. Good location shooting in and around New York captures the suburban scene with intoxicating precision. If you know this world you'll be intrigued to watch it on film. See it with *HUSBANDS*.

LUCIA. Cuba. 1969. Humberto Solas directed this view of three different women living in three separate eras of Cuban history. It was one of the influential Third World films of the late sixties and early seventies.

⚑ **LUCK OF GINGER COFFEY, THE**. Canada. 1964. Here's an outstanding example of sixties Canadian realism. Robert Shaw and Mary Ure are the couple living in Montreal trying to deal with day-to-day existence. Irvin Kershner directed.

LUST FOR LIFE. US. 1956. Can Hollywood deal with the realities of the life of a painter? Only when he's as crazy and troubled as Vincent Van Gogh. Here Kirk Douglas is the subject and Anthony Quinn is his friend Paul Gauguin. Vincente Minnelli directed this striking color film that comes pretty close, all things considered, to capturing the spirit of Van Gogh.

⚑ **M**. Germany. 1931. The landmark of film noir by a master of the genre, Fritz Lang, established the Peter Lorre character for all time. It's depressive and demanding but a stark portrait of the Berlin underworld. ▽

MACARTHUR. US. 1977. A solid biopic by Joseph Sargent, with Gregory Peck as the man who shall return. Play it together with *PATTON* and you've got a good handle on a particular kind of heroism that we celebrated during World War II. ▽

⚑ **MAD WEDNESDAY**. US. 1947. A concept picture by Preston Sturges puts Harold Lloyd and his unique character from the 1920s twenty years further down the road. The combination of Lloyd's earnest deadpan and Sturges's wild intensity is rather unusual. You don't usually see two such different comic sensibilities working together.

◉ **MADE FOR EACH OTHER**. US. 1971. Another pointed and telling comic script by Renee Taylor and Joseph Bologna. This time it's an adult romance and Bologna and Taylor star as two off-the-wall group therapy victims who fall for each other. Great local New York photography again. Robert B. Bean directed.

◉ **MADIGAN**. US. 1968. Don Siegel directed Richard Widmark and Henry Fonda in this well-remembered police drama. *Madigan* is a kind of fulcrum in its combination of day-to-day problems and the high drama of police work. It looks backwards to *DRAGNET* and forwards to *Hill Street Blues*.

MAEDCHEN IN UNIFORM. Germany. 1931. Written and directed by, and starring women, this simply-observed story about relationships, sexual and otherwise, in a girl's school was a succès de scandale at the time. Leontine Sagan directed.

MAGIC BOX, THE. UK. 1951. A man named William Friese-Greene was one of the inventors of the cinema. Although he led an unremarkable life, John Boulting made a remarkable movie about the man and his work. The film was obviously motivated by admiration—even love—for the early history of the magical invention, and nearly every British star at the time from Laurence Olivier to Glynis Johns had a part in the film. It's a unique and fitting celebration.

MAGIC FLUTE, THE. Sweden. 1974. A nicely done, intelligent TV film of the Mozart opera. Ingmar Bergman wisely yields to the composer's superior talent.

MAGICIAN, THE. Sweden. 1958. Ingmar Bergman's dark historical vision of the nineteenth century—with Max von Sydow, Ingrid Thulin, and Bibi Andersson—seemed more important at the time than it does now. ▼

MAGNIFICENT AMBERSONS, THE. US. 1942. Orson Welles didn't have full control over this film but it remains a brilliant if lesser companion piece to *CITIZEN KANE*, following the fortunes of a classic ruling family at the turn of the century. Joseph Cotten gives a brilliant performance together with the Welles stock company. ▼

MAGNIFICENT OBSESSION. US. 1954. Director Douglas Sirk became a camp cult favorite twenty years later for egregious melodramatic romances like this. It's really a sidetrack to cinema and not an admirable one but it's sort of funny to watch Rock Hudson as the drunken surgeon and Jane Wyman as his victim/patient try to carry off such silly stuff.

MAGNIFICENT SEVEN, THE. US. 1960. It's not often Americans try to mimic other countries' genres. Here's a remake of the Japanese classic *THE*

SEVEN SAMURAI with a bunch of tough western guys, including Yul Brynner, Steve McQueen, Charles Bronson, Eli Wallach, and Robert Vaughn as the hired guns who save a town from bandits.

MAJOR BARBARA. UK. 1941. Gabriel Pascal's films of George Bernard Shaw's plays were labors of love and important records. This is one of the better ones—as film—starring Wendy Hiller, Rex Harrison, Robert Morley, and Robert Newton, in Shaw's story of rich, poor, and the Salvation Army.

\⇧ **MALCOLM X**. US. 1972. We've elevated Martin Luther King to the status of national hero for his vision and rhetoric, but it would be a serious error to overlook the other great Black leader of the 1960s. Malcolm's story is an existential triumph of intelligence and reason over anger and hate. If you can't get to see Arnold Perl's film, pick up a copy of *The Autobiography of Malcolm X*. There's something riveting about a character like Malcolm, the self-made man.

◍\⇧ **MALE HUNT**. France. 1965. A French comedy memorable because it put together Jean-Paul Belmondo, Jean-Claude Brialy, Catherine Deneuve, and Françoise Dorléac. This is one we're going to save for images of lost youth. Its effect is heightened by the death of Dorléac (Deneuve's sister) shortly after.

✳ **MALTESE FALCON, THE**. US. 1941. The Dashiell Hammett private eye classic provided an opportunity for writer/director John Huston to explode on the US film scene. Today it is probably second only to *CASABLANCA* as the most shown, most watched, and most admired film of Hollywood's Golden Age. Humphrey Bogart, Mary Astor, Peter Lorre, Sydney Greenstreet, and Elisha Cook Jr. raised the Warner Bros. ensemble style to a new level of excitement. "I like doing business with a man who likes to do business!" You've probably seen it so often, why not check out the earlier version directed by Roy Del Ruth, with Ricardo Cortez in the Bogart role? Though it is a good film in its own right, it pales so in comparison with Huston's version that you begin to understand the difference between good filmmaking and great filmmaking. ◪

✳\⇧§ **MAN AND A WOMAN, A**. France. 1966. Everybody's favorite romantic movie of the mid-sixties (except, of course, the critics). Claude Lelouch directed Anouk Aimée and Jean-Louis Trintignant in what amounts to a catalogue of everything that you could possibly think of that might be romantic, including French women, American westerns, the movie business, the race car business, kids, food, wine, guitars, cigars, music, Paris, Brazil, the Samba. . . the list goes on. Pierre Barouh, who also plays in the film, apparently contributed importantly to the music. See his film *SARAVAH.* (Francis Lai built a career on the score.) At the time, Lelouch was compared unfavorably with filmmakers like Godard and Truffaut, but during the next fifteen years or so he made a number of films which seem to become more interesting each year. As a cinematographer/director he's made some important contributions to film style.

MAN ESCAPED, A. France. 1956. Hemingway once said, "it's not what you put in a story that makes it successful, it's what you leave out." Director Robert Bresson carries this tenet to the extreme, avoiding any suggestion of drama—let alone melodrama. Bresson based this film on an actual successful prison escape. His intense concentration on the job at hand is riveting. It's an existential caper film to rival *RIFIFI*.

MAN IN THE GRAY FLANNEL SUIT, THE. US. 1956. Gregory Peck is the ultimate character of the fifties, the advertising executive struggling to climb the greasy pole. Nunnally Johnson directed from Sloan Wilson's very popular novel.

MAN IN THE WHITE SUIT, THE. UK. 1951. A classic comedy which makes a quite valid economic point, posing the antithesis of planned obsolescence. Alec Guinness invents a fabric that never wears out and never gets dirty. It doesn't take long for the town to figure out that this miracle of modern science is going to destroy their economy. Alexander Mackendrick directed.

MAN OF IRON. Poland. 1980. Andrzej Wajda's sequel to *MAN OF MARBLE* carries the criticism to the present. The filmmaker is now married to the son of the mythical hero and the Polish Solidarity Movement comes into the picture. Lech Walesa appears as himself.

MAN OF MARBLE. Poland. 1977. Andrzej Wajda's politically sharp dissection of Polish national values is also cinematically remarkable for its harsh, direct style. It's the story of a fictional filmmaker who becomes fascinated with the story of a bricklayer who was "knighted" as a worker hero by the State during the 1950s.

‖ **MAN WHO CAME TO DINNER, THE**. US.
1941. William Keighley directed this adaptation of
the fine George Kaufman/Moss Hart play. Monty
Woolley reprises his parody of Alexander Woollcott,
the outrageous drama critic who is the guest who
never leaves.

◔ **MAN WHO KNEW TOO MUCH, THE**. UK.
1934. Alfred Hitchcock remade himself twenty-two
years later, and you're probably more familiar with
the 1956 Hollywood James Stewart/Doris Day
version of this film. The original stars Leslie Banks,
Edna Best, Peter Lorre, and the always inestimable
Nova Pilbeam. What it's got that the latter doesn't is
a typically British sense of humor which makes the
story of kidnapping and intrigue more resonant.

MAN WHO PLAYED GOD, THE. US. 1932.
Here's a George Arliss vehicle (John G. Adolfi
directed) that also gives us a very young Bette Davis
and an even younger Ray Milland. Arliss is a
musician losing his hearing.

◔ **MAN WHO WOULD BE KING, THE**. US. 1975.
Director John Huston took a typically thirties B-
movie adventure story (the source is Rudyard
Kipling) and managed to make it work with seventies
stars Sean Connery and Michael Caine. They play
two soldiers of fortune in the sub-continent who try
to convince the natives that the man who had been
James Bond is God.

▜ **MAN WITH THE GOLDEN ARM, THE**. US.
1957. This was a shocking film at the time. Frank
Sinatra is the heroin junkie who tries to kick the
habit. Otto Preminger directed this downbeat social
document. Considering the history of drugs during
the last twenty-five years it's sad to note we didn't
learn anything.

◔↘ **MAN WITH A MOVIE CAMERA**. USSR. 1929.
Nobody experienced the joy of the freedom the
movie camera gives nor celebrated it better than
Dziga Vertov (originally Denis Kaufman), the
Russian experimental filmmaker whose work stands
as the antithesis to Sergei Eisenstein's formalism.
Man with a Movie Camera is a collage of shots, an
encyclopedia of images that can leave you breathless
even now.

◔⛊ **MANCHURIAN CANDIDATE, THE**. US. 1962.
Richard Condon's novels evoke contemporary
political paranoia with a useful sense of humor. John

Frankenheimer directed Frank Sinatra, Laurence Harvey, and Angela Lansbury in a script by George Axelrod. It's a good assassination thriller and it's still pertinent.

MANDABI. Senegal. 1970. Ousmane Sembène, the Senegalese poet and filmmaker, directed this simple charming story which was one of the first films from native African cinema to appear in the west.

MANHATTAN. US. 1979. One of Woody Allen's better movies about himself and his friends, starring Allen and Diane Keaton, Michael Murphy, and Mariel Hemingway. It's like a coda to *ANNIE HALL*, finishing up the romance. Shot in black and white, and accompanied by a Gershwin soundtrack.

MARAT/SADE. UK. 1967. Peter Brook directed this film of his seminal stage production of the play by Peter Weiss. In combining Brechtian techniques with some of the lessons of theatrical philosopher Antonin Artaud, Weiss's play was a landmark of the sixties that seemed to be exploiting everything the theater could do that film could not. Brecht suggested distancing audiences; Artaud demanded the opposite—total involvement. You went to see the film a couple of years later only to prove that this stuff couldn't work on celluloid. In fact it does. Peter Brook is a filmmaker as well as a master of the modern theater and he, perhaps uniquely, understood how to translate something so stagey and theatrical onto film. It is, in fact, a musical with more than a dozen songs, and remains an important record of a turning point in western theater. The full title is *The Persecution and Assassination of Jean-Paul Marat as Performed by the Inmates of the Asylum of Charenton Under the Direction of the Marquis De Sade*.

MARATHON MAN. US. 1976. Graduate student Dustin Hoffman meets the evil Laurence Olivier in this thriller by William Goldman directed by John Schlesinger. No doubt it's violent, but there's a kind of black humor here, too. You'll never forget evil Nazi dentist Olivier using the most mundane techniques of the dental profession to torture young Hoffman.

MARIUS. France. 1931. Along with its sequels *FANNY* and *CESAR*, *Marius* constitutes Marcel Pagnol's great trilogy celebrating the little people of Marseille. It's a study of manners and morals that was quite popular internationally at the time and deserves attention even today, not only for its location photography but also for its honest sentiment. Alexander Korda directed *Marius*; Marc Allégret directed *FANNY*; Pagnol directed *CESAR* and wrote all three. ◪

MARK OF ZORRO, THE. US. 1940. Zorro, the California aristocrat and swashbuckling hero, has always been something of a tongue-in-cheek enterprise in its various incarnations. Perhaps it's the very idea of buckling swash in California, no matter what the historical period. Our hero here, Tyrone Power was certainly the most dashing of the various actors who've played the role. This one was directed by Rouben Mamoulian.

MARRIED WOMAN, A. France. 1964. Another seminal film from Godard. This one gives us Macha Méril as a young French woman split between her husband and her lover. The plot isn't important. The way Godard approaches it is. This is as close as you'll come to Cubist narrative filmmaking.

MARSEILLAISE, LA. France. 1938. Jean Renoir's hymn to the common people was a contribution to the popular movement in France in the 1930s. It has got more historical scope and drama than you usually see in Renoir's work and it remains an interesting document.

MARTY. US. 1955. This may be the first film based on a television play. Paddy Chayefsky won plaudits for this stylized, naturalistic story about a homely guy (Ernest Borgnine) who finally marries. "Let's go down to 72nd Street and watch the girls." ◪

MARY POPPINS. US. 1964. The Walt Disney production of the children's classic storybook, directed by Robert Stevenson, debuts Julie Andrews. Glynis Johns is here, too (see *THE COURT JESTER*), and a number of other character actors. It's *Upstairs, Downstairs* for children. The setting is upper-class Edwardian London and Poppins, of course, is the magical nanny. The score by Richard and Robert Sherman is derivative but satisfactory. ◪

MASCULINE-FEMININE. France. 1966. Jean-Luc Godard visits the world of young folk. It's interesting to watch Jean-Pierre Léaud without François Truffaut's guidance. Chantal Goya is the singer he has an affair with and Marlène Jobert is the other girl. One of Godard's more human films.   ▽

M★A★S★H. US. 1970. Follow the exploits of America's favorite Mobile Army Surgical Hospital crew as they laugh and cry, cut and sew their way through the ever-colorful Korean war! Ring Lardner Jr. wrote the screenplay for this Robert Altman classic. The television series starring Alan Alda was so enormously successful during the seventies that you're probably brainwashed by it. Altman's film is tougher, colder, and in fact funnier. The difference between the two clearly defines the difference between movies and TV. Donald Sutherland and Elliott Gould star.   ▽

MATTER OF LIFE AND DEATH, A. UK. 1946. The team of Michael Powell and Emeric Pressburger is responsible for this unusual mixture of fantasy and reality, an interesting examination of the logic of life and death set in World War II. David Niven is a pilot who thinks he's actually been beyond the pearly gates.

MATTER OF SEX, A. US. 1984. Lee Grant directed this television docudrama about the Wilmar Eight, a group of average midwestern women who struck the bank for which they worked to gain equal pay with their male counterparts. Grant's daughter, Dinah Manoff, and Jean Stapleton, star. It's an absorbing, well-made story and offers a rare and interesting comparison with a documentary—*THE WILMAR 8*—that Grant had produced previously.

MAYTIME. US. 1937. Jeanette MacDonald and Nelson Eddy are perhaps an acquired taste, but their 1930s operettas were notable at the time. This is one of the better ones, tastefully filmed, as they used to say, by Robert Z. Leonard. They sing "Sweetheart" here.

MAZE, THE. US. 1953. This may be the ultimate 3-D movie of 1953. Designer William Cameron Menzies directed and he found just the right visual structures to exploit the very limited trick of 3-D. I still remember the frog jumping out at the audience, and it's been more than thirty years now.

MCCABE AND MRS. MILLER. US. 1971. Robert Altman cast Warren Beatty and Julie Christie together with a bunch of his regulars in this neo-western. It's an atmospheric and resonant exploration of an old northwestern town in the middle of winter. Christy runs a bordello and Beatty is the smaller-than-life hero.   ▽

ME. France. 1968. Maurice Pialat is a French director who has made only a handful of films during the last twenty years, few of which have been seen outside of France but all of which are important. Pialat must rank as one of the more interesting French directors to come along since the New Wave. *Me* is about a boy put out with foster parents who has brushes with delinquency. It's coolly observed and detailed—almost distant—but Pialat displays great empathy.

MEAN STREETS. US. 1973. This is the film Martin Scorsese was born to direct and Robert DeNiro was born to act in. An on-location exploration of life in New York's Little Italy, it captures the mood of a very precise segment of society with sharp precision, good music, and some gusto. ◪

MEDIUM COOL. US. 1969. Haskell Wexler, the famous cinematographer, directed this Godardian essay in the meaning of movies on location in Chicago during the Democratic Convention of 1968. Robert Forster is a television cameraman, Peter Bonerz is his soundman, Verna Bloom is the woman from the Kentucky hills he meets and Harold Blankenship is her son. While "the whole world is watching," Forster remains unmoved by the politics or human drama of the situation. He's the ultimate artist divorced from society. "God, I love to shoot film," he declares, and it doesn't matter if the subject of his filming is an auto accident or the dramatic riots that took place in Lincoln Park that year. Through his contact with Verna Bloom and even moreso with her son, who trains pigeons, he opens up a little only to be caught in a surrealistic web of his own design at the end. At the end Wexler turns the camera on us. We're responsible, too. Spectators are just as immoral as artists. This is an extraordinary, powerful, and meaningful movie whose effect has never been duplicated. Wexler captured an unusual balance between feelings and intelligence. ◪

MEET ME IN ST. LOUIS. US. 1944. Judy Garland, Mary Astor, Marjorie Main, Margaret O'Brien, and others, directed by Vincente Minnelli in a musical set in the 1903 St. Louis World's Fair. Judy never sang better: "The Trolley Song," "The Boy Next Door," "Meet Me in St. Louis." ◪

MEET PAMELA. France. 1972. A rather pedestrian story of a young Frenchman who marries an English girl and brings her home to meet his parents, at which time the young girl and her father-in-law fall madly in love with each other, *Pamela* starred American actress Julie Baker. It stands here to remind us of the tenuous but critical relationship between French "cinema" and American "movies"—and for all films within films.

⬆ **MELVIN AND HOWARD**. US. 1980. A nice piece of Americana directed by Jonathan Demme, an as yet unsung but deserving practitioner of that art. Paul LeMat and Jason Robards with Mary Steenburgen in the story of Melvin Dummar, one of the people who thought Howard Hughes's will should have named him. Hughes is a big enough character to match *CITIZEN KANE* and Dummar is a real honest-to-goodness nebbish: the extreme contrast powers the film. ▽

⬎ **MEMORIES OF UNDERDEVELOPMENT**. Cuba. 1968. Tomàs Gutierrez Alea directed this portrait of bourgeois intellectuals in Cuba at the time of the revolution. The film became a considerable hit on the art house circuit a couple of years later in the west because it carried with it the style of the French New Wave and gave us a chance to get an inside look at Cuba. It also has some interesting political and moral implications.

◬ **MEMORY OF JUSTICE, THE**. West Germany/US. 1976. Marcel Ophuls, fresh from his triumph with the seminal documentary *THE SORROW AND THE PITY*, turned his attention to the dilemmas of nationality that he himself as a European-American must have found painful and pointed. *The Memory of Justice* juxtaposes the French experience in Algeria with the American war in Vietnam and the German Nuremberg trials. It's long and involved, and sometimes it begs the question, but so many issues are raised in such detail that it rewards repeated viewings.

↘⬆ **MEN OF BRONZE**. US. 1977. William Miles directed this seventies-style documentary about Black soldiers in World War I. It's a curious and important bit of history heightened by the interviews with the still-surviving soldiers.

MERCHANT OF FOUR SEASONS, THE. West Germany. 1971. During the seventies, Rainer Werner Fassbinder achieved a reputation internationally as an interesting filmmaker. I've never quite understood why. It seems to me he's an apolitical German Lina Wertmüller—a stylist with a very precise sensibility. . . but to what end? *The*

Merchant of Four Seasons, a portrait of a simple fruit peddler disintegrating slowly but surely, is a nicely realized emblem of what was good about Fassbinder's style. He gave us a simple, uncluttered view of the world which at its best was Brechtian.

MERRY ANDREW. US. 1958. Danny Kaye continued his string of bright musicals that young people can enjoy with this story of a teacher (Kaye) and a circus performer (Pier Angeli).

MERRY WIDOW, THE. US. 1925. This version has rather little to do with the Franz Lehar operetta. It's a good companion piece to *THE WEDDING MARCH*, full of gorgeous sets and costumes and concerned with sexual relationships. It also holds the strange honor of being the only Von Stroheim film to be released without major meddling by producers.

MERRY WIDOW, THE. US. 1934. Ernst Lubitsch mounted the Franz Lehar operetta with Maurice Chevalier, Jeanette MacDonald, and Edward Everett Horton. His fine touch makes it work. The music is quite good.

METROPOLIS. Germany. 1926. Fritz Lang's best movie is a silent science-fiction classic that gives us a rich visual parody of a mechanistic future that looks better than most futurist paintings of the time.

MIDDLE OF THE WORLD, THE. Switzerland. 1974. In the middle of the lost decade, the 1970s, in the middle of Europe, Alain Tanner tells us a simple story of a guy running for political office (Philippe Léotard) who gets into trouble because of a romantic affair. But that's not the point. The real subject of the film is the political stasis that has pertained since the 1960s. Tanner is almost alone in depicting this on film: "We are in a time of 'normalization,' where exchange is permitted, but nothing changes." It should be seen in conjunction with *JONAH, WHO WILL BE 25 IN THE YEAR 2,000*. John Berger wrote the script.

MIDNIGHT. US. 1939. Mitchell Leisen had better luck with screenwriters than most Hollywood journeymen. This one was written by Billy Wilder and Charles Brackett. Claudette Colbert, Don Ameche, John Barrymore, and Mary Astor mix it up in Paris with considerable aplomb.

MIDNIGHT COWBOY. US. 1969. Jon Voight is the cowboy and Dustin Hoffman is Ratso Rizzo, the sickly bum, in this really downbeat view of New

York's Times Square sexual scene. John Schlesinger directed. It was a bit of a scandal at the time but doesn't really make any point. ▽

◔ **MIDSUMMER NIGHT'S DREAM, A**. US. 1935. When you're making up a list of Shakespearian movies it never gets very long, so Max Reinhardt's staging of *A Midsummer Night's Dream* generally gets included. James Cagney is Bottom, if you can believe it, and Mickey Rooney is Puck. Watch it for Merle Oberon's Titania and the set design.

MIDSUMMER NIGHT'S SEX COMEDY, A. US. 1982. After doing serious Bergman in *INTERIORS*, Woody Allen attempted light Bergman with his own version of *SMILES OF A SUMMER NIGHT*, and it comes off quite well. It's also his only attempt at an historical setting (turn of the century). He stars with Mia Farrow, Mary Steenburgen, Tony Roberts, and Jose Ferrer. ▽

▜ **MIGRANTS, THE**. US. 1974. Tom Gries directed this landmark television movie, a heavily fictionalized account of migrant workers' desperate situation.

◔ **MILDRED PIERCE**. US. 1945. It's a James M. Cain novel directed by Michael Curtiz. Joan Crawford is the title character. Ann Blyth is her bitchy daughter. It was a camp classic made more interesting by the revelations in *Mommie Dearest* of Joan Crawford's own family life, where quite the reverse seems to have been true.

▜§ **MILLION, LE**. FRANCE. 1931. René Clair's most ambitious and influential film is a landmark in sound. Not because the actors sing most of the dialogue, but because he attempted to integrate action and music so thoroughly. It's also a fairly nice story about a missing lottery ticket. Of course these were Old Francs, but then people used to care about the "$64 Question" as well.

＼ **MILLIONAIRE, THE**. US. 1931. Not the television series you may remember, but a pleasant George Arliss vehicle. Here the great man is a retired businessman who likes to keep busy. Noah Beery, Florence Arliss, and James Cagney assist. John G. Adolfi directed.

MILLIONS LIKE US. UK. 1943. Good home-front propaganda during World War II by Frank Launder and Sidney Gilliat. Shows us *A Family at War*.

⊘ MINISTRY OF FEAR. US. 1944. Fritz Lang directed Ray Milland in this version of a complex and absorbing Graham Greene novel with a good feel for wartime London.

MINNIE AND MOSCOWITZ. US. 1971. This is undoubtedly John Cassavetes's friendliest and least neurotic movie, with his wife, Gena Rowlands, as the middle-aged girl who falls for a carhop, Seymour Cassel. As usual, Cassavetes gets in most of his family, too. Val Avery has a great scene as a guy out on his first date. It still holds up: Cassavetes for everybody.

MIRACLE IN MILAN. Italy. 1951. A Neorealist fantasy, if you like, by Vittorio De Sica, which satirizes Italian lifestyles after World War II.

‖ MIRACLE OF MORGAN'S CREEK, THE. US. 1944. Another good screwball by Preston Sturges with the usual cast, this time including Betty Hutton. She gets pregnant and can't remember who the father is. That's rather daring for the time.

MIRACLE ON 34TH STREET. US. 1947. This is a nice fantasy—especially for children—that works because of the reality with which the actors approach the story. Edmund Gwenn has to prove he's Santa to please kid Natalie Wood. ▽

MIRACLE WORKER, THE. US. 1962. This is a stagey adaptation of the play by William Gibson about the education of Helen Keller by Annie Sullivan. Anne Bancroft and Patty Duke star under the direction of Arthur Penn. The film was an inspiration for Truffaut's *THE WILD CHILD*.

⊘ MIRAGE. US. 1965. Here's a film that probably started out as an attempt to duplicate the success of the stylish mystery *CHARADE* a few years earlier. What we get is something quite different. Gregory Peck is the star (he's certainly not the equal of Cary Grant in light comedy), but there's no equivalent for Audrey Hepburn in *CHARADE*. Walter Matthau is here again. He does as well as he did in *CHARADE*, but here he steals the show. Edward Dmytryk directed. There's fine location shooting, mainly in New York City. The end result looks like something Hitchcock might have toyed with for a while and then rejected, but just barely.

MISERABLES, LES. US. 1935. Fredric March, Charles Laughton, and Cedric Hardwicke in the

Wilfrid Brambell, the "clean old man," with a young Ringo Starr in *A Hard Day's Night*.

Victor Hugo classic about a crime that haunts a seemingly respectable bourgeois. Generally cited as one of the better adaptations of novels in the thirties.

MISFITS, THE. US. 1961. All the ingredients are here: Arthur Miller wrote the screenplay, John Huston directed, Clark Gable and Marilyn Monroe star (it was the last film for each), but the whole doesn't add up to the sum of the parts. Monroe doesn't fit in a cowboy setting and the film goes off in too many directions.

MISSING. US. 1982. When you add all of the made-for-television films of the seventies, it's probable that the politically motivated melodrama is the most common genre of the last twenty years. In theatrical films it's been done many times, both in western Europe and the US, but never so well as in the films of Costa-Gavras. From *Z* onwards, he's had a peculiar talent for infusing his films not only with intelligence and balance, but also with deeply felt passion and a sense of the possibilities of political life. He may not be honored very often in the popular and specialist press, but his contribution to film in the last twenty-five years is a major one. Although he's of Greek origin, he's worked mainly in the French language. *Missing* is not his first film in the English language but it is his first film with American stars. It's based on the Charles Horman affair in Chile during the coup against Allende in

1973. It stars Jack Lemmon as Horman's father, searching for his missing son in Chile and gradually learning of the complicity of the American government in the coup. Sissy Spacek is Charles Horman's wife. The manner in which it takes Jack Lemmon's point of view and works very gradually to break down his unbending faith in the honesty of the American way, makes it a profoundly moving film. As always, Costa-Gavras shoots with a great sense of place, and the Chilean music of the era adds a lot. Charles Cioffi, a great character actor, plays an American official with the ingratiating untrustworthiness that is his hallmark. ▽

MISSISSIPPI MERMAID. France. 1970. Several times during his career François Truffaut seems to have attempted to recapture the romantic depth of experience of *JULES AND JIM*. He never succeeded. *Mississippi Mermaid* is one of these attempts, starring Jean-Paul Belmondo and Catherine Deneuve. It's an interesting film stylistically but it simply doesn't have the feeling of the earlier success.

⬧ **MISSOURI BREAKS, THE**. US. 1976. Thomas McGuane is an idiosyncratic novelist who is probably an acquired taste. His novels have been the source of several movies. (*Rancho Deluxe* is probably most representative.) He wrote this script especially for Arthur Penn who over-cast it with Marlon Brando and Jack Nicholson. It's pretty messy but it's interesting to watch because Brando is so out of control as an actor. You learn a lot about what the balance should be between actor and director. ▽

⬧ **MR. BLANDINGS BUILDS HIS DREAM HOUSE**. US. 1948. *IT'S A WONDERFUL LIFE* and *THE BEST YEARS OF OUR LIVES* both suggested at the end of the war America's driving fantasy: to have a home of your own. This film by H. C. Potter based on the very popular novel of the time takes that fantasy one step forward to fruition. Cary Grant is the well-to-do businessman, and Myrna Loy his wife. They're an upper-middle-class couple used to living in the gorgeous New York apartments that exist only in 1930s movies, when they decide to build a house in the country. The film still works because the fantasy still works. ▽

⬧↘ **MR. DEEDS GOES TO TOWN**. US. 1936. It's a simple idea with interesting reverberations. Gary Cooper in the role he was born to play, Longfellow Deeds, is a rather simple fellow who inherits millions of dollars (that was a lot at the time) and decides to share the wealth. This simple decision so contradicts capitalist philosophy that Deeds runs into much trouble. Frank Capra solidified his reputation with this film.

MISTER ROBERTS. US. 1955. Two master directors, John Ford and Mervyn LeRoy, worked together here to mount the film version of what is probably the great play about World War II (by Thomas Heggen and Joshua Logan.) James Cagney is the crazy Captain; Henry Fonda is the title hero. Jack Lemmon built a long-lasting career on his Ensign Pulver. This plot has got an enormous amount going for it. There's the struggle between the arbitrary authority Cagney represents and the plight of the deck hands, symbolized by Pulver. Mr. Roberts, as middle management, mediates. (It's as if he were preparing for a dull fifties corporate existence after the war.) More important, there's the focus on those who only stand and wait. It's Mr. Roberts's dream to see action during the war but he's stuck on a leaky crate. It's a sign of the unique mythology of World War II that we don't think Roberts is crazy when he finally wins his assignment.

MR. SMITH GOES TO WASHINGTON. US. 1939. It sounds like a sequel to *MR. DEEDS GOES TO TOWN*. . . if anything, it exceeds its predecessor. James Stewart is a young everyman who gets elected to the US Senate and meets and conquers the corruption that he finds there.

MRS. MINIVER. US. 1942. What *IN WHICH WE SERVE* succeeded brilliantly in doing for British fighting men during World War II *Mrs. Miniver* attempted, slightly less successfully, to do for the home front. It's very much a Hollywood film in which Greer Garson and Walter Pidgeon attempt to play Britishers for William Wyler. Yet, the film had a noticeable impact on American sentiment about the war. It showed us in the best possible light the people our boys were fighting for. (*A Family at War*, a British 52-hour television series from the 1970s, did the same thing much better. See it if you get a chance.)

MOANA. US. 1926. Though Robert Flaherty failed here to duplicate the commercial success of *NANOOK OF THE NORTH*, he topped it artistically. He went to the South Seas this time to photograph the life and rituals of Samoan Islanders. It's a more accurate film ethnographically because it's not staged and it's a more beautiful film to look at because Flaherty experimented with panchromatic stock, for which the film is notable.

MOBY DICK. US. 1956. Okay, if Herman Melville's novel weren't a masterpiece this probably wouldn't make the list, but John Huston and his cast, including Gregory Peck, Richard Basehart, Orson Welles, and Harry Andrews, have a good go at it. It has neither the historical sensibility nor the liveliness that would make a great film but probably its greatest difficulty is Gregory Peck. I admire Peck's persona as much as most people but when he wasn't *THE MAN IN THE GRAY FLANNEL SUIT* he always stuck out like a minister at a brothel. ▽

✛\⇪ **MODERN   ROMANCE**.   US.   1981. Director/writer Albert Brooks is literally the comedian's comedian since he's the son of comedian Harry Einstein ("Parkyakarkus" of the 1940s). His early routines on records were brilliant parodies of media and comedy forms and formats, and his first movie, *REAL LIFE* was cast in the same mold. In *Modern Romance* he goes further to paint not one but a gallery of portraits of contemporary characters who, in their neurotic intellectual approach to people and the world around them, are strikingly fresh. They show us that there really is something different about us now. If you look closely at Brooks's work you see what drives Woody Allen. Brooks plays a film editor in the movie and there's a good bit of incisive joking about the film medium, but the real heart of the experience is Brooks's relationship with Kathryn Harrold. James L. Brooks (no relation) puts in an appearance as does Bob Einstein (relation). Both are excellent cameos. This one's going to be with us a long time. ▽

✳§ **MODERN TIMES**. US. 1932. Yes: the ultimate Chaplin film. Charlie works on the assembly line twisting bolts and twisting lunch. The gamine, Paulette Goddard, is the girl with whom he ever so slowly walks off down the road into the sunset at the end of the film. Chaplin gave up silents only with great difficulty and *Modern Times*, although it has a soundtrack, has no dialogue. The music, which he wrote, includes the famous "Smile." The lyrics, which came later, neatly summarize not only the film but his career. ▽

✛‖ **MON ONCLE**. France. 1958. Jacques Tati's first color film introduces the themes that obsessed him later in life. Monsieur Hulot's simplicity is in stark contrast to everyone else's over-civilized existence. The gags deal almost entirely with this contrast and it's fascinating to watch Tati hold our interest with such single-mindedness. See *M. HULOT'S HOLIDAY*. ☑

MON ONCLE D'AMERIQUE. France. 1980. This is an extraordinary attempt by Alain Resnais to do a supposedly fiction film about complex psychological theories. For years he had been absorbed with the work of psychologist Henri Laborit. Jorge Semprun and Jean Gruault had both worked on the script at one time or another. (Gruault is given full credit here.) Laborit himself appears in the film, so part of it is straight documentary essay. Gérard Depardieu, Nicole Garcia, Marie Dubois, and Roger Pierre provide the dramatic illustrations of Laborit's theory of human interaction. This is exactly the sort of film that makes you see the wisdom of the invention of the videotape. You want to take it home, run it a few times, and study it—for the fun of it.

MONKEY BUSINESS. US. 1931. Pretty good Marx Brothers. Marx Brothers movies should probably be rated by the number of brothers that appear in them. That makes this a 4-Marx movie: Groucho, Harpo, Chico, and Zeppo. S. J. Perelman had something to do with the script.

M. HULOT'S HOLIDAY. France. 1951. A classic work by a great clown, Jacques Tati. Hulot is his Charlot character, a nice fellow who innocently leaves a landscape of destruction in his wake. Tati studies all the little details of a seaside vacation. There's little sound; it's very much a physical performance. ☑

MONSIEUR VERDOUX. US. 1947. Lesser and late Chaplin but Chaplin nevertheless, *Monsieur Verdoux* shows one of the most successful filmmakers of all time late in life striking out in new directions. The inventor of the sentimental Victorian Charlot clown here attempts what can only be termed a kind of black comedy. He is a bluebeard, killing off one wife after another, quite efficiently and funnily, for their money. Martha Raye is the only one who rises sufficiently to the occasion.

MONTEREY POP. US. 1969. This documentary of the famous concert in Monterey was overwhelmed quite quickly in the public consciousness by films like *WOODSTOCK* but it remains not only a successful concert musical documentary, but probably the first rock concert film. A number of documentarians, including the Maysleses and

Richard Leacock, worked on it. D. A. Pennebaker is credited with coordinating. The film includes sequences with Otis Redding, the Mamas and the Papas, the Who, Janis Joplin, the Jefferson Airplane, and Jimi Hendrix. What more could you ask?

◐‖ **MONTY PYTHON AND THE HOLY GRAIL**. UK. 1974. Is there anyone out there who can explain to me why 90% of the Python group's energy in film in the last ten years has been devoted to historical subjects, usually ancient? They've made more than half-a-dozen movies now in various combinations since their brilliant television career and they seem collectively and individually obsessed with the past. It may be Terry Jones's doing. (He and Terry Gilliam are credited with directing this film.) They seem drawn most often to medieval settings. This is the one where the Great Knight, John Cleese, refuses to admit even the possibility of defeat even though one arm, then another, one leg, then another, and finally the entire body is severed from the head. Perhaps it's a gloss on John Dryden's definition of satire, which "severs the head from the body and leaves it standing." Farce then must sever the body from the head and leave it talking. However... ▽

◐‖ **MONTY PYTHON LIVE AT THE HOLLYWOOD BOWL**. UK. 1982. . . . We do have a couple of records of the Python's original skit humor, including this one, chosen mainly because it follows alphabetically. They're all here: Graham Chapman, John Cleese, Terry Gilliam, Eric Idle, Terry Jones, Michael Palin, and even Carol Cleveland. If you've got a complete set of the original television tapes you certainly don't need this film (transferred from tape), but this is a book about film and the only legitimate way we could get Python's skits in here. They're less effective on stage and far less effective in the film of the stage presentation, but it's important to have a record of the Piranha Brothers for posterity. What the Pythons do at their best (and that's TV) is fully the equal of esthetically more acceptable comedians like Samuel Beckett. ▽

⌐ **MOON IS BLUE, THE**. US. 1953. You'll wonder what all the fuss was about, but when *The Moon Is Blue* was released in the early fifties it caused quite a furor. It used vulgar language: the invective adjective "virgin" was cited. Director Otto Preminger received great credit among the intelligentsia for daring to film this stage play by F. Hugh Herbert. The film (which stars William Holden, David Niven, and Maggie McNamara) is a cultural landmark, only for the reaction to it. This was the nadir of Hollywood censorship. After this, we began to rise from the muck of "the Code" which had held sway for twenty years.

MOONLIGHTING. UK. 1982. Polish director Jerzy Skolimowski found a way to make a Polish movie in England. It's about a group of Polish workers temporarily exiled in London whose story gives exile Skolimowski a chance to describe and comment on the anguish of that position. Skolimowski in England and Wajda in Paris were able to discuss the imposition of martial law and the destruction of the Solidarity movement only from a great distance.

MOONRAKER. France/UK. 1979. This will be heresy to most James Bond fans but *MOONRAKER*, a British-French co-production, not based on an Ian Fleming novel, seems to me on reflection to be the best of the Bond films so far. All the elements from years before are here: good gadgets, excellent locations (Venice, Rio, the jungle, and outer space), the vodka martini "stirred not shaken." (Who would regard that drink as a sign of savoir faire today?). A string of girls is here, too, but what's important is that for the first time Bond settles down with one woman (Lois Chiles). She's as beautiful as any girl in a Bond movie but she's also very, very smart. In fact, during most of the climactic sequences aboard a space station circling above the Earth, Roger Moore has to depend on her expertise and knowledge. This is the feminist James Bond film. "Where did you learn to fight like that? NASA?" "No, Vassar!" Let it be said, too, that although Sean Connery had first dibs on the role, I've always thought that Roger Moore fitted better. Partly it's his training as *The Saint*, partly it's that you can't trust a Celt like Connery as the quintessential English adventurer. Finally, this is the only Bond film—to my knowledge—in which our hero makes love on the Queen's telly (certainly a climactic gambit).

MORGAN! UK. 1966. Screenwriter David Mercer's plays have been a mainstay of the London theater for a number of years. This is the film version of his *Morgan, A Suitable Case For Treatment*. David Warner scores as the slightly crazy artist. The subject is a little coy but it was an important film at the time. Karel Reisz directed. Vanessa Redgrave is the love interest.

MORNING GLORY. US. 1933. Katharine

Hepburn is the young actress who's going to be a success, we just know it. Compare *STAGE DOOR*. ◩

MORON MOVIES. US. 1984. Like many of us— only moreso—a man from Philadelphia by the name of Len Cella amuses himself with an 8-millimeter camera. He shoots, as crudely as you or I might, ten-to-thirty-second strips that illustrate an idea or a joke. Unlike us, however, his films became cult favorites at midnight showings in his hometown. *The Tonight Show* discovered him, and since then he's had a national audience of millions. His "moron movies," as he calls them, are often very funny and usually sublime illustrations of the simplicity of visual humor. In *A Cook's Punishment in Hell* Len cracks an egg only to discover that the bowl into which it will drop is a bed of spikes. No hope for that yolk. In *The Chicken Comedian*, one of Frank Perdue's finest sits on a stage cracking bad jokes. The hook drags him off. In *Poor Man's Remote Control*, Len invents a way to turn off his television set without getting up. He uses a plumber's helper. There's two things going on here: first, Len Cella is plain funny; more important, *Moron Movies* stand here for all our home movies to remind us that it's very important—even crucial—to do it yourself.

MOSCOW ON THE HUDSON. US. 1984. A masterful, if sad, comedy about the contemporary American melting pot by Paul Mazursky. This view of a Russian emigre on the streets of New York stars Robin Williams in a most subdued, but very effective, characterization. It's a film about something we don't much talk about these days, even if it's as true now as it ever was: the magnificent, unique diversity that makes America different from all other nations. At one point late in the film, Williams, after only a few months in New York, is driving a rich Texan in from the airport and hustling him in true American fashion with digital watches and all kinds of other goodies. "Sit back and enjoy the ride," he says, "I give good limo." It's the Texan's first time in New York and he's clearly more of a stranger than the Russian emigre. That's America. ◩

MOST DANGEROUS GAME, THE. US. 1932. Ernest B. Schoedsack co-directed with Irving Pichel. Schoedsack was always concerned with the battles of nature. In this case it's a normal human being who actually hunts other human beings for entertainment on his island preserve. Joel McCrea and Fay Wray star. An interesting comparison to

KING KONG made by Schoedsack and Cooper at about the same time. Run it on a double bill with *THE TENTH VICTIM*.

MOTHER. USSR. 1926. Great camerawork by V. I. Pudovkin, the USSR's second-most important film theorist (after Eisenstein). *Mother* is based on the Maxim Gorky novel about a woman's conversion to the Communist cause after her harrowing experiences with the czarist regime.

MOTHER AND THE WHORE, THE. France. 1973. Director Jean Eustache had one great success. This is a film that delineates a generation. Jean-Pierre Léaud is the young French intellectual in love with himself and ideas and stuck between two women (Bernadette Lafont and Françoise Lebrun). The film is three-and-a-half hours long and during that time Eustache works a dizzying number of changes on the themes of commitment, direction, and rationalization. A unique document of its time and place, it is perhaps the last of the New Wave films.

MOULIN ROUGE. US. 1952. John Huston's biopic of Toulouse-Lautrec with Jose Ferrer and—believe it or not—Zsa Zsa Gabor. The film is in the rich, garish color of the early fifties which Huston comes close to molding into a representation of the work of the artist. It's a mesmerizing experience of the Pigalle mystique.

MOVIE, MOVIE. US. 1978. After ten years of watching Hollywood go gaga over kid directors who were more or less talentless, veteran Stanley Donen had a bright idea. Donen shot two short, typical 1930s programmers: *Dynamite Hands* is a black-and-white boxing story, and *Baxter's Beauties of 1933* is a breathless Busby Berkeleyish musical that crams into less than an hour's running time just about every cliche you can think of. George C. Scott stars as the impressario. While all the kid directors were attempting to mimic their elders, Donen, who came up the hard way, outclassed them. *Movie, Movie* is a fitting capstone to a successful career. ◪

MUMMY, THE. US. 1932. The horror classic with Boris Karloff as the well-wrapped undead.

MUPPET MOVIE, THE. US. 1979. After more than ten years dominating the television screens and consciousness of American children, Kermit the Frog, Miss Piggy, Fozzie Bear, Animal, and the other Muppet creations of Jim Henson and company finally decide to go Hollywood. The impetus for the film is the subject for the film as well. We discover Kermit in a swamp and we follow him and his crew all the way to success on the sound stages of mogul Orson Welles. Along the way they meet more than a dozen guest stars from Bob Hope on down. Watch for Steve Martin serving Idaho wine to Kermit and Miss Piggy in their big romantic scene and offering to smell the cap for Kermit. Check out villain Mel Brooks as he readies himself to fry the brains of the frog. James Frawley directed. ▽

MUPPETS TAKE MANHATTAN, THE. US. 1984. Jim Henson's second-in-command, Frank Oz, directed the third outing for the personable puppets. They've already been to Hollywood and London. . . what's next? This time they attempt to match the success of the first film with an assault on Broadway. We know these cloth constructions so intimately, they've taken such an active part in our contemporary mythology, that it's easy to ignore the extraordinary accomplishment of Henson and company in integrating live actors with puppets. Think of how far puppeteering had come a generation ago (Bil Baird, and even before him Edgar Bergen and Charlie McCarthy) and then consider Henson's accomplishments. The Muppets' physical construction is one step up from Señor Wences. It's not their physical appearance that enthralls us, it's the personalities behind them. What Henson has done is to find a way to bring the essence of radio to film and television: all that counts are the voices. ▽

MURDER. UK. 1930. This early Alfred Hitchcock sound film starring Herbert Marshall establishes the theme of guilt and innocence that was to haunt Hitchcock for another fifty years.

MURDER MY SWEET. US. 1944. Edward Dmytryk's film of Raymond Chandler's *Farewell My Lovely*, sets Dick Powell up as the hard-boiled Phillip Marlowe. He's no Humphrey Bogart, but almost any Chandler novel makes a good movie. ▽

MURDER ON THE ORIENT EXPRESS. UK. 1974. Sidney Lumet directed this late adaptation of Agatha Christie. It's too star-studded and colorful to match the nostalgic feel of the earlier black-and-white films of her novels, but it's still enjoyable to watch Albert Finney, Sean Connery, Jean-Pierre Cassel, Lauren Bacall, and, most of all, Ingrid Bergman.

◭◥ **MURIEL**. France. 1963. In his third feature film Alain Resnais finally found a human framework in which to explore his concerns with memory and the relationship of past life with present. Shot in a remarkably luminous color on location in Boulogne, *Muriel*is an essay in small talk among a small family centered around Delphine Seyrig. It has to do with political memory (the Algerian colonial war), too, as well as the memory function of the film medium. By the time of *Muriel*, Resnais's very ambitious experiments in film time had developed a more traditional dramatic structure which makes them all the more fascinating.

♪ **MUSIC ROOM, THE**. India. 1958. Satyajit Ray turned here to the story of an out-of-date Brahmin obsessed with music. The focus on sitar performances makes this one of Ray's most enjoyable films.

⚑ **MUSKETEERS OF PIG ALLEY, THE**. US. 1912. Lillian Gish, Harry Carey, and Jack Pickford in one of D. W. Griffith's best-remembered short films: a gangster movie set on the streets of New York. (It was filmed on West 12th Street.) It's interesting not only for its documentary view of the city in the early years of this century, but also for the panache with which Griffith paints his group of characters.

◭ **MUTINY ON THE BOUNTY**. US. 1935. This is the ultimate historical naval film, with Charles Laughton, Clark Gable, Franchot Tone, and others. Laughton's Captain Bligh is one of the most memorable characters you'll encounter. The myth of the Bounty has been treated numerous times. ▽

◥◉ **MY BODYGUARD**. US. 1980. Actor Tony Bill turned to producing in the 1960s and quietly nourished a host of young directors and screenwriters who later went on to prominence. This was his first effort at directing and it's a good little film full of attention to detail and character and setting. It's about a kid (Chris Makepeace) who hires a bodyguard to protect him from bullies. It was filmed in Chicagoland and includes welcome performances by Martin Mull, John Houseman, and Matt Dillon. Good for kids. Run it on a double bill with *THE KARATE KID*. ▽

◭ **MY BRILLIANT CAREER**. Australia. 1979. Gillian Armstrong directed this landmark Australian film starring Judy Davis and Sam Neill. It's a now classic true story of an independent-minded young woman who makes her own way in the Outback in the early 1900s. ◼

MY DARLING CLEMENTINE. US. 1946. John Ford's emblematic western with Henry Fonda as Wyatt Earp and Victor Mature as Doc Holliday gives us the ultimate western shootout at the O.K. Corral. The film is remarkable because it's so restrained; Ford lets the story speak for itself.

MY FAIR LADY. US. 1964. George Cukor's film of the most popular musical of the 1950s stars most of the original Broadway cast, including the remarkable Rex Harrison, but with the notable and contentious exception of Julie Andrews. Though she owned the role of Eliza onstage, she was thought not to have the necessary star quality for the film and Audrey Hepburn replaced her (with songs dubbed by Marni Nixon). It's not a great movie, but it is a great musical and Andrews had her revenge with a successful career in film in the late sixties and the seventies. ◼

MY FAVORITE BLONDE. US. 1942. Bob Hope without Bing and Dorothy Lamour but with Madeleine Carroll.

MY FAVORITE BRUNETTE. US. 1947. Bob Hope with Dorothy but without Bing but with Peter Lorre and Lon Chaney. Bing has a few solo films listed here. We thought we'd give Bob equal time.

‖ **MY FAVORITE WIFE**. US. 1940. Leo McCarey worked on this film directed by Garson Kanin and starring Cary Grant, Irene Dunne, Randolph Scott, and Gail Patrick. Dunne returns from the dead, Grant has remarried, and you can imagine the ensuing complications.

∖‖ **MY FAVORITE YEAR**. US. 1982. Television's *Your Show of Shows*, produced by Max Liebman and starring Sid Caesar, Carl Reiner, Imogene Coca, and Howard Morris in the early fifties is probably the major watershed in American comedy since the death of Vaudeville. It founded a dynasty that has lasted thirty years. Reiner went on to direct and produce as did his son, Rob, and the writers for the show at one time or another included Neil Simon, Woody Allen, and most of all, Mel Brooks. The experience of working on *Your Show of Shows* is captured in this winning memorial produced by Brooks, written by Norman Steinberg and Dennis Palumbo, and directed by Richard Benjamin. Mark

Linn-Baker is the Brooksian figure. Joseph Bologna plays the Sid Caesar character. Selma Diamond puts in an appearance and Peter O'Toole does a remarkable self-parody as the Errol Flynn type, Allan Swann, about whom the plot revolves. This is the way hommages should be done. ◨

MY LIFE TO LIVE. France. 1962. Jean-Luc Godard's essay on the idea of prostitution stars his then-wife Anna Karina. It's in this film that he begins to push against the limits of straight narrative, trying to shape the essay form he needs. Karina's conversations with philosophers and others in the film are important structural devices. Godard found the metaphor of prostitution fascinating for years after.

MY LITTLE CHICKADEE. US. 1940. It probably seemed like a good idea at the time to pair Mae West and W. C. Fields (they also co-wrote the script), but it just proves there's some kind of law of comedy that more is less: there's only room for one of these people on the screen, and you get crosseyed looking at the double centers. Still, individual scenes are as good as you might expect.

MY MAN GODFREY. US. 1936. Gregory La Cava directed William Powell, Carole Lombard, Gail Patrick, and Eugene Pallette in a classic screwball comedy. Powell is a millionaire. The others think he's a tramp and hire him as a butler. Screwballs with rich-folk settings like this one, produced during the middle of the great Depression, have a wealth of meaning just below the surface.

MY NIGHT AT MAUD'S. France. 1969. Eric Rohmer forged an international reputation very quickly with this third of his series of moral tales. Jean-Louis Trintignant is a provincial Catholic intellectual who almost falls for Françoise Fabian (Maud). The theme of the moral tales was to set male characters up with irresistible female temptations and see how they rationalize their way out of the situation. The later ones were progressively simpler; Trintignant works hardest at the job. Though essentially Rohmer's moral tales are complex Pascalian intellectual discussions, it's also true that they have much to look at. The men and women in Rohmer's films may not move too much while they're talking, but they are very attractive. It's an important truth of movies that you don't necessarily need a lot of action.

MYSTERY OF THE WAX MUSEUM. US.

1933. If you can find a print, this is a technical landmark shot in early two-color Technicolor. It's a classic horror story that was remade as *HOUSE OF WAX*. Michael Curtiz directed this version.

NAKED CITY, THE. US. 1948. The storyline will probably disappoint you but the location photography in New York will not. This is a seminal film directed by Jules Dassin (despite his name, he's from the Bronx), starring Barry Fitzgerald and Howard Duff. A young girl is murdered and the cops chase the killer. You could make a case that *The Naked City* set a style for policiers that has lasted on TV for thirty-five years and more.

NANA. France/Germany. 1926. This isn't one of Jean Renoir's better films but it's a fascinating melange of French and German styles that seem to mix like oil and water. Loosely based on the Zola novel, it's brooding and romantic, but doesn't quite come off.

NANOOK OF THE NORTH. US. 1922. In recent years it's been fashionable to downgrade the importance of the work of Robert Flaherty and to criticize *NANOOK* in particular for its romantic outlook. But what Flaherty did in the 1920s really is extraordinary. Almost single-handedly he was responsible for founding the genre of nonfiction filmmaking which later came to be known as documentary. With great difficulty he shot this record of the lives of an Eskimo family over a period of more than a year, living and eating and sleeping with them. When the film was finally released it met with an enormous popular reception. Remember now that this was a silent film and Flaherty had none of our modern techniques of narration to tell us what to think. Audiences were mesmerized watching real people eat, drink, work, fish, and sleep. It's an important lesson. When you remember that one of the most popular uses of the film medium during the twenties, thirties, and forties, was the travelogue, you see what an important groundbase nonfiction film has provided for Hollywood and the fiction film. The equivalent today is probably the very popular and numerous anthropological, ethnographical, and naturalist films that the BBC, PBS, and others churn out on a regular basis. For any given foot of film stock, this stuff is as exciting and even entertaining as the majority of fiction films today. In the future we're going to pay a lot more attention to it, and Robert Flaherty had the vision a very long time ago.

NAPOLEON. France. 1927. Abel Gance's great, ambitious bio-myth was recently restored to its four-hour-plus length and a multi-screen print was prepared to reproduce properly the triple-screen process that Gance pioneered. It's important technically for these inventions and its ambition, but it even works in the shorter one-and-a-half-hour version that existed previously. One of the landmarks of silent film. ▽

NARROW MARGIN, THE. US. 1950. A lot of critics regard this as one of the best B-movies ever shot: a tough cop against a bunch of hitmen on a hurtling train. Directed by Richard Fleischer.

NASHVILLE. US. 1975. If you had to save only one Robert Altman film, this is probably it. It represents all that's valuable about his work: more than any director of recent years Altman has been able to capture a multiplicity of characters on a screen rich with the possibilities of images and sounds. *Nashville*, about people, politics, and success in the capital of country music, gives us an entertaining gallery including Lily Tomlin, Michael Murphy, Barbara Harris, Ned Beatty, Shelley Duvall, Keenan Wynn, Henry Gibson, Karen Black, Ronee Blakley, and Keith Carradine. He's crammed no less than twenty-four characters into this kaleidoscope and each one of them comes across as fully-dimensioned. The songs, many of them written by the actors, are still memorable, and the celebration of the country music style and milieu is notable. For years now Altman has been making movies that may very well turn out to work better on tape than on the large screen. They're meant to be viewed, enjoyed, and savored numerous times, like good pieces of music. ▽

NATIONAL LAMPOON'S ANIMAL HOUSE. US. 1978. I know why I liked this movie: it seems to have been shot on location at my college just about the time I was there. Its scenes of fraternity life are uncannily accurate, and I think that's why it was such a success. It's exactly the kind of humor we used to perpetrate at Alpha Tau Omega back in 1962. College humor, which has been a mainstay of the British stage and television for many years, bubbles above the surface only seldom in the US. It hasn't been done as well as it is done in *Animal House* for a long while. Ivan Reitman produced, John Landis directed, John Belushi starred. ▽

NATIVE LAND. US. 1942. The Frontier Films

Organization produced this landmark political tract which never did receive a very wide distribution, probably because of its politics. It uses a combination of documentary and fictional techniques to make a passionate statement against anti-Union activity in the US during the preceding years. Leo Hurwitz and Paul Strand are credited with direction. Paul Robeson did some of the commentary and Marc Blitzstein did the music. You don't see films like this very often in the US and it's instructive to compare *Native Land* with the kind of natural propaganda Hollywood was putting out at the time. Hollywood probably did it better.

NATURAL, THE. US. 1984. Barry Levinson's interesting film version of the classic Malamud novel celebrating the mystery of baseball, America's national sport, gives Robert Redford his best role in ten years. Run it on a double bill with *DAMN YANKEES*.

NAVIGATOR, THE. US. 1924. A classic Buster Keaton collection of gags. He's a rich man stuck on a boat with only Kathryn MacGuire as company: no food, no water, no domestic help, only his own wits to guide him.

NETWORK. US. 1976. In films like *Hospital* and *Network*, playwright Paddy Chayefsky was making some rather strident comments on contemporary institutions and audiences, given the chance to yell vicariously, found the films entertaining. Faye Dunaway and William Holden are the television executives. Peter Finch is the crazy newscaster who gets us all to shout out our windows and builds his ratings to monumental proportions in the process. The film might have had a greater political effect if it were a little more laid back. The fact is although "we're mad as hell," we *are* going to take it anymore.

NEVER CRY WOLF. US. 1983. This is the more or less true story of a Canadian named Farley Mowat who set up shop in the Arctic to study wolves. Produced by Disney, it's an interesting continuation of the nature themes begun in the 1950s. Carroll Ballard directed Charles Martin Smith.

NEVER GIVE A SUCKER AN EVEN BREAK. US. 1941. This is W. C. Fields's last big movie and one of his best. There's no discernible plot, thank God, but he and Margaret Dumont, Franklin Pangborne, and Leon Errol have a wonderful time and a car chase to rival Harold Lloyd.

The "It" Girl—Clara Bow—in *It*, directed by Clarence Badger.

§ **NEVER ON SUNDAY**. Greece. 1960. Jules Dassin directed and starred with his wife Melina Mercouri in this American vision of Greek cliches. He is the intellectual; she is the prostitute he tries to reform. See it with *ZORBA* if you want to overdose on Ouzu and sweet coffee.

NEVER SAY NEVER AGAIN. UK. 1983. Irvin Kershner over-directed Sean Connery in a return to the role of James Bond after a dozen-year absence. It's a nice Bond film, but nothing special except for the spectacle of an aging Connery in the heroic role. Connery and Roger Moore are about the same age but Moore has kept his looks in a way that Hollywood stars of the Golden Age would envy.

NEVERENDING STORY, THE. West Germany. 1984. An unusual and fascinating movie for kids, directed by Wolfgang Petersen in English, combining fantasy with sophisticated moral feelings. A young boy imagines that he becomes the hero he is reading about. This is *He-Man* with soul.

NEW LAND, THE. Sweden. 1973. Also called *The Immigrants*, this is the sequel to *THE EMIGRANTS*. See *THE EMIGRANTS*.

‖ **NEW LEAF, A**. US. 1970. I don't suppose this is really a superior film but the spectacle of the money-hungry Walter Matthau attempting to deal with an incredibly sloppy Elaine May stays in the mind for a long time: two great comic talents rather well matched. In their improvised routines of the late fifties, Elaine May and Mike Nichols produced some brilliant work that remains for us only on records. Their separate film careers since have been haunted by our memory of their earlier careers on stage. May directed and wrote this film and it comes closer than any to recreating the May/Nichols magic.

NEW YORK HAT, THE. US. 1912. Anita Loos wrote the screenplay for this famous D. W. Griffith Biograph one-reeler. In a small town, Lionel Barrymore wants to buy a fancy hat for Mary Pickford and is subject to the accusations of the quaintly puritanical townsfolk.

NEWSFRONT. Australia. 1978. Phillip Noyce made this unique hommage to newsreel cameramen of the forties and fifties. The people don't do much, but the subject is so fascinating that it holds your interest and the newsreel footage integrated into the story is interesting.

NEXT STOP, GREENWICH VILLAGE. US. 1976. As a kid, director Paul Mazursky started out in Village nightclubs as a standup comic. This film is his sensitive, precisely remembered hommage to the Greenwich Village of the 1950s, home of hipsters and the Beats and the kids from the suburbs, awe-struck with books and movies, art and politics. Lenny Baker and Christopher Walken star. Baker is the Brooklyn boy very much like Mazursky who moves to the Village to get into the theater. Shelley Winters is his archetypal mother, Walken his sensitive friend. It's not what happens here that counts so much as the attention to detail. Mazursky has made the Village of 1976 an eerie duplication of the Village of the fifties. There's something to be said for a very local filmmaker. Nearly all of Mazursky's movies have at least a few scenes in Greenwich Village where he's lived, at least part-time, for the last thirty years; and he keeps finding new truths about the old streets. Every town or neighborhood should have a Mazursky. Show it on a double bill with *SHADOWS*.

NIAGARA. US. 1952. Henry Hathaway directed this murder mystery with Marilyn Monroe and Joseph Cotten as the honeymoon couple. One of Monroe's most interesting roles.

NICHOLAS NICKLEBY. UK. 1947. One of the

best Dickens adaptations of the late forties (when they were so common) was directed by Alberto Cavalcanti. The recent Royal Shakespeare Company's eight-hour plus staging of the novel was a landmark. Watch this one only when you don't have the time for the newer version.

NIGHT AND FOG. France. 1955. Alain Resnais's 31-minute film about concentration camps is probably the best film on that subject ever made and proves conclusively that length is not a virtue in the cinema. By intercutting peaceful, contemporary scenes at the camps now overgrown with weeds with the dramatic historical footage we've seen elsewhere, the film is, if anything, more shocking than those that concentrate only on history. It was also a cause celebre banned from the Cannes Film Festival in 1956 because of a shot which clearly indicated French complicity in the Nazi regime. Only after the shot was altered was the film allowed to be released. See *THE SORROW AND THE PITY*.

NIGHT AT THE OPERA, A. US. 1935. The perfect Marx Brothers film is awarded three Marxes, a Dumont, and two hard-boiled eggs.

NIGHT OF THE HUNTER, THE. US. 1955. Robert Mitchum is interesting as a psychotic here in a very allegorical film listed mainly because it was written by critic James Agee and directed by actor Charles Laughton and Lillian Gish appeared: quite a combination.

NIGHT OF THE SHOOTING STARS, THE. Italy. 1982. Vittorio and Paolo Taviani directed this mesmerizing account of a village in Tuscany during the final days of World War II. It seems to star the entire village as they move in a group trying to deal with the retreating Germans and the advancing Americans. In the process it reveals much of the best in the Italian character.

NIGHT TO REMEMBER, A. UK. 1958. Roy Baker directed this most realistic and monumental disaster movie about the Titanic. It stars Kenneth More and a bunch of young English actors who later went on to fame and fortune—including David McCallum, Honor Blackman, Alec McCowen, and George Rose.

NIGHT TRAIN TO MUNICH. UK. 1940. Carol Reed directed another winning script by Launder and Gilliat. It's a complex and snappy thriller—a wartime espionage drama—of which Hitchcock might have been proud and employs a host of fine actors including Basil Radford and Naunton Wayne as the twits you may remember from *THE LADY VANISHES* (also by Launder and Gilliat).

⊘ **NIGHTS OF CABIRIA**. Italy. 1956. A companion piece to *LA STRADA*, Fellini's *Nights of Cabiria* focuses entirely on Giulietta Masina. This time the waif is a prostitute, not necessarily with a heart of gold, but definitely with hope and spirit enough for dozens of us. When she walks down the road, the reference to Chaplin is pointed and moving.

⊘ **NINOTCHKA**. US. 1939. The great Garbo movie magnificently mounted by Ernst Lubitsch with a script by Billy Wilder and others. She's a cold Russian commissar who falls for the west, Paris, and Melvyn Douglas, not necessarily in that order. Compare it with the remake, *SILK STOCKINGS*. ▣

⚑ **NOBODY WAVED GOODBYE**. Canada. 1965. Here's a landmark Canadian road movie by Don Owen starring Peter Kastner as the kid who leaves home on an odyssey. Compare this with Coppola's *YOU'RE A BIG BOY NOW* in which Kastner reprised the juvenile role. It's the difference between Canadian realism and Hollywood movie-making.

✳\§ **NORTH BY NORTHWEST**. US. 1959. Alfred Hitchcock was at the height of his powers here and this is probably his best film. The script by Ernest Lehman has exactly the right balance between comedy and drama, romance and thrills. It also has political implications that I'm sure neither Hitchcock nor Lehman were fully aware of at the time. Twenty-five years later each scene seems filled with political commentary that we didn't hear back in 1959. Cary Grant is erstwhile agent Roger O. Thornhill. ("What does the O. stand for?" "Nothing.") It's the government against the people and the government is not entirely to be trusted. "FBI, CIA. . . what's the difference? We're all in the same alphabet soup!" Cinematically nearly every scene is a film school course, from the murder at the U.N. right on through the Illinois cornfields ("That's funny. That plane's dustin' crops where there ain't no crops!") up to the famous Mount Rushmore scene. This is the film in which The Man in the Gray Flannel Suit symbolically left the quietistic fifties forever behind and entered the activist sixties. ▣

⊘⌂ **NORTH DALLAS FORTY**. US. 1979. Nick

Nolte, Mac Davis, Charles Durning, and G. D. Spradlin (as a dead ringer for Dallas Cowboys coach Tom Landry) in Ted Kotcheff's film of the Peter Gent book about contemporary professional football. Nolte and Davis confront with considerable humor the occupational hazards of the professional sports star in the seventies and eighties: the drugs, the computerized coaches, the exploitative owners, the damage to the body and approaching age, and even the groupies. It's a dead heat between *SLAPSHOT* and *NORTH DALLAS FORTY* for sports film of the decade. ☒

NOSFERATU. Germany. 1922. F. W. Murnau's vampire was never bettered in the scores of vampire films that followed it. This is one of those early silent films that expresses clearly the ebullience of the new film medium. Murnau seems to be making stylistic discoveries in every sequence. ☒

NOSFERATU THE VAMPYRE. West Germany. 1979. Werner Herzog directed less a remake than an hommage to the Murnau classic (see above) starring Klaus Kinski and Isabelle Adjani. It's an interesting gloss on the theme.

NOTHING BUT A MAN. US. 1964. Ivan Dixon, Abbey Lincoln, and Gloria Foster star in this quiet, simple, and absorbing movie about a Black man in the south who tries to stand up to "the Man." Michael Roemer directed, Robert Young produced. I suppose we see movies like this every couple of months or so on TV now, but in the mid-sixties this was a landmark: a mainstream Black movie.

NOTHING BUT THE BEST. UK. 1964. A very stylish satire written by playwright Fredric Raphael and directed by Clive Donner with Alan Bates, Denholm Elliott, and Harry Andrews. This is the swinging London of the mid-sixties as seen by one of England's leading novelist/screenwriters. More fun than his *DARLING*.

NOTORIOUS. US. 1946. Alfred Hitchcock directs Cary Grant and Ingrid Bergman in a good spy story by Ben Hecht set in Brazil. Grant and Bergman take time out to perform what is reputedly the longest kiss in film history since the John Rice-May Irwin film *The Kiss* in the late nineties, famous to film school students. ☒

NOTTE, LA. Italy. 1962. This is lesser Michelangelo Antonioni but still worth taking a look at for the abstract existential style that had such an effect on "art" cinema in the early sixties. Jeanne Moreau is the bored wife; Marcello Mastroianni is the almost equally bored husband. Monica Vitti also stars.

⇪ **NOUS SOMMES TOUS DES ASSASSINS**. France. 1952. During the 1950s, lawyer André Cayatte directed a series of films with a moral and political punch to them which remains unique. There was no question watching a Cayatte film that the aim of the fiction was simply and directly to illustrate a political point. This one happens to be a treatise against capital punishment. The films were surprisingly popular, proving—although few noticed—that politics and ideas can sell at the box office. Charles Spaak assisted on the screenplay. See *TO DIE OF LOVE*.

⇪ **NOW ABOUT ALL THESE WOMEN!** Sweden. 1970. Right after the extraordinary series of neurotic classics of the sixties, Ingmar Bergman directed this ostensible comedy with autobiographical overtones. The artist hero is surrounded by a bunch of women, even as Bergman always was. It's so rare that Bergman ventures into comedy that he deserves to be encouraged. No, it's not all that funny, but you have to remember where he's coming from.

◉ **NOW VOYAGER**. US. 1942. "The women's film" apotheosized. Bette Davis stars as the incredibly introverted spinster who takes a cruise and falls in love with Paul Henreid. Maybe it was the cigarettes. ▼

NUMERO DEUX. France. 1975. It's not important that Jean-Luc Godard isn't making great movies any more. It's important that he's still making movies. *Numéro Deux*, which came after a series of experiments on videotape and the Dziga-Vertov period during which he dedicated himself to "political" film, marks his re-entrance into the quasi-commercial cinema. It reprises a lot of the themes of the previous seven years more accessibly.

◉ **NUTTY PROFESSOR, THE**. US. 1963. Jerry Lewis directed himself here as a nerdy college professor who has the ability to transform himself into the King of Swingers. Is this Lewis's revenge against the Rat Pack that had taken in his former partner Dean Martin and was reigning supreme at the time? This is the film French scholars of Jerry Lewis regard as his masterpiece.

⚠§ **O LUCKY MAN!** UK. 1973. The second of Lindsay Anderson's Malcolm McDowell trilogy is by far the best. It's allegorical (like its predecessor *IF. . .*): the story of the rise, fall, and rise of a young, ambitious salesman. It's got a fine score by Alan Price, proving once again the inestimable value of music to movies. ▽

OCCASIONAL WORK OF A FEMALE SLAVE. West Germany. 1974. Alexander Kluge, one of the founders of New German Cinema, made this film with his sister Alexandra. It's a fictional film that uses many of the techniques of documentary to study the life of an ordinary woman and at the time it was an important feminist statement— probably still is.

OCTOBER. USSR. 1928. Sergei Eisenstein's epic account of the Russian revolution was loosely based on John Reed's *Ten Days That Shook the World*. It's a mostly effective propaganda piece in which Eisenstein catalogued many of his cinematic concerns and techniques.

⚠‼ **ODD COUPLE, THE.** US. 1968. Gene Saks directed this definitive film of the Neil Simon play with Jack Lemmon and Walter Matthau as the fussy Felix and the sloppy Oscar. Simon has hit on a set of characters here that's going to enter the mythology: they've already been through two television series. ▽

⚠ **ODD MAN OUT.** UK. 1947. Another classic by the often underrated Carol Reed stars James Mason in the story of an Irish rebel leader on the run during the uprising. One of the most suspenseful movies ever made.

§ **ODDS AGAINST TOMORROW**. US. 1959. Robert Wise directed an unusual cast including Robert Ryan, Shelley Winters, Harry Belafonte, and Gloria Grahame in a breathless gangster story with an excellent jazz score by Miles Davis.

OF MICE AND MEN. US. 1939. Lon Chaney Jr. and Burgess Meredith in the classic film version of the John Steinbeck novel about the US underclass in the 1930s. Lewis Milestone directed.

OFFICER AND A GENTLEMAN, AN. US. 1982. Debra Winger is a real star; she's halfway to renown in *An Officer and a Gentleman*. She's the main attraction in what otherwise is a very strange movie: a fifties melodrama with all its cliches set in the eighties. Lou Gossett does a good job as the old fashioned drill sergeant. Richard Gere holds his own, but second in interest to Winger is probably the Seattle seashore. We are too intellectual about films now to review the scenery, but filmmakers know that very often the stuff in the background can lend unwarranted life and interest to the faces in the foreground. Check out this principle in *An Officer and a Gentleman*. ▽

OH! WHAT A LOVELY WAR. UK. 1969. Joan Littlewood's Brechtian theatrical extravaganza was filmed by Richard Attenborough with an all-star cast including Olivier, Gielgud, Richardson, Redgrave, John Mills, Vanessa Redgrave, Dirk Bogarde, Susannah York, Maggie Smith, and Kenneth More. It's interesting to approach anti-war drama through a bunch of musical scenes dealing with vignettes of World War I, but it was more important as a stage production than a film.

OKLAHOMA! US. 1955. The Rodgers and Hammerstein landmark musical as filmed by Fred Zinnemann is a better musical than a movie. It's studio-bound rather than location-free as the subject might suggest but it's got Gordon MacRae, Shirley Jones, Rod Steiger, and Gloria Grahame and the garish color is a hallmark of the mid-fifties. Agnes DeMille's choreography is preserved here for the future. "Oh what a beautiful morning!" ▽

OLD DARK HOUSE, THE. US. 1932. Another winner from James Whale, with Boris Karloff, Melvyn Douglas, and Charles Laughton. Karloff is the brooding butler; the rest are stuck in the house. Based on a J. B. Priestley novel.

OLIVER! UK. 1968. Carol Reed mounted the long-running Lionel Bart musical version of the Dickens novel with Ron Moody as Fagin, Oliver Reed, Mark Lester, and the always interesting Harry Secombe. Or. . .

OLIVER TWIST. UK. 1948. . . . If you prefer your Dickens straight, take this version by David Lean, with Alec Guinness (Fagin), Robert Newton, and a young Anthony Newley.

OLYMPIAD. Germany. 1936. Although it's seldom in evidence in commercial filmmaking, the relationship between sports and the film medium is crucial. Forget the acting, forget the scenery, forget the dialogue for a while. Watching great athletes perform more than justifies the invention of this recording medium. Controversial filmmaker Leni Riefenstahl was not the first to recognize the symbiotic relationship between sports and film, but her record of the 1936 Berlin Olympics remains a model for all who came after. Since that time most Olympic games have been commemorated by feature film records, but recently television coverage has been so extensive that the films seem almost beside the point. When Jesse Owens's daughter entered the stadium in Los Angeles in the summer of 1984 we were pointedly reminded of the hidden drama in Riefenstahl's movie: it was Jesse Owens with his success in the Berlin games who struck an early symbolic blow against Hitler. ∨

ON GOLDEN POND. US. 1981. Not a very good film but a great performance by Henry Fonda (his last), teamed with Katharine Hepburn (for the first time) and his daughter Jane in an often cloying drama of family relationships. Compare Fonda and Hepburn here with James Stewart and Bette Davis in *RIGHT OF WAY*. ∨

ON THE BEACH. US. 1959. Stanley Kramer directed Fred Astaire, Ava Gardner, Gregory Peck, and Anthony Perkins in this early and effective anti-nuclear war drama. It takes place in Australia. The rest of the world has been destroyed and the survivors are waiting for the other shoe to drop. ∨

ON THE TOWN. US. 1945. Another lively and refreshing Betty Comden and Adolph Green musical. This time they work with Leonard Bernstein. Gene Kelly, Frank Sinatra, and Jules Munshin are the sailors on the town in the Big Apple. Kelly and Stanley Donen co-directed this landmark of location color filming in New York City. "New York, New York, it's a wonderful town. The Bronx is up and the Battery's down. The people ride in a hole in the ground." ∨

ON THE WATERFRONT. US. 1954. At the time the critical appreciation of *On the Waterfront* was somewhat obscured by the politics of the fifties, but clear away the ideological fog and what remains is one of the great movies of the post-war era. Elia Kazan directed the Budd Schulberg script. Marlon Brando was at the height of his powers as the longshoreman and sometime boxer who "coulda been a contender." Character actors Karl Malden, Lee J. Cobb, and Rod Steiger turned in superior performances. Eva Marie Saint was the girl. It was actually shot mainly in Hoboken, New Jersey, but that's still the port of New York after all and it's a landmark of on-location photography (by Boris Kaufman, brother of Russian filmmaker Dziga Vertov). ▽

⬤ ONCE UPON A TIME IN AMERICA. US. 1984. Once again it's interesting to watch a foreign director at work in the US dealing with an American genre, this time the gangster film. Robert DeNiro and James Woods, Elizabeth McGovern and Tuesday Weld star in this lengthy example of the genre by Sergio Leone. ▽

⬤ ONCE UPON A TIME IN THE WEST. Italy/US. 1969. After his successful introduction of the spaghetti western, with a mostly Italian cast, Sergio Leone had a chance to Americanize the genre by using a greater number of American actors. Henry Fonda, Charles Bronson, Jason Robards and others contribute here. It's an unusual mixture of national approaches. ▽

ONE-EYED JACKS. US. 1961. Marlon Brando's only directorial effort is a curiosity: an unusual western starring Brando and Karl Malden as former friends now on opposite sides of the law. ▽

⇓ ONE FLEW OVER THE CUCKOO'S NEST. US. 1975. Miloš Forman's version of the popular 1960s Ken Kesey novel about the oppression of a mental hospital is more than a bit forced and formulaic by 1975 but has excellent performances by Jack Nicholson and a large supporting cast. ▽

§ ONE HUNDRED MEN AND A GIRL. US. 1937. Deanna Durbin is an acquired taste. Look at it this way: she's not Shirley Temple. Henry Koster directed this Durbin vehicle. Leopold Stokowski and Orchestra also star.

⬤ ONE MORE RIVER. US. 1934. James Whale directed this film version of a John Galsworthy novel about the social mores of divorce in the twenties, with a bunch of English actors, including the legendary Mrs. Patrick Campbell.

⬤‖ 1, 2, 3. US. 1962. One of Billy Wilder's best, this marked James Cagney's farewell appearance (before *RAGTIME*). It's a classic thirties screwball comedy in sixties garb and therefore of interest to anyone who cares about genres. It starts at a high pitch and moves breathlessly from beginning to end. A real tour de force of comic pacing—something like a piece of music by Aram Khatchurian. Noteworthy, too, is the cold war Berlin locale.

ONLY ANGELS HAVE WINGS. US. 1939. An often overlooked and underrated Howard Hawks film, with Cary Grant and Jean Arthur battling it out. (He's a pilot, she's an entertainer.) As usual in Hawks, she proves as tough as he.

OPEN CITY. Italy. 1945. This is the clarion call of the Neorealist movement shot on the desolate streets of Rome just after the German armies had retreated. Roberto Rossellini scrounged out-of-date film stock and enlisted non-actors to re-enact one of the Roman people's battles with the Gestapo during .the occupation. Anna Magnani and Aldo Fabrizzi are the professionals here. The "Neorealism" of the film was almost certainly more a matter of practicality than theory, but you have only to see a few minutes of *Open City* to realize the potential power of the style. The faces and settings are so various and alive that your attention is riveted to the screen. And the emotions behind the film are so deep-rooted that they carry you along. Fellini contributed to the script. ▩

ORDINARY PEOPLE. US. 1980. Of all the actors who've turned to directing in the last few years, Robert Redford probably had the greatest commercial success with this rather cold and certainly downbeat version of the Judith Guest novel. The film itself is far too much like Mary Tyler Moore's repressed central character to be a really good one, and it's too much in the old American tradition of "serious" filmmaking to be enjoyable. Watching *Ordinary People* you remember that there is no really superior movie that isn't basically, at least in part, in one way or another, a comedy. ▩

ORGANIZER, THE. Italy. 1964. Mario Monicelli directed this film about a labor organizer in the early years of this century, played by Marcello Mastroianni, in an unusually serious and ambitious role for that actor at the time. It's still a good essay on the subject, in the Neorealist tradition.

ORPHANS OF THE STORM. US. 1922. The Gish sisters, Dorothy and Lillian, pull out all the stops in this late D. W. Griffith feature. They're wonderful to watch, even in the mishmash of Victorian melodramatic sequences that Griffith has created to illustrate this story of separated sisters, united by their pathos.

OTHER SIDE OF THE WIND, THE. US. 19??

Orson Welles has been at work on this film, apparently, for the last fifteen years. Footage has been shot, editing has taken place, and numerous articles have been written about *The Other Side of the Wind* during that lengthy period. This sort of schedule is not unusual in the other arts. You can think of a number of novels, poems, symphonies, and even paintings, that never quite get finished. In film, such an expensive undertaking, unfinished projects are rare indeed. *The Other Side of the Wind* has become a great "unfinished movie." Does Welles realize this? Let's hope he keeps the fires of publicity smoldering but never releases the film. Then, a good number of years from now after he's gone, we can unearth the remnants to celebrate his career.

OUR DAILY BREAD. US. 1934. King Vidor produced and directed this Depression classic independently. It's about a farming cooperative started by a couple from the city who have moved to the country to forge a new life, and it celebrates exuberantly the thrill all country people know of controlling your own destiny. While everyone else was off at the movies watching unnaturally rich little girls hitchhike home from Florida, King Vidor was trying to suggest an alternative life that would last longer than an hour-and-a-half at the movies.

OUR HITLER: A FILM FROM GERMANY. West Germany. 1980. In Europe intellectual culture is protected—almost like an endangered species— because it has a well-marked role in the political scheme of things (even if that position is honored more in the breach than in the observance). In America, however, intellectuals have never been protected by the myths that support them in Europe. They've had to struggle long and hard for acceptance. The fifties was the recent nadir, a time when anybody with a Masters degree was considered an un-American egghead. For thirty years thereafter, American intellectuals have been slowly climbing the ladder of respectability. They did make a significant mess of things in the late 1960s when they failed to provide any sort of coherent progressive ideology for what was then known as the New Left. But that's okay. Nobody noticed. We all blamed it on the kids. In the seventies while no one was looking, they eased nicely and neatly into the Washington political establishment, and by the early eighties you could even watch Jerzy Kosinski sucking up to Johnny Carson on *The Tonight Show*. Then something like this *Our Hitler* comes along and sets back the cause many years. The film became a brief intellectual cause celebre early in the eighties

when Susan Sontag wrote at length about it and
Francis Coppola decided to sponsor showings of this
seven-hour collection of stagey soliloquies, false
starts, and rationalizations that we would regard as
pretentious if it weren't so utterly dumb. We're not
blaming director Hans-Jürgen Syberberg. If he can
get the money, let him fool around like this. We're
not blaming Coppola. He's never claimed to be an
intellectual; he's an artist. Sontag and the American
intelligentsia have to bear the brunt of moral
responsibility here. *Our Hitler*—or more precisely,
the critical hype of it—makes you want to cancel
your subscription to *The New York Review of Books*
and run out and join the Rotary. The only salutary
effect may be that we'll be less likely in the future to
confuse intellectualism with intelligence.

OUR TOWN. US. 1940. Sam Wood directed this
version of the Thornton Wilder classic play about
the multiple relationships among the folks in a small
New England town. The "our town" genre—studies
of the relationships that mold a community—became
a welcome staple of the movies. Give Wilder credit
for establishing an important form.

OUT OF THE PAST. US. 1947. Here's a great, if
little known, film noir with Robert Mitchum and
Kirk Douglas, directed by Jacques Tourneur. All the
elements are here: the fatalism, fast cars and loose
women, and the gangster setting. Mitchum tries to
escape them without success. This film is so aware of
its style it could pass for French.

OUTLAND. US. 1981. The first science fiction/film
noir/western of the eighties can be seen as a gloss on
the bar scene in *STAR WARS*, the most original
thing in that film. Sean Connery is the Marshall on
one of Jupiter's moons sometime in the next century.
It's mild fun to watch him clean up the corrupt
plastic planet.

PADDY THE NEXT BEST THING. US. 1933.
Harry Lachman directed this programmer with
Janet Gaynor and Warner Baxter—a romantic
comedy that's a model of early screwball.

PADRE, PADRONE. Italy. 1977. The Taviani
brothers, Paolo and Vittorio, struck an important
chord with this post-Neorealist version of the
autobiography of Gavino Ledda, a Sardinian peasant
boy who pulled himself up by his own bootstraps to
enter the twentieth century and become educated.
It's an important Italian theme and the Tavianis' use
of nonprofessional actors gives it a freshness that

successfully counters the threat of cliche.   ▽

⊘ **PAISAN**. Italy. 1946. Roberto Rossellini followed up the quick success of *OPEN CITY* with what is for him a more typical film. Six episodes trace the progress of the invading American army up the Italian peninsula. The relationship between the Italians and the Americans is still fascinating and the emphasis on the human scale of the war still impressive.   ▽

§ **PAJAMA GAME, THE**. US. 1957. Stanley Donen and George Abbott directed this film of the famous fifties Broadway musical about life on the assembly line and off, starring Doris Day, John Raitt, and Carol Haney. It's memorable especially for Bob Fosse's choreography and some good show tunes redolent of the mid-fifties.

⊹║⇧ **PALM BEACH STORY, THE**. US. 1942. Preston Sturges at full tilt, with Claudette Colbert and Joel McCrea, Rudy Vallee, and Mary Astor. Joel is a crazy young architect who has dreams of building a magnificent airport. Claudette is his adoring wife who runs away to Palm Beach with the Ale and Quail Club and meets Rudy the incredibly normal zillionaire J. D. Hackensacker III who of course falls in love with her. Rudy's sister, Mary, falls for Joel. In the end all's set right again and each Jack has his Jill. It's hard to describe Sturges's special brand of comedy. Perhaps it's realistic farce. He takes a perfectly natural action and lets it run on just too long to the point of slight but affectionate absurdity. You won't soon forget these actors and you'll be surprised to discover what a nice fellow Rudy Vallee was.

⊹╍ **PANDORA'S BOX**. Germany. 1928. G. W. Pabst directed this mythic silent version of the Lulu story, starring Louise Brooks. If you've never seen Brooks on the screen you'll be surprised at her beauty—and sexuality. For anyone under sixty, film history seems to begin in the early 1930s with the advent of sound. Unconsciously we draw the conclusion—and it seems a logical one—that attitudes toward sexuality and lifestyles have gradually "matured" over the years. We think of ourselves now as more advanced and sophisticated than earlier generations. It's a shock then to discover that much of what we think of as "contemporary" culture, from sex to drugs to politics to language, existed full-blown in the 1920s. In terms of sexual attitudes, *Pandora's Box* is a revealing landmark. Don't dismiss its seeming sophistication as purely European, the attitudes were

James Stewart as Harry Bailey just after his guardian angel Henry Travers has saved his life in Frank Capra's *It's a Wonderful Life.*

apparent in a number of American films at the time. If Louise Brooks had an American counterpart it was Clara Bow.

PAPER CHASE, THE. US. 1973. James Bridges struck a rich vein with this film about life at Harvard Law School. Although college and professional school is a common experience, it's not often treated with such detail on film. *The Paper Chase* made John Houseman a star late in life after an extraordinary career as a producer. Timothy Bottoms and Lindsay Wagner lead a fine cast of young actors. This is the model for films like it for the next ten years. ▽

PAPER MOON. US. 1973. It's not often that father and daughter get to star together in a movie and for that reason alone *Paper Moon* might be notable. This is the film that introduced Ryan's daughter, Tatum O'Neal, in a likeable story of a man and a little girl on the road in the thirties. But it's also a rather good attempt on the part of director Peter Bogdanovich to pay homage to the comic thirties road movie. ▽

PARIS BELONGS TO US. France. 1960. Jacques Rivette was responsible for this portrait of Paris intellectuals at the dawn of the New Wave. It's rather pretentious when viewed today but it was important at the time as the image of a new generation of French intelligentsia.

PARIS, TEXAS. US. 1984. For aficionados of foreign perspectives on America here's another shaggy, forlorn, but ingratiating Wim Wenders road movie, this time set in the plains and cities of Texas and the suburban hills of Los Angeles. It's a curious story about fathers and sons, husbands and wives, that will stay with you for a while after you leave the theater. Harry Dean Stanton stars with Dean Stockwell and Nastassja Kinski.

PARTIE DE CAMPAGNE, UN. France. 1936. This half-hour movie by Jean Renoir is among his best work. It's based on a Maupassant story and gives us an idyllic day in the country during which a girl and her mother are both seduced to ironic counterpoint. It's as close as Jean Renoir ever got to the romantic images that we have from his father, Auguste. It was shot by Jean's nephew, Claude Renoir, and is thus very much a family affair. Renoir had trouble finishing shooting the film and it wasn't completed and released until ten years later. We're fortunate it was.

PASSE TON BAC D'ABORD. France. 1979. Maurica Pialat (see *ME* and *WE WON'T GROW OLD TOGETHER*) in a lighter vein, focusing on a group of French schoolchildren. Sabine Haudepin, the little girl from *JULES AND JIM* now grown-up, stars.

PASSENGER, THE. Italy. 1975. What was striking about Michelangelo Antonioni's work in the 1960s seemed less interesting when he did it again ten years later. Here he's working in English with Jack Nicholson and Maria Schneider as "the girl." It has one great famous shot at the end in which in a long, slow track the camera moves from inside a hotel room to the street outside despite the very physical fact of iron bars on the windows.

PASSION OF ANNA, THE. Sweden. 1969. One of Ingmar Bergman's sad, neurotic, but beautiful island movies of the late sixties with Liv Ullmann, Bibi Andersson, Max von Sydow, and Erland Josephson. Put four human beings in a social laboratory like Bergman's beloved island and strange and sometimes interesting things happen.

PASSION OF JOAN OF ARC, THE. France. 1928. Not really a good film but a landmark. Director Carl Theodor Dreyer broke new ground with this stark portrait of the obsessive Joan. The images are striking. Long closeups, fancy tracking shots, and pans. But the drama is much less successful. It's a silent film that tries to deal with complex issues, and that's difficult.

＼‖ PASSPORT TO PIMLICO. UK. 1949. Here's a classic Ealing comedy, directed by Henry Cornelius and starring Stanley Holloway, Margaret Rutherford, and a host of favorites. The idea is simple and intriguing. Pimlico, a neighborhood of London, declares its independence from Great Britain and we watch the neighbors set up national housekeeping. It's interesting that despite the lip service we pay to nations and patriotism, we realize our gut loyalties are really with the neighborhood.

◬＼ PAT AND MIKE. US. 1952. Spencer Tracy and Katharine Hepburn take their enduring and always entertaining relationship into the sports world. She's an athlete, he's her trainer. Ruth Gordon and Garson Kanin wrote the script. George Cukor directed.

◥◬ PATHER PANCHALI. India. 1955. The first in Satyajit Ray's Apu trilogy quietly and intently studies a family in the grip of poverty. Later episodes—*APARAJITO* and *THE WORLD OF APU*—continued this fascinating portrait of the strength and complexity of Indian family life. *Pather Panchali* marks the debut of Indian cinema in the west; it won awards at film festivals in the mid-fifties. Ravi Shankar, who introduced westerners to the music of the sitar in the sixties, wrote the score. ▽

✛◈ PATHS OF GLORY. US. 1959. Stanley Kubrick's first great movie established the epic style that has served him so well since. This is a harrowing and still very effective anti-war film set during the first World War, starring Kirk Douglas, Ralph Meeker, and Adolphe Menjou. The split between officers and men has never been so sharply delineated. Three soldiers are court-martialed unjustly as an example and Kirk Douglas, the officer charged with their defense, can't get them off. The film was banned in parts of Europe when it first appeared for its anti-militarist stance. ▽

◬◈ PATTON. US. 1970. What *PATHS OF GLORY* attempted to show about the relationships between officers and men of the first World War, *Patton* in part attempts to do for the second. Patton, of course, is best remembered as the General who slapped a soldier. But George C. Scott, under the direction of Franklin Schaffner, creates a much more colorful and ambiguous portrait. Patton's eccentricity may very well have been an important ingredient of victory. You don't win wars by being reasonable or compassionate. *Patton* is a war movie of unusual depth. The screenplay was by Francis Coppola and Edmund H. North. ▣

∨‼ **PAULINE AT THE BEACH**. France. 1983. Eric Rohmer returned to the moral and philosophical concerns of the contes moreaux in the and early eighties. This one contrasts the simplicity of the sexual relationships of young people with the much more complex and naughty attitudes of their elders. It's infused with the same human intelligence that makes Rohmer's films taken together a unique and superior body of work. For twenty years he has been celebrating the better part of ourselves—our ability to think and act ethically and morally—while at the same time he gently parodies our excesses in this regard. His films are not only infectious comedies, they are also restorative tonics.

◉ **PAWNBROKER, THE**. US. 1965. Sidney Lumet's dark study of Sol Nazerman, a refugee from the Holocaust trying to survive the remainder of his life in Harlem, is still a gripping drama of memory and courage. The film is based on the novel by Edward Lewis Wallant. Boris Kaufman photographed in black and white. ▣

§ **PENNIES FROM HEAVEN**. US. 1981. This is a failed experiment but an interesting one nevertheless. It's based on the British TV series of the same name which, in most respects, was more successful. Steve Martin plays a sheet-music salesman in the 1930s. Bernadette Peters, Christopher Walken, and Jessica Harper also star. The songs that Martin sells are full of love and hope. His life is quite the opposite. The actors mouth the lyrics as we hear the original recordings. The photography by Gordon Willis is fitting and evocative of the styles of the 1930s, especially Edward Hopper. ▣

⇪ **PENTHOUSE**. US. 1933. An unsung comedy by W. S. Van Dyke starring Warner Baxter and Myrna Loy. He's a lawyer; she's a lady of the night. There are dozens of good little movies like this from the 1930s, the welcome surprises that reward you for prospecting among the programmers.

◉👁 **PEPPERMINT SODA**. France. 1977. In a sense, this is *THE 400 BLOWS* for girls. Director Diane Kurys shows a sure hand telling a mainly autobiographical story about puberty with all of the elements.

PERFECT COUPLE, A. US. 1979. Late Robert Altman, but good Altman nevertheless. Paul Dooley and Marta Heflin are the title couple and of course they're not perfect at all. He's incredibly stuffy; she's a would-be rock 'n' roll star. It gives Altman a chance to explore a gallery of weird but pleasant characters. You have to know that he doesn't take the eccentricities seriously. Good music.

PERMUTATIONS. US. 1970. John Whitney and his brother James have been important figures in abstract film since the early 1940s, responsible for many technical experiments that later yielded much fruit in commercial cinema. Most important was their early and effective use of computer techniques in abstract filmmaking. John Whitney hooked the optical printer directly to the computer for this landmark short and it's a fascinating visual experience if you're not jaded by the abstract computer images that bombard us daily today. Despite the enormous advances in the technology during the last fifteen years, no one has really done this stuff better than the Whitneys.

PERSONA. Sweden. 1966. This is Ingmar Bergman's chaste exploration of psychosis. It's not a horror story but a poem, and remarkable for that. Liv Ullmann is the actress who stops talking in the middle of her performance. Bibi Andersson is the nurse who cares for her, gradually becoming one with the patient. The shot of the two faces merged near the end of the film is one of the great images of cinema.

PERSONAL BEST. US. 1982. Legendary screenwriter Robert (*SHAMPOO*) Towne turned to directing with this unusual and absorbing portrait of women athletes. Mariel Hemingway and Patrice Donnelly are competing runners who also happen to have an affair. The sex may be there as a crowd pleaser but it is a real part of the athletic scene and it makes these characters more than just physical machines. The attention to detail is exceptional here. You can smell the locker rooms. Run it on a double bill with *DOWNHILL RACER*.

PETER PAN. US. 1953. Walt Disney's animated features of the fifties were unsuccessful at the box office, perhaps because Disney's studio technique had not progressed since the late thirties, and perhaps because audiences sensed the lack of a real passionate commitment. Perhaps simply because animation can't sustain feature performances. Nevertheless, this is a classic children's story and the film isn't released very often.

PETRIFIED FOREST, THE. US. 1936. One of the variants on the *GRAND HOTEL* theme halfway between the pleasant comings and goings at that hostelry and the screaming disasters of, say, *The Poseidon Adventure*. From a famous Robert Sherwood play. Here we have the group held hostage. Archie Mayo directed Leslie Howard, Bette Davis, and Humphrey Bogart. ▽

PETULIA. US. 1967. Richard Lester's best film has had a devoted following of cognoscenti for fifteen years. The elegantly melodramatic script by Lawrence B. Marcus remains the best portrait of the hip sixties we have to date. Returning to the US after fifteen years in Europe, Lester saw in 1967 what we weren't able to see about ourselves: the curious mixture of good intentions and mistaken opportunities that gave that decade its character— and always with the Vietnam War quietly, painfully in the background on television. George C. Scott and Shirley Knight, Richard Chamberlain and Julie Christie are the very models of modern Marin County marriages. These slightly sad stories were repeated countless times in the seventies. Lester never did this sort of thing again.

PHANTOM OF LIBERTY, THE. France. 1974. A summary of Luis Buñuel's surrealistic concerns in a collection of anecdotes starring Jean-Claude Brialy, Michel Piccoli, and Monica Vitti.

PHANTOM OF THE OPERA, THE. US. 1925. Lon Chaney's finest hour as the underground Parisian composer with a grudge.

PHILADELPHIA STORY, THE. US. 1940. Katharine Hepburn is the society dame who's got a lot to learn about real life. Cary Grant's her ex, and James Stewart is the reporter who covers the brouhaha and falls in love with his subject. George Cukor directed the film of the Philip Barry play. It's lively and wonderfully predictable. See *HIGH SOCIETY*. ▽

PICKPOCKET. France. 1959. Another transcend-ental meditation by Robert Bresson, this one about an intellectual criminal who has wonderfully rationalized his career. The photography of Paris is stylized but absorbing.

THE CONNOISSEUR'S GUIDE 209

PICKUP ON SOUTH STREET. US. 1953. Nobody makes gutsier, tougher, or more hard-boiled movies than Sam Fuller. This one's a steak-and-potatoes spy thriller starring Richard Widmark, Jean Peters, and Thelma Ritter. At the end of their run, B-movies were better than ever.

PICNIC. US. 1955. This is the classic William Inge play about romantic dramas in Kansas. The theme song of the film was one of the theme songs of the fifties. Joshua Logan directed William Holden, Kim Novak, Rosalind Russell, and Cliff Robertson.

PICNIC AT HANGING ROCK. Australia. 1975. Three Australian schoolgirls at the turn of the century vanish during a picnic on a beautiful summer day. Director Peter Weir turns this simple story into a hushed and evocative cinematic experience. With this film and *The Last Wave* he established one of the more unusual film sensibilities of the seventies. These are existential thrillers.

PICTURE OF DORIAN GRAY, THE. US. 1945. Oscar Wilde established a modern myth with his novel about the man whose portrait ages while he remains the same. Hurd Hatfield, Donna Reed, and George Sanders star in this nice period piece directed by Albert Lewin.

PIERROT LE FOU. France. 1965. This is Jean-Luc Godard's poetic B-grade road gangster movie painted in brilliant primary colors: Godard very near the height of his powers. Jean-Paul Belmondo, Anna Karina, and Jean-Pierre Léaud improvised their way to the south of France in this existential poem. Godard's hero, Sam Fuller, even puts in an appearance to lend his tough-guy cachet to the enterprise.

PILLOW TALK. US. 1959. There's no doubt that the 1950s is the most cramped, constrained, and introverted era in US twentieth-century social history. There's always a sense in movies of the 1950s that the people aren't telling you something; that there's more going on than meets the eye. Sexual relations had regressed to the point of pre-teendom and that's only emphasized by the fact that doll-like Marilyn Monroe was the great sex symbol of the period. At the end of the fifties, *Pillow Talk*, with Doris Day and Rock Hudson, seemed to be a little daring, opening a slight crack in the rigid facade, although you'll probably never notice that from a contemporary vantage point. It's all pink and gray and a good summary of the styles of the fifties. Rock and Doris share a party line leading to the inevitable confusion and eventually true love.

PINK PANTHER, THE. US. 1964. Blake Edwards hit paydirt with the character of Inspector Clouseau, a Tati-like police inspector in an over-large trenchcoat who is sublimely indifferent to the physical realities that surround him. Peter Sellers brought magnificent life to this character and it lasted through a number of movies until Sellers's death. (Clouseau has occasionally been played by others.) By now *The Pink Panther* is probably second only to James Bond as a long-running contemporary movie series.

PINOCCHIO. US. 1940. The Disney technique was still fresh when this film was released and the story of the puppet who earns real life by learning to be good was an unusual choice. With both *FANTASIA* and *Pinocchio* in release in 1940, the future must have seemed bright and interesting at the Disney studios. Then came *Dumbo* and *Bambi* and a long stretch of declining success with animated features from which Disney was not able to recover artistically.

PIZZA TRIANGLE, THE. Italy. 1966. Monica Vitti and Marcello Mastroianni in an unpretentious but nicely made comedy about a love triangle. Directed by Ettore Scola.

PLACE IN THE SUN, A. US. 1951. Not a great movie but based on a classic novel, Theodore Dreiser's *An American Tragedy*, and an early opportunity for some stars of the fifties to work together. George Stevens directed Montgomery Clift, Shelley Winters, Raymond Burr, and Elizabeth Taylor.

PLAY IT AGAIN, SAM. US. 1972. By the end of the 1960s when Woody Allen wrote the play on which this film was based we had become thoroughly conscious of film history thanks in part to the influence of the French New Wave. From that point on, movies themselves have been an important part of the material a filmmaker works with. Allen is as much aware of this self-centered, self-referential world as anyone and *Play It Again, Sam*, directed by Herbert Ross, gives us Woody as the film fan trying to act out his Humphrey Bogart fantasies in his relations with the opposite sex. Friends Diane Keaton and Tony Roberts assist.

PLAYTIME. France. 1967. A long, elegant, and precise late work by Jacques Tati. "Monsieur Hulot" simply wanders around the contemporary streets of Paris getting himself into one Tati fix after another. This is a Paris that is indistinguishable from New York or Rio or Kansas City, Missouri— all glass and steel. At one point Hulot opens a door (in Paris) and the glass reflects the New York skyline. ◪

POCKETFUL OF MIRACLES. US. 1961. The new Hollywood meets the old in Frank Capra's swan song, a Damon Runyon story starring Bette Davis with Peter Falk, Ann-Margret, and Hope Lange.

POINT BLANK. US. 1967. A classic thriller of the sixties directed by John Boorman, giving Lee Marvin one of his best opportunities to portray the jut-jawed tough guy he did so well in a breathtaking drama of revenge. Great location shooting in Los Angeles.

POINT OF ORDER. US. 1963. Give him enough rope and he'll hang himself. Quietly and simply, filmmaker Emile De Antonio allows Senator Joe McCarthy to bang his own last nails in his coffin. There's nothing here but kinescopes of the TV coverage of the Army/McCarthy hearings of 1954, but they make a scathing indictment. Even if you think you remember that crucial moment in television and social history, you'll be struck by the vivid portrait of McCarthy painted here. This film should be shown at every voter registration drive. Compare *TAIL-GUNNER JOE*. ◪

POLTERGEIST. US. 1982. Steven Spielberg co-wrote and co-produced what may look like just another experience in masochistic horror. It isn't. Craig T. Nelson, JoBeth Williams, and their children are a typical young American family living in the Los Angeles suburbs. Their house is invaded by presences and in fact their five-year-old girl is kidnapped by the spirits. Sounds horrific, but the Spielberg script treats it with an unusual and very welcome sense of humor. Beatrice Straight leads an exorcist team from the university who are almost good enough to join the *GHOSTBUSTERS*. ◪

POOR COW. UK. 1967. Based on the novel by Nell Dunn, this is a typical Ken Loach survey of working-class family life and something of a feminist document because of its point of view. Carol White and Terrence Stamp star.

◬ **POSTMAN ALWAYS RINGS TWICE, THE**.
US. 1946. This James M. Cain novel has been filmed
at least four times in the US, France, and Italy, so it
seems right that at least one version should be listed
here. The French film doesn't count and Luchino
Visconti's 1942 *Ossessione* is a messy, sloppy,
overrated film. Bob Rafelson's 1981 remake is more
faithful to the novel. (It stars Jack Nicholson and
Jessica Lange.) But on balance we have to vote for
the 1946 cleaned-up Hollywood version directed by
Tay Garnett and starring John Garfield and Lana
Turner as the doomed lovers. It's a classic story of
guilt and passion, and the forties setting fits.

⟰ **POSTO, IL**. Italy. 1961. Exceptional late Italian
Neorealist document about the search for a job ("Il
Posto") directed by Ermanno Olmi, a sensitive and
intelligent filmmaker, and perhaps one of the most
underrated of contemporary Italian directors.

✳ **POTEMKIN**. USSR. 1925. This one's de rigeur in
film classes around the world but it would rivet your
attention even if you caught it on TV late at night
between commercials. It's a moving and popular
story of the 1905 Russian uprising which
foreshadowed the revolution. Sergei Eisenstein was
without a doubt the most prolific and thoughtful film
theorist of the early years of cinematic history. You
might expect that the movies he made would turn
out theory-ridden. In fact, the theories work
surprisingly well in practice. Compare the Odessa
steps sequence here to Woody Allen's later parody of
it in *BANANAS*. ▼

✛⟍⟰ **PRAISE MARX AND PASS THE
AMMUNITION**. UK. 1969. This remarkable
comedy about leftist politics comes as close as any
film in this book to being unique. More's the pity,
for filmmaker Maurice Hatton exhibits here a
breadth of vision and a human and humorous—even
wise—attitude towards politics and the reasons for
them that we wish more of us had absorbed by now.
A full-length color feature shot for less than £25,000
in 1968 and 1969, *Praise Marx and Pass the
Ammunition* follows Dom (John Thaw), a
rambunctious, rhetorical Marxist-Leninist revolutionary who was kicked out of the Communist
party at fifteen and has founded his own new
"Revolutionary Party of the Third World." Dom
lives in an elegant and decidedly un-revolutionary
Bloomsbury flat, spends time in good restaurants,
and raises the consciousness of a succession of
women in bed. He's full of facts and figures and the

film pauses every once in a while in the midst of a very rich comic fabric to insert documentary details—little essays on the painful, humiliating disparity between rich and poor. *Praise Marx*, in no sense a rightist movie, also offers a perceptive analysis of the events of May, 1968 in France. You have to know something about the highly developed culture of the left during the last hundred years to fully appreciate all the comedy of *Praise Marx*. In deflating the pretensions and the rhetoric of leftists Hatton performed a monumental political good. The failure of the New Left in the 1960s still haunts us. In retrospect, after fifteen years, *Praise Marx* seems to suggest that we won't make significant progress until somehow the anachronistic labels of left and right have been buried once and for all in history. Hatton forecast the wisdom of the late eighties fifteen years before.

⊘ PRETTY POISON. US. 1968. This is a nice offbeat script by Lorenzo Semple Jr., directed by Noel Black. Anthony Perkins is an inveterate criminal who meets sweet and sexy teenager Tuesday Weld. It turns out she's the real criminal personality.

⊘ PRIDE AND PREJUDICE. US. 1940. Robert Z. Leonard directed this well-made film of the Jane Austen novel about property, love, and marriage in Regency England. Laurence Olivier stars with Greer Garson.   ▽

⟍ PRIDE OF THE YANKEES. US. 1942. If the name Lou Gehrig means something to you you're already a fan of this film about him written in part by Herman J. Mankiewicz. If it doesn't you've got a nice surprise coming in this best of the baseball biopics. Teammate Babe Ruth appears in the film. Gary Cooper plays old #4 of the Yankees. Sam Wood directed.   ▽

⊘⟍⇧ PRIME CUT. US. 1972. "I give 'em things to stick in their arm and things to rub their bellies with," says meat packer/gangster Gene Hackman at one point in this very funny and on the mark parody of gangster films directed by Michael Ritchie. The conceit here is to put the gangsters in the middle of the wholesome American plains and let them look like fresh-faced farmers, and it's a very effective trick. There's one magnificent sequence in a cornfield: Lee Marvin and Sissy Spacek are running for their lives, pursued by a fat-faced farmboy in a giant combine harvester. It's almost as suspenseful as the cornfield scene in *NORTH BY*

NORTHWEST, but much funnier because it's so mundane.

⬤ **PRINCE OF THE CITY**. US. 1981. Once again Sidney Lumet takes up the challenge of the complex New York scene, this time with an intricate story of police morality and ethics. He wrote the script with Jay Presson Allen. Here's another cop (it's a true story) who turns whistle-blower during the early seventies investigations into police corruption, but he's no *SERPICO*. In fact, he may be the opposite. Treat Williams and Jerry Ohrbach star. The story may be true, but this is not the only viewpoint. For another, nearly opposite, see *A QUESTION OF HONOR*. ▽

PRISONER OF ZENDA, THE. US. 1937. Ronald Colman, Madeleine Carroll, Mary Astor, and Douglas Fairbanks Jr. star in this most effective of at least five versions of the famous novel set in a middle-European fantasy kingdom. This is what we used to call "kitsch" in the sixties.

⚑ **PRIVATE LIFE OF HENRY VIII, THE**. UK. 1933. An early British attempt at the grand historical subject by Alexander Korda and starring Charles Laughton, this film may have set the tone for a genre popular now for fifty years in British film and television. ▽

⬤ **PRIVATE SCHOOL**. US. 1983. Certainly the most curious development in the long history of cinematic exploitation of eroticism has been the recent series of teenage "porn." The most execrable of these—so far—has been the very popular *Porky's*, real pornography with no redeeming social value (except perhaps that it's an authentic recreation of the worst behavioral patterns of teenagerhood). *Private School*, directed by Noel Black and starring Phoebe Cates—the Hedy Lamarr of eighties adolescence—and Sylvia Kristel, sex star of the seventies who adds historical resonance, seems to me to be a fairly healthy exploitation of kids' eroticism— if that's not a contradiction in terms. The same crass adolescent psychology is apparent here but it's handled with some artistic distance. Director Black has come a long, hard way from the magical and enticing pre-teen romance of his short *Skater-Dater* in the mid-sixties. ▽

⊶╪‖ **PRODUCERS, THE**. US. 1968. Mel Brooks's first, wildest, and funniest movie was a landmark in its time. Zero Mostel, Gene Wilder, Kenneth Mars, and Dick Shawn star. Mostel as Max Bialystock forms a partnership with milquetoast Gene Wilder to con a bunch of old ladies into investing in a guaranteed Broadway flop: "Springtime for Hitler." Here's another film that proves the worth of VCRs: everytime you watch this one it gets better. "I'm hysterical! I'm wet and I'm hysterical! I'm in *pain* and I'm wet and I'm hysterical!" ▽

PROMISED LAND, THE. Chile. 1973. In the late sixties and very early seventies Chile was rocked by an explosion of talent in music and film that coincided with the Allende regime. Director Miguel Littin is perhaps the best-known of the filmmakers whose renaissance was cut short by the brutal coup of September 1973. This film was begun before the coup and never fully completed. Using documentary techniques, it forms an essay about class differences in Chile. The effect is very much heightened by the use of the music of the time.

PROVIDENCE. UK. 1977. Probably it's a good idea to have seen and studied and thoroughly appreciated a couple of Alain Resnais's earlier movies before you approach *Providence*. It's a complex and involuted set of wordplay and image-play that undoubtedly draws a confused blank from most viewers unfamiliar with Resnais's concerns with time and memory in film. But if you do know something about these, *Providence* is a fascinating experience. It stars John Gielgud, Dirk Bogarde, Ellen Burstyn, David Warner, and Elaine Stritch. Gielgud is Clive Langham, a writer almost eighty who's keeping himself alive with good Chablis (the real stuff, not the California kind), and with the full force of his imagination. Every scene in the film is cockeyed: we're watching the writer at work on a first draft. It's a daring approach by Resnais and writer David Mercer. Miklòs Rosza did the music. ▽

PSYCHO. US. 1960. Here's a pandora's box: this most popular film by Alfred Hitchcock has spawned such dreck—and sadistic dreck at that—during the last twenty-five years that you might almost wish it hadn't been made. So many people have been slashed, mutilated, and generally cut to pieces in the genre that *Psycho* seems to have established, that Hitchcock must bear some guilt. Wherever he is, he probably appreciates the guilt and the irony of it. But *Pyscho* itself is not at all like the many movies that tried to imitate it. It's got a sense of black humor that more than redeems it and there's no doubt that it's great filmmaking. Hitchcock himself approached it almost as a technical joke: he wanted to see what would happen to audiences if you killed off a star in the first reel. That's how Janet Leigh got into the shower with Anthony Perkins. ▽

PUBLIC ENEMY. US. 1931. William Wellman directed James Cagney in the prohibition-era gangster role that made him a star. It's not the best of the early gangster movies but it was influential at the time. ▽

PUMPKIN EATER, THE. UK. 1964. Jack Clayton directed the Harold Pinter script (from the novel by Penelope Mortimer). Anne Bancroft puts in quite an interesting and affecting performance as a woman who doesn't depend on her husband(s), and finds the current one cheating on her. In the mid-sixties this was a feminist statement.

PURSUIT OF D. B. COOPER, THE. US. 1981. D. B. Cooper jumped out of a plane with a lot of money several years ago and has never been seen since. Roger Spottiswoode directed this very thoughtful and enjoyable film version of the modern legend of a successful renegade. Treat Williams stars as the hijacker. There's nothing particularly unusual about the film, it's just a good solid story with good solid acting and, of course, gorgeous scenery. ▽

PYGMALION. UK. 1938. Leslie Howard and Wendy Hiller in the landmark film of the George Bernard Shaw play about a Cockney flower girl who becomes a lady. Compare it with *MY FAIR LADY*. Anthony Asquith and Howard directed.

Q-PLANES. UK. 1938. A pleasant spy movie with Laurence Olivier and Ralph Richardson—both very young—playing roles you're not accustomed to seeing them in. Aeronautical secrets have been stolen; Richardson cracks the case.

QUEST FOR FIRE. Canada. 1982. Jean-Jacques Annaud is responsible for this certainly unique cult movie. The model for the film is the first sequence of *2001*. A pack of prehistoric humans loses its fire and doesn't know where to find another one. They use a language invented by Anthony Burgess, a kind of quasi-pre-proto-Indo-European. Desmond Morris was called in to consult on body language. (Since the actors worked long hours mostly naked in cold swamps, the dominant dialect is the shiver.) ▽

QUESTION OF HONOR, A. USA. 1982. Sonny Grosso, one of the real cops in *THE FRENCH CONNECTION* case, has since built a career in the media as writer and producer. This film, based on Grosso's and Philip Rosenberg's book *Point Blank*, treats the same material as Sidney Lumet's *PRINCE OF THE CITY*, but from quite a different viewpoint. Grosso knew the cops involved personally and he takes the point of view of one of the victims of the "hero" of Lumet's film. Budd Schulberg wrote the script with Philip Rosenberg. With Ben Gazzara, Paul Sorvino, Robert Vaughn, and Tony Roberts.

QUIET MAN, THE. US. 1952. You can see where the title comes from: this is a very subdued role for John Wayne. The motivation for the film may have been the chance it afforded Wayne, John Ford, Barry Fitzgerald, and Maureen O'Hara to spend some time pleasantly shooting a movie in gorgeous Irish scenery. We appreciate it with them and it's not a bad story, either, about an American boxer who moves to a village in Ireland and gradually wins his place in the tight-knit society. ▾

QUO VADIS? US. 1951. An early herald of fifties historical spectacle, this involved, Neronian story pre-dated CinemaScope by several years but set the tone for the decade for historical romances. Mervyn LeRoy directed. Robert Taylor, Deborah Kerr, and the ubiquitous Peter Ustinov starred.

RA EXPEDITIONS, THE. Norway. 1971. For Thor Heyerdahl fans (see *KON-TIKI*), the master of the rafts sets out again twenty years later, this time in a boat made of papyrus to cross the Atlantic from South America in an attempt to prove pre-Columbian peoples could have crossed the Atlantic. The building of the "paper" boat makes for some fascinating sequences. What's next, Thor?

RACING WITH THE MOON. US. 1984. Actor Richard Benjamin proved his directorial success in *MY FAVORITE YEAR* was no fluke with this pleasant and perceptive recreation of the early forties set in smalltown America on the California coast, starring Elizabeth McGovern and Sean Penn. ▾

RAGING BULL. US. 1980. Thirty or forty years ago the rough and depressing life of boxer Jake LaMotta would have been cleaned up for a standard Hollywood biopic. Martin Scorsese and Robert DeNiro give us LaMotta as the anti-hero, warts and all. It's a tough, tight, direct portrait. The only problem is that you may find yourself asking: why should we be interested in this guy? Paul Schrader and Mardik Martin wrote the script. ▾

✛ ↖ ⇪ **RAGTIME**. US. 1981. Directed by a Czechoslovak (Miloš Forman), produced by an Italian (Dino de Laurentiis), and filmed mainly in Britain, *Ragtime* is one of the great movies about America. It is, perhaps, the only film by whites that really captures the essence of the Black American experience. Partly because it's by outsiders, it sets that experience in context better than most other attempts. Coalhouse Walker joins Bigger Thomas (of *Native Son*) and The Invisible Man in the pantheon of Black American literary heros. The successful novel by E. L. Doctorow does all this (and much more) but, ironically, the film does it better. The conceit of the novel was to tell a number of stories involving historical characters. Because of time constraints of the movie, much of the rich subplot material was left on the cutting-room floor. The net effect was positive: to make the central story clearer. Because it knits together history and fiction, *Ragtime* has much of the same resonance that *CITIZEN KANE* does. ▾

RAIDERS OF THE LOST ARK. US. 1981. There's no denying that this magnificent pastiche of 1940s adventure serials is great fun. Steven Spielberg directed; George Lucas produced. Harrison Ford comes as close as any actor working today to capturing the insouciance and mock-heroism of stars of the past like Clark Gable, Errol Flynn, and "Tim Tyler." Lawrence Kasdan fashioned the meaty script. ▾

⇪ **RAILROAD MAN, THE**. Italy. 1956. A Neorealist classic about a rail worker by Pietro Germi, starring himself and Sylva Koscina.

📬⇪ **RAISIN IN THE SUN, A**. US. 1961. Lorraine Hansberry's play about a Black family in Chicago was a milestone in the history of the development of Black Theater. Daniel Petrie directed this film version starring Sidney Poitier, Ruby Dee, Diana Sands, Ivan Dixon, Claudia McNeil, and Louis Gossett.

↖ **RAMPARTS OF CLAY**. Algeria/France. 1971. Jean-Louis Bertucelli directed this simple and powerful story of a woman who gets involved in political action. The North African setting is the star. ▾

RANDOM HARVEST. US. 1942. Ronald Colman working well with Greer Garson under the direction of Mervyn LeRoy in a pleasant MGM melodrama

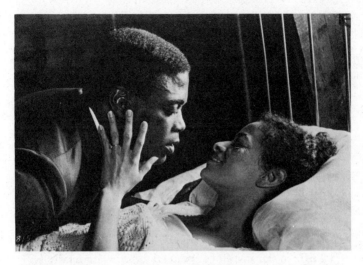

Howard E. Rollins asks Debbie Allen to become his wife in *Ragtime*.

about the aftereffects of World War I.

RASHOMON. Japan. 1951. This Akira Kurosawa classic introduced the Japanese film to the west after the war. Toshiro Mifune is the star, and the conceit is that the same crime is remembered by several people from quite different points of view.

REAL LIFE. US. 1979. Albert Brooks's first feature is a film about Albert Brooks, the documentarist, who sets out to make a movie about a real-life American family that includes Charles Grodin. Now we know that no real-life American family would ever include Charles Grodin, but nevertheless we're taken in. It doesn't work all the way but it's a sharp parody of documentary style. (Remember the PBS series of the early seventies, *An American Family*.) See *A MODERN ROMANCE*.

REAR WINDOW. US. 1954. House-bound with a broken leg, photographer James Stewart wiles away the time watching the many lives of his neighbors in the CinemaScope windows across the courtyard from his apartment in Greenwich Village. His voyeurism is interrupted only by romantic interludes with his girlfriend, Grace Kelly, and his nurse, Thelma Ritter. Then he sees what looks like a murder and he must deal with it from his wheelchair with only his wits. *Rear Window* is one of Alfred

Hitchcock's most charming movies and a great emblem for the filmgoing experience. Cornell Woolrich wrote the novel on which this is based. ▣

⬥ **REBECCA**. US. 1940. This is at least as much a David O. Selznick film as it is an Alfred Hitchcock movie. Based on the mildly Gothic novel by Daphne Du Maurier, it provides Laurence Olivier with his greatest romantic role. Joan Fontaine, George Sanders, and Judith Anderson also star. Elegantly photographed, the film works out the classic Gothic fantasy of a helpless young woman haunted by her husband's ex-wife, Rebecca. ▣

⚑ **REBEL WITHOUT A CAUSE**. US. 1955. Nicholas Ray directed this centerpiece movie of fifties sensibility. James Dean, Natalie Wood, and Sal Mineo star in a story about friendship and family that still has many emotional hooks for teenagers, and at the time captured the spirit of a restless generation. ▣

⬥ **RED BALLOON, THE**. France. 1956. A classic short children's film about a boy who finds a red balloon with a life of its own. The balloon leads him an idyllic chase through the streets of Paris. Invitingly photographed in fifties color. ▣

⬥ **RED DESERT**. Italy. 1964. Monica Vitti is the neurotic, bored, but nevertheless elegant and beautiful upper-middle-class woman who can't escape from a magnificently photographed milieu. This is Michelangelo Antonioni's first color film and probably his most approachable movie.

⬥⚑ **RED RIVER**. US. 1948. A great western by Howard Hawks with John Wayne in one of his more interesting roles and Montgomery Clift in his first film. It's a drama set against a cattle drive, magnificently photographed, and scored by Dimitri Tiomkin. ▣

⬥ **RED SHOES, THE**. UK. 1948. A classic by Michael Powell and Emeric Pressburger. Moira Shearer, Anton Walbrook, and Robert Helpmann star in everybody's favorite ballet film. Shearer is the young ballerina at the center of the drama torn between music and choreography. Stunning newly-struck Technicolor prints are available.

✳⟍§ **REDS**. US. 1981. Probably the most ambitious American film in ten or fifteen years, Warren Beatty's complex re-telling of the story of American journalist John Reed and writer Louise Bryant, their romance and involvement in radical politics, is remarkably resonant. In the first place, it's a grand romantic drama that has been compared with films like *DOCTOR ZHIVAGO* (probably because of the Russian scenes), but it's also a crucial historical story about progressive American politics on the one hand, and the failures of the Soviet revolution on the other. The comparison—and the problems—started in 1917 and they're still continuing. Then, too, Louise Bryant's story (Diane Keaton plays her) is a classic early feminist tale. And finally, Beatty has punctuated the grand sweep of this romantic historical drama with brief interviews with many American political activists who have survived from those days. Here he's linking the present with the past in a fashion that reminds us that there's nothing new under the sun, that the world that was forged during the years of the great war and the twenties still very much pertains today. This interview technique had been used to great effect in historical documentaries made during the seventies. Beatty makes it work in a real Hollywood movie. *Reds* is in the end a remarkable film and an unusually thoughtful one. Show it with *PRAISE MARX AND PASS THE AMMUNITION* and you'll have enough material for a semester-long course in the passionate but unfulfilled politics of the left in the twentieth century. ◪

◬ **REGION CENTRALE, LA**. Canada. 1970. There's a kind of filmmaking that used to be known as "avant-garde." It's done mainly by people who consider themselves artists rather than directors or cinematographers or writers. It's often of some interest esthetically, but it's not often of great interest cinematically. Michael Snow is one of the very few "conceptual" filmmakers in the last thirty years whose work is consistently interesting in both regards. *La Région Centrale* is one of his most ambitious pieces. He mounted a camera on a complicated automatic pan and tilt device in the middle of the Quebec tundra and let it revolve and gyrate for several hours. That's the "central region" of the title, and it's an interesting idea, believe it or not.

◬ **REMBRANDT**. UK. 1936. Another classic biopic by Alexander Korda starring Charles Laughton, Elsa Lanchester, and Gertrude Lawrence. Rembrandt happens to be the one great painter that side of Franz Kline whose work can be successfully evoked in a black and white movie.

◤ **RESCUED BY ROVER**. UK. 1905. At least five

countries lay claim to inventing cinema, and students in each of them study its early history from insular national points of view. In the US we're taught that Edwin S. Porter first experimented with some of the basic techniques. In the UK, however, filmmakers Robert W. Paul and Cecil Hepworth were by all reports doing more interesting work. Nearly all of Paul's films were destroyed, but this interesting experiment in editing by Hepworth survives.

RETURN OF THE SECAUCUS 7. US. 1980. The biggest low-budget hit of the last twenty years. Writer/director John Sayles gives us a reunion of friends from the 1960s. Compare it with the expensive *THE BIG CHILL*. Sayles reputedly made this movie for less than $100,000. ▼

REVOLUTIONARY, THE. US. 1970. One of the least-known young directors of the late sixties and early seventies was Paul Williams (not to be confused with the musician). In *Out Of It* and *The Revolutionary* he made two important movies for the new generation: they never got the attention they deserved and his career went nowhere after that. This film has a script by novelist Hans Königsberger. It's about a student who gets drawn into politics and it's a curiously Brechtian investigation of the emotions involved in that experience. Jon Voight, Jennifer Salt, and Robert Duvall star.

RHAPSODY IN BLUE. US. 1945. It's an old-fashioned story but the subject of this biopic, George Gershwin, is so important and interesting that you'll want to take a look at this film directed by Irving Rapper and starring Robert Alda, Alexis Smith, and Oscar Levant.

RICH KIDS. US. 1979. That rare thing, a really honest and direct movie from a kid's point of view. Pre-teener Trini Alvarado's parents are divorcing and the film traces the development of her friendship with Jeremy Levy during the course of the events. This is a view from the opposite side of *KRAMER VS. KRAMER* with great New York location photography. Robert M. Young directed.

RICHARD III. UK. 1956. This is a magnificent staging of the Shakespeare play directed by and starring Laurence Olivier. It's undoubtedly the best film version of Shakespeare ever made and certainly ranks among the great performances in any medium over the last three hundred years. Olivier perfectly catches the ambiguous and strangely modern character of the hunchbacked king in a great balance of villainy and victimization. Now is the winter of our discontent made glorious summer by this colorful, adventurous, intelligent, and immensely enjoyable movie. If you want to know why people in so many different cultures honor William Shakespeare *Richard III* may show you.

RIDE THE HIGH COUNTRY. US. 1962. Despite its date, this is the last of the great color westerns of the fifties. Sam Peckinpah expertly directed two old western hands, Randolph Scott and Joel McCrea, as over-the-hill gunslingers. The presence of Mariette Hartley and Warren Oates connects us with the future, and the nouveau westerns of the sixties. The western was the great unsung genre of the fifties and you see why here. Widescreen and widespread color photography gave the genre a new breadth of vision which very much suits it.

RIDER ON THE RAIN. France. 1970. A nice French suspense piece by René Clément and an interesting union of French and American characters. Marlène Jobert stars with Charles Bronson and Jill Ireland.

RIDERS OF THE PURPLE SAGE. US. 1925. Here's a classic Zane Grey western story starring the durable Tom Mix. It stands here as representative of all the enjoyable western series and B-westerns that followed for thirty-five years.

RIFIFI. France. 1954. Bronx-born Jules Dassin directed this breathless and enjoyable caper movie which founded the genre. The elaborate robbery they've planned takes place without any dialogue; it's a classic sequence that lasts almost twenty minutes.

RIGHT OF WAY. US. 1983. This was one of the first made-for-cable movies. It's important because it puts Bette Davis and Jimmy Stewart together for the first time, at the end of their careers. Any occasion to watch either at this stage is notable. The premise is interesting; two old people decide to end their lives, and to take control at the end. The execution is rather plain, but again, here's Davis and Stewart.

RIGHT STUFF, THE. US. 1983. *The Right Stuff* is about three different movies rolled into one. It seems to go on forever. It turns test pilot Chuck

Yeager into a western hero. He rides a horse as often as he rides an X-1 test plane. Then it drops Yeager (played by Sam Shepard) and goes on to the story of the Mercury 7 astronauts. Contrary to popular opinion, it doesn't paint them at all as heroes. It paints them as media creations, pseudo-heroes who have to live up to their fellow Americans' expectations of them. If there's any drama in the film, this is it. It has about seven climaxes. First, Shepherd's suborbital flight, then Glenn's orbital flight, then Grissom's orbital flight, and finally back to Yeager again. It's also got great aerial and space photography. It's about a vital and exciting subject. Director Philip Kaufman continues to try new things. ▽

RIO BRAVO. US. 1959. Howard Hawks's best western and a classic of the fifties form, with John Wayne, Dean Martin, Angie Dickenson, and Walter Brennan. Sheriff Wayne stands alone protecting the rule of law with only a bunch of riffraff to help him. See also *EL DORADO*. ▽

RIO GRANDE. US. 1950. *Rio Grande* and *RED RIVER* opened up the western of the 1950s. John Ford directed this one with John Wayne and Maureen O'Hara. Like *RED RIVER* it's in black and white but it shows the scope and epic proportions that were crying out for widescreen and color. This is a Civil War story. ▽

RIO LOBO. US. 1970. This was Howard Hawks's last film. John Wayne stars as an over-the-hill Union soldier with a bunch of young actors who don't add much, but the Hawks magic is still there.

RISE OF LOUIS XIV, THE. France. 1966. This began the epic series of historical dramas with which Roberto Rossellini ended his career. All were made ostensibly for European television; this is the only one that had a significant theatrical run. Taken together they form one of the great accomplishments of contemporary cinema. Rossellini used nonprofessionals, a technique which connects these films with the early days of Neorealism. Much work was done on location but he also utilized sophisticated matting techniques to combine real settings with painted backdrops. The technique works very well. Technically, these films may be the equal of *2001*. Though they take us on an eerie trip to other times and places with resonance and color, Rossellini's essays in historical intelligence, are more dramas of ideas than of action. We still have a lot to learn from this masterful series of films.

◐ **RIVER, THE**. India. 1951. Jean Renoir's masterful staging of the Rumer Godden novel about English children growing up in India. Superbly photographed by Claude Renoir.

◣⇧ **ROAD HOUSE**. US. 1948. Ida Lupino has long been overlooked and underrated not only as a director (her work in television is an accomplishment that any history of women in film must include), but also as a star. She's not as outgoing and ingratiating as, say, Rosalind Russell, but she has the same rare combination of intelligence, sensibility, and physical beauty. In this noirish melodrama she's torn between enemies Cornel Wilde and Richard Widmark. Jean Negulesco directed.

ROAD TO RIO, THE. US. 1947. We've picked one of the Bob Hope/Bing Crosby road movies to stand for the series. None of these are really great comedies, but together they mark the final flowering of the Vaudeville tradition in movies. Like the Marx Brothers movies before them (and to a lesser extent Abbott and Costello and Laurel and Hardy), they are more variety shows than plotted dramas: a little singing, a little dancing, lots of comedy, and a few skits. Hope and Crosby (and Lamour) are playing Hope and Crosby who are playing lackadaisical roles in the current movie. It's more like a radio show of the forties than a fiction film: we're certainly more interested in the personalities of the entertainers than the characters they portray. In their television series, George Burns and Gracie Allen raised this form to a very sophisticated level.

◐ **ROARING TWENTIES, THE**. US. 1939. This is a classic Raoul Walsh movie just this side of the B's. Humphrey Bogart and James Cagney thrash their way with considerable energy through the cliches of the jazz age and prohibition. ▼

⚑ **ROBE, THE**. US. 1953. Okay, it's here mainly because it's the first CinemaScope feature, and that's significant. But it's also a decent historical spectacle of the sort that was quite important in the fifties. The plot: the crucifixion of Christ and its aftermath. Henry Koster directed Richard Burton, Victor Mature, and Jean Simmons.

⇧ **ROBERT ET ROBERT**. France. 1978. Director Claude Lelouch has never been a favorite of the critics, but over the last twenty-five years he's produced an interesting and more or less consistent body of work with a very special attitude that deserves attention. He's criticized for being sentimental, but more often than not he's discussing valid sentiments. This one with Charles Denner, Jean-Claude Brialy, Jacques Villeret, and Macha Méril is a novel story of two very different fellows named Robert, whose lives and loves are intertwined. ◩

◬ **ROBIN AND MARIAN**. UK. 1976. James Goldman wrote this post-romantic latter-day historical romance. Richard Lester directed Sean Connery and Audrey Hepburn in the title roles, along with Robert Shaw, Nicol Williamson, and Richard Harris. A view of Robin Hood as middle-aged, this is a quietly attenuated movie, but all the more haunting if you pay close attention. The dream is over. ◩

⚑ **ROCCO AND HIS BROTHERS**. Italy. 1960. Alain Delon and Annie Girardot in Luchino Visconti's long, elaborate, and moving study of southern Italians migrating to Milan in the north. The historical subject was central to the Italian experience in the fifties and the sixties and *Rocco* gains added resonance from this fact. Nino Rota did the music.

⚑♪ **ROCK AROUND THE CLOCK**. US. 1956. It should have been made three years earlier just at the dawn of the Rock 'n' Roll era, but this platform for the music of Bill Haley and the Comets was, even in 1956, a thrilling overture to the age of Rock 'n' Roll. There were better bands and better singers but this is the theme song of the generation. It's curious that classical fifties Rock 'n' Roll had such a limited effect on the movies. Aside from musicals like this you see very little evidence of the music of a generation on soundtracks between 1953 and 1965. It wasn't really until *AMERICAN GRAFITTI*—when the music had nostalgic significance—that it became common to build evocative soundtracks around it. Leading Rock 'n' Roll d.j. Alan Freed appears.

⚑◬ **ROCKY**. US. 1976. In the middle of the age of the anti-heroes, a relatively unknown actor named Sylvester Stallone invented this character—a struggling boxer—for himself, wrote a snappy, affecting script—about his rise to success—and got the film produced against all odds. His own story is probably more heroic in contemporary terms than Rocky's. He gave us back the idea of heroes after Vietnam and we'll be grateful for a long time. Maybe the truth is larger and more complex, but the sentiments *Rocky* evokes must be part of it. It doesn't matter that success is difficult, complex, and discounted; it matters that it's still possible. The only negative element to this spirited movie is the underlying potential racism involved in the story of a Great White Hope. Stallone seemed to address this in the sequels, and all three of the *Rocky* films are imbued with the irony of the Black experience in the US: it's better to play second banana than not to be a banana at all. This one should have been dedicated to Terry Malloy. ▼

ROLLERBALL. US. 1975. College professor William Harrison wrote the script for this film from his own story and the academic provenance shows. It's very much a concept movie, but the concept is so enticing that you don't mind the rather crude execution. James Caan is the sports superstar of the next century. He plays rollerball, an ingenious combination of hockey, jai alai, roller derby, and bowling, and a quite violent sport meant to serve as a pressure valve for a sedated society. The drama is rather beside the point. "Rollerball" is such a fascinating idea that I'm surprised we haven't formed at least one professional "Rollerball" league during the ten years since the film was released. What this world needs is more new sports! Australian rules football and indoor soccer won't suffice. ▼

ROMA. Italy. 1972. After *FELLINI SATYRICON* Federico Fellini settled down to do a pleasant series of essays: hommages to the life-affirming Italian culture he represents so well. *THE CLOWNS*, *Roma*, and *AMARCORD* are quite unusual and sophisticated experiments in narrative style. He does it with such ease that we tend to overlook the sophistication. *Roma* stands in the middle: *THE CLOWNS* is more documentary; *AMARCORD* is more fictional; but all three combine fictional and nonfictional techniques in a fascinating essay form. This one's a memory of the Eternal City, of course.

ROMAN HOLIDAY. US. 1953. Audrey Hepburn's first big role as a princess escaping to the world of commoners fully exploited her unique gamine quality. Gregory Peck was her foil, William Wyler her director. ▼

RONDE, LA. France. 1950. Give most of the credit to Arthur Schnitzler whose play *Reigen* served as the basis for this, and at least one other movie. It's an attractive conceit: to tie together a series of little stories in a chained circle. In this case Jean-Louis

Barrault, Gérard Philipe, Simone Simon, Simone Signoret, Danielle Darrieux, Fernand Gravet, and others, are involved in a series of stories about love affairs, each one linked to the last by a shared character and coming full circle at the end. Anton Walbrook ties it all together. For cinephiles, this Max Ophüls movie has a number of the grand, gliding, tracking shots for which he is famous. It's surprising this technique—doing numerous little stories about the same subject—hasn't been used more often. ⊻

⊘ **ROOM AT THE TOP**. UK. 1958. John Braine's popular novel was filmed by Jack Clayton with Laurence Harvey and Simone Signoret. It was an instructive story at the time about class structure and making it in the corporate world. In a way it's the British *MAN IN THE GRAY FLANNEL SUIT* but tougher and more moral. See *NOTHING BUT THE BEST* for a more sardonic view of the battle to get ahead. ⊻

‼ **ROOM SERVICE**. US. 1938. William A. Seiter directed the Marx Brothers this time out with Lucille Ball and Ann Miller. Morrie Ryskind wrote the script which is more straightforward and less Vaudevillian than earlier Marx Brothers movies. They're down-and-out Broadway producers, struggling in business through sheer inventiveness. Compare *THE PRODUCERS*. ⊻

⊘ **ROPE**. US. 1948. Long out of circulation until it was re-released in 1983, this Alfred Hitchcock experiment with James Stewart, John Dall, and Farley Granger succeeds fairly well as drama. Two boys have killed a friend of theirs for the hell of it and the corpse is hidden. Hitchcock shot the film in complete ten-minute (one reel) takes and edited those takes into a seamless flow just to see what would happen. If Edison's first experiments to record images on disks like audio records had succeeded, the movies would have developed along quite different technical lines, much more like *Rope*. No montage, all mise-en-scene. It wasn't until the late forties, just about the time of *Rope*, that audio technicians had the same capability to edit sound on tape that film technicians had enjoyed for fifty years. ⊻

⌐ **ROSEMARY'S BABY**. US. 1968. Ira Levin's play filmed by Roman Polanski with Mia Farrow, John Cassavetes, and Ruth Gordon. Levin took a root neurotic fear that all parents share to one extent or another and turned it into a modern classic of the horror film. The nightmare is: what if your child turns out to be evil? This fantasy reflects a classic separation anxiety: the realistic (and well-founded) fear that your child will be different from you. In retrospect, *Rosemary's Baby* seems like an intelligent staging of this fantasy, especially as compared with the more extreme and quite sadistic treatment of the same theme in *THE EXORCIST*. What's really fascinating is that these two popular horror movies of the late sixties and early seventies and all their imitators are obsessed with a fear of children. This does not bode well: call in the Ghostbusters or apply liberal quantities of Muppets as an antidote. ▣

‼ **ROTTEN TO THE CORE**. UK. 1965. A nice Boulting Brothers caper comedy with Charlotte Rampling, Ian Bannen, and Eric Sykes.

‼ **ROYAL FLASH**. UK. 1975. Richard Lester mounted this film version of the popular classic George MacDonald Fraser novel. Fraser wrote the script. He hit early in the seventies with his *Flashman* series of swashbuckler parodies and they're amusing, novel twists on the genre. Malcolm McDowell stars; the presence of Alastair Sim and Michael Hordern is more than welcome.

⊘ **ROYAL WEDDING**. US. 1951. Stanley Donen directed Fred Astaire, Jane Powell, and Keenan Wynn in a rather boring story with no really good songs, that seems to have been constructed all too quickly to hang on the hook of Queen Elizabeth's marriage, scenes of which are interpolated. It's redeemed by one classic sequence: in his hotel room Fred dances his way across the floor, up the wall, back across the ceiling, and down the wall again. The third or fourth time you watch this you see how very cautious Fred is while working in this revolving barrel, but it's fun anyway. ▣

RUDD FAMILY GOES TO TOWN, THE. Australia. 1938. Just to show you that Australian movies weren't invented in the 1970s, here's a sample of the *Rudd Family* series, directed by Ken G. Hall, that can match most of the B-movies being done in Hollywood or London at the time.

⊘‼ **RUGGLES OF RED GAP, THE**. US. 1935. Charles Laughton is the haughty English butler won on a bet by the uncouth Charlie Ruggles and shanghaied out west in a simple but classic comedy of the clash of lifestyles. Leo McCarey directed.

✳ **RULES OF THE GAME**. France. 1939. The masterpiece by Jean Renoir harks back to the comedies of Beaumarchais. It's a nearly unique mixture of farce and realism that not only brilliantly illustrates social rules but also makes telling comments on class differences by contrasting the affairs of the haute bourgeoisie and their working-class servants during a long weekend in the country. ▾

⊺‼ RUNNING, JUMPING, AND STANDING-STILL FILM, THE. UK. 1959. Television director Richard Lester took radio actor Peter Sellers out into the country and turned on the camera. Sellers lived up to the title for five or ten minutes and the result is, second-for-second, one of the funniest short movies ever made.

SABOTAGE. UK. 1936. This is Alfred Hitchcock's film of Joseph Conrad's *Secret Agent*, a novel about London's political underworld. Oscar Homolka is the spy, and Sylvia Sidney is his suspicious wife. The film has one of the most suspenseful scenes in all Hitchcock: the boy with the bomb on the bus. ▾

＼⇧ SABOTEUR. US. 1942. One of the more unusual Hitchcock thrillers, *Saboteur* reiterates the theme of the unjustly accused. Robert Cummings is the defense worker who has a false rap pinned on him and has to evade the police as he chases the real saboteurs. This is the film with the famous Statue of Liberty scene. In some ways it's an ideological model for *NORTH BY NORTHWEST*. Dorothy Parker had a hand in the script. ▾

✳＼‼ SAFETY LAST. US. 1923. The ultimate Harold Lloyd film has all the elements: he's a serious young man who always seems to be behind everybody else but wins out in the end. Nothing phases him in his dogged determination to be successful. *Safety Last* includes one of his famous building-climbing routines. Lloyd was a superior stuntman and did all his own stunts.

⇧ SAINT JACK. US. 1979. Peter Bogdanovich took Ben Gazzara, Denholm Elliott, and James Villiers on location in Singapore to film a story of the Singapore underworld in the early seventies. Gazarra is a pimp, amiably servicing American soldiers on R and R. This metaphor surprisingly has more relevance to the Vietnam experience than such epic but apolitical films as *The Deer Hunter*. ▾

◬＼ SAKHAROV. UK/US. 1984. This made-for-cable biography of Soviet dissident hero Andrei Sakharov stars Jason Robards as Sakharov and Glenda Jackson as his wife Yelena Bonner. Jack Gold directed. All of them quietly put their talents at the service of the story and the result is a moving and telling film essay. Sakharov is a character worth at least three more movies. This one captures with considerable understanding the historical dilemma of the USSR, a nation paralyzed by a failed revolution now receding rapidly into the past.   ▽

SALAMANDRE, LA. Switzerland. 1971. An early and humorous film by the very original Swiss director Alain Tanner. Bulle Ogier is accused of murder. A writer (Jean-Luc Bideau) investigates, and we learn much about journalistic approaches to truth.

SALT OF THE EARTH. US. 1953. This is a mostly nonfiction film about Mexican-American mine workers in the southwest (sponsored by their union). Though the film may seem unexceptional now, it hit at the height of McCarthyism and caused a furor. The director, Herbert Biberman, and the leading Mexican actress were both imprisoned. The screenwriter, Michael Wilson, and the producer, Paul Jarrico, were both blacklisted.

SALVATORE GIULIANO. Italy. 1962. Giuliano Salvatore was a real Sicilian outlaw who was hunted down by the authorities. Francesco Rosi's powerful Neorealist re-telling of the story raised significant questions not only about the Sicilian society pervaded by the authority of the Mafia, but also more importantly about official Italian corruption. It's also good drama. This is the same character Mario Puzo fictionalizes as "Salvatore Guiliano" [sic] in *The Sicilian*.

SAMSON AND DELILAH. US. 1949. Late but classic Cecil B. De Mille extravaganza. It's hairy Victor Mature's great role, with Hedy Lamarr, George Sanders, and Angela Lansbury.   ▽

SAN FRANCISCO. US. 1936. Anita Loos wrote this musical adventure directed by W. S. Van Dyke. Clark Gable, Spencer Tracy, and—surprisingly—Jeanette MacDonald star in a film whose point is to climax with the great earthquake.

SANSHO THE BAILIFF. Japan. 1954. Director Kenji Mizoguchi is the third of the triumvirate, with Kurosawa and Ozu, of modern Japanese master filmmakers whose work is well-known in the west. Like Ozu, he developed a remarkable contemplative and restrained visual style—lots of long shots, little cutting, few closeups. Like Kurosawa he was fascinated by Japanese history. *Sansho the Bailiff*, his study of feudal Japan, is balanced and elegant. ▽

SARAVAH. France. 1968. One of the great musical inventions of the last thirty years has been the "new beat" or Bossa Nova of the Brazilian Samba. It's more than just a style of music, it's a way of life. Romantic but human and humane, tuneful and jazzy, the music has had a significant if minor presence in the US for twenty years through the work of Stan Getz, João Gilberto, and a few others, but the French have taken the Brazilian originals more to heart. Filmmaker and musician Pierre Barouh made this documentary about the music, the musicians, and the way of life in the mid-sixties. He was influential in introducing the Saravah style to France. See *A MAN AND A WOMAN*.

SATURDAY NIGHT AND SUNDAY MORNING. UK. 1960. From Alan Sillitoe's classic Angry Young Man novel, script by Sillitoe, and directed by Karel Reisz. Albert Finney is the A.Y.M. trying to burst the bounds of bourgeois convention and bridge class barriers. Shirley Anne Field and Rachel Roberts are the women he romances.

SATURDAY NIGHT FEVER. US. 1977. This is a pretty good contemporary musical film by director John Badham, most significant for turning John Travolta from a television star into a film star—at least for a while. It also made a ton of money and popularized disco music—at least for a while. The Bee Gees' music might be derivative, but so is most other music of the late seventies and eighties. Some good location shooting in Brooklyn adds to the effect. What Travolta is doing here is what he did on TV: keeping the teenager myths of the fifties alive long after they should have been put to rest. ▽

SCAR OF SHAME, THE. US. 1927. Here's a representative example of a thriving genre in the 1920s that few know existed. Produced by the Colored Players Film Corporation and starrng Lucia Lynn Moses this was one of a number of films produced way outside of Hollywood, by Blacks for Blacks and about Blacks. It's time to unearth more of them.

SCARFACE: THE SHAME OF A NATION. US. 1932. Tough, loud, and powerful, *Scarface*, produced by Howard Hughes and directed by Howard Hawks is the ultimate gangster film of all time. Paul Muni is the Al Capone figure; Anne Dvorak, George Raft, and Boris Karloff also star. It's full of unusual touches and in tone is well ahead of its time. It was filmed in 1930 but censors delayed its release for two years. ▽

⇩ **SCARLET EMPRESS, THE**. US. 1934. If you want to find out what Josef von Sternberg was all about, this is the film to see. It's full of garish lighting, ornate sets, and performances to match. Marlene Dietrich is the empress surrounded by brash cinematic effects. Von Sternberg should be every sophomore's favorite filmmaker: when you're just learning about artistic style, this effulgent display is quite impressive. Later, you learn there's less here than meets the eye.

↘ **SCARLET PIMPERNEL, THE**. UK. 1934. If you're ranking bright red movies made in 1934 this one is better. Alexander Korda produced. Leslie Howard and Merle Oberon star in the tale of an English aristocrat's double life during the French Revolution.

🚩◬ **SCENES FROM A MARRIAGE**. Sweden. 1973. This 6-part TV miniseries squeaks in only because Ingmar Bergman re-edited it to feature length for showing outside Sweden. It's as painful an expose of the relationships of men and women as any of the earlier Bergman films but the more naturalistic style of television gives him a chance to explain more, and that leads to a catharsis that's often missing from the highly-charged symbolic movies. With Liv Ullmann, Erland Josephson, and Bibi Andersson. ▽

◬↘ **SEA HAWK, THE**. US. 1940. Here's your classic Errol Flynn movie. (Directed by Michael Curtiz.) It's full of naval adventure and dashing romance and crazy swashbuckling. Erich Wolfgang Korngold wrote the score. ▽

◬ **SEA WOLF, THE**. US. 1941. Michael Curtiz again. This time it's the Jack London novel with excellent performances by Edward G. Robinson, John Garfield, and Ida Lupino in a story that delineates the cramped world that a ship at sea becomes.

✳↘ **SEARCHERS, THE**. US. 1956. John Ford's most poignant and in many ways most ambitious western. Natalie Wood is the girl kidnapped by Indians. John

Wayne is the man who searches for her half a lifetime. It's a sentimental story that Ford handles with great reserve. The film provides an opportunity for numerous striking portraits of John Wayne set against the western vistas in color and widescreen. If you had to pick an ultimate western still, it would probably come from this film. ▽

△ **SECONDS**. US. 1966. John Frankenheimer directed a script by Lewis John Carlino, a playwright before and filmmaker after. Rock Hudson, John Randolph, and Will Geer star in a strange and still fascinating fantasy. Hudson's a middle-aged man-in-a-gray-flannel-suit who buys himself youth and a new identity. Hokey, but absorbing.

‼ **SECRET LIFE OF WALTER MITTY, THE**. US. 1947. Danny Kaye, on a roll, is cast as the legendary James Thurber everyman. Virginia Mayo and Boris Karloff assist under the direction of Norman Z. McLeod.

⤢ **SECRET OF NIMH, THE**. US. 1982. This is one of the most successful attempts at animation to come along in a long time. By Don Bluth and other graduates of the Disney studio, here is an intelligent, humane, interesting and unpretentious morality play for children, as well as adults. A group of intelligent rats, victims of The National Institutes of Mental Health, set up their own sensible society and help a mouse meet the challenge of living. Good music for this sort of thing, too. ▽

△⟍ **SEDUCED AND ABANDONED**. Italy. 1964. Another tough and funny essay on Sicilian lifestyles by Pietro Germi (*DIVORCE ITALIAN STYLE*). Stefania Sandrelli is the gorgeous young Sicilian girl who's the object of the title. Sicilian comedies prove once again that the more it hurts the more you laugh.

SEDUCTION OF MIMI, THE. Italy. 1974. One of Lina Wertmüller's more successful melanges of sex and politics, once again with Giancarlo Giannini and Mariangela Melato. Giannini is Mimi, the macho worker who makes a false move at every step, whether in sex or politics. ▽

⟍ **SEMI-TOUGH**. US. 1977. A typical Michael Ritchie comedy based on the novel by Dan Jenkins about a couple of professional football players (Burt Reynolds and Kris Kristofferson), their girl (Jill Clayburgh), and their strange careers in the absurd world of pro sports. Compare *NORTH DALLAS FORTY*. ▽

SENSE OF LOSS, A. Northern Ireland. 1972. Essayist Marcel Ophuls turned his attention here to the political embroglio in Northern Ireland. Although this is a solid portrait of the complex and various factions involved in the Irish Civil War it's disappointing because it doesn't suggest a clear analysis of the situation. Bernadette Devlin stars.

SEPTEMBER 30, 1955. US. 1977. James Bridges fashioned this view of teenage life in the mid-fifties by focusing on the day James Dean died and the effect that had on a group of southern college students. It's an interesting idea.

SERGEANT YORK. US. 1941. Howard Hawks directed Gary Cooper in the title role. It's a perfect opportunity for Cooper to display the naive but attractive simplicity which was his best quality. York was the celebrated World War I hero who was a pacifist until he was drafted. Compare *FRIENDLY PERSUASION*.

SERIAL. US. 1980. Columnist Cyra McFadden produced a series of essays in the late 1970s on the curious lifestyles of Marin County, north of San Francisco, which achieved some considerable success. They were collected into a "novel" and published in book form. This is an attempt to capture the unusually precise and telling social commentary on film and it comes close to succeeding in a difficult task. Bill Persky directed. Martin Mull, Sally Kellerman, Tuesday Weld, Bill Macy, Tom Smothers, Christopher Lee, Peter Bonerz, and numerous others star in the series of vignettes. Compare it with *PETULIA* to see the historical roots.

SERPICO. US. 1973. Sidney Lumet made this version of the Peter Maas book about the real-life police renegade Frank Serpico. At least in New York now, cops seem like regular people. To understand the impact of the Serpico myth of the early seventies you have to remember that it came just a few years after a time in which cops and hippies saw themselves as sworn enemies. For Serpico to break the cop's code and lead a "hippie" lifestyle was one thing. (Any middle-class yuppie would find this lifestyle totally unexceptional today.) For him to become a hero to civilians because of his testimony in front of the Knapp Commission investigating police corruption, was quite something else. Frank Serpico and the media myth that was created around him are in no small part responsible for humanizing police work during the 1970s. ☑

SERVANT, THE. UK. 1963. Joseph Losey directed this early Harold Pinter script. The relationships between Dirk Bogarde and James Fox, servant and employer, are typically knotty, but much of the sense of humor of Pinter's plays at the time seems to be missing. ☑

SETUP, THE. US. 1949. Robert Wise directed this stagey but still interesting experiment in film time. Robert Ryan is the over-the-hill boxer who tries to stay straight. As in *CLEO FROM 5 TO 7*, film time is real time. ☑

§ **SEVEN BRIDES FOR SEVEN BROTHERS**. US. 1954. This wasn't an especially popular Stanley Donen musical at the time, but it has stayed around. Howard Keel and Jane Powell star. Johnny Mercer wrote the music. Michael Kidd choreographed a lot of exciting dances. Jacques D'Amboise performs. The plot? Keel and his six brothers decide to get married and do. ☑

SEVEN DAYS IN MAY. US. 1964. Another political melodrama by John Frankenheimer based on a popular novel of the time. The premise is the threat of a military coup in the US. Burt Lancaster and Kirk Douglas are the generals; Fredric March is the President. With hindsight, the irony of this film is that during the ten years that succeeded it, the military *did* stage a kind of symbolic coup, keeping successive governments obsessed with an unwinnable war in Vietnam. It didn't last seven days; it lasted more than seven years. ☑

☛ **SEVEN SAMURAI, THE**. Japan. 1954. Akira Kurosawa's epic samurai masterpiece has been imitated many times. It's full of great action sequences and pervaded with a spiritual sense, but it may be most important historically for beginning a period of cultural rapprochement between Japan and the United States. We all could see that this samurai movie was really a western and we began to realize that "the Japs" weren't so very different from you and me. Could Sony have succeeded without *The Seven Samurai*? ☑

⇧ **SEVEN YEAR ITCH, THE**. US. 1955. A George Axelrod script directed by Billy Wilder, this may be Marilyn Monroe's best film. She's still a dumb blonde but somehow Axelrod and Wilder give her a humanity she wasn't often allowed. This one includes the emblematic scene of Marilyn with her full skirt blowin' in the wind from the subway grating. Tom Ewell is the neighbor who gets the itch for Marilyn while his wife is away on vacation. ◧

SEVENTH SEAL, THE. Sweden. 1956. Ingmar Bergman's medieval mystery film with Max von Sydow as the knight who plays chess with Death was and is beloved by all English teachers because it is highly symbolic; because its literary antecedents are clear and present; and because it offers much to translate, explain, and analyze. It was a movie they and others could accept as art and it began the fifteen-year process of legitimizing the art of film in academia. Today, it may seem overburdened with allegory, but it's still visually striking. ◧

SEVENTH VEIL, THE. UK. 1945. James Mason, Ann Todd, and Herbert Lom in a solid forties melodrama interesting for Todd's proto-feminist character and Mason's performance as her guardian. She leaves her family to become a pianist.

SEX HYGIENE. US. 1941. During the war John Ford, like Frank Capra and a number of other filmmakers, turned his talents to the war effort, producing a number of instructional films. This one is notorious for its graphic depiction of the terrors that awaited the soldiers and sailors who weren't careful. Everyone who served in the war saw it and nobody forgot it. It stands here as an emblem of all the great instructional movies that aren't touted in the newspapers or studied in the universities.

SHADOW OF A DOUBT. US. 1943. Thornton Wilder worked on this Alfred Hitchcock script and that may be the reason this is a funnier, calmer, and less frenzied Hitchcock movie. Wilder has added a good dose of small-town Americana to this story of Teresa White's wonderful Uncle Charley (Joseph Cotten), who turns out to be a killer. Compare *OUR TOWN*.

SHADOWS. US. 1959. This is a landmark in US independent filmmaking. John Cassavetes shot it on a shoestring on location in Greenwich Village and the film has none of the pacing or dialogue or character that we expect from a Hollywood movie: it's fascinating. Lelia Goldoni stars as a light-skinned Black girl caught between the races. The film does have a plot but the interest lies in the way it uses the rough realism we associate with home movies. This film is as important in its way in marking the dawn of a new age in film history as the art house classics from Europe shown during the same year.

SHAFT. US. 1971. In the early seventies it looked as if *Shaft*, a Black private eye movie directed by Gordon Parks, was going to be only the first in a continuing series of films that would give Black actors, technicians, and filmmakers more work in Hollywood. The trend lasted for only two years before producers discovered that Black audiences were just as likely to spend money on, say, *THE GODFATHER* or *THE EXORCIST* as on films starring and directed by Blacks. The death of the Black Hollywood movie is curious when you realize that the influence of Blacks in legitimate theater, which started about the same time, has grown over the years. In any event, *Shaft*, with Richard Roundtree, Moses Gunn, and Charles Cioffi, is still a good uptown private eye movie. It was followed by a couple of equally good sequels. ▨

SHAKESPEARE WALLAH. India. 1965. Another James Ivory/Ismail Merchant film that plays on the mixture of English and Indian characters. Shashi Kapoor and Madhur Jaffrey star. This time the twist is Shakespeare as we follow an English company touring India.

SHALL WE DANCE. US. 1937. "They All Laughed," "Let's Call the Whole Thing Off," and other Gershwin tunes stud this Fred Astaire, Ginger Rogers, Edward Everett Horton show directed by Mark Sandrich. ▨

SHAME. Sweden. 1968. Another of Ingmar Bergman's Island movies with Liv Ullmann, Max von Sydow, and Gunnar Björnstrand. This time the background is civil war. Compare *THE PASSION OF ANNA*.

SHAMPOO. US. 1975. Warren Beatty was the driving force behind this minor landmark with a script by Robert Towne, directed by Hal Ashby. The aim is to satirize southern California lifestyles in the late sixties. Beatty's a hairdresser with numerous attractive customers. See *I LOVE YOU ALICE B. TOKLAS* for another view of the same time, or *SERIAL*, to compare Marin with L.A.

SHANE. US. 1953. If you were a kid in the fifties you probably identified with Brandon de Wilde, the kid in *Shane* who finds a friend in gunslinger Alan Ladd. Here's a moral western (directed by George Stevens) that in its own way matched *HIGH NOON* as a distillation of "western" philosophy.

SHANGHAI EXPRESS. US. 1932. Von Sternberg idealizes Marlene Dietrich as Shanghai Lil in China during the Civil War. The plot is the sort of fodder that fed many reels of Saturday morning serials during the thirties but Von Sternberg squeezes every ounce of visual cinema out of it.

‼ **SHE DONE HIM WRONG**. US. 1933. "Whyancha. . . come up and see me sometime?" intones Mae West to Cary Grant. This best of the West movies (directed by Lowell Sherman) was based on her own stage play. Here she's Diamond Lil in the gay nineties.

⊘ **SHE WORE A YELLOW RIBBON**. US. 1949. John Ford directs John Wayne and the usual cast in this second of his cavalry trilogy. Great color photography at the time. See *FORT APACHE*, *RIO GRANDE*.

‼ **SHERLOCK JR**. US. 1924. This is the great Buster Keaton movie about movies. Buster is the projectionist who falls asleep dreaming about being a famous detective, jumps up and runs onto the screen, and in the process is liberated to perform some of his greatest stunts. It's a breathless fifty-seven minutes.

SHOESHINE. Italy. 1946. Together with *OPEN CITY*, *Shoeshine* marked the explosion of Neorealism after the war. Vittorio De Sica directed the script by Cesare Zavattini and others that tells in stark, well-paced terms the story of two kids who barely survive in Rome during the allied occupation. It's angry and direct but also profoundly humane: just the qualities that made Neorealism far more than an esthetic approach.

SHOGUN. US. 1981. Originally an eight-and-a-half-hour miniseries, *Shogun* has been re-edited as a feature-length film, apparently for the home video audience. The saga, based on the James Clavell novel about a British sailor in feudal Japan, was a landmark in television history. Throughout much of its eight-and-a-half-hours most of the cast spoke Japanese. Its popularity proved that American audiences hungered for exposure to Japanese culture, at least when it was presented as an exciting adventure and romance. Richard Chamberlain starred with Toshiro Mifune and Yoko Shimada. See *THE SEVEN SAMURAI*.

SHOOT THE PIANO PLAYER. France. 1960. What set out to be a small hommage to the American film noir became one of François Truffaut's most memorable movies. The story of piano player Charlie Kohler has become a romantic classic thanks in great part to the music by Georges Delerue. Charles Aznavour is Charlie, the down-and-out piano player who gets involved with gangsters. Marie Dubois is his girlfriend. If this had been an American film it would have been much tougher and downbeat. Truffaut who sees the story from a greater distance, adds humor, warmth, and restraint. �

SHOOTIST, THE. US. 1976. You can't escape the references here in Don Siegel's post-western: John Wayne stars as the aging gunfighter who learns from his doctor, James Stewart, that he has cancer. Lauren Bacall and Richard Boone are also here to remind us of movie history. The film uses clips of Wayne as a young man. It's a great coda to a magnificent career. ▽

SHOP AROUND THE CORNER, THE. US. 1940. One of Ernst Lubitsch's most charming and amiable movies. James Stewart and Margaret Sullavan star as two workers in a Viennese dry goods shop who fall in love with each other—unknowingly—by mail. Frank Morgan is the ingratiating shopkeeper.

SHOT IN THE DARK, A. US. 1964. Blake Edwards's second Inspector Clouseau (*PINK PANTHER*) comedy is probably the best. Peter Sellers had worked out the timing and the series hadn't yet jaded. This is the one with the nudist colony scene. ▽

SHOWBOAT. US. 1936. If Paul Robeson singing "Old Man River" isn't enough. . . you may not be particularly interested in *Showboat* except for its significance in the history of the musical. James Whale directed.

SILENT WORLD, THE. France. 1956. Jacques-Yves Cousteau not only a long and memorable career here, but also contributed to the founding of one of the major forms of cinema during the last thirty years: the nature documentary. Considering the importance and vitality of this sort of filmmaking, you have to rank even a popularist like Cousteau many rungs higher than most fiction filmmakers. The "art" of film may be the subject of study in universities, but the simple craft has the power to teach and discover in a way that can be far more influential.

§ **SILK STOCKINGS**. US. 1957. Rouben Mamoulian directed Fred Astaire and Cyd Charisse in this Cole Porter musical of *NINOTCHKA*, a last vestige of the classic thirties Hollywood style.

⬟ **SILKWOOD**. US. 1983. Karen Silkwood was a worker in a nuclear power plant and a union activist who may or may not have been murdered in 1976 by agents of the Kerr-McGee Corporation. In its way it's as important a story as 3-Mile Island (or *THE CHINA SYNDROME*) about atomic energy, the quiet killer. For years, various filmmakers (including Jane Fonda) had tried to film the Silkwood story. Mike Nichols finally succeeded. But it's a curiously distant film that focuses at least as much attention on Silkwood's seventies lifestyle as on the dangers of nuclear proliferation and the drama of her situation. Thirty years ago the Silkwood character would have been cleaned up for the movies, and maybe it's all to the good she's shown as a realistic young woman here, but the political effect of the film is certainly muted by this apparently conscious attempt to avoid melodrama. ▽

‼ **SILVER STREAK**. US. 1976. Colin Higgins wrote this entertaining latter-day screwball that gives Gene Wilder and Richard Pryor a chance to let out all the stops. The Silver Streak, of course, is a train, and you'll never forget its landing in Chicago. Jill Clayburgh is the love interest. ▽

⬟ **SINCE YOU WENT AWAY**. US. 1944. David O. Selznick wrote and produced, Max Steiner scored, and John Cromwell directed what is one of the great domestic melodramas of the Golden Age. We follow the fortunes of a family during World War II. Claudette Colbert, Jennifer Jones, Joseph Cotten, and Monty Woolley are among the stars.

✳‖§ **SINGIN' IN THE RAIN**. US. 1952. This is, most people will agree, the perfect Hollywood musical. Betty Comden and Adolph Green, any of whose screenplays is worth not one but several looks, constructed an emblematic story about Hollywood at the dawn of the talkies. The songs, all of them winners, were chosen from a large catalogue of Arthur Freed/Nacio Herb Brown songs that had been written for earlier movies. Gene Kelly and Stanley Donen directed. Kelly plays Don Lockwood, the hero star who makes the transition to sound successfully. Jean Hagen is Lena Lamont, his incredibly dumb leading lady who doesn't. Debbie Reynolds is Kathy Selden, the fresh-faced and spunky girl he falls in love with. Donald O'Connor is Cosmo Brown, the ultimate sidekick. It's got satire, it's got nostalgia, it's even got revenge. And the songs, including "Make 'Em Laugh," "Singin' in the Rain," and "Good Mornin'," are the kind that wake you up, make you feel good, and get you back on the right track. It all comes together here. "What a glorious feeling, I'm happy again!" ▽

SITTING PRETTY. US. 1948. Clifton Webb has got to be the strangest Hollywood leading man of thirty years. His fussy—even prissy—character should have been relegated to a minor supporting role but he hit paydirt here as Mr. Belvedere, the man who becomes a fulltime babysitter. Several other Belvedere films followed and he concluded with Mr. Pennypacker, an equally strange role.

SIX AMERICAN FAMILIES. US. 1977. We're cheating here. This was an independent television series in six parts, produced by Paul Wilkes. It was never re-edited like *SHOGUN* or *SCENES FROM A MARRIAGE* into theatrical feature, but it represents such an important vein of filmmaking that we're breaking the rules. Wilkes and his crews went to live with six different American families and the portraits that emerge are fascinating. This technique could work anywhere, but in the US—so diverse and various—it's even more appropriate. There's none of the hype that attached to *An American Family*, the PBS series several years before this that made the Loud family a household word and even turned Mom into a professional actress. Watching the families watch themselves as they do at the end of each film, we realize the inherent drama between filmmakers and film subjects. This is a series that should have run forever, until the last one of us had been filmed.

SIX IN PARIS. France. 1964. Producer Barbet Schroeder conceived this anthology film shot quickly and cheaply in 16mm by Jean-Luc Godard, Claude Chabrol, Eric Rohmer, Jean Rouch, and others. It remains a useful survey of the French New Wave at a certain point in time. Chabrol's sketch—"La Muette"—is a fifteen-minute distillation of his weirdly comic sensibility. Rohmer's "Place de l'Etoile" serves equally well as an emblem of his work.

SIX OF A KIND. US. 1934. George Burns, Gracie

Allen, W. C. Fields, and Charlie Ruggles combine under the direction of Leo McCarey in an underrated comic classic. The setting is an hilarious cross-country automobile trip—not so easy to do in 1934. Don't miss Fields's pool-playing scene.

SLAP SHOT. US. 1977. Paul Newman's the over-the-hill star of a very minor hockey team, Michael Ontkean is the young star, and Jennifer Warren and Lindsay Crouse are their women in this well-paced and knowing satire of professional sports. Nancy Dowd wrote the script. George Roy Hill directed. It's good fun. ☑

SLEEPER. US. 1973. Woody Allen and Diane Keaton together again for the first time in an unusual and successful attempt at slapstick science fiction. Woody is thawed out in 2173 after a 200-year freeze. It's a model situation for physical comedy in the tradition of Buster Keaton and Jacques Tati. Our hero also has trouble dealing with the world around him, and the futuristic setting allows Allen considerable freedom to build that world in the funniest way possible. ☑

SLEUTH. US. 1972. Joseph L. Mankiewicz mounted this version of Anthony Shaffer's successful West End mystery puzzle with Laurence Olivier as the mystery writer and Michael Caine as his victim. There's no depth here, but it's so exceptionally well made that it's great fun. ☑

SLIGHT CASE OF MURDER, A. US. 1938. Here's a real sleeper, based on a Damon Runyon play, with Edward G. Robinson as a gangster who tries to go straight at the end of Prohibition. As an honest brewer he's a magnificent and funny failure. Lloyd Bacon directed. It's interesting that Robinson, who played gangsters straight so often and so well, is so funny here.

SMALL CHANGE. France. 1976. Throughout most of the seventies François Truffaut was busy with a series of rather dark, forlorn visions, but here he returned to the subject of children with a remarkably winning portrait of the kids of a small French town. Most of them are younger than Antoine Doinel of *400 BLOWS* fame, but Truffaut's touch with the material is, if anything, wiser and more sophisticated than it was before. Truffaut sees children from their own point of view. Something hardly anyone else has done. *Small Change* is full of bright touches and unusual moments and it should be fascinating to watch children relate to it. After the closing credits they may very well pick up a camera themselves. ▼

SMILE. US. 1975. The wonderful characters in Michael Ritchie's portrait of a northern California town probably haven't the slightest idea what those people in *SERIAL* are doing. It's not that they live so far away, it's simply that they're of a different class. No one as yet has picked up the mantle laid down by Frank Capra, but if anyone could—on the evidence of *Smile* and a couple of other films—it's Ritchie. He has an affection for car salesmen and manufacturers of bowling trophies that's enormously infectious. Bruce Dern, Barbara Feldon, Michael Kidd, and Nicholas Pryor are the grownups here. The kids in the beauty contest which is our town's pride and joy, include Joan Prather, Annette O'Toole, and Melanie Griffith. Don't be misled by McDonald's; smalltown Americana survives.

SMILES OF A SUMMER NIGHT. Sweden. 1955. If you've been exposed to the musical *A Little Night Music*, rest assured that Ingmar Bergman did it better in the original. It's his sanest, most self-assured, and in the process perhaps most mundane movie: a romantic comedy set at the turn of the century in which Ulla Jacobsson, Eva Dahlbeck, Harriet Andersson, Gunnar Björnstrand, and Jarl Külle match step for step and line for line any Hollywood actors who might have done this sort of film at the time. Solid and serene.

SMOKEY AND THE BANDIT. US. 1977. Southern drive-in movies as a genre had existed before this, but Burt Reynolds, Sally Field, Jackie Gleason, and director Hal Needham raised them to a new and higher level with this funny and affectionate road movie full of wonderful stunts. Gleason is the sheriff, Reynolds is "the bandit," and the chase is a classic piece of American movie-making. For the real sequel, see *HOOPER*.

SNOW WHITE AND THE SEVEN DWARFS. US. 1937. The first of Walt Disney's animated features may still be the best. It has a freshness and authenticity which gradually disappeared from that studio's work as it became a children's animation factory.

SOCRATES. Italy. 1970. Roberto Rossellini turns his critical intelligence to an essay on the ancient Greek philosopher/teacher.

SOFT SKIN, THE. France. 1964. François Truffaut's first try at domestic melodrama is stylish

Henry Fonda gazes wistfully at Barbara Stanwyck in Preston Sturges's *The Lady Eve.* The corpulent gentleman with his back to us is Eugene Pallette.

and evocative. Jean Desailly is the middle-aged businessman, Nelly Benedetti is his wife, and Françoise Dorléac his lover. Dorléac was killed in an auto accident shortly after.

🜂 **SOME LIKE IT HOT**. US. 1959. Director/writer Billy Wilder and writer I. A. L. Diamond managed to take a traditional European comedy turn—dressing in drag—and make it into a thoroughly American experience here. Jack Lemmon and Tony Curtis star as two musicians on the lam who disguise themselves by joining an all-female band. They fall for Marilyn Monroe and Joe E. Brown, and the usual, hilarious, fast-paced Wilder complications ensue. ▼

SONS AND LOVERS. UK. 1960. It's surprising that D. H. Lawrence's novels haven't proved better sources for the movies. Here's one—about the struggles of a cultured young man in a rough Welsh coal-mining town—that works pretty well. Directed by Jack Cardiff with Trevor Howard, Wendy Hiller, Dean Stockwell, and Mary Ure.

📵 **SOPHIA LOREN: HER OWN STORY**. US. 1980. If nothing else this is a landmark in self-referential cinema since Sophia Loren stars not only as herself, but also as her mother. (John Gavin is Cary Grant, Rip Torn is Carlo Ponti, and Edmond Perdom is Vittorio De Sica.) In fact, Loren's life story, even if idealized, is a worthy subject of a movie biography. She is without a doubt the most self-confident and powerful woman film artist since Mary Pickford; she's had a long and interesting career in not one but three separate countries and languages (Italian, English, and French); she's been close to the centers of powers of both European and American cinema; and she's led a far more interesting life than businesswoman Pickford (or most other stars you can point to). Mel Stuart directed from the autobiography written by A. E. Hotchner.

*¶ **SORROW AND THE PITY, THE**. Switzerland. 1970. A four-and-a-half-hour five-part essay about French complicity during the Nazi occupation, this landmark documentary was originally intended for television. It appeared in theaters only after being banned on TV. Marcel Ophuls, son of the late Max Ophüls, had had a fairly colorless career as a fiction director in France until this remarkable effort put him on the cinematic map for all time. There's a kind of intellectual diffidence that marks Ophuls's documentaries and that hurts them some, but the material here is so powerful that that soft political focus is not noticeable. *The Sorrow and the Pity* proved like no other film before it that cinema was a tool for dealing with ideas, fully the equal of prose. Few books have had such a profound effect on French cultural politics during the last twenty years.

$ **SOUND OF MUSIC, THE**. US. 1965. All right, it's not great cinema and it's not even among Rodgers and Hammerstein's best works, and it's undoubtedly corny, but this nearly three-hour musical directed by Robert Wise and starring Julie Andrews and Christopher Plummer is still one of the most popular films ever made. The story of the Trapp family singers has all the necessary ingredients: music, children, World War II, and the flavor of Gothic romance. For Julie Andrews fans it has the added attraction of coming hard on the heels of *MY FAIR LADY*. Producers had rejected her as Eliza Doolittle because of her apparent lack of star quality. Only months later she was the lead in a smashing blockbuster.

¶ **SOUNDER**. US. 1972. Perhaps sentimental, but a landmark nevertheless, *Sounder* marked the final acceptance of Black characters as central figures in American movies made for general audiences. Cicely Tyson, Paul Winfield, and Kevin Hooks starred in the story of a sharecropper family. Director Martin

Ritt provides another sensitive portrait of the south. Compare *NOTHING BUT A MAN*. ▽

✛ **SOUTHERNER, THE**. US. 1945. Jean Renoir's best US film is a distilled moral tale about a southern farmer and his family attempting to revive an abandoned farm and meeting with the usual disasters of everyday rural life. It's not unlike the director's earlier *TONI* and could serve as an early model for the recent spate of "country" films with the same moral lesson. Zachary Scott, Betty Field, and J. Carroll Naish star. ▽

◑⭫ **SPARTACUS**. US. 1960. This long and colorful movie starring Kirk Douglas as the title character, is as close as Stanley Kubrick has ever come to making a standard Hollywood movie. Laurence Olivier, Charles Laughton, Tony Curtis, and a host of others support. It's based on the Howard Fast re-telling of the Spartacus legend so you know it's got some political underpinnings as well: Spartacus, a Roman slave who led a rebellion against the Republic, could be a model for contemporary political action. ▽

⬥ **SPECIAL BULLETIN**. US. 1983. This is a technical landmark: not the first made-for-television movie shot on tape rather than film, but the one where that choice had the greatest effect. It's presented as a real television newscast about terrorists threatening a nuclear disaster. It was intended to have the same effect as Orson Welles's famous radio broadcast of *The War of the Worlds*. Perhaps the ethics of that intention should be carefully examined, especially given the extraordinary psychological power of contemporary media. Edward Zwick directed.

⬥ **SPELLBOUND**. US. 1945. Lesser Hitchcock but nevertheless Hitchcock with a somnolant Gregory Peck as the patient and a restrained Ingrid Bergman as the psychiatrist. At the time its psychologizing was regarded as avant-garde; today it seems superficial and simplistic. Miklòs Rosza wrote a score using the early electronic instrument, the theramin. Salvador Dali did the special effects. ▽

SPIDER'S STRATAGEM, THE. Italy. 1970. This curious, mysterious investigation into the residue of fascism by Bernardo Bertolucci solidified his reputation as a new film artist. It's gorgeously photographed by Vittorio Storaro, but on repeated viewings there is less here than meets the eye.

⭫ **SPIRIT OF ST. LOUIS, THE**. US. 1957. An

unusual choice for director Billy Wilder, this absorbing study of Charles Lindbergh's epic flight across the Atlantic gives James Stewart the opportunity of a lifetime: it's almost a solo movie. Excellent fifties color. ▽

‖⬆ SPRINGTIME IN THE ROCKIES. US. 1942. A classic Twentieth Century-Fox musical in violent early forties Technicolor, starring Betty Grable, John Payne, Carmen Miranda, César Romero, and Charlotte Greenwood, with Harry James and the band. Good fun.

◬ SPY WHO CAME IN FROM THE COLD, THE. US. 1965. Richard Burton stars as the anti-heroic secret agent of the John le Carré novel under Martin Ritt's direction. Supporting cast includes Claire Bloom, Oscar Werner, and Michael Hordern. This was the first of le Carré's post-modernist spy novels to be turned into a latter-day film noir. At the time it seemed a sophisticated advance on the sentiments of an earlier generation. Although le Carré's success in film and television has continued to grow, climaxing in the early eighties with *Tinker, Tailor, Soldier, Spy*, the fact is that these downbeat depressive plots now seem to pall. They may be important as emblems of a curious English national psychological depression but we keep wishing that Smiley and his people could find other work since spying seems so painful, unrewarding, and ultimately useless to them.

◬ STAGE DOOR. US. 1937. This is the George S. Kaufman/Edna Ferber play directed by Gregory La Cava. Set in a boarding house, it's a *GRAND HOTEL* for actors. Katharine Hepburn is the little rich girl we know will make it. The rest of the cast includes Ginger Rogers, Gail Patrick, Lucille Ball, and Eve Arden, among others. "The Calla lillies are in bloom again!" ▽

STAGE FRIGHT. US. 1950. Despite the presence of Marlene Dietrich and lots of good English actors (the film was made in London), this was not a great success for Alfred Hitchcock. It's a rather dull story about murder in the world of the theater and audiences reacted strongly to the gimmick of the film. In the first reel Hitchcock shows us a scene which turns out not to be true. There is no visual indication that the scene is hypothetical and that leaves the audience without the proper information to solve the mystery themselves. We're including *Stage Fright* here just for that trick. Hitchcock projected an avuncular image as a folksy story-teller in his appearances on his television series, but that's only part of the Hitchcock persona. He may be your portly uncle but he was also an intensely analytical filmmaker. Most of the questions of narrative were explored in his more than fifty films, and most of the theories of mise-en-scene and montage have been tried out. He's a complete film course all by himself and *Stage Fright* is one of the lectures. ▽

STAGECOACH. US. 1939. The classic western of the thirties starred John Wayne, Andy Devine, Thomas Mitchell, and John Carradine under the direction of John Ford. What was significant about *Stagecoach* at the time was the attention paid to the interplay of character and action. ▽

STALAG 17. US. 1953. World War II was such an overwhelming and pervasive experience that it gave rise to not one but several genres in film. *Stalag 17* is the ultimate POW movie. We've been exposed to so much low-level POW comedy on television since 1953 that it may be difficult to recapture the excitement that *Stalag 17* caused as play and film in the early fifties. Billy Wilder directed William Holden, Otto Preminger, Harvey Lembeck, and Peter Graves. The very idea of making a comedy about the POW experience was striking at the time. ▽

STANLEY & LIVINGSTONE. US. 1939. Spencer Tracy was such an urban character that it's always interesting to see him in an outdoor adventure like this one. Here he's the intrepid reporter searching for Cedric Hardwicke's famous missing missionary in Africa. Henry King directed.

STAR IS BORN, A. US. 1937. Movies about movie-making may seem self-centered and self-important, but the fact is the subject is significant. Since the days of Douglas Fairbanks and Mary Pickford, actors have played a powerful role in society. As celebrities they serve functions that used to be performed by royalty. *A Star Is Born*, remade several times, is a classic examination of the Hollywood myth. The relationship between an actress on the rise and an actor whose prime is well past touches a raw Hollywood nerve. This version starred Fredric March and Janet Gaynor under the direction of William Wellman; Dorothy Parker had a hand in the screenplay. It's a great example of thirties Technicolor. ▽

STAR IS BORN, A. US. 1954. Here's a case where a film and its remake run neck and neck. Moss Hart wrote this script and it's nicely punctuated with Harold Arlen tunes. Judy Garland and James Mason star under the direction of George Cukor. (In the seventies the film was remade yet again by Frank Pierson with a rock music setting. Barbra Streisand and Kris Kristofferson starred.) ▽

STAR TREK III: THE SEARCH FOR SPOCK. US. 1984. Of the three *Star Trek* features so far, this one comes closest to recapturing the special qualities of the notorious television series. You will remember that Spock (played by Leonard Nimoy), the hero of a generation, logically sacrificed himself for the greater good of the Enterprise back in *Star Trek—the Wrath of Khan*. When you die in the movies you go behind the camera: Leonard Nimoy directed this episode. Gene Roddenberry's creation has been the object of a large and enthusiastic cult following for twenty years now for very good reasons. It's not the collection of characters on the bridge of the Starship Enterprise (although they are simple enough to offer the pleasures of pulp fiction). It's rather that the format allowed writers to treat all of the classic myths as the Enterprise roved from Stardate to Stardate, and also to invent a few of their own. It's the most liberating sort of science fiction and enormously attractive to young people looking for stories that explain the world: which is what myths do. ▽

STAR WARS. US. 1977. There's no denying the appeal of this historic blockbuster. George Lucas has done more than anyone except Jim Henson (and perhaps Walt Disney) to establish the gallery of characters who now populate contemporary childhood. What's fascinating from a cinematic point of view is the magnificently derivative nature of the film. It's an enormous summary of characters, styles, and plot points that surveys forty years of film history. There's probably not a frame in it that doesn't have some cinematic antecedent, which is not to criticize *Star Wars*: it brought back for a new generation a lot of the elements of Hollywood movie-making that were attractive to their parents and it did so in breathless anthology form. ▽

STARTING OVER. US. 1979. Alan J. Pakula directed this incisive and touching script by James L. Brooks, one of the creators of the masterful *Mary Tyler Moore Show*. Burt Reynolds is a small, introverted fellow who has anxiety attacks in department stores. Jill Clayburgh is the girl he falls for, and Candice Bergen is magnificent as his ex-wife who's learning to sing. These are contemporary characters with a vengeance. This is the way we live now. ⊻

⊘ **STATE OF SIEGE**. France. 1973. Shot in English with mostly French stars, this is another striking docudrama by Costa-Gavras which deals with covert US political involvement in South American politics: this time an assassination in Uruguay. Costa-Gavras has the almost unique ability to combine sensible and complex political commentary with taut and effective melodrama. Yves Montand and Jean-Luc Bideau star. ⊻

⛫ **STATE OF THE UNION**. US. 1948. Frank Capra worked with Spencer Tracy and Katharine Hepburn to mount this Howard Lindsay/Russel Crouse play about Presidential and family politics.

⛫ § **STAVISKY. . .** France. 1974. This is the closest Alain Resnais has ever come to a straight movie. Jean-Paul Belmondo is the fascinating historical character Stavisky; Charles Boyer, Anny Duperey, François Périer assist. The photography is excellent and so is the score by Stephen Sondheim. Yet it's more than just a biopic of a colorful entrepreneur/swindler involved in the politics of the thirties, for Resnais plays particular attention to the role of the media in the *Stavisky* story. A fascinating and underrated film.

§ **STING, THE**. US. 1974. After the success of *BUTCH CASSIDY*, director George Roy Hill brought Paul Newman and Robert Redford back together again in this stylish entertainment. David S. Ward wrote the slick caper comedy which also stars Robert Shaw as the stingee. The 1930s Chicago settings are done on a shoestring but what really turned this film into a major hit was the use of Scott Joplin's ragtime music for the score. Sure it's anachronistic, but it shows you that sometimes it's the little decisions that mean a lot to the success of a film. ⊻

✳ **STOLEN KISSES**. France. 1968. This is the third episode of François Truffaut's five Antoine Doinel films and the high point not only of the series but of romantic filmmaking in the sixties and seventies. Jean-Pierre Léaud is Doinel, who started out ten years earlier as Truffaut's alter ego in *THE 400 BLOWS*. Now he's left the army and begins to shape a life for himself. Claude Jade is the girl he falls in love with, and Delphine Seyrig is the older woman. Paris locations have never been more evocative. This is a romance of exceeding charm that has deep and abiding roots in the real world: an extraordinary accomplishment.

§⇧ **STORMY WEATHER**. US. 1943. Before the sixties, Blacks got into American movies in exactly the same way they got into American mainstream life: as maids or entertainers. The latter is certainly far preferable. Here's a rare Hollywood movie featuring a large number of major Black entertainers of the day, including Bill "Bojangles" Robinson, Cab Calloway, Fats Waller, Dooley Wilson (of *CASABLANCA* fame), dancer Katherine Dunham, and Lena Horne. *Stormy Weather* captures a number of the classic music and dance routines on film.

STORY OF G.I. JOE, THE. US. 1945. William Wellman directed this portrait of the famous war reporter Ernie Pyle. Burgess Meredith stars in the title role. A mythic World War II movie.

◐ **STORY OF LOUIS PASTEUR, THE**. US. 1936. This is the first of William Dieterle's classic 1930s biopics. Paul Muni plays the title role with his usual stagey presence and projection. (Muni is second only to George Arliss in this sort of acting in the thirties.) Compare *DR. EHRLICH'S MAGIC BULLET*.

✳§ **STRADA, LA**. Italy. 1956. The heart of Italian film since World War II—and it is a great one—has been Neorealism. The tradition has lasted under whatever label for more than thirty-five years now. Paradoxically, however, the two most famous Italian filmmakers during that period—Fellini and Antonioni— both have exceptionally strong streaks of fantasy in their work. *La Strada* is a magical combination of the romantic dream world of Fellini and the traditions of Neorealism. The score by Nina Rota, always so important to a Fellini film, makes this one well nigh operatic. Anthony Quinn is the lone circus strongman touring the countryside. Giulietta Masina is the waif who follows him. Richard Basehart is the acrobat they meet. The settings are Neorealistic, but the mood is an exhilarating affirmation of the spirit. ▼

◐ **STRANGE LOVE OF MARTHA IVERS, THE**. US. 1946. This Barbara Stanwyck vehicle is second only to *MILDRED PIERCE* in a ranking of 1940s soap operas. Kirk Douglas and Judith Anderson assist in quite an absorbing melodrama. Martha is haunted by the memory of a murder long ago. Lewis Milestone directed.

◒ STRANGER, THE. US. 1946. This is not the landmark existential novel by Albert Camus. It is Orson Welles's fascinating portrait of a Nazi in hiding in smalltown America. Welles is the fugitive: Loretta Young is the woman he wants to marry; Edward G. Robinson is the cop. Compare *SHADOW OF A DOUBT*.

⛟ STRANGER, THE. France/Italy. 1967. This is the film version of the Camus novel that helped form the existential sensibilities of a generation of intellectuals in the fifties and sixties. Marcello Mastroianni stars in the title role and the reverberations we feel from his previous roles help a great deal. Anna Karina also stars. Luchino Visconti directed with unusual and welcome restraint. The Algerian setting is evocative.

◒ STRANGERS ON A TRAIN. US. 1951. The Patricia Highsmith thriller novel as staged by Alfred Hitchcock. Farley Granger and Robert Walker are an unusual and effective pair. One of them is crazy. Memorable for its carousel sequence.   ▽

⬱ STREET SCENES 1970. US. 1970. A group of filmmakers calling themselves the New York Cinetracts Collective shot this anthology of documentary scenes of political action at a time when politics in the US was pervasive, passionate, and sometimes deadly. It's an important record of a time and place for anyone trying to understand the youth culture of the late sixties and early seventies. Martin Scorsese was part of the group whose name is an obvious reference to French filmmakers who took to the streets during the events of May 1968.

⬲ STREETCORNER STORIES. US. 1978. Film-maker Warrington Hudlin found a barbershop in New Haven, Connecticut that serves as a kind of Community Center for the men of the Black neighborhood surrounding it. He hung out with his camera and recorder and the interviews he collected form a unique and moving portrait of the Black culture of poverty in the US. There is a culture here: a fine art of story-telling whose roots date back hundreds of years. The contrast of the hope reflected in the art and the hopelessness of poverty is striking.

◒ STRIKE. USSR. 1924. Coming out of Sergei Eisenstein's theatrical experiences, *Strike* is full of stagey caricature and humor. The story of a strike in Czarist times, and its harrowing aftermath, it's also an important record of the theatrical ferment of the early twenties.

STRONGMAN FERDINAND. West Germany. 1976. Director Alexander Kluge was one of the earliest proponents of what came to be known in Germany as Das Neue Kino. He led a group of young German filmmakers in making a landmark statement against what the French called "Le cinéma du papa" in 1962 at the Oberhausen Festival. *Strongman Ferdinand* is his most traditional film, a strange and remarkably humorous story about a security guard whose power intoxicates and obsesses him. It is a strong parable about the modern police state.

STROSZEK. West Germany. 1977. A curious sometime entertainer by the name of Bruno S. is the star here in Werner Herzog's interesting attempt to treat the myth of emigration to the New World. Stroszek travels from Germany to Chicago in search of the dream and as usual Herzog exploits the tension between the reality of his actors and the fiction of his characters.

STUDENT PRINCE, THE. US. 1954. This is a shlocky but nevertheless loveable filming of the Sigmund Romberg operetta, celebrating student days at Heidelberg. Especially attractive for Ann Blyth fans, it's redolent of the fifties. Mario Lanza's voice can be heard: "Drink, drink, drink!"

STUNT MAN, THE. US. 1978. Here is a highly unusual movie, part satire, part black comedy, written by Lawrence Marcus of *PETULIA* fame and directed by Richard Rush (see *GETTING STRAIGHT*). Steve Railsback is a fugitive who gets caught up in a film production after the death of the chief stunt man. Peter O'Toole is the crazy director, and the two gradually confuse reality and imagination in one of the best movies about the film business ever made. Producer/director Rush worked on the project throughout most of the seventies, finished shooting in 1978, then spent two years desparately attempting to get the film released. It cost him a heart attack in the process. Life imitates art.

SUCH A GORGEOUS KID LIKE ME. France. 1972. François Truffaut's most unusual movie is a pleasurable comedy about a woman murderer (Bernadette Lafont) who enjoys describing her career to a student of Sociology. Claude Brasseur, Charles Denner, and Philippe Léotard are among the victims. Script by Jean-Loup Dabadie.

⇪ SUGARLAND EXPRESS, THE. US. 1974. Steven Spielberg's first theatrical movie—with Goldie Hawn, Michael Sacks, and William Atherton—about a young fugitive couple on the run and the hundreds of Texas cops who chase them. It's such an absorbing little story that it makes you wish he hadn't turned to major themes and blockbusters later. Hal Barwood and Matthew Robbins wrote the script, supposedly based on real events. The shot of these people being pursued by a highway full of Texas Rangers is unforgettable. ▽

⊹\‼ SULLIVAN'S TRAVELS. US. 1941. Joel McCrea is the title character, a famous film director, who decides to do something "important" with his life in one of Preston Sturges's most pointed achievements. Sullivan sets out on a research trip to find out what it's like to be poor. On the way he runs into Veronica Lake, a hard-up would-be starlet. The Sturges nuttiness is a bit more subdued here and the satire more socially relevant. Sullivan learns that "comedy isn't much, but it's better than nothing in this cockeyed caravan."

⧓ SUMMER OF '42, THE. US. 1971. At just about the time Robert Mulligan made this successful romantic remembrance of adolescence during the war, nostalgia became a way of life—one of the underlying principles of contemporary American popular culture. Art and music, films, and even literature had reached the point where the idea of progress—the "avant garde"—was no longer relevant. As a result the culture turned in upon itself. Increasingly movies were made about old movies and even the rebellious music of the fifties and sixties became a commodity that could be repeated and sold again and again. The fulcrum for our nostalgia was and remains World War II. Halfway between the cultural revolution of the twenties and its reprise in the sixties, it was a time when beautiful young women like Jennifer O'Neill sometimes wore jeans and daddy's white shirts and intricately-sewn brassières. ▽

SUMMERTIME. US. 1955. David Lean directed this romance with Katharine Hepburn as the American woman, Rossano Brazzi as the Italian, and Venice in full color as the stage.

\ SUNDAY IN NEW YORK. US. 1963. This is what standard Broadway comedies were like in the sixties. A very young and fetchingly awkward Jane Fonda stars here, discovering the glamour of New

York and love with Rod Taylor and Cliff Robertson. Peter Tewksbury directed the Norman Krasna script.

SUNRISE. US. 1927. If you can find a good print, this is an extraordinary example of black-and-white filmmaking. It's reputedly one of the first Hollywood products to use Panchromatic stock, and director F. W. Murnau packed it with scenes in brilliant chiaroscuro. The famous trolley scene is a landmark in the art of tracking, and the giant urban set evokes the German expressionist style. Murnau started with a good story of attempted murder and infidelity.

SUNSET BOULEVARD. US. 1950. Everybody remembers this Hollywood classic about Hollywood for its delicious melodrama: Gloria Swanson as the half-crazed Norma Desmond, faded star of the silent era, and William Holden as Joe Gillis, the screenwriter as Everyman. In fact, it's also very funny. The only good screenwriter is a dead screenwriter floating in the swimming pool. Billy Wilder got people like Cecil B. De Mille, Hedda Hopper, and Buster Keaton to appear in cameos as themselves which helps to make it a very sharp satire on the Hollywood of the 1920s. It's the obverse of *SINGIN' IN THE RAIN*.

SUNSHINE BOYS, THE. US. 1975. Neil Simon's exceptional comedy is a fitting hommage to the Vaudeville tradition. Walter Matthau and George Burns are the aging comics who are brought back together again for one last stand. It's great to watch them work together: Burns, who now carries the torch for Vaudeville single-handedly, and Matthau, a generation younger, trained mainly as a film actor. Burns's presence gives it added resonance, of course.

SUPERMAN II. US. 1980. This is, after all, a cartoon and it could barely hold the weight of the early television series. Screenwriters David and Leslie Newman (with the aid of Robert Benton and perhaps Mario Puzo) managed to give it freshness in the first *Superman* (1978, directed by Richard Donner). Here, working with director Richard Lester, they take it one daring step forward: Superman and Lois Lane finally climb into bed together—they even marry. We've been waiting for for this for decades. It's always interesting to twist a myth to see what new truths can be wrung from it.

⬆ **SURVIVORS, THE**. US. 1983. Michael Ritchie back in excellent form again with Walter Matthau and Robin Williams. A typical Ritchie story about regular people who get caught up in a chain of satiric events, *The Survivors* succeeds because of the interesting chemistry between Matthau and Williams, representing two very separate comic generations. These two everymen from the outer boroughs get caught up in a survival training course. As usual in Ritchie, even the villains are nice guys here. Michael Ritchie movies are usually full of people you'd like to spend time with. This is no exception. ▽

SUSPICION. US. 1941. Alfred Hitchcock reprised the gothic situation of *REBECCA* here more on his own terms, with Cary Grant as the potentially evil husband, and Joan Fontaine as the helplessly weak wife. Hitchcock's original intention was that Grant be guilty, but the Code insisted otherwise. This is the one with the evil glass of milk. ▽

◒⬆ **SWEET SMELL OF SUCCESS**. US. 1957. A tough sardonic script by Ernest Lehman (with the assistance of Clifford Odets) portrays the New York media world in all its reputed squalor. Alexander Mackendrick directed; Burt Lancaster and Tony Curtis star; James Wong Howe was the cinematographer.

⚑◒ **SWEET SWEETBACK'S BAADASSSSS SONG**. US. 1971. A landmark in Black filmmaking in the US, this angry, extravagant, loud, and belligerent movie reaches a high pitch early on and stays there. It's written, directed, photographed, scored by, and stars Melvin Van Peebles who'd always wanted to be a filmmaker, went to France to do a conventional film, came back to try his hand in Hollywood, and finally wound up here, an independent in full control of the product. He later went on to have a significant influence on Broadway musicals in the seventies and to work on television movies and series before quitting the media to become a stockbroker. In its own way, this story of a pimp on the run is as Black as a film can get. . . a cinematic equivalent of *Native Son*. Run it on a double with *GANJA AND HESS*. "Keep this nigger boy running!" ▽

⬇ **SWEPT AWAY. . . BY AN UNUSUAL DESTINY IN THE BLUE SEA OF AUGUST**. Italy. 1975. For reasons I've never fully understood, there was a vogue for Lina Wertmüller in the mid-seventies. Her films were always a mixture of sex and politics, but the aim was never quite clear. This one's essential Wertmüller with her stars Giancarlo Giannini and Mariangela Melato as a sailor and his rich, bitchy employer, stuck on an island with no other characters to divert them. They're both attractive actors and the sexual byplay is interesting, but in the end we are left with the uneasy feeling that Wertmüller is simply exploiting the characters and the situation. ☑

SWING TIME. US. 1936. When the object is singing and dancing, the less plot you have the better. Fred Astaire was always most at his ease when he was playing a dancer, as he does here. George Stevens directed him and Ginger Rogers and the film includes Jerome Kern favorites "The Way You Look Tonight," "Pick Yourself Up," "A Fine Romance," and "Bojangles." ☑

SWISS FAMILY ROBINSON. US. 1960. John Mills and Dorothy McGuire star in this version of the Johann Wyss classic—my favorite book when I was a kid. Ken Annakin directed. There's also an earlier version directed by Edward Ludwig (1940) with Thomas Mitchell and Edna Best. Whichever one you choose, it's a primal children's fantasy full of marvelous opportunities: building your own house, finding your own food, creating your own civilization. ☑

TABU. US. 1931. Shot in Tahiti by the strange pair of Robert Flaherty and F. W. Murnau, *Tabu* is an excellent travelogue that's interesting to watch for the clash of sensibilities. Murnau won, so the film is fictional. He died a few days before the film was released.

TAIL-GUNNER JOE. US. 1977. This made-for-television film showcases Peter Boyle in a biopic of Senator Joseph McCarthy. It's surprising the story has never been done in features. Boyle is superb in the title role and a number of excellent of actors, including Burgess Meredith, Jean Stapleton, and Ned Beatty support him. Judd Taylor directed.

TAKE ME OUT TO THE BALL GAME. US. 1949. Frank Sinatra, Gene Kelly, and Jules Munchin try out for *ON THE TOWN* under the direction, curiously, of Busby Berkeley. This time they're baseball players in the gay nineties whose team is bought by Esther Williams (on dry land). It's got some good songs you've probably never heard before.

‖ **TAKE THE MONEY AND RUN**. US. 1969. Woody Allen eased into film gradually. After the experiment of *WHAT'S UP TIGER LILY?* he devised a kind of documentary--a film version of the kind of routine he used to do on stage. Here he's a compulsive thief, the subject of a thoughtful television documentary. Because its ambitions are simple, it's among his funniest films.   ☑

⛰ **TAKING OF PELHAM 1-2-3, THE**. US. 1975. Here's a great, if relatively unknown, thriller that starts with an absurd premise: a subway train is hijacked and a group of vicious criminals led by Robert Shaw holds the passengers for ransom. It's funny, tough, perfectly paced, and thoroughly effective. Peter Stone wrote the screenplay; Joseph Sargent directed; Walter Matthau, Martin Balsam, Hector Elizondo, and a number of other New York types star.   ☑

⊛ **TAKING OFF**. US. 1971. Miloš Forman's first American movie very much follows the patterns of his Czech films. It's a restrained affectionate portrait of middle-class Americans. More important, foreigner Forman chose as his subject a theme most American filmmakers avoided. Buck Henry and Lynn Carlin are parents whose teenage girl runs away. Looking for her they have to confront the youth culture of the 1960s. The scene where they and an auditorium full of similarly troubled parents learn to smoke pot is memorable.

⚑ **TALE OF TWO CITIES, A**. US. 1935. At least five film versions of this Dickens classic about the French Revolution exist. This is the best. The historical drama, rather unusual for Dickens, fit Hollywood's needs much better than the gallery of comic characters and Victorian melodrama that make up most of the other great Dickens novels. Ronald Colman stars with a large and effective cast. "'Tis a far, far better thing I do. . . ."   ☑

⛰ **TALK OF THE TOWN**. US. 1942. Jean Arthur and Cary Grant are paired together with Ronald Colman in an unusual mixture of comedy and drama. Grant's a fugitive on the run given unwitting shelter by, and discussing law with Professor Colman. Novelist Irwin Shaw wrote the script with Sidney Buchman. George Stevens directed. A sleeper.

♪ **T.A.M.I. SHOW, THE**. US. 1964. Here's a rare early wonderful record of a time when "rock 'n' roll" was becoming "rock." James Brown, Chuck Berry, Marvin Gaye, the Rolling Stones, the Supremes, Smokey Robinson, and even Lesley Gore performed at this concert in Santa Monica.   ⋁

TASTE OF HONEY, A. UK. 1961. Shelagh Delaney's play was second only in importance to *LOOK BACK IN ANGER* in marking a change in cultural attitudes during the late fifties and early sixties. Tony Richardson directed this film version starring Rita Tushingham, Robert Stephens, Dora Bryan, and Murray Melvin. Teenager Tushingham has an affair with a Black man, becomes pregnant, and talks it out with her homosexual friend. The mixture of sexual and racial elements was startling at the time.

TAXI DRIVER. US. 1976. Paul Schrader wrote and Martin Scorsese directed this movie which made quite a stir at the time. It remains an emblem of much of what was most disturbing about American filmmaking in the 1970s. There's no denying its technical accomplishment. Robert DeNiro never had a more meaty role than Travis Bickle, the crazy homicidal taxi driver. But what's the point? It's violent and uncaring. Writer Schrader later admitted he, too, thought it was sophomoric. "You talkin' to me?" That's DeNiro's great line, but Bickle and the film aren't. They're just out to gun us down.   ⋁

TEMPEST. US. 1982. Paul Mazursky's self-indulgence—a project he had been working on for many years—contains a nice irony. John Cassavetes, who plays the Mazursky role, quickly invades the film and puts his stamp on it. It turns out to be a Cassavetes movie, not a Mazursky movie, and if you take it in that light it's quite interesting. It was not a success when it was released, but it's one of those movies that's going to come back again and again. Most of us never feel the way that the Cassavetes/Mazursky architect does during his mid-life crisis, but most of us think artists are supposed to feel that way. The gorgeous Greek scenery is a large part of the haphazard success of *Tempest*.   ⋁

10. US. 1981. *10* isn't a good movie. It's too dishevelled to be that, but it's an interesting one because it brings back sexual attitudes of the fifties, almost thirty years later. It made Dudley Moore a star and Bo Derek a starlet. Like most Blake Edwards movies of the last fifteen years, it's most interesting for Julie Andrews's performance. She's much more attractive in her mid-forties than Bo

Derek in her corn rows. Compare *30 IS A DANGEROUS AGE, CYNTHIA*. ▾

TEN COMMANDMENTS, THE. US. 1956. The great Biblical epic of the 1950s and Cecil B. De Mille's swan song stars Charlton Heston, Yul Brynner, Edward G. Robinson, and it seems, most of the actors currently then working. At over three hours, it's grandiose, colorful, and the kind of film that made movies fun for kids during that decade. There's not much thought here, but there probably doesn't need to be. ▾

TEN FROM YOUR SHOW OF SHOWS. US. 1973. Producer Max Liebman strung together ten kinescopes of classic routines from the seminal television show of the 1950s, starring Sid Caesar, Imogene Coca, Carl Reiner, and Howard Morris. The kinescopes are scratchy and a lot is lost, but it's an important relic of the great age of television comedy. You'll especially enjoy the movie parodies. See *MY FAVORITE YEAR* for the fictional treatment of these people.

TENDER MERCIES. US. 1983. This is an extraordinary movie that sneaks up on you quietly, invades your sensibility, and leaves you breathless. Horton Foote wrote a screenplay about an over-the-hill alcoholic country singer who slowly rejoins the land of the living thanks to the love of a good woman—and a good kid. Robert Duvall stars with a balanced, understated, and rich portrait that totally obviates its potential cliches and reminds you what the magic of acting is all about. Australian Bruce Beresford directed and brings a fresh and invigorating vision of the Texas plains, shooting skies across the sun. Somehow he makes them look like the Australian outback. Even the songs, which Duvall wrote for the film, are memorable. Tess Harper and Betty Buckley also star. This movie holds a lot of surprises. ▾

TENTH VICTIM, THE. Italy. 1965. This is an Italian science-fiction film, a rarity worth our attention. Marcello Mastroianni and Ursula Andress star under the direction of Elio Petri. The concept was fifteen years ahead of its time: the film posits a society in which murder has become a legal sport. In the early eighties college kids in the US took to playing this game (they didn't really kill anybody) and shortly thereafter "Manhunt" camps opened in California. *ROLLERBALL* may be a better science-fiction sport, but *ROLLERBALL* doesn't have Ursula Andress's .45-calibre breasts. ▾

TERMS OF ENDEARMENT. US. 1983. While *TENDER MERCIES* was mostly being ignored in 1983, *Terms of Endearment* garnered considerable attention—and it deserves it. Based on the quirky, affectionate, and wise novel by Larry McMurtry, the film was scripted and directed by James L. Brooks. The testy but intimate relationship of mother Shirley MacLaine and daughter Debra Winger over the years as they attempt to come to terms with the men in their lives—or the lack of them—just skirts cliche at every turn, reminding us that cliches are born because they carry some real part of the truth. Shirley MacLaine in her fifties is, if anything, more fascinating as a woman and actress than she was thirty years ago. Debra Winger is the most interesting, intelligent, and attractive actress to come along in decades. And Jack Nicholson, as the debauched former astronaut and love interest for MacLaine, enjoys himself immensely trying to steal the film away from these two powerhouses. He almost makes it. There is nothing new about this film (except perhaps the emphases) but there's nothing that needs to be. Hollywood lives! ▽

TERRY FOX STORY, THE. Canada. 1983. Terry Fox caught the imagination of his fellow Canadians several years ago when, after having lost a leg to cancer, he took it into his head to run clear across Canada raising money for cancer research. This is an intelligently made movie of the story starring Eric Fryer, who is also an amputee, and Robert Duvall as the public relations type who takes him in tow. Fox's own "rage against the dying of the light" was heroic and director Ralph Thomas and the other filmmakers understand it. Fox never made it all the way to Vancouver. He died before finishing the run. At the time he fell he had already passed the 3,000-mile mark and had about 2,000 miles more to go. It seems to me a particularly telling comment on the nature of Canadian culture that had Fox been an American running from New York to L.A. he would have finished easily. ▽

TEX. US. 1982. Three movies have been made of S. E. Hinton's "young adult" novels, two by Francis Coppola (*The Outsiders*, *Rumble Fish*), one (*Tex*) by the Disney organization. This one's superior. Matt Dillon stars again in a classic childhood fantasy: the parents are gone and the kids are trying to raise themselves. ▽

THAT HAMILTON WOMAN. US. 1941. An American-made British movie directed by

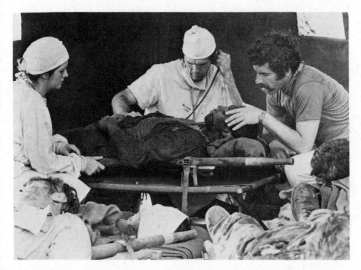

M*A*S*H: Elliott Gould and crew almost overwhelmed by the body count.

Alexander Korda and starring Vivien Leigh and Laurence Olivier. *That Hamilton Woman* celebrates the British spirit at the opening of World War II with a version of the romance of Lord Nelson and Lady Hamilton. It proves once again how culturally useful it is to own a history full of colorful characters.

THAT MAN FROM RIO. France. 1964. Philippe DeBroca directed a string of French comedies in the sixties. This one is superior. Jean-Paul Belmondo stars as a Bondian superhero chasing his prey from Paris to Rio to Brasilia. It's got lots of colorful photography and Françoise Dorléac.

THAT'S DANCING! US. 1985. A worthy successor to *THAT'S ENTERTAINMENT!* The focus this time is even more precise. You realize quite quickly what a great effect the film medium has had on the development of dance. The techniques of film don't do all that much for music. In fact, some would say any live musical performance is better than a filmed record of it. But editing, closeups, and the ability to do multiple takes until you get it right bring an entirely new dimension to the art of choreography.

THAT'S ENTERTAINMENT! US. 1974. MGM always had the reputation of being the classiest Hollywood studio and in its heyday it was the most unified. This is a super compilation film celebrating the history of MGM musicals with newly-minted clips from scores of your favorites and scores more that you probably never saw before. It's a fascinating collection, and like those late-night TV record commercials that offer you a complete history of rhythm and blues for only $9.95 plus tax, it's irresistible. The only problem of course, is that it's limited to MGM. Why haven't Paramount, Warners, and Fox performed this excellent service for us as well? Stars include, but are not limited to, Astaire, Crosby, Kelly, O'Connor, Reynolds, Rooney, and Sinatra. ▽

THAT'S ENTERTAINMENT PART 2. US. 1976. Gene Kelly and Fred Astaire appear in welcome roles as the hosts of this sequel which includes MGM non-musicals as well as musicals, so that Tracy and Hepburn, the Marx Brothers, and others, get into the act as well. ▽

THEY DRIVE BY NIGHT. US. 1940. As François Truffaut once pointed out, director Raoul Walsh was unsurpassed at describing and celebrating the jobs men do. This is one of his best: a tough movie about truck drivers who get a hell of a kick out of their work and fighting for what's right. George Raft, Humphrey Bogart, Ida Lupino, and Ann Sheridan star. ▽

THEY LIVE BY NIGHT. US. 1949. Nicholas Ray's first film, with Farley Granger, Cathy O'Donnell, and Howard da Silva: three fugitives on the lam in the thirties. Ray's realistic style was notable at the time. Robert Altman shot a later version of the same novel in the seventies: *THIEVES LIKE US*. ▽

THEY WERE EXPENDABLE. US. 1945. Most World War II movies were B-grade or only slightly above. This one is A-grade, directed by John Ford with a sense of perspective on the war, and starring John Wayne, Robert Montgomery, and Donna Reed. Excellent action in the Pacific on PT-boats during the losing battle for the Philippines.

THIEF OF BAGHDAD, THE. UK. 1940. Alexander Korda produced, Michael Powell and others directed this breathtaking attempt to capture the Arabian knights on film. It's an early example of outstanding Technicolor work and has recently become a cult favorite among young Hollywood directors. Conrad Veidt and Sabu star.

THIEVES LIKE US. US. 1974. Robert Altman's

version of the novel which also served as a source for *THEY LIVE BY NIGHT* has thirties atmosphere so thick you can ladle it with a spoon. Keith Carradine, Shelley Duvall, and John Schuck star as the trio on the run. It's unusually restrained for Altman but as rich as his more energetic films.

THIN MAN, THE. US. 1934. Perhaps because it was Dashiell Hammett with a lighter than usual touch, this film caught the imagination of the country. William Powell and Myrna Loy starred as Nick and Nora Charles, the happily married and classy couple who occasionally took it into their heads to play detective. The mysteries give this and the five succeeding films in the series a plot to hang their hats on, but the real attractions were Nick and Nora. There's a secret thrill of watching a handsome man and an attractive woman of equal and balanced intelligence and sophistication enjoying their lives— and even more important—their marriage! It's everyone's unexpressed fantasy. Of course, characters like this can be boring, too: there's very little drama in a happy situation. That problem was handled by the ingenious device of the murder mysteries. It's remarkable that this heady romance had its roots in the work of downbeat Dashiell Hammett. The basic concept served as an impetus for a dozen television series from *Ozzie and Harriet*, to *McMillan and Wife* and *Hart to Hart*, but was never done as well again. Compare Tracy/Hepburn movies.

THING, THE. US. 1951. This classic fifties science fiction horror film was also the first chronologically. It's remembered for the slimy alien presence (James Arness) that invades the arctic station, but in fact its most important accomplishment is the character of the men who fight "the thing." The fast-paced banter of men working together to get a job done gives us a great sense of their camaraderie. It's very much a film of its producer, Howard Hawks, although Christian Nyby was credited with its direction. These guys are the first in a long line of Ghostbusters. ◩

THINGS TO COME. UK. 1936. H. G. Wells wrote the script of this depressive portrait of a despotic future from his novel *The Shape of Things to Come*. Designer William Cameron Menzies directed with considerable panache. Excellent to look at even if the plot isn't one of Wells's best.

THIRD MAN, THE. UK. 1949. Another great Graham Greene novel, this time set in Vienna immediately after World War II. It's got just the right touch of world-weariness and character. Orson Welles is the mysterious Harry Lime, Joseph Cotten the novelist on his trail. The zither music, which has burned an image of this film in everyone's memory, was by Anton Karas. Carol Reed directed. ▮

30 IS A DANGEROUS AGE, CYNTHIA. UK. 1968. Joseph McGrath's comedy with Dudley Moore (and Peter Cook) makes a nice prelude to Moore's later success in romantic comedies after he passed age forty. It's about how short guys get girls. What neither Cynthia nor Dudley knew was that—basically—short guys get girls after they're rich and famous. Moore was too young at the time. He had to wait for *10*. *30 is a Dangerous Age, Cynthia* is also a nice example of British comedy in the sixties. It's got that freshness and spirit that marked the brief reign of "swinging London" between the Ealing comedies of the fifties and Monty Python of the seventies. ▮

39 STEPS, THE. UK. 1935. Alfred Hitchcock's best-known British film set a style for thriller/comedy/romance that has lasted for many years. Madeleine Carroll stars with Robert Donat as the innocent man accused who, like so many after him in Hitchcock's work, can depend on no one but himself to catch the real criminal. ▮

THIS GUN FOR HIRE. US. 1942. A lesser Graham Greene novel proves a good vehicle for a partnership of Alan Ladd and Veronica Lake. Ladd is a quiet and reserved gun-for-hire who single-mindedly pursues the man who double-crossed him, intent on revenge. ▮

THIS IS CINERAMA! US. 1953. We are jaded now by widescreen epics like *STAR WARS* and *SUPERMAN*, but once upon a time before television, movies were small and almost square and black-and-white. As a result, we paid more attention to people and to talk and the story. When Lowell Thomas on a tiny black-and-white screen at the beginning of this film intoned magnificently "THIS IS CINERAMA!" and the space around him on all sides burst into overwhelming and monumental color, a new age was born. From then on movies were more often than not spectacles, the greatest of them trips that took us where we'd never been before: to the moon, to Jupiter, and beyond. The widescreen technique of Cinerama, invented by Fred Waller, has never been fully exploited even now, thirty years later. Occasional World's Fair-type exhibitions experiment with advanced projection technology, but it's surprising we have made so little technical progress in sixty years. The real Cinerama age may be just about to dawn.

⬣ **THIS IS SPINAL TAP**. US. 1984. Rob Reiner created this telling and precise parody of a documentary about an over-the-hill British rock group on tour. We've seen so many of these tours the last fifteen years we're just as tired of them as Reiner must be. It's an unusual and ambitious little satire with Reiner himself as the director of the film within the film. ▽

◣ **THIS IS THE ARMY**. US. 1943. Here's the famous Irving Berlin patriotic revue as filmed by Michael Curtiz and Warner Bros. stalwarts with an interesting lead-in referring to Berlin's similar World War I musical *Yip, Yip Yaphank*.

⬆ **THIS MAN IS NEWS**. UK. 1938. Alastair Sim stars in a nicely mounted and entertaining light drama about a jounalist who is framed and has to catch the thieves.

⬣⬆ **THIS MAN MUST DIE**. France. 1970. Another remarkably stylish melodrama from Claude Chabrol at the height of his career, starring Michel Duchaussoy, Jean Yanne, and Caroline Cellier. Chabrol's studies of bourgeois mores seem more attractive as each year passes. No one on either side of the Atlantic has been able to duplicate his combination of stylish mise-en-scene and tongue-in-cheek but sharply observed social detail. Duchaussoy is a father out to take revenge on hit-and-run driver Yanne who has killed his son.

⬣ **THIS SPORTING LIFE**. UK. 1962. David Storey wrote this kitchen-sink drama about a miner who climbs the greasy pole by becoming a professional rugby player. Richard Harris stars with Rachel Roberts. Lindsay Anderson directed.

THREE CABALLEROS, THE. US. 1945. Walt Disney's contribution to the "good neighbor policy." Donald Duck and some interesting animation combined imaginatively with live action. ▽

⬣⬆ **THREE DAYS OF THE CONDOR**. US. 1975. Sydney Pollack is an intelligent filmmaker who's often underrated. *Three Days of the Condor* with Robert Redford was one of his many workmanlike successes of the seventies and early eighties. It's a standard political thriller from the popular novel, till near the end. There's a certain paradox that presents itself with political filmmaking: If the hero wins, your response is "Thank God, glad that's over with!" If the hero loses, your response might equally be, "If Robert Redford can't do it, how the hell can I?" Unlike most other political films, *Three Days of the Condor* skirts this paradox and strikes the right note at the end. Redford has won something, but not enough. We know that we must participate, that he needs our help, and we join him. This is a classic film of the seventies: workmanlike, absorbing, but not overwhelming. ▼

§ **THREE LITTLE WORDS**. US. 1950. Just to show you that MGM musicals weren't always masterpieces, here's a nice, if unexceptional, biopic about songwriters Burt Kalmar and Harry Ruby. (Their songs include "I Wanna Be Loved By You," Who's Sorry Now?" and the title song. Fred Astaire and Red Skelton star. Debbie Reynolds makes an appearance. Richard Thorpe directed.

THREE MUSKETEERS, THE. US. 1948. Of the four or five versions of the classic story, we've chosen two. This one starred Gene Kelly and June Allyson under the direction of George Sidney. It's in gorgeous Technicolor and, of course, Kelly's presence gives the goings-on a special rhythm. (You may also want to take a look at Allan Dwan's 1939 burlesque with Don Ameche and the Ritz Brothers.)

▲ **THREE MUSKETEERS, THE**. UK. 1974. Richard Lester directed this spirited and witty re-telling of the story. The script is by George MacDonald Fraser, and in fact, two films were made at the same time, although released separately. The sequel is *THE FOUR MUSKETEERS*. The large cast includes international stars like Charlton Heston and Richard Chamberlain, and old Lester hands like Spike Milligan and Roy Kinnear. ▼

▲ **THREE SMART GIRLS**. US. 1937. Deanna Durbin's debut includes Ray Milland and Binnie Barnes. Durbin's musicals stand out in Hollywood history because they focus so intently on her own character. It's interesting to compare her with Judy Garland, a better singer and actress, who nevertheless never achieved such a strong persona as Durbin. Here, the kid brings her feuding parents back together.

▲§ **THREEPENNY OPERA**. Germany. 1931. The theatrical dissonance of the Bertolt Brecht/Kurt

Weill musical based on John Gay's eighteenth-century play about the London underworld is mostly lost in this film version (and Brecht protested strongly). But director G. W. Pabst stages it stylishly and you get a chance to watch the great Lotte Lenya in fine form. Wherever they are, Brecht and Weill must be appreciating the irony that Mack the Knife turned into a cute upbeat standard for the likes of Sammy Davis Jr. and Bobby Darin. Nothing could be further from the tough mood they wished to convey. ☒

THRILLER. US. 1983. The title song from singer Michael Jackson's record-breaking album isn't the best of the new pop videos by far, but it was the first to list pretentious full credits for the "filmmakers." (John Landis directed.) This fifteen-minute filmlet stands here for all pop videos, the newest form of filmmaking, yet to find its real style but full of brash experimentation. The real problem with all videos is that the music seldom rises above the level of B+, but that's not the fault of the filmmakers. ☒

TILLIE'S PUNCTURED ROMANCE. US. 1914. In an age when comedy clearly belonged to actors, Mack Sennett made a name for himself behind the camera. His Keystone Kops were just as important in setting styles for silent comedies as was his erstwhile star Charlie Chaplin. This one, an ambitious, landmark full-length feature, includes the Kops, Chaplin, Marie Dressler, Mabel Normand, and Chester Conklin.

TIME AFTER TIME. US. 1979. Here's our candidate for the ultimate concept film: what if Jack the Ripper (David Warner) were really an old friend of H. G. Wells (Malcolm McDowell) and what if H. G. Wells actually invented a time machine and what if Jack the Ripper used it to escape to San Francisco circa 1979 and what if H. G. Wells figured out a way to follow him? What if H. G. fell in love with a kooky bank officer (Mary Steenburgen) and what if Jack tried to kill her? It's involuted and the plot device that allows Wells to follow Jack is laughable, but it's such a conscientious undertaking you might as well take a look. Meyer tried this historical twist previously with *The Seven-Percent Solution* in which Sherlock Holmes meets Sigmund Freud. I like this one better. For a really adult treatment of time travel, see *JE T'AIME, JE T'AIME*. ☒

TIME IN THE SUN. Mexico. 1933. In 1930 Sergei Eisenstein received an invitation from Paramount to make a movie in Hollywood. Of course when he arrived he was branded an undesirable Commie and Paramount lost their nerve. He raised funds from Upton Sinclair and his wife and went to Mexico to shoot a film which was to be called *Que Viva Mexico!* He never had a chance to finish the film: this is what's left. The violent, almost surrealist melange of imagery has its own intrinsic interest. The story surrounding the making of the film is so dramatic and curious it's surprising no one's ever treated it on celluloid.

● **TIME MACHINE, THE**. US. 1960. The special effects in this version of the H. G. Wells classic were famous at the time. Rod Taylor is the inventor of the Edwardian science-fiction engine. Yvette Mimieux is the girl of the future. Not a great movie, but a nostalgic one. Compare it to *TIME AFTER TIME*. ▼

TIME OF YOUR LIFE, THE. US. 1948. William Saroyan's play about hangers-out in a San Francisco bar is a classic of the American theater and well staged here by H. C. Potter. With James Cagney, William Bendix, Broderick Crawford and others.

╲ **TIME PIECE**. US. 1966. Long before anyone had ever heard of Kermit D. Frog, Jim Henson made this marvelous short film starring himself. (No puppets in sight.) It's a simple but remarkably winning experiment in montage. Editing the image in time with the rhythms of the soundtrack may be a simple trick, but it's fascinating. If a print still exists of this film, it ought to be unearthed.

⊹▀ **TIN DRUM, THE**. West Germany. 1979. Günter Grass's 1959 novel about the little boy Oskar who existentially refuses to grow up when the Nazis come to power in Germany is certainly one of the very few landmark novels written during the last forty years. Its understated but gripping realism spiced with a strong but simple dose of fantasy presents a unique view of an historical phenomenon that is by its very nature difficult to deal with. It's one of those novels that you sense while you read it could never be made into an effective film. This makes Volker Schlöndorff's cinematic version all the more remarkable. With David Bennent as the boy, Angela Winkler, Heinz Bennent, and Charles Aznavour, it's simply one of the best adaptations of a novel ever to be filmed. A straightforward movie made by a well-endowed and intelligent filmmaker. ▼

§ **TIN PAN ALLEY**. US. 1940. Alice Faye, Betty Grable, Jack Oakie, John Payne, and other B+/A-cast members work their way through this eventually winning story about songwriters during the early years of this century. Watch for the Nicholas brothers!

⚠‼ **TO BE OR NOT TO BE**. US. 1942. Perhaps Ernst Lubitsch's most inspired piece of filmmaking casts Jack Benny as the head of a Polish theater troupe fighting the Nazis. Carole Lombard also stars. Because the heroes here are little people quite diffident about their politics, their victory is exhilarating—and also very funny. ▼

‼ **TO BE OR NOT TO BE**. US. 1983. All remakes should be as effective as this one. It may seem heresy, but Mel Brooks is more effective as actor/hero than Jack Benny in the Lubitsch original. His manic sense brings new life to the role. Brooks and director Alan Johnson (he choreographed "Springtime For Hitler" in *THE PRODUCERS*) stick close to the original script and have an excellent time with it. Anne Bancroft in the Carole Lombard role matches her husband Brooks step for step. Songs include "Sweet Georgia Brown" in Polish. ▼

↘ **TO CATCH A THIEF**. US. 1955. Lesser Alfred Hitchcock but any film with Grace Kelly and Cary Grant, filmed on the Riviera, is worth spending time with. He's a reformed cat burglar. Grace took a liking to the locale. ▼

⇧ **TO DIE OF LOVE**. France. 1972. Based on true events, this is an absorbing combination of politics and melodrama by André Cayatte. Annie Girardot plays a provincial schoolteacher who becomes quite naturally involved with a teenage student. She is driven to suicide by the reaction of the community. Cayatte makes some pointed and passionate comments on the rigidity of middle-class mores.

TO HAVE AND HAVE NOT. US. 1944. A lot of talent combines here: Hemingway wrote the novel, Faulkner and Jules Furthman scripted, Howard Hawks directed; Humphrey Bogart, Lauren Bacall, and Hoagy Carmichael star. Bogart's a fisherman who gets involved with the French Resistance. It's a standard Hollywood movie and it looks like a remake of *CASABLANCA*, but Bogart and Bacall bring it off.

⇧ **TO KILL A MOCKINGBIRD**. US. 1962. Robert Mulligan directed with his usual sensitivity, Horton Foote wrote the script from the popular novel of the time, and Alan J. Pakula produced. The social consciousness (defending a Black man accused of murder in the south) has palled quickly, but the attention to detail makes it still interesting. ▽

✛ **TOKYO STORY**. Japan. 1953. On balance, Yasujiro Ozu is one of the world's most remarkable filmmakers. He always tells exceedingly simple stories. (This one is about an old couple who visit their young and busy children in Tokyo and get mistreated.) And he does so with such sensible wisdom that the films are haunting. He is one of very few filmmakers whose presence is always felt: we can feel the storyteller with us. Moreover, we sense he is enormously respectful of his characters. He loves these very human creations dearly. Only Ozu and Truffaut have been able to project this invaluable sensibility consistently.

👁🏠 **TOM BROWN'S SCHOOLDAYS**. UK. 1951. The classic Victorian novel by Thomas Hughes is well mounted, with Robert Newton and Diana Wynyard taking the leads. Tom Brown is the nice boy at a British public school in the middle of the last century who is beleaguered by the bully Flashman. In the end a kindly, intelligent Matthew Arnold figure takes over as Headmaster and Flashman gets his comeuppance. . . but not before escaping into the fertile imagination of George MacDonald Fraser— see *ROYAL FLASH*.

🍷$ **TOM JONES**. UK. 1963. Tony Richardson hit a gusher with this adaptation (by John Osborne) of the classic novel by Henry Fielding. It was a great box office hit and you can still see why. The trick here is the dramatic clash between naturalistic eighteenth-century backgrounds (that would later inspire the Pythons) and the breathless slapstick pace of the comedy. What *THE THIRD MAN* did for the zither, *Tom Jones* did for the harpsichord. ▽

🔺$ **TOMMY**. UK. 1975. Ken Russell finally found a project that fit his extremist style: the "rock opera" by The Who. Roger Daltrey, Ann-Margret, Oliver Reed, Elton John, Eric Clapton, Tina Turner, The Who, and Jack Nicholson star in an incredibly loud and wonderfully garish visualization of the music.

🔺🏠 **TONI**. France. 1934. Jean Renoir on location in southern France with a story about immigrant workers which is refreshingly realistic, unusually so for the time. Often cited as a precursor to Neorealism, the film has a delicate political undertone. ▽

⬇ **TOOTSIE**. US. 1982. One of the more

disappointingly overrated films of the last five years, *Tootsie* seems to have achieved its remarkable success simply from the hype that surrounded the spectacle of Dustin Hoffman in drag. The script (partly by Larry Gelbart) has the germ of an idea: Hoffman is an obstinate actor who finally lands a role—as a woman. Jessica Lange and Teri Garr are quite attractive as the real women, but Hoffman at the center is silly. Tony Curtis was more convincing in drag in *SOME LIKE IT HOT*. What's most disappointing about the success of *Tootsie* is that people took it as a feminist statement. Hoffman finds himself a better person as a woman. Think about that for a while. ⊻

TOP HAT. US. 1935. Irving Berlin supplied the music, Fred Astaire supplied the "top hat, white tie, and tails," and Ginger Rogers the "cheek to cheek," under the inevitable direction of Mark Sandrich. Probably more music and dancing to the inch than any other Astaire musical, and welcome for it. ⊻

TOPAZ. US. 1969. An unusual choice for Hitchcock late in life, this is based on the Leon Uris historical novel about Soviet involvement set in Paris, Havana, and New York. The settings may have been unremarkable for Hitchcock, but the political nature of the material is rare in his more than fifty films. John Forsythe and Frederick Stafford star. Several French actors including Philippe Noiret, Claude Jade, and Michel Piccoli, are notably effective working in English. Hitchcock had never worked on this a broad a canvas before. Run it on a double bill with *NORTH BY NORTHWEST*. ⊻

TOPKAPI. US. 1964. Jules Dassin tried to repeat his *RIFIFI* success with what may be the second most interesting caper in movies, although the rest of the film doesn't match its centerpiece, the theft of a precious dagger from the fortress-like Topkapi Museum in Istanbul. Melina Mercouri, Maximilian Schell, Peter Ustinov, and Robert Morley star. ⊻

TOPPER. US. 1937. A classic fantasy about a couple of dead young people, Cary Grant and Constance Bennett, who come back to haunt the stuffy Topper (Roland Young) and his wife (Billie Burke). The gimmick here is obvious: the ghosts are young and sophisticated. In fact, the Kirbys would make a perfect match with Nick and Nora Charles at a dinner party. ⊻

TOUCH OF EVIL. US. 1958. Orson Welles makes

a 1950s melodrama and he does so with such typical panache and intense stylization that an unremarkable story becomes interesting. It's nowhere near early Welles but then it would be unfair to ask him to match his work in the forties. Welles himself plays a large and sleazy sheriff in a seedy border town. The cinematography is certainly brilliant and the unlikely casting of Charlton Heston, Janet Leigh, and Marlene Dietrich ought to draw a chuckle. After this they ran him out of town.

TOUT VA BIEN. France. 1972. Jane Fonda and Yves Montand in Jean-Luc Godard's comeback film. It's still got the political obsessions of the Dziga-Vertov period, but the ideas are beginning to come together now. He handles them in a more summary fashion and brings back some of the humor and much of the dazzling cinema of the mid-sixties. It has something important to say about the function of media in contemporary politics and the magnificent tracking shot in the supermarket (second only to the traffic jam in *WEEKEND*) is a poignant joy. For thirteen years now I've thought of Godard everytime I've entered the checkout line.

TRADING PLACES. US. 1983. As graduates of TV's *Saturday Night Live*, Dan Aykroyd and Eddie Murphy represent the generation of the 1980s. *Trading Places* sets them both in a thirties classic comedy of social class. Aykroyd is a rich Philadelphia commodities broker. His girlfriend, his clothes, his house, his office come to us right out of 1937. You expect to see Franklin Pangborne hanging around. Murphy's streetwise Billy Ray Valentine is the modern touch. No Black actor would have got that role in 1937. But the aim is the same: to see how "the other half lives." If, someday, someone's looking for a movie to serve as an emblem for the Reagan years, this one, with its mix of eighties language and thirties themes, may be the best candidate. John Landis directed.

TRAFFIC. France. 1970. Jacques Tati takes Monsieur Hulot on an ingeniously devised auto journey. It's a one-joke film— intentionally so—that may very well hold your interest since you want to see what else he can do with a car. Compare *WEEKEND*.

TRAIN, THE. US. 1965. John Frankenheimer scored here with a sharp World War II action adventure film about a train full of French paintings on its way to Germany and the successful campaign of French Resistance fighters to put a stop to the infamous journey. Burt Lancaster, Michel Simon, Jeanne Moreau, and Paul Scofield star. ☑

TRANSATLANTIC TUNNEL. UK. 1935. It's the idea that counts here, and the sets that illustrate it. What a wonderfully absurd undertaking!—to dig from England to the US. Maurice Elvey directed. There should have been many sequels: "The Bridge Over the Caribbean," "The Pakistan Canal," "The Condos of Mt. Everest." The only one who seems to have picked up on this fantastic concept is cartoonist Bruce McCall. (See his book *Zany Afternoons*.)

TRAVIATA, LA. Italy. 1982. An excellent record of the Verdi opera with stars Placido Domingo and Teresa Stratas. Directed by Franco Zefferelli. ☑

TREASURE ISLAND. US/UK. 1950. There are numerous versions of the Robert Louis Stevenson story of pirates and hidden treasure. Victor Fleming did a nice one in the thirties with Wallace Beery and Jackie Cooper, but your kids will probably enjoy this Disney version more. It's in color with a better sense of pace. Byron Haskin directed, Robert Newton stars. ☑

TREASURE OF THE SIERRA MADRE, THE. US. 1948. There's gold in them thar hills and Humphrey Bogart, Walter Huston, and Tim Holt are hell-bent to find it. The rather preachy B. Traven novel about greed and its tragic consequences is made more lively and much more human by the father-and-son team of actor Walter Huston and director/writer John, with the able assistance of Bogart. What a nice present to give your father at the end of his career. ☑

TREE GROWS IN BROOKLYN, A. US. 1945. Elia Kazan mounted this film version of the popular Betty Smith novel about a young girl growing up in Brooklyn tenements at the turn of the century. Peggy Ann Garner stars with Dorothy McGuire and Joan Blondell.

TREE OF THE WOODEN CLOGS, THE. Italy. 1979. This is a quiet, magnificent, arresting portrait of life in a small Italian village at the very end of the last century. My great uncle tells me stories about his childhood in a similar place just a few years later that attest to the truth of Ermanno Olmi's masterpiece. The vivid class conflict that Bernardo Bertolucci exploits in *1900* may have been true at the time, but that was only part of the truth. In my uncle's village and in Olmi's, landlords weren't very important.

The classical rhythms of the peasant's year really controlled life and most of the time it worked: people grew their own food and ate very well indeed, enjoyed their children, took pleasure in the natural surroundings, and generally dealt with life quite well. This may sound like romantic pastoral fantasy but, in fact, those villages didn't change much over the course of three hundred years because they were successful social organizations. It's not too "Ecotopian" to suggest that they may even turn out to be models for the future. Olmi's film is irresistible because it paints this natural portrait (including flaws) without either dramatizing or symbolizing the truth. There's a welcome absence of didacticism here: the life speaks for itself. In late winter, just as other food supplies were running low, it was time to kill the pigs. The slaughters were communal affairs and each family chose a different time in order that the meat could be shared. (It thus wasn't necessary to try to preserve your own fresh pork.) Everything but the squeal was used. From pig's blood and chocolate you make a delicious concoction known as "sanguinaccio." It's the customary treat of the Festival of San Giuseppe in March. That confection—literally "big blood"—is emblematic of the simplicity and richness of the life Olmi captures here.

TRIAL OF JOAN OF ARC, THE. France. 1961. A rigid and difficult experiment in cinema, this is Robert Bresson's simple staging of Joan's trial based on the actual records. He has to make drama out of her simple and direct intelligence and he almost succeeds.

TRISTANA. Spain. 1970. This is a classic Luis Buñuel film starring Catherine Deneuve as a young Spanish woman at the turn of the century trying to extend the cramped limits placed on her independence. Fernando Rey is the uncle. It's simpler than the movies in French settings like *BELLE DE JOUR* (also with Deneuve) that followed it in the seventies and darker in tone, recalling the Buñuel of earlier years.

TRIUMPH OF THE WILL. Germany. 1936. As an historical record of the Nuremberg rallies (organized to celebrate Nazism), perhaps it's necessary to preserve *Triumph of the Will*. Film teachers often cite it as a great propaganda film. It is not. Director Leni Riefenstahl may have been a good filmmaker (see *OLYMPIAD*), but she doesn't show it here; she simply records the grandiose, but awfully effective pageantry devised by Goebbels. He's the "artist" who should be given credit.

Edina Ronay and John Thaw argue about their kidnapping victim in Maurice Hatton's remarkable *Praise Marx and Pass the Ammunition*.

TROUBLE IN PARADISE. US. 1932. An early thirties comedy by Ernst Lubitsch with a script by Samson Raphaelson and Grover Jones, with Herbert Marshall, Kay Francis, Miriam Hopkins, and Charles Ruggles. About two jewel thieves, their lives and loves, this is a model for sophisticated comedy in the 1930s.

TROUBLE WITH HARRY, THE. US. 1955. Writer John Michael Hayes was responsible for several of Hitchcock's best films. At the time this one was regarded as a black comedy. The trouble with Harry is that he's dead and he won't stay put. Shirley MacLaine, John Forsythe, and Edmund Gwenn star.

TRUE GRIT. US. 1969. John Wayne is the old marshall and Kim Darby the kid he helps in a movie that allows Wayne to play the old western hero role over again with respect as well as parody. Henry Hathaway directed.

TUNES OF GLORY. UK. 1960. A kind of model for much of what would be best about British television during the next twenty years, this is a characterful and well-made story about Army life in Scotland starring Alec Guinness, John Mills, Susannah York, and Gordon Jackson (later of *Upstairs, Downstairs* fame) under the direction of

Ronald Neame.

TWELVE ANGRY MEN. US. 1957. This is the Reginald Rose teleplay brought to film by Sidney Lumet. The idea of the play was to stick twelve jurors in a room and listen to them argue a case. That it works on film is to Lumet's credit and to the credit of actors Henry Fonda, Lee J. Cobb, E. G. Marshall, Jack Klugman, Jack Warden, Martin Balsam, and others.

TWENTIETH CENTURY. US. 1934. Ben Hecht and Charles MacArthur wrote the script from their play and it's hard to find a more effective screwball comedy. John Barrymore and Carole Lombard star under the direction of Howard Hawks. Barrymore has made Lombard a star and she turns against him. He spends a long train trip on the "Twentieth Century" express to Chicago trying to win her back.

20,000 LEAGUES UNDER THE SEA. US. 1954. The best Disney family drama of the fifties based on Jules Verne's classic novel about underwater life, starring Kirk Douglas and James Mason under the direction of Richard Fleischer. Run it on a double bill with *THE SILENT WORLD*.

TWO ENGLISH GIRLS. France. 1971. Truffaut reversed the sexual equation of *JULES AND JIM* here and the result is a lighter but still interesting romance between a young French writer (Jean-Pierre Léaud) and two British sisters played by Kika Markham and Stacey Tendeter.

TWO FOR THE ROAD. UK. 1967. Frederic Raphael (*DARLING*) wrote the script for this superior study of a trying twelve-year marriage. Audrey Hepburn and Albert Finney star as the wife and husband who have had the strength to survive. The film uses numerous flashbacks with great aplomb to give the full portrait over time. Compare *BETRAYAL*. Stanley Donen directed with great verve.

TWO-LANE BLACKTOP. US. 1971. Monte Hellman was responsible for a series of three or four cult movies in the late sixties and early seventies. *Two-Lane Blacktop* was featured on an *Esquire* magazine cover as potentially the best film of 1971. It bombed at the box office but it's still deserving of at least some of *Esquire*'s accolades. It's a mysterious, intense, and quiet movie about a road race from the southwest to the northeast between an old Chevrolet and a new GTO. James Taylor and Dennis Wilson man one car, Warren Oates the other. Worth a look.

✳ ↘ **TWO OR THREE THINGS THAT I KNOW ABOUT HER**. France. 1968. Jean-Luc Godard's most representative film, full of the poetry and anguish that marked his best. "Her" is Paris and Juliet (Marina Vlady). "Her" is consumerism in the US and politics and structuralism. *Two or Three Three Things That I Know About Her* is crammed with the kinds of images and sounds that are the special gifts of Godard. There's one long shot of bubbles in a coffee cup that will always remain an emblem of the director's concerns: Godard, the iconoclast, continually smashing images and sounds to make new meanings. *Two or Three Things* reminds us that, in the sixties, the art of film used to be exciting.

✳ **2001: A SPACE ODYSSEY**. US. 1968. John Lennon said of *2001* when it was first released, that the film ought to be shown in a temple 24 hours a day. He was right. It is above all else a religious experience. You have to take it on faith. People (mainly Frenchmen) have written whole books about the subject. We can't do that here. Suffice it to say that whether you see it in 70mm widescreen, or on a black-and-white TV, *2001* still has the power to mystify and thrill. It's about tools, intelligence, and lack of faith, and rebirth. It is also, among other things, definitely the most influential film of the last twenty years. All the special effects that make movies so successful today were first tried out by Douglas Trumbull and his crew for *2001* and of course, this is the progenitor of all the space operas that have kept George Lucas and others busy for so long. It's got to rank with *CITIZEN KANE* and *THE GODFATHER* as an essential representative American film. Show it on a double with *THE RIGHT STUFF* to demonstrate the triumph of fiction-before-the-fact versus fiction-after-the-fact. Kubrick's "on location" photography on the moon pre-dated Neil Armstrong and company by more than a year—and had it exactly right. Only one small item seems archaic today, more than fifteen years later: The HAL 9000 computer's memory bank is large enough to hold Keir Dullea as he floats graciously through, de-braining the untrusting machine. We now know HAL's memory would fit in a teacup. "Dave, my mind is going, my mind is going, I can feel it, I can feel it. . . !" ◪

TWO WOMEN. Italy. 1961. Based on the novel by Alberto Moravia, this is the story of a mother (Sophia Loren) and a daughter who are raped by soldiers during the second World War and survive through an intense struggle. It's one of Loren's best roles (she won an Oscar). Raf Vallone and Jean-Paul Belmondo assist. Vittorio De Sica directed.

UGETSU. Japan. 1953. Kenji Mizoguchi's sixteenth-century ghost story. Beautifully photographed, it was a prize winner at Western Film Festivals that helped introduce Japanese films to occidentals. It's a meditation on samurai values.

UMBERTO D. Italy. 1952. Another Vittorio de Sica Neorealist classic. About an old man and his dog, it's simply told and moving.

UMBRELLAS OF CHERBOURG, THE. France. 1964. The French they are a funny race and *The Umbrellas of Cherbourg* is evidence of that. Semi-New Wave director Jacques Demy had the idea to do a musical with little or no dialogue. A very young Catherine Deneuve stars and the music by Michel Legrand, who later became a Hollywood stalwart, is good enough. The color photography is a palate of brilliant pastels. Rather remarkable.

UNDER FIRE. US. 1983. I suppose this might have been a better film than it is, but director Roger Spottiswoode has nevertheless fashioned quite an unusual movie set in Nicaragua during the Sandinista Revolution. Nick Nolte, Gene Hackman, and Joanna Cassidy are American journalists covering the war who get involved—perhaps a little too quickly and easily—in the politics. It's an interesting and thoughtful combination of approaches: a bit of a war movie, a little romance, some politics, some international intrigue. Run it on a double bill with *MEDIUM COOL*. Joanna Cassidy is remarkably attractive and it's surprising that this film didn't make her a major star.

UNFAITHFULLY YOURS. US. 1948. Rex Harrison is a musical conductor who thinks his wife is cheating on him in this last of Preston Sturges's Hollywood films. Rudy Vallee, Lionel Stander, Linda Darnell, and Edgar Kennedy are terrific in supporting roles. (The film was remade in 1984 by Howard Zieff with Dudley Moore and Nastassja Kinski.)

UNINVITED, THE. US. 1944. A pleasant and mildly suspenseful ghost story with a nice moral to make, starring Ray Milland, Ruth Hussey, and Donald Crisp. It's another haunted house by the sea and goes well with *THE GHOST AND MRS.*

MUIR. The theme song is "Stella by Starlight."

⚠ **UNION PACIFIC**. US. 1939. A Cecil B. De Mille western with Joel McCrea, Robert Preston, Barbara Stanwyck, and many others. It's action filled and all in all a pretty good saga about the joining of east and west with the first transcontinental railroad.

⚠ **UNMARRIED WOMAN, AN**. US. 1978. Jill Clayburgh in the title role has to learn to take control of her life when her schlump of a husband, beautifully played by Michael Murphy, walks out on her. Set in the New York milieus Mazursky knows so well, it has some great insights and was considered something of a feminist statement at the time. Mazursky populates the film with his usual, very real and attractive modern characters, but you may think it cops out in the end when Jill Clayburgh luckily falls into the arms of romantic SoHo painter Alan Bates. ▽

⇪ **UPTOWN SATURDAY NIGHT**. US. 1974. Sidney Poitier turned to directing with this film and managed to get a little series going starring himself, Bill Cosby, and Harry Belafonte. (Richard Pryor and Flip Wilson lend support.) It's light stuff but they bring it off quite well. The series, including *Let's Do It Again*, lasted longer than the genre of early seventies Black films. ▽

⚠ **URBAN COWBOY**. US. 1980. James Bridges directed this film version of a famous magazine story by Aaron Latham about the fabled Gilley's Bar outside of Houston. John Travolta stars but Debra Winger steals the show. What's interesting about the film is indicated in the title: though the old myths of the west are dead, young people in these curiously disappointing big western cities are still trying desperately to recapture them, even resorting to mechanical bulls in beer bars like this one. These are the same people that populate *SILKWOOD* and they're worth a couple more movies. ▽

⇪ **USED CARS**. US. 1980. Robert Zemeckis directed this script by Bob Gale and himself which has become a cult classic. The singular, obsessive theme is used-car dealer promotions and it builds to a properly outrageous climax. ▽

↘ **VARIETY LIGHTS**. Italy. 1951. Giulietta Masina in Fellini's early celebration of the world of musical performers shows us much of the spirit that would appear in his later films. Alberto Lattuada co-directed.

VERA CRUZ. US. 1953. Robert Aldrich directed this solid, representative western starring Burt Lancaster, Gary Cooper, Ernest Borgnine, and Charles Bronson. It's set in Mexico. The plot to overthrow Emperor Maximilian gives it a historicity that most westerns don't have. ☒

VERDICT, THE. US. 1982. Playwright David Mamet adapted the novel on which this Sidney Lumet film is based. It's Paul Newman's best role in a very long time. He's a dissolute Boston lawyer who decides finally to summon up the courage to fight for justice when he gets handed a particularly upsetting negligence case. He has to fight Judge Milo O'Shea's court as well as the well-heeled opposition of lawyer James Mason and his client, the Church. Sounds like a plot from the thirties, but Lumet makes it surprisingly contemporary. ☒

VERONIQUE, OU L'ETE DE MES TREIZE ANS. France. 1975. Director Claudine Guilemain made a brief splash in the mid-seventies with this charming and irresistible story of a thirteen-year-old French girl on holiday. It's one of the few films about young teenagers that's shot from their point of view and thus offers younger filmgoers the shock of recognition. Adults will be reminded of an approach to life that they've long forgotten. Compare *PEPPERMINT SODA*.

VERTIGO. US. 1958. Although there's no doubt this is top-notch Hitchcock, it may also be his most overrated film since so many critics regard it as his best. James Stewart is the cop who can't climb ladders who falls for Kim Novak. Lots of great sequences including Hitchcock's own favorite, the tower "vertigo" scene, but it doesn't have the vigor or wit that Hitchcock showed in his best films like *NORTH BY NORTHWEST*. One of Bernard Herrmann's better scores. ☒

VICTIM. UK. 1961. Dirk Bogarde stars as a homosexual lawyer who confronts blackmailers. The film was remarkable at the time for its homosexual subject matter. Basil Dearden directed.

VICTORY AT SEA. US. 1954. Here's a theatrical anthology of the documentary television series about the naval history of World War II. It loomed large in the history of 1950s TV. Score by Richard Rodgers. ☒

VIKINGS, THE. US. 1958. Not a great film but a

classic fifties outdoor adventure with a little swashbuckling, a little history, and lots of great photography. Kirk Douglas, Tony Curtis, and Ernest Borgnine star, and you're probably laughing already. Richard Fleischer directed.

VILLAGE OF THE DAMNED. UK. 1960. The pedophobia that came to a head a decade later with *ROSEMARY'S BABY* and *THE EXORCIST* may have started with this generally well-regarded thriller about an English village filled with zombie children. ◪

VINCENT, FRANCOIS, PAUL, ET LES AUTRES. France. 1975. Claude Sautet directed some of the more notable French films of the 1970s—which may be damning with faint praise. This one is a pleasant and telling portrait of four middle-aged friends and their wives. Not much happens but I'd rather watch this than *THE FOUR SEASONS*. Yves Montand, Michel Piccoli, Gérard Depardieu, Stéphane Audran, and Marie Dubois star.

VIRGIN SPRING, THE. Sweden. 1959. The best of Ingmar Bergman's morality tales gives us a medieval peasant girl who is suddenly raped and murdered. This magnificently photographed film with Max Von Sydow and Gunnel Lindblom comes quite close to reproducing the feel and magic of the Ancient Scandinavian Sagas. Compare *HAGBARD & SIGNE*.

VIRIDIANA. Spain. 1961. Luis Buñuel returned in triumph to Spain after his long exile to shoot this masterful allegory. With hindsight it shows some touches of the humor that was to come in the later French films. At the same time it puts a cap on the criticism of religion that had obsessed him earlier. Fernando Rey is the evil uncle. ◪

VITELLONI, I. Italy. 1953. Federico Fellini's critical celebration of life in a provincial town. "I Vitelloni" are a bunch of out-of-work young men who hang out until one of them—Moraldo—takes off for Rome and adulthood. Fellini did not return to the village until *AMARCORD*.

VIVA ZAPATA! US. 1952. Marlon Brando's most heroic role as the peasant who rises to be President of Mexico. An exciting and interesting film written by John Steinbeck and directed by Elia Kazan. Anthony Quinn and Jean Peters support.

VOYAGE TO THE MOON. France. 1903. It's somehow fitting that one of the very first special effects experiments in film (by Georges Méliès) dealt with space travel. The two have been linked ever since. Show it on a double bill with *STAR WARS*.

W. R.—MYSTERIES OF THE ORGANISM. Yugoslavia. 1971. Director Dusan Makavejev seemed like a one-man Yugoslavian New Wave in the late sixties and early seventies. This one was banned by Yugoslav officials and taken up as a cause in the west. It's a kaleidoscopic mixture of plot and interviews that tries to use the theories of Wilhelm Reich to sexually liberate Communist party philosophy. In the sixties people did things like this.

WAGES OF FEAR, THE. France. 1952. Henri-Georges Clouzot is responsible for this crackerjack and classic European suspense adventure. It follows the exploits of four men driving trucks filled with nitroglycerin at breakneck speed across all but non-existent South American roads. Yves Montand stars. (William Friedkin remade it in the seventies as *Sorcerer*, not a bad film itself.)

WAIT UNTIL DARK. US. 1967. Over the last twenty years suspense plays like this Frederick Knott Broadway production filmed by Terence Young have become a sub-genre of some interest (compare *SLEUTH*). They're generally limited to one set as befits a modern theatrical production and that presents a very interesting limitation which both writer and filmmaker must deal with. Audrey Hepburn is great here as the blind potential victim, and Alan Arkin has his best role as the villain. You'll remember this one.

WAKE ISLAND. US. 1942. A classic World War II B-movie like many others. Directed by John Farrow, starring Brian Donlevy, Robert Preston, Macdonald Carey, and William Bendix. It's simply the story of the fight to hold that island at the beginning of the war. It stands here for all those B-movies made during the war that also served the cause.

WALK IN THE SUN, A. US. 1945. A good end-of-the-war-movie (by this time we were interested in the effects of war and not just chronicles of battle) about American soldiers attacking a German stronghold in Italy. Lewis Milestone directed; Dana Andrews, Richard Conte, and many other character actors star.

WALKABOUT. Australia. 1971. Before the burgeoning Australian film industry began to market images of their fascinating country to the rest of the world, British cinematographer Nicolas Roeg directed this classic outback story. Two lost white kids team up with a young aborigine and learn survival techniques. It's a great travelogue and a good kid's film.

WALKING TALL. US. 1973. This was a very popular movie at the time and re-introduced a vigilante theme that has become an important current in contemporary American culture during the last twelve years. Joe Don Baker re-enacts the exploits of real-life Sheriff Buford Pusser wreaking vengeance on the bad guys with his baseball bat. The film was sharply criticized by liberal critics at the time but it expressed a real deep-seated need for revenge. Phil Karlson directed.

WANDERERS, THE. US. 1979. Philip Kaufman directed this celebration of Bronx teenagerhood circa 1963. Full of the sentiments you may remember, it's a nostalgic classic.

WAR AND PEACE. USSR. 1967. Nearly eight hours in length, this is the definitive theatrical film version of Tolstoy's novel, the epic portrait of Russia during the Napoleonic Wars. Sergei Bondarchuk directed. Probably better is the twenty-hour BBC television serial which proves definitively the special ability of TV and its series form to capture the breadth and depth of great novels.

WAR GAME, THE. UK. 1966. Much ahead of its time this film originally intended for the BBC, but banned, is based on a simple and devastating concept. Director Peter Watkins shot a portrait of life after a nuclear holocaust as if it were a real television documentary. Nearly twenty years later, *THE DAY AFTER* reprised the subject with astonishing impact and *SPECIAL BULLETIN* borrowed the documentary technique to the same effect. An important landmark.

WAR OF THE WORLDS, THE. US. 1953. George Pal produced (and Byron Haskin directed) this superior example of fifties sci fi—a version of the H. G. Wells fantasy of a Martian invasion. It may seem to be the same paranoid script that was repeated so many times in the fifties but at least it has the literary antecedent.

WARGAMES. US. 1983. An interesting solution to the problem of dealing with nuclear war in the film *Wargames* is also a very good movie. It's the kid, Matthew Broderick, with hope, who beats the grownup cynic who's programmed the computer for ultimate destruction. The film maintains a light, affirmative tone throughout most of the story. Interestingly enough, it's not men versus computers, either. The computer is smarter. The last scene, in which the computer learns that nuclear war is a no-win situation, is not only moving but profoundly instructive. Here's a classic Hollywood movie that makes a sharp political point and does it with wit and reserve; an all too rare occurrence. ▼

WARRIORS, THE. US. 1979. The idiosyncratic Walter Hill came up with this strange fantasy which follows a New York teenage gang as they wend their way home clear across the city through foreign lands belonging to rival gangs. It has little to do with reality but it's interesting to watch Hill's apocalyptic vision of street culture. ▼

WATCH ON THE RHINE. US. 1943. Dashiell Hammett wrote the script of the Lillian Hellman play about Nazi goings-on in the US during World War II. Paul Lucas is the secret patriot and Bette Davis his wife. It was effective propaganda at the time. ▼

WAVELENGTH. Canada. 1967. Here's a lovely "avant-garde" experiment by Michael Snow. It consists of a single imperceptibly slow zoom shot from one side of a large room to the other and then into a closeup and a detailed shot of a photograph of waves. It lasts forty-five minutes and you'll enjoy many of them.

WAY AHEAD, THE. UK. 1944. A classic British World War II drama with a nice point to make: united we stand. . . . Carol Reed directed the script by Eric Ambler and Peter Ustinov; David Niven and Stanley Holloway star. We follow a group of civilians as they are drafted and trained and sent to North Africa. Contrast *HOW I WON THE WAR*.

WAY DOWN EAST. US. 1920. D. W. Griffith's Victorian melodrama is a classic of the silent era, in part for Lillian Gish's performance as a wronged waif and a memorable scene in which she works her way across an ice-filled river.

WAY OUT WEST. US. 1937. Most critics agree

Diane Keaton and Warren Beatty as Louise Bryant and John Reed almost lost in the landscape of the Russian revolution in *Reds*.

this is Stan Laurel's and Oliver Hardy's best effort. The western setting sharpened their by-then classic comic duet.

WAY TO THE STARS, THE. UK. 1945. What Noel Coward did for naval officers and men during World War II in *IN WHICH WE SERVE*, Anthony Asquith does here for the R.A.F. John Mills, Michael Redgrave, Stanley Holloway, and Trevor Howard star. Terence Rattigan had a hand in the script.

WAY WE WERE, THE. US. 1973. Director Sydney Pollack and stars Barbra Streisand and Robert Redford do a good job of bringing the Arthur Laurents script to the screen. It's a great romance and it does tell something about the way we were from the thirties to the fifties, but a lot of the politics of the Blacklist period are missing from the film, apparently cut just before release. Streisand's an activist; her lover Redford is apolitical.

WE ALL LOVED EACH OTHER SO MUCH. Italy. 1977. This is a great movie about movies by Ettore Scola. Three friends are involved with the same woman (Stefania Sandrelli) over more than twenty years, giving Scola a chance to comment on the Italian filmmaking scene from the forties to the sixties at the same time that he tells a sharply observed and moving story of men and women.

WE WON'T GROW OLD TOGETHER. France. 1972. This is Maurice Pialat's remarkable portrait of a man and a woman—Jean Yanne and Marlene Jobert—who can't live with each other and can't live without each other. It's a brilliant portrait of a marriage gone wrong that would have been perhaps funnier if Claude Chabrol had directed it. Pialat's style is serious—almost humorless—but you know that he's not exploiting these people and that he has tremendous compassion for them and their situation. There's never been a better film about the tough side of marriage.

WEDDING, A. US. 1978. Robert Altman's second-most-interesting film has even more "major characters" than *NASHVILLE*. Carol Burnett, Desi Arnaz Jr., Vittorio Gassman, Geraldine Chaplin, Mia Farrow, Paul Dooley, Lauren Hutton, John Cromwell, Lillian Gish, Howard Duff, Peggy Ann Garner, John Considine, Viveca Lindfors, and even others, attend the celebration. This kind of thing is quite hard to do, but Altman makes it look easy. There's a wonderful balance to the huge set of characters and the images and sounds are as rich as in any of Altman's films. At one point late in the film during a major dramatic scene we hear lush Howard Duff far off-screen, two floors below, very quietly reply when asked if he wants another drink: "Just to the brim, please!" It's the most thrown-away of all great throwaway lines in movies.

WEDDING MARCH, THE. US. 1926. Erich Von Stroheim tackled the middle European milieu once again in *The Wedding March*, which exhibits the usual Von Stroheim concerns of class conflict and behavior. The film was originally planned to be at least six hours long. Something more than three hours exist in a form close to what Von Stroheim may have envisioned. He stars with Fay Wray and ZaSu Pitts.

WEE WILLIE WINKIE. US. 1937. John Ford handles Shirley Temple with the help of Victor McLaglen in a Kipling story about India that yielded a classic thirties movie for children.

WEEKEND. France. 1967. Jean-Luc Godard's most ambitious and vociferous "revolutionary" movie before he retired to the shelter of the Dziga-Vertov group is full of funny anti-bourgeois set-pieces including one of the great sequences in all cinema: a full reel, ten-minute tracking shot that proceeds with a stately pace past a very, very long line of stalled automobiles on a French country highway lined with poplars. Compare the supermarket scene in *TOUT VA BIEN*.

⊘ **WELCOME TO L.A.** US. 1977. This is too precious to be a really good film but it's an interesting study in the Altman style of a bunch of over-the-edge Angelenos, including Keith Carradine, Sally Kellerman, Harvey Keitel, and Viveca Lindfors. Altman produced; Alan Rudolph directed without Altman's sense of humor. ∨

⇧ **WERNER HERZOG EATS HIS SHOE.** US. 1981. German filmmaker Werner Herzog bet somebody he'd eat his shoe. He lost the bet and set up a special performance at a Berkeley theater. American filmmaker Les Blank decided to record the event and the result is as insightful about contemporary artistic characters as it is funny. Blank later trailed Herzog through South American jungles as he shot *Fitzcarraldo*. See *BURDEN OF DREAMS*.

⎯⬦⎯⨎ **WEST SIDE STORY.** US. 1961. A good film record of one of the major Broadway musicals of the last thirty years. Robert Wise and Jerome Robbins directed. Natalie Wood, Rita Moreno, and Russ Tamblyn star in the Romeo and Juliet saga set on New York's upper west side. Leonard Bernstein and Stephen Sondheim wrote the songs and Arthur Laurents the play. ∨

‼⇧ **WHAT A WAY TO GO!** US. 1964. An underrated farce written by Betty Comden and Adolph Green, directed by J. Lee Thompson, and starring Shirley MacLaine as the woman with the uncanny luck to marry a long succession of rich men who each quickly die, contributing to her personal balance sheet. The men include Dick Van Dyke, Paul Newman, Robert Mitchum, Gene Kelly, and Dean Martin.

‼ **WHAT'S NEW, PUSSYCAT?** US. 1965. Clive Donner was nominally in control as director of this classic sixties comedy. Woody Allen wrote it and starred in it with Peter O'Toole, Romy Schneider, and Peter Sellers. It has some of the wildness that was the hallmark of a generation just waking up to new possibilities. Compare *CASINO ROYALE*. Burt Bacharach and Hal David wrote the catchy title tune. ∨

‼⇧ **WHAT'S UP, DOC?** US. 1972. Believe it or not, this is as close as anyone's come in a long time to reproducing the feel and pace of a classic 1930s Hollywood screwball comedy. Peter Bogdanovich directed an hommage to *BRINGING UP BABY*. Ryan O'Neal and Barbra Streisand star with Madeline Kahn. There are some really good chase scenes. Ryan O'Neal, the pretty boy from *Peyton Place*, proves he's a real actor here. ⬇️

‼️ **WHAT'S UP TIGER LILY?** US. 1966. Woody Allen bought the rights to a cheap Japanese detective story, recut the footage, and dubbed some very funny dialogue in English. It's an interesting experiment and it was his entree to feature film direction. ⬇️

＼‼️⬆️ **WHEELER-DEALERS, THE**. US. 1963. Here's an underrated early sixties comedy with Lee Remick, James Garner, Jim Backus, and Phil Harris. About investors who don't take their avocation seriously, it has a lot to say about the contemporary financial world and in this regard was years ahead of its time. Arthur Hiller directed.

🚩 **WHERE THE BOYS ARE**. US. 1960. A teenage classic about spring vacation in Fort Lauderdale, this film founded a genre and became the model for dozens of similar celebrations of adolescent sexual exploration. Henry Levin directed Jim Hutton, Paula Prentiss, Connie Francis, and Barbara Nichols. ⬇️

🚩⬆️ **WHISTLE, THE**. US. 1921. William S. Hart is known now, if at all, as an early western star on the order of Tom Mix. While it's true he was a great western star (see *HELL'S HINGES*), he had a much wider range. He is perhaps second only to Chaplin—who, like Hart, also had a stage background—as a truly accomplished actor of the silent cinema. *The Whistle* is a sharply moving story of a father and a son which exhibits Hart's intelligence and art to great effect. The emotions here are complex and sophisticated—not at all what one expects from "silent movies." Of course, Hart—and *The Whistle*—were not alone. Our image of silent film as emotionally simplistic is a distortion that comes from having been exposed to so little of its range.

§ **WHITE CHRISTMAS**. US. 1954. Michael Curtiz's variation on the themes of *HOLIDAY INN* with Bing Crosby, Danny Kaye, Rosemary Clooney, and Vera-Ellen. It's not as good as its predecessor, but it's nostalgic of the fifties. And it has an ample quantity of Irving Berlin songs.

WHITE HEAT. US. 1949. "Top of the world, ma!" James Cagney is the crazy gangster in love with his mother in this tough no-nonsense gangster movie by Raoul Walsh that harks back to the thirties.

WHITE SHEIK, THE. Italy. 1951. Alberto Sordi and Giulietta Masina in Fellini's first film on his own. It's minor Fellini but it chronicles the world of the Fumetti (comic books with photographs of actors instead of drawings) in which his talent was forged.

WHO'S AFRAID OF VIRGINIA WOOLF? US. 1966. Mike Nichols's film record of the famous Edward Albee play that was a landmark in the early sixties. The film was notable on its own since it paired Richard Burton and Elizabeth Taylor as the intensely self-destructive couple. On second viewing you wonder why these people don't just get a divorce or take separate vacations.

WHY WE FIGHT. US. 1943. Frank Capra's sensible, intelligent, yet pointedly effective series of US World War II propaganda films speaks volumes about the cultural importance of that war which served as a crucible of US national sensibility. Capra's passionate yet balanced attitude represents much of what is best in the American character. The title of the series was intended at the time as a simple description of documentary intent. Now it has an extra dimension: we fought, and still fight, in large part because of the qualities in the American character Frank Capra represents.

WILD BUNCH, THE. US. 1969. Sam Peckinpah's classic late western about out-of-date outlaws in the early twentieth century was notable at the time, like *BONNIE AND CLYDE*, for its controversial "poetic" violence. Today it's just a good solid story with William Holden, Ernest Borgnine, Robert Ryan, and Warren Oates.

WILD CHILD, THE. France. 1970. This is certainly François Truffaut's most ambitious film. A simple, restrained, and elegant essay on the strange true story of *Victor of Aveyron* by Jean Itard, who discovered the boy who had spent most of his youth in the woods, and took him into his home to try to civilize him. Truffaut himself stars as Itard, and with good reason. This modern myth has exceptional resonance: it's about parents and children, and teachers and students, and even filmmakers and actors. It's about language and images and— forgive the expression—semiotics. Nestor Almendros photographed the film in elegant black and white. Jean Gruault wrote the screenplay. (Consider his script for Resnais's *MON ONCLE D'AMERIQUE* as a sequel.) Truffaut's concerns with children, moral sentiment, and the idea of civilization far transcend the existential platitudes that passed for French philosophy in the fifties and early sixties. Truffaut's seemingly simple cinematic concerns are also keys helpful in understanding the real significance of the recent past period of French philosophy and its obsession with language. *The Wild Child* is among the wisest of films.

WILD PARTY, THE. US. 1929. Dorothy Arzner directed Clara Bow as a sexy twenties college student who has an affair with her professor (Fredric March). The style is archaic jazz-age, but the subject has proved a small goldmine for semi-erotic kid's movies in the eighties. Compare *PRIVATE SCHOOL*.

WILD STRAWBERRIES. Sweden. 1958. This is Ingmar Bergman's best film. A balanced, intelligent portrait of the life of an elderly professor, played by Swedish director Victor Sjöström (with the assistance of Ingrid Thulin, Bibi Andersson, and Gunnar Björnstrand). It's full of precisely observed touches and shows the same intense psychology as the later films but with measurably more spirit and understanding of the broader world outside than we see in the succeeding films. ☒

WILLIE AND PHIL. US. 1980. Here's a seriously underrated movie by Paul Mazursky. It's inspired by Truffaut's classic love triangle *JULES AND JIM*. Willie and Phil are played by Michael Ontkean and Ray Sharkey. Margot Kidder is the Jeanne Moreau character, and that's the problem with the film: she doesn't show the magic Moreau did. What Mazursky is really about, however, is investigating the folkways of the sixties and seventies. This doesn't tell the whole story of the way we lived then but it tells a good part of it and it does so with remarkable understanding and affection.

WILMAR 8, THE. US. 1980. This is a strong documentary about eight Minnesota women who struck the bank where they worked to achieve equal pay. They received little support from the national unions and less from the community, but they refused to quit. It's both an inspiring story and a painfully instructive one: they were asking for so little, so late in the twentieth century. Compare *A MATTER OF SEX*, the fictional version of the story, also by Lee Grant.

WILSON. US. 1944. A curious but solid biopic about the President, directed by Henry King and starring Alexander Knox, Charles Coburn, Geraldine Fitzgerald, and Thomas Mitchell.

⏺ **WING AND A PRAYER, A**. US. 1944. Here's a good World War II action movie. This time it's Navy pilots on a carrier. Don Ameche and Dana Andrews star, Henry Hathaway directed with his usual aplomb.

🚩 **WINGS**. US. 1927. It's not a great film but it won the first Oscar. It stars Clara Bow (with Buddy Rogers and Richard Arlen), and it has terrific aerial photography of the Army Air Corps during World War I. That's probably enough. ▼

⏺😊 **WINNIE THE POOH**. US. 1965. This is the Disney version of the extraordinary children's stories by A. A. Milne. If you love the whimsy of the only children's book ever to become a best-seller in Latin translation, you may be disappointed the first time you see this. The *Winnie the Pooh* stories are so literarily sophisticated the animated film is hard-pressed to match them. It doesn't have the quaint Englishness of the original. It does try, however, to translate the elaborate narrative structure to the screen. The second time you see it you'll think, "Well, I guess for Disney it's a pretty conscientious job." Drawn by lots and lots of people, and Mr. Shepard didn't help. ▼

WINSLOW BOY, THE. UK. 1948. Here's a Terence Rattigan play (directed by Anthony Asquith) with Robert Donat and Margaret Leighton. It's a cut above the average courtroom drama—about a boy accused of theft—and a perennial favorite of English-movie fans.

🏠 **WINTER KILLS**. US. 1979. William Richert directed this cult favorite about the aftermath of a Presidential assassination. It's full of strange dark comedy touches. Maybe it doesn't work after all, but it was worth the try. Jeff Bridges, John Huston, Anthony Perkins, and Sterling Hayden star. ▼

🚩 **WINTER SOLDIER**. US. 1972. If you want to know what Vietnam was all about, check out this documentary record of veterans' testimony during a Vietnam Veterans Against the War hearing. It's worth all the fiction films about the war so far put together, giving a harrowing description of sublime stupidity.

WISE BLOOD. US. 1979. John Huston translated this Flannery O'Connor story to the screen with masterful adroitness. It's full of the southern gothic elements—cripples, religious fanatics, and assorted oddballs—for which American southern novels have been famous for for fifty years. A curious choice for Huston, it's almost a self-test in translation.

WITH BABIES AND BANNERS. US. 1978. Here's a superior example of the effective seventies documentary format that mixed historical footage with contemporary interviews. Lorraine Gray's subject is the Women's Emergency Brigade which worked to support the General Motors Sitdown Strike of 1937. You'll love these women, both then and now. It's an important piece of American history neatly and intelligently put together. Compare *THE LIFE AND TIMES OF ROSIE THE RIVETER*.

WITNESS FOR THE PROSECUTION. US. 1958. Everyone's favorite courtroom drama, from the Agatha Christie play, directed by Billy Wilder and starring Marlene Dietrich, Tyrone Power, Charles Laughton, and Elsa Lanchester. It's a model for the inherent and paradoxical drama of the courtroom: in courts everyone sits around asking and answering questions. There is no physical action, but nevertheless the result can be riveting and suspenseful.

WIZARD OF OZ, THE. US. 1939. I can't give you much help here. Everyone's favorite children's film has always left me cold. I know the music's nice and it's very colorful and Judy Garland and friends are cute, but I've never understood why it takes so long to get to Oz. We learn so little along the way from the Munchkins and the Witches. It's a dream, of course, but it's like one of those dreams where everything happens in slow motion. I'd much prefer annual television showings of *THE COURT JESTER*.

WOBBLIES, THE. US. 1979. Here's another fascinating seventies documentary combining contemporary interviews and historical footage. Filmmakers Stewart Bird and Deborah Shaffer captured another important American political movement on film just in time before the witnesses passed on. Unlike other examples of this genre (*WITH BABIES AND BANNERS*), this one gives us more-or-less famous historical characters.

WOMAN IN THE DUNES. Japan. 1964. This is

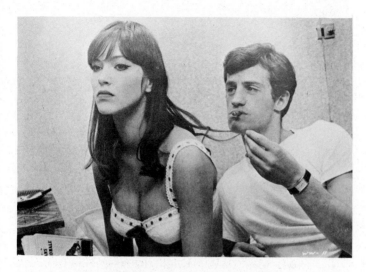

Anna Karina and Jean-Paul Belmondo in bed in *A Woman Is a Woman*,
Jean-Luc Godard's *hommage* to the American musical.

the kind of symbolic drama that ought to be claptrap.
It's not. Somehow director Hiroshi Teshigahara
makes this dream of a woman trapped in a sand pit
(from a novel by Kobo Abe) memorable and
involving. Partly it's the mesmerizing cinematography, partly it's the raw emotion. ▼

WOMAN IN THE WINDOW, THE. US. 1944.
Fritz Lang directed this unusual Nunnally Johnson
script that turns the action of a simple melodrama in
upon itself as a commentary on the medium. Worth
thinking about. Edward G. Robinson and Joan
Bennett star.

WOMAN IS A WOMAN, A. France. 1960. This
may seem rather thin now, but it was a marvelous
experience at the time: Jean-Luc Godard's very
Parisian attempt at sketching an American musical.
Jean-Paul Belmondo, Jean-Claude Brialy, and Anna
Karina form the triangle. They want to be Cyd
Charisse and Gene Kelly, and they want
choreography by Bob Fosse. There isn't much
music. "Hello, Joe, whaddaya know?" But it's got
the breath of youth about it in a still-romantic Paris.

WOMAN OF THE YEAR. US. 1942. This is the
first of the Spencer Tracy/Katharine Hepburn
movies. She's a famous reporter, he's a lowly sports
writer. The romance crackles with wit and spunk.
(The 1976 Renee Taylor/Joseph Bologna remake

isn't bad either.)

⬆ **WOMAN TIMES SEVEN**. US. 1967. Shirley MacLaine under the direction of Vittoria De Sica, is an oddity that shouldn't be missed. She stars in seven separate episodes, some good, some not so good. The men in her life include Peter Sellers, Vittorio Gassman, and Rossanno Brazzi.

WOMAN UNDER THE INFLUENCE, A. US. 1974. For John Cassavetes fans (okay, there aren't many), here's a portrait of a wife who's losing her grip and her worker husband's reactions to the events. Gena Rowlands and Peter Falk star.

WOMEN, THE. US. 1939. Not at all to be confused with any of the "women" films we've just cited, this is the famous Clare Boothe Luce play about catty rich "girls" in the thirties. Rosalind Russell, Joan Crawford, Joan Fontaine, and Paulette Goddard star. Anita Loos had a hand in the screenplay.

⊘ **WOMEN IN LOVE**. UK. 1969. Ken Russell restrained himself with this quite good adaptation of the D. H. Lawrence novel about a pair of love affairs. Glenda Jackson, Eleanor Bron, Alan Bates, and Oliver Reed star. This is the one with the famous nude wrestling sequence.

⬇ **WOMEN'S ROOM, THE**. US. 1980. Marilyn French's popular feminist novel is translated faithfully to the screen with Lee Remick, Colleen Dewhurst, Patty Duke Astin, and others in the roles of a bunch of 1950s women, college friends observed through the course of two decades. It's too downbeat to be topnotch: we need more women heroes here. Compare *THE GROUP*. In my fantasy, Katharine Hepburn, Rosalind Russell, and Barbara Stanwyck show up from the 1940s to shape these women into an effective spirited fighting force—with a sense of humor.

WONDER MAN. US. 1945. Danny Kaye in a dual role here with Virginia Mayo, S. Z. Sakall, and Vera-Ellen. As the stuffy brother, he's forced to take the place of his entertainer brother. H. Bruce Humberstone directed this colorful comedy of conflicting character.

⬛$ **WOODSTOCK**. US. 1970. Were you there? You are here with three hours plus of multi-screen images and sounds distilled from the many thousands of feet that were shot during the historic weekend in upstate

New York. Michael Wadleigh directed this celebration of a generation (now more obviously a conclusion than a beginning) which includes performances by the Jefferson Airplane, Joe Cocker, Santana, the Who, Jimi Hendrix, Arlo Guthrie, and Joan Baez, among many others. 🔲

WORLD IN HIS ARMS, THE. US. 1952. I haven't seen this in more than thirty years, but I still remember it as a breathtaking, quintessentially fifties color adventure. Gregory Peck buckles swash as the sea captain. The beauteous Ann Blyth is the object of his affection. Anthony Quinn adds color. The teeming San Francisco of the middle of the nineteenth century is the setting. Raoul Walsh directed.

WORLD OF APU, THE. India. 1959. This is the concluding part of Satyajit Ray's Apu Trilogy (after *PATHER PANCHALI* and *APARAJITO*), and a majestic and moving conclusion it is. Apu marries here, his wife dies, and he arrives at a point very near wisdom.

WORLD OF HENRY ORIENT, THE. US. 1964. The New York sensibility is captured perfectly here in the screenplay by Nunnally and Nora Johnson. It may have started out to be a Peter Sellers movie (he's a famous pianist), but two unknown pre-teens—Tippy Walker and Merrie Spaeth—thoroughly steal the show. They are irresistably ingratiating as teenybopper proto-groupies. Both were signed to long-term contracts after the film but I don't believe either was ever seen on film again. George Roy Hill directed. Paula Prentiss, Angela Lansbury, and Tom Bosley add support.

WRONG BOX, THE. UK. 1966. This is a masterful Victorian farce based, believe it or not, on a Robert Louis Stevenson story. The inestimable Larry Gelbart and Burt Shevelove wrote the script. Bryan Forbes directed. John Mills, Ralph Richardson, Peter Cook, Dudley Moore, Michael Caine, and Peter Sellers star in the story of a tontine (that's a mutual bet amongst a group of people in which the last to survive wins the pot). It's far funnier than the serial murders of *KIND HEARTS AND CORONETS*.

WRONG MAN, THE. US. 1957. Hitchcock on location in New York City to do a docudrama, if you will, about Manny Balestrero, a real club musician who was falsely accused of robbery. It's Hitchcock's most uncharacteristic film but it adds an important footnote to his work because of its real-life roots. Henry Fonda is the mouse-like musician in his most unusual role, Vera Miles his wife. ▾

WUTHERING HEIGHTS. US. 1939. The ultimate Gothic novel done to a turn by director William Wyler and stars Laurence Olivier, Merle Oberon, and David Niven. Gregg Toland was responsible for the exceptional photography on the Hollywood backlot heath.

YAKUZA, THE. US. 1975. Paul Schrader wrote the script for this unusual American attempt at a Japanese gangster genre. Robert Mitchum is the perfect choice as the American set down in the Tokyo underworld. The clash of cultures works quite well. Sydney Pollack directed. ▾

YANKEE DOODLE DANDY. US. 1942. A tour-de-force performance by James Cagney as the legendary George M. Cohan, a wealth of good, simple musical routines, and a bit of biography add up to a classic Hollywood entertainment. Michael Curtiz directed. ▾

YELLOW SUBMARINE. UK. 1968. A unique animated celebration of Beatles music, *Yellow Submarine* is far more than just a rock exploitation film. The animation was magnitudes more sophisticated than anything else done in commercial features at the time. The plot is enough to hold your attention, and the way it showcases the Beatles verbal wit and music is unbeatable. George Dunning coordinated as director. It's poignant now to say, "twenty years ago today, Sergeant Pepper taught the band to play."

YOJIMBO. Japan. 1961. Akira Kurosawa's most human samurai epic gives us Toshiro Mifune as a very "western" hero. ▾

YOU CAN'T CHEAT AN HONEST MAN. US. 1939. W. C. Fields jests with Edgar Bergen, Charlie McCarthy, and Eddie Anderson, in this most sustained of the Fields movies. He runs a circus full of snappy bits of business and one-liners.

YOU CAN'T TAKE IT WITH YOU. US. 1938. Why don't we give George S. Kaufman the credit that's due him? Any sensible list of great American playwrights of the twentieth century should certainly rank Kaufman very close to the top. Here he was working with Moss Hart to paint a portrait of domestic contentment and strength with a gallery of weird and wonderful characters. Frank Capra directed. James Stewart, Lionel Barrymore, Jean Arthur, Edward Arnold, and Eddie Anderson star.

YOUNG AND INNOCENT. UK. 1937. Perhaps Hitchcock's most overlooked and underrated film, this is a pleasant and charming mystery starring the cute Nova Pilbeam and Derrick de Marney. He's accused of murder, but innocent, of course. They find the real culprit at a dance disguised in blackface as the drummer. The tracking shot from one end of the hall to the other moving into a detailed closeup of the drummer's twitching eyes is one of the great shots in all Hitchcock. Compare *WAVELENGTH*.

YOUNG AT HEART. US. 1954. Gordon Douglas directed this tearjerker, a satisfactory musical, with Frank Sinatra, Doris Day, and Gig Young. During Sinatra's long and often distinguished career he has established himself as the best American popular singer of three generations and an interesting actor as well. He has richly earned the sobriquet "Chairman of the Board." The curious thing is that we have so little of his music on film. He's made only a handful of musicals and that's going to prove a disappointment to future generations. Given the sparseness of his musical output, *Young at Heart* just makes the list.

YOUNG CASSIDY. UK. 1965. Jack Cardiff and John Ford both worked on this gorgeous color biopic of Dublin playwright Sean O'Casey set in the years before World War I. Rod Taylor, Julie Christie, and Maggie Smith star. It's a winning combination.

YOUNG FRANKENSTEIN. US. 1974. Mel Brooks's most successful genre parody of the seventies takes apart Frankenstein movies with great affection and fun. In black and white it manages to reproduce surprisingly well the feel of an early thirties movie. Gene Wilder, Madeline Kahn, Marty Feldman, and Peter Boyle star.

YOUNG IN HEART, THE. US. 1938. Here's an overlooked but charming story of a group of not quite so honest—con artists who go straight—eccentrics that is a lesson in fine ensemble playing from Douglas Fairbanks Jr., Paulette Goddard, Janet Gaynor, Roland Young, and Billie Burke. Richard Wallace directed.

YOUNG LIONS, THE. US. 1958. A long and

generally intelligent re-telling of the Irwin Shaw novel comparing German and American battle experiences in World War II. Edward Dmytryk directed Marlon Brando, Montgomery Clift, Dean Martin, and Maximilian Schell.

YOUNG MR. LINCOLN. US. 1939. A solid historical study from John Ford, with Henry Fonda as the young Abe learning to be a lawyer.

YOUNG WINSTON. UK. 1972. Richard Attenborough cut his directorial teeth with this attractive biography of the early years of Winston Churchill. It's the sort of thing you might better expect from British television but Attenborough gives it added value with superb color photography (he experimented with "flashing" techniques here, exposing the film before shooting to get subtle color tints) and a broad painterly hand. Simon Ward, Anne Bancroft, Robert Shaw, and John Mills star.

YOU'RE A BIG BOY NOW. US. 1966. Francis Coppola eases into the director's chair with an adolescent memory of growing up in New York and its suburbs. Peter Kastner is the boy from Great Neck (Coppola's hometown) who learns about life and sex from Elizabeth Hartman in the New York Public Library. The Lovin' Spoonful score is still memorable, and the location photography in New York is becoming nostalgic.

Z. France. 1969. Costa-Gavras established the leading film and television genre of the seventies and eighties with this tough, rhythmic, breathless and enormously effective docudrama about a Greek political assassination. Jean-Louis Trintignant stars as the investigating magistrate, Yves Montand is the victim. A bunch of great French character actors assist. The music by Mikis Theodorakis is an integral part of the emotional and political effect as is the exceptional photography by Raoul Coutard. Costa-Gavras is of Greek origin and this is his outraged condemnation of the military coup of 1967 that extinguished democracy in its homeland. Important cinema and more important history. Jorge Semprun wrote the script. Mikis Theodorakis was responsible for the exceptional music.

ZABRISKI POINT. US. 1970. This highly visual enterprise may yet turn out to be Michelangelo Antonioni's best film. The revolutionary American youth culture of the late sixties is seen through the wrong end of a telescope by a man from another country from another generation from another class.

He perceives quite clearly and with unusual detail the tension between American middle-class lifestyles and the spiritual revolt of us kids at the time, but he uses an exaggerated metaphorical technique to express it. When the film was released people dismissed it as arty. Now, what seems like a lifetime later, we may be able to see that this was his most pointed and therefore most useful film. In the ultimate scene, Antonioni explodes an entire suburban house in slow motion from seventeen angles: cereal boxes, toasters, and coke bottles float majestically and graciously through the air. It was for me a breathtaking emotional experience, and it may be still for you. That was the urgent psychological fantasy that was at the root of the sixties counter-culture. ⊻

ZANDY'S BRIDE. US. 1974. This story of a mail-order bride in California in the last century can be tacked onto *THE EMIGRANTS* and *THE NEW LAND* as the third element in director Jan Troell's trilogy of the American immigration experience. Here he takes his star Liv Ullmann (playing a different character) from the midwest to the far west to serve as helpmate to pioneer Gene Hackman. There are some dramatic problems, but it's a fascinating portrait of the old west as seen through Swedish eyes. Compare the very similar plot of *HEARTLAND*.

ZAZIE DANS LE METRO. France. 1960. This is a great film by Louis Malle totally outside the mainstream of French or any other cinema at the time. He took a very verbal comic novel by Raymond Queneau and turned it into a dazzlingly visual film about a ten-year-old girl's wild exploits on a visit to Paris. It's a great farce that children will take to immediately because of its spirit, but it's also full of inside jokes and illusions that repay third, fourth, and fifth viewings. It's also a colorful celebration of the city of light and cinema.

ZERO FOR CONDUCT. France. 1933. Jean Vigo's unsurpassed masterpiece about children at a boarding school who rebel magnificently against the regimentation. Why have the French made so many of the great films about children? The pillow fight is an image that will remain with you forever, a bit of cinema you'll enjoy remembering as you snuggle deep into the covers just before going to sleep. ⊻

ZIEGFELD FOLLIES. US. 1946. Before TV, movies had to serve the traditions of Vaudeville and variety, and they did so quite well. This is probably the best of those revue films, directed by Vincente Minnelli and starring William Powell, Judy Garland, Lucille Ball, Fred Astaire, Fanny Brice, Lena Horne, and Red Skelton. An important record of popular entertainment at the time. ▽

△ **ZORBA THE GREEK**. Greece. 1964. Anthony Quinn's best role: the apotheosis of the life force. Michael Cacoyannis directed this celebration of quaint, and perhaps cliched, Greek lifestyles from the Nikos Kazantzakis novel. The Mikis Theodorakis score adds significantly to the experience. Lila Kedrova, Alan Bates, and Irene Papas support Quinn nicely. ▽

Jean-Pierre Léaud and Claude Jade steal a moment and a kiss in the wine cellar in Truffaut's *Stolen Kisses.*

Alternate Titles

Key: orig = original, alt = alternate, UK = United Kingdom, US = United States titles.

<--> (orig): see BACK AND FORTH.

A BOUT DE SOUFFLE (orig): see BREATHLESS.

AFFAIR OF THE HEART, AN (alt): see LOVE AFFAIR, OR THE CASE OF THE MISSING SWITCHBOARD OPERATOR, THE.

AKIBI YORI (orig): see LATE AUTUMN.

ALBERO DEGLI ZOCCOLI, L' (orig): see TREE OF THE WOODEN CLOGS, THE.

ALICE IN DEN STADTEN (orig): see ALICE IN THE CITIES.

ALL THAT MONEY CAN BUY (alt): see DEVIL AND DANIEL WEBSTER, THE.

ALL THESE WOMEN (alt): see NOW ABOUT ALL THESE WOMEN.

AMANTS, LES (orig): see LOVERS, THE.

AMERIKANISCHE FREUND, DER (orig): see AMERICAN FRIEND, THE.

AMOUR EN FUITE, L' (orig): see LOVE ON THE RUN.

AMOUR, L'APRES-MIDI, L' (orig): see CHLOE IN THE AFTERNOON.

AND WOMAN. . . WAS CREATED (UK): see AND GOD CREATED WOMAN.

ANGEL EXTERMINADOR, EL (orig): see EXTERMINATING ANGEL, THE.

ANIMAL HOUSE (alt): see NATIONAL LAMPOON'S ANIMAL HOUSE.

ANNEE DERNIERE A MARIENBAD, L' (orig): see LAST YEAR AT MARIENBAD.

ANSIKTET (orig): see MAGICIAN, THE.

APUR SANSAR (orig): see WORLD OF APU, THE.

ARANYER DIN RATRI (orig): see DAYS AND NIGHTS IN THE FOREST.

ARGENT DE POCHE, L' (orig): see SMALL CHANGE.

AS USUAL, UNKNOWN (TV): see BIG DEAL ON MADONNA STREET.

ASHANI SANKET (orig): see DISTANT THUNDER.

AU MILIEU DU MONDE (orig): see MIDDLE OF THE WORLD, THE.

BABIES AND BANNERS (alt): see WITH BABIES AND BANNERS.

BADGE OF HONOR (alt): see QUESTION OF HONOR, A.

BAISERS VOLES (orig): see STOLEN KISSES.

BALLAD OF JOE HILL, THE (alt): see JOE HILL.

BALLON ROUGE, LE (orig): see RED BALLOON, THE.

BANK DETECTIVE, THE (UK): see BANK DICK, THE.

BATTAGLIA DI ALGERI, LA (Italy): see BATTLE OF ALGIERS, THE.

BATTALIA DE CHILE, LA (orig): see BATTLE OF CHILE, THE.

BATTLESHIP POTEMKIN (alt): see POTEMKIN.

BAXTER'S BEAUTIES OF 1933 (episode): see MOVIE, MOVIE.

BELLE FILLE COMME MOI, UNE (orig): see SUCH A GORGEOUS KID LIKE ME.

BELLE ET LA BETE, LA (orig): see BEAUTY AND THE BEAST.

BERLIN, DIE SYMPHONIE EINER GROSSTADT (orig): see BERLIN—SYMPHONY OF A GREAT CITY.

BIG CARNIVAL, THE (alt): see ACE IN THE HOLE.

BIG DAY, THE (alt): see JOUR DE FETE.

BIG DEAL, THE (alt): see BIG DEAL ON MADONNA STREET.

BIG HEART, THE (UK): see MIRACLE ON 34TH STREET.

BLAUE ENGEL, DER (orig): see BLUE ANGEL, THE.

BLECHTROMMEL, DIE (orig): see TIN DRUM, THE.

BLONDE BOMBSHELL, THE (UK): see BOMBSHELL.

BLOOD COUPLE (alt): see GANJA AND HESS.

BOAT, THE (US): see BOOT, DAS.

BOUDU SAUVE DES EAUX (orig): see BOUDU SAVED FROM DROWNING.

BRONENOSETS 'POTYOMKIN' (orig): see POTEMKIN.

BUECHSE DER PANDORA, DIE (orig): see PANDORA'S BOX.

BUILD MY GALLOWS HIGH (UK): see OUT OF THE PAST.

BUTCHER, THE (US): see LE BOUCHER.

CABINETT DER DOKTOR CALIGARI, DAS (orig): see CABINET OF DR. CALIGARI, THE.

CABIRIA (UK): see NIGHTS OF CABIRIA.

CACCIA AL MASCHIO (Italian): see MALE HUNT.

CACCIA ALLA VOLPE (Italian): see AFTER THE FOX.

CARNETS DU MAJOR THOMPSON, LES (orig): see FRENCH, THEY ARE A FUNNY RACE.

CARROSSE D'OR, LE (orig): see GOLDEN COACH, THE.

CASE OF THE MISSING SWITCHBOARD OPERATOR, THE (alt): see LOVE AFFAIR, OR THE CASE OF THE MISSING SWITCHBOARD OPERATOR, THE.

CELINE AND JULIE GO BOATING (US): see CELINE ET JULIE VONT EN BATEAU.

CENTRAL REGION, THE (alt): see REGION CENTRALE, LA.

C'ERA UNA VOLTA IL WEST (Italian): see ONCE UPON A TIME IN THE WEST.

C'ERAVAMO TANTI AMATI (orig): see WE ALL LOVED EACH OTHER SO MUCH.

CHAGRIN ET LA PITIE, LE (orig): see SORROW AND THE PITY, THE.

CHARME DISCRET DE LA BOURGEOISIE, LE (orig): see DISCREET CHARM OF THE BOURGEOISIE.

CHASSE A L'HOMME, LA (French): see MALE HUNT.

CHELOVEK S KINOAPPARATOM (orig): see MAN WITH THE MOVIE CAMERA, THE.

CHRONIQUE D'UN ETE (orig): see CHRONICLE OF A SUMMER.

CINERAMA! (alt): see THIS IS CINERAMA!

CIOCIARA, LA (orig): see TWO WOMEN.

CLANSMEN, THE (orig): see BIRTH OF A NATION, THE.

CLEO DE CINQ A SEPT (orig): see CLEO FROM 5 TO 7.

CLOUDS OVER EUROPE (US): see Q-PLANES.

COMPAGNI, I (orig): see ORGANIZER, THE.

CONDAMNE A MORT S'EST ECHAPPE, UN (orig): see MAN ESCAPED, A.

CONFORMISTA, IL (orig): see CONFORMIST, THE.

COUP DE FOUDRE: see ENTRE NOUS.

COUSINS, THE (US): see COUSINS, LES.

CRIME DE M. LANGE, LE (orig): see THE CRIME OF MONSIEUR LANGE.

CRISTO SI E FERMATO A EBOLI (orig): see CHRIST STOPPED AT EBOLI.

CUTTER AND BONE (alt): see CUTTER'S WAY.

CZLOWIEK Z MARMARU (orig): see MAN OF MARBLE.

CZLOWIEK Z ZELAZA (orig): see MAN OF IRON.

DAS BOOT: see BOOT, DAS.

DAY IN THE COUNTRY, A (alt): see PARTIE DE CAMPAGNE, UNE.

DECIMA VITTIMA, LA (orig): see TENTH VICTIM, THE.

DERNIER METRO, LE (orig): see LAST METRO, THE.

DERNIER TANGO A PARIS, LE (orig): see LAST TANGO IN PARIS.

DESERTO ROSSO, IL (orig): see RED DESERT.

DETECTIVE, THE (alt): see FATHER BROWN.

DEUX ANGLAISES ET LE CONTINENT, LES (orig): see TWO ENGLISH GIRLS.

DEUX OU TROIS CHOSES QUE JE SAIS D'ELLE (orig): see TWO OR THREE THINGS THAT I KNOW ABOUT HER.

DIABOLIQUES, LES (orig): see DIABOLIQUE.

DIARY OF MAJOR THOMPSON, THE (UK): see FRENCH, THEY ARE A FUNNY RACE, THE.

DIVORZIO ALL'ITALIANA (orig): see DIVORCE ITALIAN STYLE.

DOES, THE (US): see BICHES, LES.

DOKTOR MABUSE, DER SPIELER (orig): see DR. MABUSE.

DOMICILE CONJUGALE (orig): see BED AND BOARD.

DORADO, EL: see EL DORADO.

DOUBLE, THE (alt): see KAGEMUSHA.

DOUBLE POSSESSION (alt): see GANJA AND HESS.

DOWN WENT MCGINTY (UK): see GREAT MCGINTY, THE.

DRAMA OF JEALOUSY AND OTHER THINGS, A (alt): see PIZZA TRIANGLE, THE.

DRAMMA DELLA GELOSIA—TUTTI I PARTICOLARI IN CRONACA (orig): see PIZZA TRIANGLE, THE.

DREIGROSCHENOPER, DIE (orig): see THREEPENNY OPERA.

DU RIFIFI CHEZ LES HOMMES (orig): see RIFIFI.

DUVE, DE: see DE DUVE.

DYNAMITE HANDS (episode): see MOVIE, MOVIE.

E LA NAVE VA (orig): see AND THE SHIP SAILS ON.

EMILE ZOLA (alt): see LIFE OF EMILE ZOLA, THE.

ENEMIES OF THE PUBLIC (UK): see PUBLIC ENEMY.

ENFANCE NUE, L' (orig): see ME.

ENFANT SAUVAGE, L' (orig): see WILD CHILD, THE.

ENFANTS DU PARADIS, LES (orig): see CHILDREN OF PARADISE.

ENIGMA OF KASPAR HAUSER, THE (UK): see EVERY MAN FOR HIMSELF AND GOD AGAINST ALL.

ESCAPE TO HAPPINESS (UK): see INTERMEZZO.

ET DIEU CREA LA FEMME (orig): see AND GOD CREATED WOMAN.

ETAT DU SIEGE (orig): see STATE OF SIEGE.

ETRANGER, L' (orig): see STRANGER, THE (1967).

EVERYBODY'S CHEERING (UK): see TAKE ME OUT TO THE BALL GAME.

EXTASE (orig): see ECSTASY.

EXTRATERRESTRIAL, THE (alt): see E. T.: THE EXTRATERRESTRIAL.

FACE, THE (alt): see MAGICIAN, THE.

FADNI ODPOLEDNE (orig): see BORING AFTERNOON, A.

FALSTAFF (alt): see CHIMES AT MIDNIGHT.

FANTOME DE LA LIBERTE, LE (orig): see PHANTOM OF LIBERTY, THE.

FANTOME OF LIBERTY (alt): see PHANTOM OF LIBERTY, THE.

FAREWELL MY LOVELY (UK): see MURDER MY SWEET.

FATHER AND MASTER (alt): see PADRE, PADRONE.

FELLINI'S ROMA (alt): see ROMA.

FEMME EST UNE FEMME, UNE (orig): see WOMAN IS A WOMAN, A.

FEMME MARIEE, LA (orig): see MARRIED WOMAN, A.

FERROVIERE, IL (orig): see RAILROAD MAN, THE.

FIENDS, THE (UK): see DIABOLIQUE.

FOR BETTER, FOR WORSE (TV): see ZANDY'S BRIDE.

G.I. JOE (alt): see STORY OF G.I. JOE, THE.

GANG WAR (US): see ODD MAN OUT.

GATTOPARDO, IL (orig): see LEOPARD, THE.

GELEGENHEITSARBEIT EINER SKLAVIN (orig): see OCCASIONAL WORK OF A FEMALE SLAVE.

GENOU DE CLAIRE, LE (orig): see CLAIRE'S KNEE.

GENTLE CREATURE, A (alt): see FEMME DOUCE, UNE.

GESTAPO NIGHT TRAIN (alt): see NIGHT TRAIN TO MUNICH.

GIARDINO DEI FINZI-CONTINI, IL (orig): see GARDEN OF THE FINZI-CONTINIS, THE.

GIRL WAS YOUNG, THE (alt): see YOUNG AND INNOCENT.

GIRLS HE LEFT BEHIND, THE (UK): see GANG'S ALL HERE, THE.

GIRLS IN UNIFORM (alt): see MAEDCHEN IN UNIFORM.

GIULIETTA DEGLI SPIRITI (orig): see JULIET OF THE SPIRITS.

GOD CREATED WOMAN (alt): see AND GOD CREATED WOMAN.

GOLDEN MARIE (US): see CASQUE D'OR.

GREGORIO CORTEZ (alt): see BALLAD OF GREGORIO CORTEZ, THE.

GUNS IN THE AFTERNOON (UK): see RIDE THE HIGH COUNTRY.

GYPSY BLOOD (alt): see CARMEN.

HAENDLER DES VIER JAHRZEITEN, DER (orig): see MERCHANT OF FOUR SEASONS, THE.

HANDLE WITH CARE (alt): see CITIZEN'S BAND.

HER OWN STORY (alt): see SOPHIA LOREN: HER OWN STORY.

HITLER, A FILM FROM GERMANY (alt): see OUR HITLER: A

FILM FROM GERMANY.

HITLER: EIN FILM AUS DEUTSCHLAND (orig): see OUR HITLER: A FILM FROM GERMANY.

HOLLYWOOD COWBOY (UK): see HEARTS OF THE WEST.

HOLLYWOOD! HOLLYWOOD! (foreign): see THAT'S ENTERTAINMENT PART 2.

HOMME DE RIO, L' (orig): see THAT MAN FROM RIO.

HOMME ET UNE FEMME, UN (orig): see MAN AND A WOMAN, A.

HORI, MA PANENKO (orig): see FIREMEN'S BALL, THE.

HOUNDS OF ZAROFF (UK): see MOST DANGEROUS GAME, THE.

HOW TO STEAL A DIAMOND IN FOUR UNEASY LESSONS (UK): see HOT ROCK, THE.

HULOT'S HOLIDAY (alt): see M. HULOT'S HOLIDAY.

ILLUMINACJA (orig): see ILLUMINATION.

IM LAUF DER ZEIT (orig): see KINGS OF THE ROAD.

IMMIGRANTS, THE (alt): see NEW LAND, THE.

IMMORTAL BATTALION, THE (alt): see WAY AHEAD, THE.

IN THE WOODS (alt): see RASHOMON.

INDAGINE SU UN CITTADINO AL DI SOPRA DI OGNI (orig): see INVESTIGATION OF A CITIZEN ABOVE SUSPICION.

INVADERS, THE (US): see FORTY-NINTH PARALLEL, THE.

IVAN GROZNYI (orig): see IVAN THE TERRIBLE, PART 1.

JAG AR NYFIKEN (GUL) (orig): see I AM CURIOUS (YELLOW).

JE VOUS PRESENTE PAMELA (orig): see MEET PAMELA.

JEALOUSY ITALIAN STYLE (TV): see PIZZA TRIANGLE, THE.

JEDER FUR SICH UND GOTT GEGEN ALLE (orig): see EVERY MAN FOR HIMSELF AND GOD AGAINST ALL.

JEUX INTERDITS (orig): see FORBIDDEN GAMES.

JOB, THE (alt): see POSTO, IL.

JOB, THE (episode): see BOCCACCIO '70.

JOHNNY IN THE CLOUDS (alt): see WAY TO THE STARS, THE.

JONAS—QUI AURA 25 ANS EN L'AN 2000 (orig): see JONAH, WHO WILL BE 25 IN THE YEAR 2000.

JOURNAL D'UN CURE DE CAMPAGNE, LE (orig): see DIARY OF A COUNTRY PRIEST.

JUNGFRUKALLAN (orig): see VIRGIN SPRING, THE.

JUSTE AVANT LA NUIT (orig): see JUST BEFORE NIGHTFALL.

KABINETT DER DOKTOR CALIGARI, DAS (alt): see CABINET OF DR. CALIGARI, THE

KAGI NO KAGI (alt): see WHAT'S UP TIGER LILY?

KASPAR HAUSER (alt): see EVERY MAN FOR HIMSELF AND GOD AGAINST ALL.

KILLER! (UK): see THIS MAN MUST DIE.

KIZINO KIZI (orig): see WHAT'S UP TIGER LILY?

KNACK, THE (orig): see KNACK. . . AND HOW TO GET IT, THE.

LADRI DI BICICLETTE (orig): see BICYCLE THIEF, THE.

LADY DANCES, THE (TV): see MERRY WIDOW, THE.

LADY HAMILTON (alt): see THAT HAMILTON WOMAN.

LASKY JEDNE PLAVOVLASKY (orig): see LOVES OF A BLONDE.

LAUREL AND HARDY IN TOYLAND (alt): see BABES IN TOYLAND.

LES GIRLS (alt): see GIRLS, LES.

LETZTE MANN, DER (orig): see LAST LAUGH, THE.

LIFE IS A NOVEL (alt): see LIFE IS A BED OF ROSES.

LION HUNTERS, THE (US): see CHASSE AU LION A L'ARC, LA.

LJUBAVNI SLUCAJ ILI TRAGEDIJA SLUZBENICE P.T.T. (orig):
    see LOVE AFFAIR, OR THE CASE OF THE MISSING
    SWITCHBOARD OPERATOR, THE.

LOIN DU VIETNAM (orig): see FAR FROM VIETNAM.

LOST HORIZON OF SHANGRI-LA (orig): see LOST HORIZON.

LOUIS XIV (alt): see RISE AND FALL OF LOUIS XIV, THE.

LUCI DEI VARIETA (orig): see VARIETY LIGHTS.

LULU (alt): see PANDORA'S BOX.

MA NUIT CHEZ MAUD (orig): see MY NIGHT AT MAUD'S.

MAARAKAT ALGER (orig): see BATTLE OF ALGIERS, THE.

MACARTHUR THE REBEL GENERAL (alt): see MACARTHUR.

MAGNIFICENT SEVEN, THE (alt): see SEVEN SAMURAI, THE.

MAMAN ET LA PUTAIN, LA (orig): see MOTHER AND THE
    WHORE, THE.

MAN ALONE, A (TV): see KILLERS, THE.

MAN OF IRON (alt): see RAILROAD MAN, THE.

MARCH OF THE WOODEN SOLDIERS, THE (alt): see BABES IN
    TOYLAND.

MARY NAMES THE DAY (UK): see DOCTOR KILDARE'S
    WEDDING DAY.

MASH (alt): see M*A*S*H.

MAT (orig): see MOTHER.

MEET WHIPLASH WILLIE (UK): see FORTUNE COOOKIE,
    THE.

MEMORIAS DEL SUBDESAROLLO (orig): see MEMORIES OF
    UNDERDEVELOPMENT.

MIMI METALLURGICO FERITO NELL'ONORE (orig): see
    SEDUCTION OF MIMI, THE.

MIRACLE OF LIFE, THE (UK): see OUR DAILY BREAD.

MIRACOLO A MILANO (orig): see MIRACLE IN MILAN.

MODERN HERO, A (UK): see KNUTE ROCKNE, ALL
    AMERICAN.

MORTE A VENEZIA (orig): see DEATH IN VENICE.

MOURIR D'AIMER (orig): see TO DIE OF LOVE.

MOVING TARGET, THE (TV): see HARPER.

MUPPET CAPER (alt): see GREAT MUPPET CAPER, THE.

MURDER IN THORNTON SQUARE (UK): see GASLIGHT.

MURDER, INC. (UK): see ENFORCER, THE.

MURDER ON THE BRIDGE (alt): see END OF THE GAME.

MURIEL, OU LE TEMPS D'UN RETOUR (orig): see MURIEL.

MY AMERICAN UNCLE (US): see MON ONCLE D'AMERIQUE.

MY UNCLE, MR. HULOT (US): see MON ONCLE.

MYSTERIES OF THE ORGANISM (alt): see W. R.—MYSTERIES
    OF THE ORGANISM.

MYSTERY OF KASPAR HAUSER, THE (alt): see EVERY MAN
    FOR HIMSELF AND GOD AGAINST ALL.

NAVE VA (alt): see AND THE SHIP SAILS ON.

9/30/55 (alt): see SEPTEMBER 30, 1955.

NIGHT, THE (alt): see NOTTE, LA.

NOSFERATU, EINE SYMPHONIE DES GRAUENS (orig): see
    NOSFERATU

NOSFERATU PHANTOM DER NACHT (orig): see NOSFERATU
    THE VAMPYRE.
NOSFERATU, THE VAMPIRE (alt): see NOSFERATU.
NOTTE DI SAN LORENZO, LA (orig): see NIGHT OF THE
    SHOOTING STARS, THE.
NOTTI DI CABIRIA, LE (orig): see NIGHTS OF CABIRIA.
NOUS NE VIELLIRONS PAS ENSEMBLE (orig): see WE WON'T
    GROW OLD TOGETHER.
NOW FOR SOMETHING COMPLETELY DIFFERENT (alt): see
    AND   NOW   FOR   SOMETHING   COMPLETELY
    DIFFERENT.
NOW IT CAN BE TOLD (alt): see HOUSE OF 92ND STREET, THE.
NOZ W WODZIE (orig): see KNIFE IN THE WATER.
NUIT, LA (French): NOTTE, LA.
NUIT AMERICAINE, LA (orig): see DAY FOR NIGHT.
NUIT ET BROUILLARD (orig): see NIGHT AND FOG.
NYBYGGARNA (orig): see NEW LAND, THE.
OKTYABR' (orig): see OCTOBER.
OLYMPISCHE SPIELE (orig): see OLYMPIAD.
ORFEU NEGRO (orig): see BLACK ORPHEUS.
ORO DI NAPOLI, L' (orig): see GOLD OF NAPLES, THE.
OTTO E MEZZO (orig): see 8 1/2.
OUTSIDERS, THE (US): see BANDE A PART.
OVER THE RIVER (UK): see ONE MORE RIVER.
PAISA (orig): see PAISAN.
PARAPLUIES DE CHERBOURG, LES (orig): see UMBRELLAS OF
    CHERBOURG, THE.
PARIS NOUS APPARTIENT (orig): see PARIS BELONGS TO US.
PARIS VU PAR. . . (orig): see SIX IN PARIS.
PASSAGER DE LA PLUIE, LE (orig): see RIDER ON THE RAIN.
PASSION, A (alt): see PASSION OF ANNA, THE.
PASSION, EN (orig): see PASSION OF ANNA, THE.
PASSION DE JEANNE D'ARC, LA (orig): see PASSION OF JOAN
    OF ARC, THE.
PASTEUR, LOUIS (alt): see STORY OF LOUIS PASTEUR, THE.
PATTON—LUST FOR GLORY (UK): see PATTON.
PAULINE SUR LA PLAGE (orig): see PAULINE AT THE BEACH.
PEAU DOUCE, LA (orig): see SOFT SKIN, THE.
PEPPERMINT FRAPPE (orig): see PEPPERMINT SODA.
PER UN PUGNO DI DOLLARI (orig): see FISTFUL OF
    DOLLARS, A.
PERSECUTION AND ASSASSINATION OF JEAN-PAUL
    MARAT AS PERFORMED BY THE INMATES OF THE
    ASYLUM OF CHARENTON UNDER THE DIRECTION OF
    THE MARQUIS DE SADE, THE (orig): see MARAT/SADE.
PERSONS UNKNOWN (UK): see BIG DEAL ON MADONNA
    STREET.
PETIT THEATRE DE JEAN RENOIR, LE (orig): see LITTLE
    THEATRE OF JEAN RENOIR, THE.
PLEURE PAS LA BOUCHE PLEINE (orig): see DON'T CRY WITH
    YOUR MOUTH FULL.
POCKET MONEY (alt): see SMALL CHANGE.
POPIOL Y DIAMENT (orig): see ASHES AND DIAMONDS.
POTE TIN KYRIAKI (orig): see NEVER ON SUNDAY.
PRIMA DELLA RIVOLUZIONE (orig): see BEFORE THE

REVOLUTION.

PRISE DE POUVOIR PAR LOUIS XIV, LA (orig): see RISE OF LOUIS XIV, THE.

PROCES DE JEANNE D'ARC, LE (orig): see TRIAL OF JOAN OF ARC, THE.

PROFESSIONE: REPORTER (orig): see PASSENGER, THE.

PUGNI IN TASCA, I (orig): see FIST IN HIS POCKET.

400 COUPS, LES (orig): see 400 BLOWS, THE.

QUATRE NUITS D'UN REVEUR (orig): see FOUR NIGHTS OF A DREAMER.

QUE LA BETE MEURE (orig): see THIS MAN MUST DIE.

QUEEN'S DIAMONDS, THE (alt): see THREE MUSKETEERS, THE.

RAFFLE, THE (episode): see BOCCACCIO '70.

REBEL WITH A CAUSE (alt): see LONELINESS OF THE LONG DISTANCE RUNNER, THE.

RED MANTLE, THE (alt): see HAGBARD & SIGNE.

REGLE DU JEU, LA (orig): see RULES OF THE GAME.

REMARKABLE MR. KIPPS, THE (US): see KIPPS.

REMPARTS D'ARGILE (orig): see RAMPARTS OF CLAY.

REVENGE OF MILADY, THE (alt): see FOUR MUSKETEERS, THE.

RICHTER UND SEIN HENKER, DER (orig): see END OF THE GAME.

RING-A-DING RHYTHM (alt): see IT'S TRAD, DAD!

RISO AMARO (orig): see BITTER RICE.

ROBIN HOOD (alt): see ADVENTURES OF ROBIN HOOD, THE.

ROBINSON CRUSOE: see ADVENTURES OF ROBINSON CRUSOE.

ROCCO E I SUOI FRATELLI (orig): see ROCCO AND HIS BROTHERS.

ROEDE KAPPE, DEN (orig): see HAGBARD & SIGNE.

ROMA, CITTA APERTA (orig): see OPEN CITY.

ROME, OPEN CITY (alt): OPEN CITY.

ROSIE THE RIVETER (alt): see LIFE AND TIMES OF ROSIE THE RIVETER, THE.

SALAIRE DE LA PEUR, LE (orig): see WAGES OF FEAR, THE.

SATYRICON (alt): see FELLINI SATYRICON.

SCARFACE (orig): see SCARFACE: THE SHAME OF A NATION.

SCEICCO BIANCO, LO (orig): see WHITE SHEIK, THE.

SCENER UR ETT AKTENSKAP (orig): see SCENES FROM A MARRIAGE.

SCIUSCIA (orig): see SHOESHINE.

SE PERMETTE, PARLIAMO DI DONNE (orig): see LET'S TALK ABOUT WOMEN.

SEARCH FOR SPOCK, THE (alt): see STAR TREK III: THE SEARCH FOR SPOCK.

SEDOTTA E ABBANDONATA (orig): see SEDUCED AND ABANDONED.

SEE YOU IN HELL, DARLING (UK): see AMERICAN DREAM, AN.

SEPARATE BEDS (UK): see WHEELER-DEALERS, THE.

SEPT FOIS FEMME (French): see WOMAN TIMES SEVEN.

SETTE VOLTE DONNA (orig Italian): see WOMAN TIMES SEVEN.

SETTLERS, THE (alt): see NEW LAND, THE.
SHADOW WARRIOR, THE (US): see KAGEMUSHA.
SHERLOCK HOLMES (UK): see ADVENTURES OF SHERLOCK
    HOLMES, THE.
SHERLOCK   HOLMES   (alt):   see   HOUND   OF   THE
    BASKERVILLES.
SHICHININ NO SAMURAI (orig): see SEVEN SAMURAI, THE.
SHIP SAILS ON: see AND THE SHIP SAILS ON.
SILENT VOICE, THE (UK): see MAN WHO PLAYED GOD, THE.
SIN OF HAROLD DIDDLEBOCK, THE (alt): see MAD
    WEDNESDAY.
SINS OF LOLA MONTES, THE (alt): see LOLA MONTES.
SIRENE DU MISSISSIPPI, LA (orig): see MISSISSIPPI
    MERMAID.
SJUNDE INSEGLET, DET (orig): see SEVENTH SEAL, THE.
SKAMMEN (orig): see SHAME.
SKULL ISLAND (alt): see MOST DANGEROUS GAME, THE.
SMULTRONSTALLET (orig): see WILD STRAWBERRIES.
SOLITI IGNOTI (orig): see BIG DEAL ON MADONNA STREET.
SOMMARNATTENS LEENDE (orig): see SMILES OF A SUMMER
    NIGHT.
SONG OF STYRENE, THE: see CHANT DU STYRENE, LE.
SOUND BARRIER, THE (UK): see BREAKING THE SOUND
    BARRIER.
SPACE ODYSSEY, A (alt): see 2001: A SPACE ODYSSEY.
SPINAL TAP (alt): see THIS IS SPINAL TAP.
STACHKA (orig): see STRIKE.
STAIRWAY TO HEAVEN (US): see MATTER OF LIFE AND
    DEATH, A.
STARKE FERDINAND, DER (orig): see STRONG MAN
    FERDINAND.
STORY OF DR. EHRLICH'S MAGIC BULLET, THE (UK): see DR.
    EHRLICH'S MAGIC BULLET.
STRANIERO, LO (orig): see STRANGER, THE (1967).
STRATEGIA DEL RAGNO (orig): see SPIDER'S STRATAGEM,
    THE.
SUITABLE CASE FOR TREATMENT, A (alt): see MORGAN!
SUMMER MADNESS (UK): see SUMMERTIME.
SUNO NO ONNA (orig): see WOMAN IN THE DUNES.
SUNRISE—A SONG OF TWO HUMANS (alt): see SUNRISE.
TEMPTATION OF DR. ANTONIO, THE (episode): see
    BOCCACCIO '70.
TEN DAYS THAT SHOOK THE WORLD (alt): see OCTOBER.
THEIR FIRST TRIP TO TOKYO (alt): see TOKYO STORY.
THING FROM ANOTHER WORLD, THE (orig): see THING, THE.
THIS MAN REUTER (UK): see DISPATCH FROM REUTERS.
TIERRA PROMETIDA, LA (orig): see PROMISED LAND, THE.
TIREZ SUR LE PIANISTE (orig): see SHOOT THE PIANO
    PLAYER.
TOKYO MONOGATARI (orig): see TOKYO STORY.
TOM SAWYER (alt): see ADVENTURES OF TOM SAWYER, THE.
TRAVOLTI DA UN INSOLITO DESTINO NELL'AZZURRO
    MARE D'AGOSTO (orig): see SWEPT AWAY. . . BY AN
    UNUSUAL DESTINY IN THE BLUE SEA OF AUGUST.

TRIUMPH DES WILLENS (orig): see TRIUMPH OF THE WILL.
TROLLFLOTTEN (orig): see MAGIC FLUTE, THE.
TUNNEL, THE (orig): see TRANSATLANTIC TUNNEL.
TWISTED ROAD, THE (UK): see THEY LIVE BY NIGHT.
UCCIDERO UN UOMO (Italian): see THIS MAN MUST DIE.
UGETSU MONOGATARI (orig): see UGETSU.
ULTIMO TANGO A PARIGI, L' (orig): see LAST TANGO IN PARIS.
UNFAITHFUL WIFE, THE (UK): see FEMME INFIDELE, LA.
UNVANQUISHED, THE (alt): see APARAJITO.
USUAL UNIDENTIFIED THIEVES, THE (alt): see BIG DEAL ON MADONNA STREET.
UTVANDRARNA (orig): see EMIGRANTS, THE.
VENT SOUFFLE OU IL VENT, LE (alt): see MAN ESCAPED, A.
VERLORENE EHRE DER KATHARINA BLUM, DIE (orig): see LOST HONOR OF KATHARINA BLUM, THE.
VIE EST UN ROMAN, LA (orig): see LIFE IS A BED OF ROSES.
VILLEGGIATURA, LA (orig): see BLACK HOLIDAY.
VISKNINGAR OCH ROP (orig): see CRIES AND WHISPERS.
VIVEMENT DIMANCHE (orig): see CONFIDENTIALLY YOURS.
VIVRE SA VIE (orig): see MY LIFE TO LIVE.
VOINA I MIR (orig): see WAR AND PEACE.
VOYAGE DANS LA LUNE, LE (orig): see VOYAGE TO THE MOON.
WAR IS OVER, THE (US): see GUERRE EST FINIE, LA.
WE ARE ALL ASSASSINS (alt): see NOUS SOMMES TOUS DES ASSASSINS.
WEDDING BELLS (UK): see ROYAL WEDDING.
WHAT A MAN (UK): see NEVER GIVE A SUCKER AN EVEN BREAK.
WHAT LOLA WANTS (UK): see DAMN YANKEES.
WHISPERS AND CRIES (alt): see CRIES AND WHISPERS.
WHITHER GERMANY? (alt): see KUEHLE WAMPE.
WOMAN ALONE, A (US): see SABOTAGE.
WOMAN X 7 (alt): see WOMAN TIMES SEVEN.
WOODEN SOLDIERS (alt): see BABES IN TOYLAND.
WORLD AND HIS WIFE, THE (UK): see STATE OF THE UNION.
YEAR ONE (UK): see ANNO UNO.
YOUR SHOW OF SHOWS: see TEN FROM YOUR SHOW OF SHOWS.
ZAUBER FLOTE, DIE (alt): see MAGIC FLUTE, THE.
ZAZIE (alt): see ZAZIE DANS LE METRO.
ZELIG: see THE CHANGING MAN.
ZEMLYA (orig): see EARTH.
ZERO DE CONDUITE (orig): see ZERO FOR CONDUCT.
ZOLA (alt): see LIFE OF EMILE ZOLA, THE.
ZORMBA (orig): see ZORBA THE GREEK.
ZORRO (alt): see MARK OF ZORRO, THE.

MASTERPIECES

The Big Sleep
Breathless
Casablanca
Citizen Kane
City Lights
The Court Jester
The Crime of Monsieur Lange
Dr. Strangelove
8 1/2
The 400 Blows
A Funny Thing Happened on the Way to the Forum
The Godfather
A Hard Day's Night
Intolerance
It Happened One Night
It's a Wonderful Life
Jules and Jim
The Maltese Falcon
A Man and a Woman
Medium Cool
Modern Times
Nashville
North by Northwest
Open City
Petulia
Potemkin
Rear Window
Reds
Richard III
Rules of the Game
Safety Last
The Searchers
Singin' in the Rain
The Sorrow and the Pity
Stolen Kisses
La Strada
The Tree of the Wooden Clogs
Two or Three Things That I Know about Her
2001: A Space Odyssey
Z